Body Movement and Nonverbal Communication

An Annotated Bibliography, 1971–1981

ADVANCES IN SEMIOTICS

General Editor: THOMAS A. SEBEOK

Body Movement
and
Nonverbal Communication

An Annotated Bibliography, 1971–1981

EDITED BY

Martha Davis and Janet Skupien

Indiana University Press   Bloomington

Manufactured in the United States of America

Library of Congress Cataloging in Publication Data
Main entry under title:

Body Movement and nonverbal communication.

   (Advance in semiotics)
   Includes indexes.
   1. Movement, Psychology of—Bibliography. 2. Nonverbal communication (Psychology)—Bibliography.
I. Davis, Martha. II. Skupien, Janet. III. Series.
Z7204.M66b62   [BF295]   016.1536   81-7881*
ISBN 0-253-34101-9   AACR2
1 2 3 4 5 86 85 84 83 82

To
Susan Morance and Louis Forsdale

CONTENTS

About the Bibliography

This work takes up where *Understanding Body Movement: An Annotated Bibliography* left off in mid-1971. The reader is encouraged to consult that work and other bibliographies cited in it for earlier references. We have followed its format, punctuation style, and indexing. Unlike the first volume, however, this bibliography includes published work only, has foreign titles, and is written by a number of annotators; there are, accordingly, variations in abstract writing style. Although this bibliography is composed of original annotations except where noted, and efforts have been made to avoid phrases and expressions from the original sources unless quoted, they may of course sound in many ways like authors' abstracts or summaries.

The principal objective of this bibliography is not to evaluate works so much as to give readers enough information to determine that the work is relevant to their interests. The criteria for including a work is that it be published, that it be written in one of seven languages we were able to annotate (English, Spanish, German,

French, Italian, Dutch, and Portuguese), and that it be directly about the psychology or anthropology of body movement. Of course, certain subject areas border or overlap the area of the movement aspects of nonverbal communication, such as, dance therapy, motor learning, dance ethnology, motor physiology, psycholinguistics, ethology, and physical education, to name a few important ones. We have tried to include articles or books from these areas only when they deal in some way with behavioral aspects of movement *per se*, when they are clearly on "body language," and particularly *research* in body language as opposed to clinical or training program reports. Number of titles per author or abstract length is not necessarily an expression of the work's value. Practical considerations such as time, availability of the work, and individual differences in annotator speed and style have determined the final number and character of the annotations. In the case of about 40 "key" authors, we asked annotators to select their major works because there were so many, and several are largely represented by their books, not their journal articles.

We used many sources to find titles: textbook reference sections, existing bibliographies, computer searches, systematic searches through key journals, and so on. We limited selections to published works partly because these are easier to obtain, partly to keep the project within manageable proportions. When annotators could not find a work, we have, in rare cases, cited it anyway if it appeared clearly relevant. In these cases we tried to verify source information from *Books in Print* or from corroborating reference lists. We are hopeful that the great majority of researchers and writers on nonverbal communication and kinesics are represented here but refer the reader to Appendix II: "For Further Reference." Omissions are inevitable but merit our apologies to the authors nonetheless.

Twelve annotators wrote the abstracts and subject-indexed the sources. Titles were selected primarily by the editors who then edited the annotations, wrote the introduction, and compiled the index and appendixes. A small number of annotations were written from prepublication information or by the authors themselves and are so designated. Over 50 abstracts were reprinted from *The Journal of Nonverbal Behavior*, and we gratefully acknowledge Human Sciences Press, New York City, for permission to reprint them. In virtually all cases the annotations were done from the original sources except for dissertations. One person, Mona Daleo, was responsible for subject indexing and writing brief additional notes on the dissertations from Dissertation Abstracts.

In every way the present volume has been a team effort. We cannot stress enough the essential role of the annotators. They subject indexed the works, made the final decision whether to include them, and wrote the abstracts. They also checked our editings for accuracy. Some annotators covered specific topics, others were assigned diverse works, and one concentrated on the Dissertation Abstracts. We are indebted to them, for this is in great measure their work: Jennifer Andt, Mona Daleo, Patrick Garner, Sarah C. Greenfield, James Hannan, Madeleine Kando, Michael Knoerzer, Jane Daniels Moffett, Francis O'Brien, Jr., Claire Oppenheim, Carlotta Willis, and Christy Wilson. The annotators are a select group: college and high school teachers, dancers, dance therapists, graduate students, social workers. While they did the annotations because they were very interested in the subject, it was still laborious work, especially when combined with busy work or study schedules. We are particularly grateful to Sarah C. Greenfield who also did several title searches for us, to Christy Wilson whose remarkable contribution at the eleventh hour was a blessing, and to Anne Heimlich for her work on the authors index.

This bibliography project has been sponsored by the Institute for Nonverbal Communication Research in New York City and funded by an anonymous grant from a very generous and appreciated person. Those who have supported the Institute itself — the Board of Directors, Advisory Council, and members — have made the project possible. We are most grateful for their support. Susan Morance, one of the people to whom this book is dedicated, worked on Institute projects and on this book, with an intelligence and stamina that made all the difference. Most of all we know that the project would not have come to fruition without the help of our husbands, Sergio and Frank.

Martha Davis and Janet Skupien

Introduction:

Nonverbal Communication in the 1970s

This book is the sequel to *Understanding Body Movement: An Annotated Bibliography* (New York: Arno Press, 1972; reprint Bloomington: Indiana University Press, 1982). When that work was completed ten years ago, it was easy to predict that publications would increase exponentially. The number of dissertations alone has grown 100-fold in ten years. The number of books on nonverbal communication published in this decade has created a small crisis in title selection—there are just so many ways one can say "a book on nonverbal communication."

It was also apparent in 1971 that there would be a massive shift to traditional experimental design and away from the few films-observed-endlessly studies of the 1960s. This bibliography shows the dominance in the 1970s of research psychologists who applied more rigorous methods of assessment, sampling, manipulation, and statistical analysis to the study of nonverbal behavior. It is also a decade of few-variables research. The subject index shows the overwhelming number of annotations devoted to gaze and/or personal distance measures alone. Studies which assess several parameters usually do so in a fairly simple way (for example, number of gesticulations, open or closed body positions, frequency of eye contact, number of head nods).

What couldn't be so clearly predicted in 1971 were the subtle shifts in content and emphasis. At that time it seemed useful to overview the "field" in terms of traditional academic disciplines or major subjects within them: developmental patterns, expression of the emotions, personality and psychodiagnosis, psychological interpretation of gesture, interaction and communication, cultural characteristics, and animal behavior (Davis, 1972). Scanning the work now, it seems a decade of special topics that captured the imagination and energy of many and that reflected the social concerns of the 1970s.

In the 1971 bibliography there were 68 subject-index entries for "sex differences"; in this one there are 239. More important, however, sex differences are no longer side observations in studies dealing basically with other subjects. They are the key topics of many studies in the 1970s, and no doubt this reflects the influence of the women's movement. The works on gender differences in nonverbal communication reported here create a motion picture of what different social worlds men and women occupy; how minutely and constantly they differ in all manner of nonverbal behavior—visual, facial, spatial, tactile, postural, and so on, and how pervasive are the interaction contrasts and complementarities between men and women.

Facial expression of emotion remains a principal area of research, led by the work of Paul Ekman and Wallace V. Friesen. The debate concerned with whether there are a few universally recognized facial expressions has given way to study of facial movement patterns as they occur in varying contexts and to the development of extremely refined observation techniques for assessing the nuances of expression.

In the 1970s a considerable body of literature formed on the subject of "intimacy" or interpersonal closeness—how it is established, defended against, regulated. In this topic, gaze and distance measures—the most commonly studied variables throughout the nonverbal communication research of the 1970s—are usually examined together. For example, in the "equilibrium theory" extensively tested in '70s research, a relationship is posited between increased interpersonal contact (often literally moving closer to) and defense (often seen as decreasing or averting mutual gaze).

Another key topic is nonverbal "leakage" and "clues" to deception. Although body language has been regarded as a source of cues to unconscious or unintended communication at least since Freud analyzed "chance acts," studies of cues to conscious deception have become rigorous and extensive in the 1970s. Also, a rich literature has accumulated in a related area—which "channels" of communication (such as vocal, visual, tactile) take precedence when messages are discrepant between channels, and what are the relationships between various channels in impression formation, person perception, and message "encoding" processes.

The distinction between "decoding" and "encoding" nonverbal behavior is a common one in the 1970s literature. Encoding ability (as in facility in expressing affect, degree of animation, nonverbal social skills) is increasingly examined. Decoding ability (patterns of perceiving, recognizing, interpreting nonverbal behavior) has been researched particularly by Robert Rosenthal and his colleagues. Rosenthal's Profile of Nonverbal Sensitivity (PONS) is the most extensively tested and utilized instrument in nonverbal communication research. Work on the PONS, in particular, and nonverbal aspects of person perception, in general, is generating new evidence of how different groups perceive the same behavior.

Despite the proliferation of single-variable studies, there are signs already in the 1980s of a trend toward a synthesis of the elaborate multivariable film studies of the 1960s and the experimental rigor of the 1970s. Some have begun to do rich sequential recordings, computer analyzed for pattern and/or assessed with more sophisticated multivariate statistics. This trend is particularly clear in sophisticated mother-infant interactions research in which microanalysis of films is a well-established approach. Careful, repeated viewing of the intricacies of facial expression, touch, orientation and spacing, synchrony and echoing of actions between infant and mother appears most salient for studies concerned with bonding and rapport. Developmental psychologists have discovered a structure of "proto-conversation" in the interaction of mother and infant and have begun to look at action and gesture within the context of interaction for an understanding of the way in which language is acquired. There is also a growing body of knowledge of "developmental kinesics," although the bulk of the studies on developmental stages of nonverbal communication are limited to personal space measures. Within the observational studies of classroom, cafeteria, and playground there are a notable number on handicapped children, particularly those who are retarded.

The influence of the ethological approach and method is evident in the mother-infant and developmental studies and in the careful study of face-to-face interaction, particularly adult conversational behavior. Naturalistic observation, from Charles Darwin on to Birdwhistell (1974) and Scheflen (1972), has been essential to body-movement research, and modern ethological study continues this tradition best through the experimentalism of the '70s. Studies of the organization of face-to-face interaction reveal how speech and body movement are subtly integrated in communication. Along these lines, research on conversational behavior describes the ways in which verbal interaction is maintained and regulated by extra-verbal cues. This is the decade in which terms such as "back-channel" behavior, "turn-taking cues," "monitoring," "interactional synchrony" and "mirroring" became the focus of many special studies. Language and gesture have seemed to move closer together in this decade. There have been an increasing number of studies of the role of gestures in the production and facilitating of speech, the relationship of movement to thought and cognitive processes, and the investigation of body and eye movements in relation to brain laterality and verbal or visual tasks.

Movement and language are integrated in a unique way in gestural language. Specialists in semiotics and in sign-language study have in this decade produced a fascinating literature on nonverbal signs and formal sign languages. Embedded in this literature are clues to how body movement can reflect and help structure thought; can possess a syntax and "vocabulary"; can cue intent, subliminal reinforcements, and so on. Since William Stokoe's seminal work in the 1960s there has been a flowering of studies on aboriginal, Native American, monastic, and job-related sign languages, as well as investigations of the linguistic properties of American Sign Language (ASL).

Interest in sign language has been spurred on in the '70s by an interest in the communicative abilities of animals, especially primates. The controversial attempts to teach language to apes, especially with signs, has generated speculation on the original emergence of language from gesture. Apart from these theories and studies dealing with language, the investigation of the many nonverbal channels through which animals communicate continues to receive a great deal of attention.

Much research on nonverbal communication in the 1970s can be characterized as a proliferation of few-variable studies scattered piecemeal through diverse journals. But as a whole it adds up to overwhelming support for the role of nonverbal behavior in the maintenance of gender differences, the expression of rapport and liking/disliking, the regulation of social encounters, and the delineation of cultural identity, to name a few of the most powerful results of the

Paul Byers

Albert E. Scheflen

Ray L. Birdwhistell

research. It has in the past decade become an established topic, important to educators, counselors and psychotherapists; specialists in intercultural communication training; environmental psychologists; and many others. The profession of dance therapy which came of age in this decade depends on this research and has begun to contribute greatly to it. It is a regular part of communication courses and in-

Eliot D. Chapple

Irmgard Bartenieff

creasingly is accepted within academic circles as a serious subject, not a trivial fad. Books on communication seem obliged now to have a chapter on nonverbal communication. Although grant funding has been tight, especially since the late '70s, researchers do not have to defend so vigorously the relevance and importance of the subject as the pioneers had to just a few years ago.

By 1980 it was possible to look back and identify those who directly or indirectly pioneered the curent heyday of nonverbal comunication research. Some of them — Ray L. Birdwhistell, Eliot Chapple, Irmgard Bartenieff, Erving Goffman, Edward Hall, Paul Ekman, William Condon — continue to generate an astonishing range of ideas and fruitful research. Others — Margaret Mead, Albert E. Scheflen, Gregory Bateson — have died. Perhaps it's the halo effect of time, but these who initiated so much seem more colorful personalities, more daring and innovative minds. They were visionaries even when they seemed hopelessly mired in two seconds of a single encounter on film. Their influence on the nonverbal communication research of the 1970s is everywhere to be seen.

Looking ahead to a new decade of research, it is tempting to make predictions that are half educated guess and half wish. The signs of the times point to a synthesis of advanced statistical methods and complex descriptions of the ongoing behavior stream. "Developmental kinesics" and the study of "kinesics acquisition" as pioneered by

Edward T. Hall

Paul Ekman

Walburga von Raffler-Engel and her colleagues should come of age in the 1980s. By 1990 there should be far more documentation of cultural differences in nonverbal communication and rich descriptions of diverse cultural movement styles such as were promised as early as Boas' work with the Kwakiutl in the 1930s and Efron's dissertation on Italian and Jewish gestures in the early 1940s. Specialists in intercultural communication will increasingly demand good research in this area. The 1980s should be a decade for development of curricula and training in nonverbal communication research. Training films and videotapes are badly needed. Hopefully, many sophisticated films and videotapes on this subject which requires visual presentation will be produced in the next 10 years. And finally it is tempting to predict that the field will grow from the "this topic would be good for (psychotherapists, teachers, business people, diplomats, and so on)" stage to specialized training programs that are tested for value and effectiveness.

In 1972 Davis wrote: "A bibliography of literature on body movement is really words about words about what is nonverbal; thus, there is a danger of losing sight of the original event." This still seems a problem and one that is exacerbated by the fact that in the current bibliography there are so many more experimental studies. But reading between the dry lines of sample procedure and experimental interventions, statistical assessment and predictable results, one can see the liveliness and excitement of the subject anyway. The behavioral study of body movement is not an abstruse subject. It's as vital as a greeting, a glance, and a smile.

Body Movement and Nonverbal Communication

An Annotated Bibliography, 1971–1980

Bibliography

1. **Abbey, David S.** *Now See Hear! Applying Communication to Teaching.* Ontario, Canada: Ontario Institute for Studies in Education, 1973. 74. pp. Illus.

A brief review of communication theory for educators, this book provides a basic model of communication, a practical introduction to kinesics and proxemics, and a comparative analysis of various instructional media. It discusses interactional, transactional, and verbal-immediacy analyses of interpersonal communication, and offers ideas for discussion and demonstrations in the classroom. An annotated list of suggested readings concludes each chapter.

2. **Abecassis, Jeanine.** "A propos de la communication non verbale chez l'enfant d'âge pré-scolaire: étude de certains aspects de la communication gestuelle." *Bulletin de Psychologie* 26 (1972-73) : 506-512.

A report of a study of the evolution of certain affective gestures among three groups of children in a nursery school in Strasbourg. Gestures that ask for help, hugging gestures, and gestures of giving gifts were found to diminish, whereas hand shaking and giving help gestures increase. It includes a discussion of two theoretical points, namely, that the nonverbal communication system is completely interdependent, that is, changing one element influences the whole in contrast to, say, the structure of language, and that gestures have multiple meanings dependent on the situation or context. Written in French.

3. **Abramovitch, Rona, and Daly, Eleanor M.** "Children's Use of Head Orientation and Eye Contact in Making Attributions of Affiliation." *Child Development* 49 (1978) : 519-522.

Reports on two studies investigating children's use of head orientation and eye contact as cues for judging affiliation. Forty preschool children, 18 about 3½ years old and 22 about four years, participated in the first study. Judgments that facing dyads liked each other while those not facing did not like each other were confirmed for both groups. In the second study 30 preschoolers about four years old and 32 grade-school children with a mean age of about six were asked to indicate their preference for a woman who was videotaped making eye contact or not with the viewer. The preschoolers showed no preference. The grade-school children preferred the eye contact.

4. **Achilles, Charles M., and French, Russell L.** *Inside Classrooms: Studies in Verbal and Nonverbal Communication.* Danville, Illinois: The Interstate Printers and Publishers, Inc., 1977. 83 pp.

This is a report of the University of Tennessee studies of the observation system for teacher behavior IDER (Indirect/Direct-Encouraging/Restricting) based on the framework of N.A. Canders system of interaction analysis. The design procedures and rationale of the project using videotapes of grade-school classroom interaction are described, including an analysis of sex differences in student-teacher interaction, teacher behaviors toward children of different social classes, and toward delinquents. There are reports of comparisons of black and white perceptions of teacher behavior and discussion of the implications of the research for education and recommendations for future directions.

5. **Adams, Robert M.**, ed. "Human Ethology Abstracts III." *Man-Environment Systems* 9 (1979) : 57-164.

This excellent annotated bibliography contains over 560 abstracts on various topics in human ethology such as social spacing, courtship, sex roles, child/adult and child/child interactions. There are a good number of entries specifically on facial expression, gaze, gesture, touch, and posture. A good supplement to the current bibliography, it is one of a series regularly published in *Man-Environment Systems*.

6. **Adams, Robert M.** "Nonverbal Social Signals and Clinical Processes." In *The Evolution of Human Social Behavior,* edited by J.S. Lockard, pp. 239-256. New York: Elsevier, 1980.

This chapter provides an overview of some of the literature on the relevance of nonvocal behavior to the causes, assessment, and treatment of certain interpersonal problems requiring psychotherapy. The author also examines a specific problem area, assertiveness. The author points out that while clinical practitioners have traditionally been concerned with the verbal behavior of clients as the primary means of their assessment, there has been a growing emphasis on the overt nonverbal behavior of the client, not only for assessing problems, but for treating them.

7. **Adams, Robert M.; Hammeke, Thomas A.; and DeHaven, Everett D.** "Goal Gradient in Locomotor Behavior: Field Studies." *Perceptual and Motor Skills* 46 (1978) : 675-678.

Three studies compared walking speeds of subjects approaching a location assumed to contain a reward with walking speeds of subjects who passed by the reward location. No evidence was found for acceleration of walking speeds in the rewarded groups.

8. **Adams, Robert M., and Kirkevold, Barbara.** "Looking, Smiling, Laughing, and Moving in Restaurants: Sex and Age Differences." *Environmental Psychology and Nonverbal Behavior* 3 (1978) : 117-121.

Three hundred and twenty-eight diners in three restaurants were observed for three minutes each and the frequencies of six behaviors recorded: looking and glancing away from the table and companions, smiling, laughing, gross movements, and standing. Males looked more than females, and females smiled and laughed more than males. Significant age differences were found for smiling, laughing, movement, and standing. Significant interactions were found in looking for sex by with or without a companion. Significant age by sex interactions were found for smiling, laughing, and standing.

9. **Adler, Ron; Rosenfeld, Lawrence B.; and Towne, Neil.** *Interplay: The Process of Interpersonal Communication.* New York: Holt, Rinehart & Winston, 1980. 352 pp. Illus.

This is a college-level text which has, among others, chapters on self-disclosure, listening, and nonverbal communication. To enliven the text there are interesting photos, quotes, and anecdotes inserted throughout as illustrations. The book deals with broad categories in a conversational tone, with only occasional reference to specific researchers.

10. **Aiello, John R.** "Male and Female Visual Behavior as a Function of Distance and Duration of an Interviewer's Direct Gaze: Equilibrium Theory Revisited." Ph.D. dissertation, Michigan State University. 1972. 114 pp. (Order No. 73053-12)

Distance and duration of interviewer's visual attention were manipulated in interviews with male and female subjects. Seven hypotheses concerning sex differences in looking behavior were tested and confirmed, including a linear increase in looking behaviors with increased distance for males and a curvilinear relationship between distance and looking for females, with more looking at the intermediate distance than at the closer or farther distance.

11.   **Aiello, John R.** "A Further Look at Equilibrium Theory: Visual Interaction as a Function of Interpersonal Distance." *Environmental Psychology and Nonverbal Behavior* 1 (1977) : 122-140. Illus.

This paper presents a study that examined the relationship between visual interaction and interpersonal distance as it relates to an equilibrium theory of social interaction. Differential boundaries were found to exist for the effect of distance on five highly related male and female visual behaviors, exemplifying different overall equilibrium levels for the sexes. While males looked more as distance increased, females looked less after an intermediate distance of 6.5 feet. These data support a modified equilibrium model that posits that eye contact functions to regulate the comfort of an interaction and is also a response to the degree of interaction comfort; further, comfortable interaction distances promote eye contact and, more importantly, uncomfortable distances diminish it. Because women tend to be more oriented toward inclusive relationships, they are more comfortable at closer interaction distances and, hence, look more at these distances.

12.   **Aiello, John R., and Aiello, Tyra DeCarlo.** "The Development of Personal Space: Proxemic Behavior of Children 6 through 16." *Human Ecology* 2 (1974) : 177-189.

The participants in this study were 424 white American children from grades one, three, five, seven, nine, and 11 in same-sex dyads. Observations were made of the children's interpersonal distance and body orientation (axis) while interacting. Results indicate that distance between interactants increased with age up to about seventh grade, at which time it stabilized at societal norms. There were no distinctive sex differences in distance or orientation in the earlier grades, but by early adolescence males stood further apart and at greater angles than females.

13.   **Aiello, John R., and Baum, Andrew,** eds. *Residential Crowding and Design.* New York : Plenum Press, 1979. 252 pp.

Several teams of investigators have used multiple methodologies in their examination of physical density and the psychological experience of crowding. Going beyond studies which yield moderate correlational relationships between census tract density and various social and physical pathologies, this collection focuses on mediating factors as well as the consequences of crowding, particularly the mediating influences of architectural design. The buildings that we shape in turn shape us. Several papers in this volume are concerned with the relationship between architectural design and high-density residential settings, with studies that show the effects of crowding. The book contains 14 essays, including a chapter on the problems which accompany attempts to ameliorate negative effects of high-density living.

14.   **Aiello, John R., and Cooper, Ralph E.** "Use of Personal Space as a Function of Social Affect." *American Psychological Association Proceedings* 7 (1972) : 207-208.

Eighth-grade boys and girls were grouped into 40 same-sex dyads according to reciprocal positive or negative choices on a sociometric form. Interpersonal distance and angle of orientation were recorded in a naturalistic situation. Results indicated a significant relationship between affect and distance, with students who liked each other interacting at closer distances. There was a tendency for students who did not like each other to widen the axis of orientation over time.

15.   **Aiello, John R.; DeRisi, Donna T.; Epstein, Yakov M.; and Karlin, Robert A.** "Crowding and the Role of Interpersonal Distance Preference." *Sociometry* 40 (1977) : 271-282.

Thirty-two female undergraduates were stratified on the basis of far or close personal space preference. They then experienced either a crowded or uncrowded situation. Various physiological measures were taken. Subjects found to prefer far interpersonal distances were most physiologically stressed by crowding and displayed lower performance levels on creativity tasks.

16.   **Aiello, John R.; Epstein, Yakov M.; and Karlin, Robert A.** "Effects of Crowding on Electrodermal Activity." *Sociological Symposium* 14 (1975) : 42-57.

Arousal and adaptation during and after varying degrees of crowding were measured with skin conductance readings and their change over time. Two studies are reported. In experiment I groups of six same-sexed subjects were placed in both small and large rooms and skin conductance levels for each subject were recorded every 105 seconds. In experiment II the method and measure were the same except that only one person was placed in each of the two rooms. Results indicate that crowded subjects were more aroused, males and females did not differ in degree of arousal, and the presence of others in conjunction with the size of the room is the major contributor to the arousal effect.

17.   **Aiello, John R., and Jones, Stanley E.** "Field Study of the Proxemic Behavior of Young School Children in Three Subcultural Groups." *Journal of Personality and Social Psychology* 19 (1971) : 351-356.

Two hundred ten same-sex dyads of children aged 6-8 were selected from black, Puerto Rican, and white subcultures in New York City. The children were observed on their school playgrounds. Interaction distance and shoulder axis were recorded. Results showed middle-class white children to stand farther apart than lower-class Puerto Rican or black children. In the white culture males stood further apart than females. Black children faced each other less directly than did the white children. There was a difference across cultures between shoulder axis for males and females.

18.   **Aiello, John, and Thompson, Donna.** "Personal Space, Crowding, and Spatial Behavior in a Cultural Context." In *Human Behavior and Environment, Volume 4: Culture and Environment,* edited by I. Altman, J. Wohlwill, and A. Rapoport, pp. 107-171. New York: Plenum Press, 1980.

The authors explore the personal space phenomenon from several aspects. First, they talk about the construct in general, its definition, models, methodologies, and measures. Next, they examine cultural studies (both interactional and projective types) of personal space. A portion of the paper is devoted to crowding and culture. It is concluded with a discussion of environmental design.

19.   **Ainsworth, Mary D. Salter.** "Attachment as Related to Mother-Infant Interaction." In *Advances in the Study of Behavior,* Vol. 9, edited by J.S. Rosenblatt, R.A. Hinde, C. Beer, and M.C. Busnel, pp. 1-51. New York: Academic Press, 1979.

Data from a longitudinal study done in 1963 of 26 mother-infant pairs are discussed in relation to individual differences and the effect of the mother on infant attachment formation. Mothers' interaction behaviors were stable during the first year whereas infant behaviors were unpredictable during the first three months. Infants with deviant behavior (anxious, avoidant) at the end of the one-year study had mothers with deviant behavioral patterns; infants who were normally attached had mothers who were appropriately sensitive. The author concludes that the mother's behavior has more influence on the mother-infant interaction than the infant's behavior.

20. **Ainsworth, Mary D. Salter; Blehar, Mary C.; Waters, Everett; and Wall, Sally.** *Patterns of Attachment: A Psychological Study of the Strange Situation.* Hillsdale, New Jersey: Lawrence Erlbaum, 1978. 391 pp. Illus.

This book is a detailed and highly interesting presentation of information about the attachment of infants to their mothers. Manifestations of attachment behavior of one-year-olds in the laboratory (unfamiliar or strange) situation are compared with manifestations of attachment observed at home. Origins and development of the behaviors, individual and national differences, and ethological-evolutionary theory of attachment behavior are key topics covered.

21. **Akeret, Robert U.** *Photoanalysis.* New York: Pocket Books, 1973. 311 pp. Illus.

A popularized book from the publishers of the 1970 *Body Language* on how to interpret the hidden psychological meaning of personal and public photographs. Hundreds of photos are reproduced here and accompanied by the author's interpretations.

22. **Alcock, John.** "The Evolution of Behavior." In *Animal Behavior: An Evolutionary Approach,* by J. Alcock, pp. 360-394. Sunderland, Massachusetts: Sinauer Associates, 1979. Illus.

By comparing the behavior of closely related species it is possible to trace the "likely" evolutionary history of an unusual behavior pattern. Employing the comparative method, one can explain the evolutionary history of complex communication signals in some insect species. For example, one can trace the history of honeybee communication. Diversity of communication signals may stem from variation in the effectiveness of signals in different sensory channels to carry a particular kind of message from sender to receiver.

23. **Allgeier, A.R., and Byrne, Donn.** "Attraction Toward the Opposite Sex as a Determinant of Physical Proximity." *Journal of Social Psychology* 90 (1973) : 213-219.

This study of ten male and ten female undergraduates showed a significant relationship between attitude similarity and chosen seating distance for both sexes. Analysis of variance showed that subjects who sat closer to the confederate had lower self-reported ratings of anxiety, hostility, and depression.

24. **Alloway, Thomas; Krames, Lester; and Pliner, Patricia,** eds. *Communication and Affect: A Comparative Approach.* New York: Academic Press, 1972. 155 pp. Illus.

The papers in this volume were originally delivered at the first Symposium on Communication and Affect at the University of Toronto. Included is "The Language of Love" by Harry F. Harlow and Margaret K. Harlow which deals with the communication channels and behaviors involved in the development of affection between mother and infant rhesus monkeys, the role of play in development, and the learning of sex-differentiating behaviors. Jacob L. Gewirtz, in "Attachment and Dependence: Some Strategies and Tactics in the Selection and Use of Indices for Those Concepts," discusses the great variety of behavioral indexes used to operationalize attachment and dependence, the assumptions that underlie their use, and related strategic considerations. Edward S. Klima and Ursula Bellugi discuss the use of sign language with chimpanzees and the acquisition of sign language by a deaf child as compared to the acquisition of spoken language in "The Signs of Language in Child and Chimpanzee." J.P. Scott and V.J. DeGhett have contributed "Development of Affect in Dogs and Rodents."

25.　**Als, Heidelise.** "The Newborn Communicates." *Journal of Communication* 27 (1977) : 66-73. Illus.

Thirty-one pairs of primaparous mothers and their newborns were observed during their first encounter after birth and once on the second and third days. The author postulates a three-layered communication system. The first level is state control communication during which the newborn makes its needs known for state adjustment; the second level is affectionate communication, during which newborn alertness is a signal of readiness for eye contact, visual following, yawning, vocalizations, and so on that elicit talking, kissing, nodding, and smiling from the mother. The third level is cognitive communication and readiness for input from the mother, which can only occur during the calm, alert state of the infant.

26.　**Altman, Irwin.** *The Environment and Social Behavior: Privacy, Personal Space, Territory, Crowding.* Monterey, California: Brooks/Cole Publishing Company, 1975. 256 pp. Illus.

This book is an analysis of the concepts of privacy, personal space, territory, and crowding in humans. After an introduction, the author examines privacy in terms of its definitions, properties, mechanisms, and functions. The author then examines personal space — its nature, theoretical approaches toward it, methods for its study, compensatory aspects of it, and the nature of its intrusion. Conceptual issues and relevant research related to territorial behavior are examined next. Finally, crowding is discussed with regard to its meaning, methods of research, theory, and effect. Implications of this discussion for environmental design are also noted.

27.　**Altman, Irwin.** "Research on Environment and Behavior: A Personal Statement of Strategy." In *Perspectives on Environment and Behavior*, edited by D. Stokols, pp. 303-323. New York: Plenum Press, 1977.

The author argues that although there is a great deal of research on environment and behavior, not enough energy has been spent studying social units such as couples, teams, and families. He then discusses several aspects of a research strategy for social-unit analysis, including a focus on several levels and patterns of behavior and the systemlike and dynamic qualities of social units.

28.　**Altman, Irwin, and Vinsel, Anne.** "Personal Space: An Analysis of E.T. Hall's Proxemics Framework." In *Human Behavior and Environment: Advances in Theory and Research,* Volume 2, edited by I. Altman and J. Wohlwill, pp. 181-254. New York: Plenum Press, 1977.

The authors discuss the nature of E.T. Hall's proxemic schema and its cross-cultural variation. They also provide an extensive review of research in proxemics. They survey research to date in five areas: effects of spatial intrusion, interpersonal liking, attraction, similarity or dissimilarity, individual variations in distance patterns, distance as related to other behaviors, and culture and distance. Literature in the field is integrated into Hall's schema and is seen as validating it in most areas. Finally, the authors stress new directions for research.

29.　**Altman, Irwin, and Wohlwill, Joachim,** eds. *Human Behavior and Environment: Advances in Theory and Research* vol. 2. New York: Plenum Press, 1977, Illus.

This anthology explores the relationship between human behavior and the physical environment. Topics include research methodologies, a review of professional media, environmental stress, applied behavior analysis, personal space, methodological issues, and environmental planning. Authors addressing these problems include R. Golledge, D. Appleyard, R. Lazaraus, J. Cohen, J. Cone, S. Hayes, I. Altman, A. Vinsel, S. Klausner, and S. Mann.

30. **Altman, Irwin, and Wohlwill, Joachim,** eds. *Human Behavior and Environment: Advances in Theory and Research. Vol. III, Children and the Environment.* New York: Plenum Press, 1978. 300 pp. Illus.

This anthology is a study of children as they interact with their environment. In Chapter 1 Yi-fu Tuan examines children and the natural environment. The child's home environment is studied in Chapter 2 by Ross Parke. Robin Moore and Donald Young explore the child outdoors from the viewpoint of social ecology in Chapter 3. Chapter 4 by Paul Gump deals with the school environment. Maxine Wolf discusses children and privacy in the next chapter. The last two chapters examine the child's cognitive structuring of geographic space and the child's ability to be an environmental planner.

31. **Altman, Irwin; Wohlwill, Joachim; and Rapoport, A.,** eds. *Human Behavior and Environment: Advances in Theory and Research, Vol. IV, Culture and Environment.* New York: Plenum Press, 1980. Illus.

In this volume John Aiello and Donna Thompson discuss personal space from a cultural perspective; John Bennett examines human ecology and behavior; and John Berry writes on "Cultural Ecology and Individual Behavior." Richard Brislin examines cross-cultural research methods and strategies, and Sidney Brower writes on territoriality in urban context. Environmental design is discussed in cultural context by Amos Rapoport; Miles Richardson notes the "Cultural Change and Urban Form"; Ignacy Sachs has an article in this anthology entitled "Culture, Ecology and Development"; Gilbert White and John Sorenson discuss cross-cultural differences in response to natural hazards in a final chapter. (From prepublication information.)

32. **Anandam, Kamala, and Highberger, Ruth.** "Child Compliance and Congruity Between Verbal and Nonverbal Maternal Communication—A Methodological Note." *Family Process* 11 (1972) : 219-226.

Six mother-preschool-son dyads were videotaped during a play activity. The mothers were instructed to prohibit the child from playing with certain toys available in the room. The sessions were rated independently for positive and negative maternal verbal and nonverbal communication and child compliance. The children's compliant behavior was more associated with congruent, positive maternal verbal and nonverbal communication, although the sample was too limited for conclusive results. The authors discuss the value of videotapes for such research.

33. **Andersen, Peter A., and Leibowitz, Kenneth.** "The Development and Nature of the Construct Touch Avoidance." *Environmental Psychology and Nonverbal Behavior* 3 (1978) : 89-106.

Development of two touch-avoidance measures via factor analysis are reported. Touch avoidance is a nonverbal communication predisposition that consists of two dimensions, same-sex touch avoidance and opposite-sex touch avoidance. The results are replicated across two distinct samples with consistent reliability of measurement. Touch avoidance is then related to communication apprehension, self-disclosure, self-esteem, and a series of cultural role variables. The cultural role variables seem to have the greatest relationship with the two measures of touch avoidance. A program for future research on touch avoidance is also discussed.

34. **Anderson, David R.** "Eye Contact, Topic Intimacy, and Equilibrium Theory." *Journal of Social Psychology* 100 (1976) : 313-314.

Thirty-six same-sex dyads discussed topics rated low, medium, or high in intimacy.

There was no significant effect for topic intimacy, but eye contact tended to be higher with medium-intimacy topics.

35. **Angelini, Diane J.** "Nonverbal Communication in Labor." *American Journal of Nursing* 78 (1978) : 1221-1222. Illus.

Facial expression, eye, and body movements of the pregnant woman in labor are discussed in relation to the progression of the labor and the need for the attending nurse to be sensitive to nonverbal cues.

36. **Angenot, Marc.** "Les traites de l'eloquence du corps." *Semiotica* 8 (1973) : 60-82.

The author describes works from 17th- and 18th-century France, elaborating a theory of natural and formalized gesture and a typology of gestural practice.

37. **Apple, Marianne M.** "Kinesic Training for Blind Persons: A Vital Means of Communication." *The New Outlook for the Blind* 66 (1972) : 201-208.

Blind persons may be hindered in developing interpersonal relationships by their use of a nonverbal communication system differing from that of sighted individuals. The author reviews some nonverbal communication literature concerning kinesics, emotional development and the arts, and concludes with a list of facial expressions and gestures to be taught to the blind individual.

38. **Archer, Dane, and Akert, Robin M.** "Words and Everything Else: Verbal and Non-verbal Cues in Social Interpretation." *Journal of Personality and Social Psychology* 35 (1977) : 443-449.

In a decoding study of how verbal (transcript) and nonverbal (full-channel) messages are interpreted, two groups of undergraduates were given two versions of the Social Interpretations Task (SIT). The SIT consists of a 30-minute videotape of 20 natural sequences of behavior showing one or more people in unposed situations (for example, two women playing with a seven-month-old baby), and a multiple-choice questionnaire about the people in each scene or their relationship (for example which woman is the baby's mother). The verbal transcript version was given to 76 subjects and the verbal-plus-nonverbal version to 370 subjects. Among the results it was found that full-channel subjects were significantly more accurate than transcript subjects.

39. **Arend, Susan, and Higgins, Joseph R.** "A Strategy for the Classification, Subjective Analysis, and Observation of Human Movement." *Journal of Human Movement Studies* 2 (1976) : 36-52.

This strategy involves three phases: preobservation (investigating the environment, movement, and essential features of the performer), observation (systematic approaches to viewing and recording the movement), and postobservation (evaluating the efficiency of the movement, environmental influences, and giving feedback to the performer). The strategy is directed toward teachers, students, and researchers and attempts to integrate current knowledge in the field of human movement. Detailed and abbreviated worksheets are provided for the observer.

40. **Arensberg, Conrad M.** "Introduction." In *Interaction and Social Structure*, edited by O. Collins and J. Collins, pp. 9-20. The Hague: Mouton, 1973.

Interaction theory asserts the indispensability for the human sciences of the systematic observation of interpersonal behaviors as an integral part of social sciences: interaction theory seeks new ways to order and make sense of the immense data accumulated by researchers. This theory begins with an observation of interpersonal events and employs a method which dates back to 1940. In his introduction,

Arensberg traces briefly the application of this theory and method and outlines some of the advantages and complications of its usage. He concludes by judging the Collins' paradigm as both new and restated.

41. **Argyle, Michael.** "Non-Verbal Communication in Human Social Interaction." In *Non-Verbal Communication,* edited by R. Hinde, pp. 243-269. Cambridge: Cambridge University Press, 1972. Illus.

A general survey of the field of nonverbal communication. The first part has to do with various research methods in the field. Next, the author talks about specific forms of nonverbal behavior: body contact, proximity, orientation, appearance, posture, head nods, facial expression, gestures, looking, and paralanguage. He notes the function of nonverbal behavior in the social setting and its role in social interaction. Notably, nonverbal behavior can influence attitudes, perceptions, emotions, and interaction; and setting can influence nonverbal behavior as can individual differences. Argyle concludes by surveying various theoretical explanations of nonverbal behavior.

42. **Argyle, Michael,** ed. *Social Encounters: Readings in Social Interaction.* Chicago: Aldine Publishing Company, 1973. 416 pp. Illus.

This book is an anthology of readings in social psychology. Seven of the 28 readings in the book deal directly with nonverbal behavior. Watson and Graves' study of proxemic differences between Arabs and Americans is included in this compilation. Adam Kendon has an article discussing the functions of gaze in interaction. Ray Birdwhistell has put in a short summary of his approach to kinesics. Albert Mehrabian's study of one's ability to infer communicator attitudes from posture, orientation, and distance is included. P. Ekman and W.V. Friesen have an article on nonverbal deception and leakage. The reciprocity of approving nonverbal behavior (smiles and head nods) is studied by H. Rosenfeld, and Michael Argyle and Janet Dean's examination of the interrelations among eye contact, distance, and affiliation is included.

43. **Argyle, Michael.** *Bodily Communication.* New York: International Universities Press, Inc., 1975. 403 pp. Illus.

This book is a discussion of nonverbal behavior from three aspects. In Part One the author discusses the biological-cultural backgrounds of nonverbal behavior in humans and animals. In Part Two Argyle enumerates the different uses of bodily communication in emotion, expression, attitude formation, information about personality, speech, ritual, ceremony, and politics. In Part Three he examines the various types of bodily signals including the face, gaze, gesture, posture, touch, spatial behavior, clothes, physique, and vocalizations.

44. **Argyle, Michael, and Cook, Mark.** *Gaze and Mutual Gaze.* Cambridge: Cambridge University Press, 1976. 210 pp. Illus.

The purpose of this book is to examine to date the research on gaze to " . . . see how far it adds up to a coherent picture of the role of gaze in human social behavior." To accomplish this task, the authors examine gaze behavior from several vantages. They explore the biological-cultural basis of gaze, the measurement of gaze, the reaction of gaze to interpersonal attitudes and emotions, the perception and interpretation of gaze, the role of gaze in the sequence of interaction, individual differences in gaze, and the role of gaze in visibility in social interaction.

45. **Argyle, Michael, and Graham, Jean Ann.** "The Central Europe Experiment: Looking at Persons and Looking at Objects." *Environmental Psychology and Nonverbal Behavior* 1 (1976) : 6-16.

Gaze at objects, another person, and background was measured for 15 dyads which constituted five different experimental groups in which task and situational factors were varied. The findings were that background stimuli had an unreliable effect on gaze; a very simple object relevant to the subject's task attracted a great deal of gaze and greatly reduced gaze at the other person. This effect was even stronger with a complex relevant object, where visual attention was almost completely transferred from the other person to the object. There was evidence of forces to avoid too much gaze at the other person.

46. **Argyle, Michael; Lefebvre, Luc; and Cook, Mark.** "The Meaning of Five Patterns of Gaze." *European Journal of Social Psychology* 4 (1974) : 125-136.

Forty subjects conversed with confederates using five gaze conditions (continuous, looking while talking, looking while listening, normal gaze, and nearly zero gaze). Conversations were role played as either first meetings with a stranger or an interview situation with the confederate playing the ingratiating interviewee. Subjects then completed rating scales of the confederate's personality. High-gaze conditions were related to positive ratings in general and potency and self-confidence in particular. The ingratiation condition was not related to personality ratings. The meanings and sex differences in gaze patterns are reviewed in more detail.

47. **Aronow, Edward; Reznikoff, Marvin; and Tryon, Warren W.** "The Interpersonal Distance of Process and Reactive Schizophrenia." *Journal of Consulting and Clinical Psychology* 43 (1975) : 94.

Four distance measures showed no significant difference between 61 process and 43 reactive schizophrenics and 30 normal males.

48. **Asante, Molefi Kete; Newmark, Eileen; and Black, Cecil A.**, eds. *Handbook of Intercultural Communication.* Beverly Hills, California: Sage Publications, 1979. 479 pp.

This wide-ranging handbook covers a variety of theoretical approaches and practical applications in intercultural communication. In "Theoretical Dimensions for Intercultural Communication" William S. Howell discusses an interactive dyadic model of interpersonal communication integrating verbal and nonverbal behaviors. Jerry L. Burk and Janet G. Lukens describe a taxonomy of nonverbal behaviors that impede intercultural relations in their article on cognitive anthropology and ethnomethodology. In an article entitled "Integrating Etic and Emic Approaches in the Study of Intercultural Communication," Stanley E. Jones reviews research on proxemic behavior and argues that an "emic" analysis of contextual factors should precede an "etic" or comparative analysis. In "Nonverbal Behavior: An Intercultural Approach," Sheila J. Ramsey provides a review of research on nonverbal dimensions and cites the need for an analysis of contexts. V. Lynn Tyler, Peggy Hall, and James S. Taylor have contributed an article in which they discuss sources, methods, and strategies for data acquisition in intercultural communication, as well as methods of validation. Robert Shuter discusses still photography as a research tool in Chapter 15. In "Black-White Communication: An Assessment of Research" Dorothy L. Pennington discusses nonverbal differences found in the literature and the differences between existential and experimental methodologies. And in "Counseling Clients from Other Cultures: Two Training Designs" Paul Pedersen describes two experiences for counselor training using videotaped feedback.

49. **Ashcraft, Norman, and Scheflen, Albert E.** *People Space: The Making and Breaking of Human Boundaries.* Garden City, New York: Anchor Press/Doubleday, 1976. 185 pp.

The first part of this book explores how people use space in various contexts and at various points of interaction and how this use is repeated and replicated at different levels from conversational settings, to the spatial layouts of rooms, to entire cities. With many references and descriptions of gaze and proxemic behaviors from different cultures, the authors elucidate the meaning of territory and the related concepts of privacy, intrusion, defense, constraints, and crowding. The second part focuses on the repercussions of these elements within human problems such as poverty, scarcity of resources, and violence.

50.   **Ashear, Victor, and Snortum, John R.** "Eye Contact in Children as a Function of Age, Sex, Social, and Intellective Variables." *Developmental Psychology* 4 (1971): 479.

The authors examined developmental changes and sex differences in relation to eye contact and eye pattern communication in 90 preschool and school-age children. Different patterns of eye communication based on the age and sex of the child were found. For example, females were found to make significantly more eye contact than males when speaking.

51.   **Athanasiou, Robert, and Yoshioka, Gary A.** "The Spatial Character of Friendship Formation." *Environment and Behavior* 5 (1973) : 43-65. Illus.

The authors collected the data at a housing project which contained 427 dwelling units of varying size and arrangement. They interviewed women residents about their friendship patterns, activity patterns, life styles, previous residence site development preference, and children's activities. Their results showed that propinquity plays a part in the formation and maintenance of friendships among women who may have little in common.

52.   **Ayers, Harold J.** "Observers' Judgments of Audience Members' Attitudes." *Western Speech* 39 (1975) : 40-50.

A three-minute videotape was made of each of four pretested audiences consisting of six men and women with high ego involvement in the program presented to them and six women and men with low ego involvement in the program. Sixty-two college students were shown the audience videotapes and asked to complete a semantic differential-type scale for each audience member. They were also asked to rate each audience member's ego involvement on a Likert-type scale. Following the assessment task each observer indicated his or her own attitude toward the subject of the program. The results indicated that female audience members' attitudes were more accurately assessed than male audience attitudes. Highly ego-involved audience members were more accurately assessed than low ego-involved members. No relationship was found between the observers' self-perceived social desirability or their attitudes toward the program and their judgments of the audience members' attitudes.

53.   **Babcock, Barbara A.** "The Semiotics of Subordination." *Semiotica* 24 (1978) : 149-156.

A book review and description of Erving Goffman's *Gender Advertisements.*

54.   **Badler, Norman I., and Smoliar, Stephen W.** "Digital Representations of Human Movement." *Computing Surveys* 2 (1979) : 19-38. Illus.

There are many different approaches to the representation within a digital computer of information descriptive of human body movement. In order to extract some primitive movement concepts which can be used to animate a realistic human body on a graphics display, the authors examine one particular notation system, Labanotation. This notation system has led to the design of a "machine language," and programs in this language can be interpreted by a simulator to produce an animated display of human movement.

55. **Bailey, Kent G.; Hartnett, John J.; and Gibson, Frank W. Jr.** "Implied Threat and the Territorial Factor in Personal Space." *Psychological Reports* 30 (1972) : 263-270.

Forty male and 40 female undergraduates served as experimental subjects and took an anxiety measure and a heterosexuality scale. In some cases a male or female confederate walked toward the subject until the subject felt uncomfortable. In other instances the subject walked toward the confederate until he or she (the subject) felt uncomfortable. Subjects tended to keep greater distance from the male confederate. Males approached by a female confederate allowed the closest approach. Amount of anxiety seemed to influence the distance kept by females and the heterosexuality score seemed related to male distance patterns.

56. **Bailey, Kent G.; Hartnett, John J.; and Glover, Hilda W.** "Modeling and Personal Space Behavior in Children." *Journal of Psychology* 85 (1973) : 143-150.

Fifth and sixth graders from a school in a southern city were assigned to the Model Far (18 males, 18 females). Model Close (18 males, 18 females), or the No Model (15 males, 15 females) condition. The model was a popular male peer who approached or was approached by a female adult, either at a close or far distance. Results show a strong tendency to model, with subjects following the spatial behavior of the peer. Both modeling conditions tended to attenuate the sex differences, girls keeping greater distance than boys, found in the control group.

57. **Baker, Charlotte.** "Regulators and Turn-Taking in American Sign Language Discourse." In *On the Other Hand: New Perspectives on American Sign Language*, edited by L.A. Friedman, pp. 215-236. New York: Academic Press, 1977.

Two same-sex dyads conversing in American Sign Language were noted to use hand rest positions as regulators. Males and persons posing questions tended to rest hands at or above waist level, while females tended to use rest positions at or below the waist. Touching or quick gestural movements were used to obtain requisite eye contact for the initiation of conversation. As with normals, a return to eye contact during sign conversation served to check the other participant's decoding, signal conversation boundaries, and the termination of encoding. In contrast to normals, deaf individuals participated in longer periods of mutual gaze and more frequent facial activity. The author suggests introducing these differences in nonverbal communication when teaching sign language to hearing individuals.

58. **Baldwin, Lori A.; Duttro, M. Kathleen; and Telek, Geza,** eds. *Films: The Visualization of Anthropology* 1980. University Park, Pennsylvania: The Pennsylvania State University Audiovisual Services, 1980. 164 pp.

This catalog is a descriptive listing of 16 mm films from the collection of Audiovisual Services at the Pennsylvania State University. Films are listed with descriptions of their contents according to the subdisciplines of anthropology (cultural, archaeology, and so on.)

59. **Ball, Donald W.** *Microecology: Social Situations and Intimate Space.* Indianapolis, Indiana: Bobbs-Merrill, 1973.

60. **Ball, Howard Guy.** "Educable Mentally Retarded Students' Perceptions of Teachers' Nonverbal Behavior." Ph.D. dissertation, Ohio State University. 1972. 214 pp. (Order No. 73-1930)

Seven categories of Galloway's Continuum of Teachers' Non-Verbal Behaviors were presented on videotape by two white and two black female teacher-actors and viewed by 84 educable mentally junior high school students. Subjects successfully differentiated the eight categories, with students of each race rating teacher-actors of their own race higher.

61. **Bär, Eugen.** *Semiotic Approaches to Psychotherapy.* Bloomington, Indiana: Indiana University Publications, 1975. 177 pp.

The author describes the behavior theories of J. Lacan (with emphasis on his notion of the unconscious), C.G. Jung (emphasis on individuation), H. Shands, J. Ruesch, and A.E. Scheflen, categorizing their approaches in terms of connotative or denotative semiotic systems.

62. **Barakat, R.A.** *The Cistercian Sign Language: A Study in Non-Verbal Communication.* Kalamazoo, Michigan: Cistercian Publications, 1975. 220 pp. Illus.

This dictionary of the Cistercian Sign Language provides an illustrated list of signs, examines the historical record, and contributes to the basic study of gestures, particularly technical gestures. The author, in addition to tracing a brief history of the use of gesture in speech, classifies Cistercian sign language into five groups: pantomimic signs, pure signs, qualitative signs, feature signs, and speech signs. The alphabet and syntax of the sign language, and an authorized list of signs with accompanying photographs are presented.

63. **Barakat, Robert A.** "Arabic Gestures." *Journal of Popular Culture* 7 (1973) : 749-787. Illus.

In order to register reactions to events and peoples, or to communicate silently, Arabs extensively rely on a vast variety of gestures and body movements. Although the data available on autistic, culture-induced, and technical gestures remains meager, the data on semiotic gestures offers cautious but rich generalizations. The article concludes with a catalog of 247 Arabic gestures and an explanation of their usage.

64. **Barakat, Robert A.** "On Ambiguity in the Cistercian Sign Language." *Sign Language Studies* 8 (1975) : 275-289.

This article describes the sign language used in Cistercian monasteries for about a thousand years. The language has taken on some characteristics of natural languages but, because of its ambiguity, can be frustrating.

65. **Barash, David P.** "Human Ethology: Personal Space Reiterated." *Environment and Behavior* 5 (1973) : 67-72.

Among many animals, personal space varies with internal, physiological conditions, but it is likely there are less important influences on personal space among humans. Rather, humans develop an expectation of personal space based upon assessment of the per capita space available which enables them to avoid discomfort and/or uneasiness; that is, unlike animals they utilize cognitive capacities which mediate personal space patterns.

66. **Barefoot, John C.; Hoople, Howard; and McClay, David.** "Avoidance of an Act which Would Violate Personal Space." *Psychonomic Science* 28 (1972) : 205-206.

This is a study of 508 male users of a water fountain in a public building. A female or male confederate was seated at one of three distances from a water fountain. Subjects drank less often when the confederate was seated nearest to the fountain, supporting the previous research on spatial invasions.

67. **Barker, Roger G.** *Habitats, Environments, and Human Behavior.* San Francisco, California: Jossey-Bass, 1978. 327 pp.

This book is the product of work at the Midwest Psychological Field Station which was established to study the everyday behavior and psychological situations of the children of Midwest towns. Part one of the work presents the fundamental issues of ecological psychology and a treatment of the problems of ecobehavioral science. Part two addresses methodological, analytical, and conceptual problems of research in ecological psychology and presents some findings. The studies demonstrate the values of field-station research with its phenomena-centered data. The studies presented in Part three deal with "behavior settings," procedures for measuring environmental extent and variety, and methods of measuring dynamic properties of behavior settings.

68. **Barnes, Susan Vanden Hoek.** "The Use of Sign Language as Technique for Language Acquisition in Autistic Children." Ph.D. dissertation, California School of Professional Psychology. 1973. 95 pp. (Order No. 74-7093)

Sign language was used as a possible technique for treating autism. In this study the children were able to learn sign language, and their vocabularies increased, as did interaction with others in their environment.

69. **Barnett, Kathryn E.** "A Survey of the Current Utilization of Touch by Health Team Personnel with Hospitalized Patients." *International Journal of Nursing Studies* 9 (1972) : 195-209.

After a brief review of the literature to support the therapeutic importance of touch to reduce psycho-physiological stress, the author describes a study of the occurrence of "nonnecessary" touch routinely utilized by health care personnel at two hospitals. Significant differences in the occurrence of touching were associated with the age range and race of both patients and personnel. Nurses and nursing students most utilized "nonnecessary" touch. Touching most often occurred in pediatric, obstetrical, and intensive care units and more often at the publicly funded than the privately funded hospitals. This latter finding was interpreted in terms of the socioeconomic level of the patients at the two hospitals. While patients' extremities were the areas most often touched at both hospitals, the abdomen of the patients at the publicly funded hospital was also often touched. Notably, patients in serious or critical condition were touched less than half as often as patients in good or fair condition.

70. **Barrel, James J.** "Sexual Arousal in the Objectifying Attitude." *Review of Existential Psychology and Psychiatry* 13 (1974) : 98-105.

Sexual arousal in the "objectness position" (that is, when the viewer sees the other as an object apart from the world) reveals two important dimensions: the dialectic of "concealment-revealment"; and the polar opposites of "aliveness/deadness." While the former concerns the viewing of a potential to be expressed in the future, the latter deals with the body as either possessing sexual vitality or as a structure without function. Both these elements are necessary to the type of sexual arousal found within an objectifying attitude.

71. **Bartee, Neale King.** "The Development of a Theoretical Position on Conducting Using Principles of Body Movement As Explicated by Rudolf Laban." Ph.D. dissertation, University of Illinois at Urbana-Champaign. 1977. 218 pp. (Order No. 78039-30)

Laban's theory of movement was examined as a basis for improving the use of body movement in conducting.

72. **Bartenieff, Irmgard.** "Dance Therapy: A New Profession or a Rediscovery of an Ancient Role of the Dance?" *Dance Scope* Fall/Winter (1972/73) : 6-18.

Using brief descriptions of the work of dance therapy innovators, this article presents an historical overview of the field, starting with its roots in the modern dance revolution of the 1930s and 40s. Major themes discussed are the varying degree and type of cooperation between dance therapists and psychiatrists or psychologists, the relationship of Effort/Shape analysis to dance therapy, and the importance of dance as social interaction as well as individual therapy.

Dance is often regarded as such a separate category of movement experiences that it is excluded, unnecessarily, from the training and experience of other disciplines. The framework of Labananalysis does not maintain so sharp a separation. There are differences in intention, choice, and degree of body usage, but the components of all body movements are the same. Since dance provides combinations of the components at heightened intensities, any student of body movement for any reason can incorporate the observations from dance analyses.
Irmgard Bartenieff with Dori Lewis. *Body Movement: Coping with the Environment.* New York: Gordon & Breach, 1980. P. ix.

73. **Bartenieff, Irmgard.** *Notes from a Course in Correctives.* New York: Dance Notation Bureau Press, 1977. 37 pp. Illus.

Five lectures on postural correctives, described in Laban terms and accompanying exercises, are presented in this introductory course description. The fine opening chapter discusses muscular functioning from the perspective of biomechanics and neurophysiology as well as Laban's work. Ensuing chapters include detailed information on the lower unit as regards initiation from center of weight, locomotion, change of level; the rotary element in movement; and the upper unit as regards counterbalance, exploration, orientation, manipulation, communication, and breathing.

74. **Bartenieff, Irmgard with Lewis, Dori.** *Body Movement: Coping with the Environment.* New York: Gordon and Breach Science Publishers, 1980. 289 pp. Illus.

A beautifully written and illustrated book on "what the body can do, how it does it, how it relates to space, and how the quality of its movement affects function and communication—coping." Based on the work of the inventor of the major dance notation, Rudolf Laban, and his student and colleague, Irmgard Bartenieff, the book is the primary source of "Labananalysis," a quantitative and qualitative vocabulary, for describing human movement which includes the concepts and terms of Labanotation and Effort-Shape Analysis of movement. Following a history of Irmgard Bartenieff's work in dance, physical therapy, and dance therapy, there are chapters on the "body architecture," carving shapes in space, "effort" dynamics or intensity aspects of movement, rhythm and phrasing, special aspects of patterning, and group interaction. There is a chapter on cross-cultural study of movement styles and a series of diverse applications of Labananalysis. The book concludes with an appendix on Bartenieff fundamentals of movement training. Examples from everyday life, the arts, and research are woven throughout this complex book.

75. **Bass, Marian H., and Weinstein, Malcolm S.** "Early Development of Interpersonal Distance in Children." *Canadian Journal of Behavioural Science* 3 (1971) : 368-376.

This study attempts to identify the interpersonal distance behaviors of children and the influence of sex, age, degree of acquaintance, and setting upon such behaviors. An interviewer tested 113 children between the ages of five and nine using cut-out silhouettes which the child arranged in different room drawings. Results indicate that by age five children have acquired interpersonal distance preferences. Their proxemic choices reflect awareness of the effect of age, setting, degree of acquaintance, and specific interactions between these variables on interpersonal distance behaviors. No significant sex differences in the interpersonal space preferences were found.

76. **Bassett, Ronald E., and Smythe, Mary-Jeanette.** *Communication and Instruction.* New York: Harper & Row, 1979.

This text for student teachers contains a section on "nonverbal communication and teaching effectiveness" that discusses research such as that of J.A. Civikly, A. Love, and J. Roderick and T. Willet on research of teacher nonverbal behavior.

77. **Batchelor, James P., and Goethals, George R.** "Spatial Arrangements in Freely Formed Groups." *Sociometry* 35 (1972) : 270-279.

Twenty groups of four high school students, each with four males and four females, were asked to make either collective or individual decisions on a problem. Members of the groups were free to place their chairs wherever they wanted. Distances between subjects' chairs, number of other subjects each subject could see, and distance to the nearest person were calculated. Groups making collective decisions sat significantly closer together and had greater visual contact. All collective decision groups showed similar spatial arrangements. There was great variation among groups making individual decisions, but within groups individual distances tended to remain constant.

78. **Bate, Brian R.** "Effects of Various Social Reinforcers on Interviewee Eye Contact." Ph.D. dissertation, Case Western Reserve University. 1971. 190 pp.

Experiments were designed to examine the effects of head nodding, vocal approval, and smiling on amount of eye contact during three periods in an interview.

79. **Bates, John E.** "The Effects of Children's Nonverbal Behavior Upon Adults." *Child Development* 47 (1976) : 1079-1088.

Sixty-four college student subjects were given the task of teaching four elementary mathematical principles in one-to-one interactions. Four 11 year old boys were trained to perform the same on objective tests and to display nonverbal cues of either "high positivity" (high amount of looking and smiling) or "low positivity" (looking 25 percent of time and no smiling) while interacting with college student subjects given the task of teaching them math principles. Results indicate that high level of child positivity produced higher levels of adult positivity and more favorable written evaluations of the child's intellectual and social abilities than did the low level of positivity, despite identical objective performance by the confederates. Sequential analyses were performed and are reported in terms of adult-child reciprocity. The results are discussed in terms of real-life instructional situations.

80. **Bateson, Gregory.** *Steps to an Ecology of Mind.* San Francisco, California: Chandler Publishing Company, 1972. 541 pp. Illus.

This important collection brings together most of Bateson's writings before 1971, dealing with anthropology, art, psychiatry, biology and evolution, systems theory, epistemology, and ecology. Included here are Bateson's influential papers on the double bind and schizophrenia, logical types in communication, analogical and digital coding, animal communication, and play as communication. There is also a comprehensive list of the published books, reviews, articles and films by Bateson.

81. **Bateson, P.P.G., and Hinde, R.A.,** eds. *Growing Points in Ethology.* Cambridge: Cambridge University Press, 1976. 548 pp.

Articles based on proceedings from the 1975 conference on ethology at the University of Cambridge at Madingley. The causes, evolution, biological function, and development of animal behavior patterns are addressed by essays in the first three sections of the book. The role and organization of specific behaviors as they relate to survival, adaptation, communication, and perception are examined closely. The final section focuses on links between human social relationships and ethology, providing a valuable perspective for viewing human behavior. Authors included in the volume are: R. Dawkins, D.J. McFarland, R.J. Andrew, J. Fentress, J. Hall-Craggs, T.H. Clutton-Brock, P.H. Harvey, P. Marler, B.C.R. Bertram, N.K. Humphrey, A. Manning, J.S. Rosenblatt, M.J.A. Simpson, P.P.G. Bateson, N.G.B. Jones, R.A. Hinde, J. Stevenson-Hinde, J. Dunn, and P.B. Medawar.

82. Battison, Robbin, and Jordan, I. King. "Cross-Cultural Communication with Foreign Signers: Fact and Fancy." *Sign Language Studies* 10 (1976) : 53-68.

From personal interviews and observation, the authors conclude that signs vary considerably from country to country, and that receptive skills exceed expressive skills in cross-cultural signing.

83. Battle, Esther S., and Lacey, Beth. "A Context for Hyperactivity in Children, Over Time." *Child Development* 43 (1972) : 757-773.

This study examined the motor activity over time of 31 females and 43 males drawn from the Fels Longitudinal Study. Observational data from recorded interactions with mother and with peers during childhood and interview data from adolescence and young adulthood, as well as standardized test data, were used. Examination of the data found higher hyperactivity scores for males only in the age six-to-ten period. IQ test performance and academic and verbal performance were not significantly related to hyperactivity. However, significant sex differences in the antecedents and correlates of hyperactivity were observed. For example, during the period from birth to age three disapproving and unaffectionate behavior in mothers is correlated with subsequent hyperactivity in males but not in females. From age three to six hyperactive children interacted more with peers than nonhyperactive children, but females did so in a positive way and males in a negative way. The authors argue against a general systemic view of motoric impulsivity and for the parental and environmental contributions to hyperactivity in children.

84. Bauer, Robert E.L. "Verbal and Motor Components of Leader Behavior in a Leaderless Group Discussion." Ph.D. dissertation, University of Tennessee. 1972. 183 pp. (Order No. 72-27, 447)

Verbal and motor behaviors of a videotaped six-person group were analyzed using an ethological approach. The author stresses the importance of the measurement process used in research and critiques earlier approaches to the study of leadership.

85. Baum, Andrew; Aiello, John R.; and Clesnick, Lisa E. "Crowding and Personal Control: Social Density and the Development of Learned Helplessness." *Journal of Personality and Social Psychology* 36 (1978) : 1000-1011.

One hundred twenty residents who lived in either long-corridor (crowded, large group) or short-corridor (uncrowded, moderate group) dormitories participated in the study. Measures were taken following one, three, or seven weeks of residence. It was anticipated that the crowded dormitory residents would display increased helplessness over time. The residents completed surveys or played a Prisoner Dilemma game designed to assess competitiveness, cooperativeness, and withdrawal. Residents of long-corridor dorms were more competitive and less cooperative than short-corridor residents. Further, long-corridor residents showed a significant increase in withdrawal responses after seven weeks.

86. Baum, Andrew, and Epstein, Yakov, eds. *Human Response to Crowding.* Hillsdale, New Jersey: Lawrence Erlbaum Associates, 1978. 418 pp.

As stated by the editors, this book is an attempt to "describe theoretical developments, examine research methods and consider evidence" related to human response to crowding. The book, divided into three sections, presents a series of papers by researchers well known for their contributions to study of crowding. In Section One data generated from crowding research during the period 1970-76 is reviewed, integrated, harmonized, interpreted, and placed into conceptual frames. Section

Two reviews research results and fits them into some specific models of crowding and density-related stress. Section Three papers derive and empirically test hypotheses which spring from various theoretical approaches to crowding and the personal space construct.

87.   **Baum, Andrew, and Greenberg, Carl I.** "Waiting for a Crowd: The Behavioral and Perceptual Effects of Anticipated Crowding." *Journal of Personality and Social Psychology* 32 (1975) : 671-679.

Forty male and 40 female undergraduate subjects were told they were to be in an uncrowded or crowded room. After a subject remained alone in the room for two minutes, two confederates arrived and sat close to or far away from the subject. Five dependent variables were measured: position taken by the subject, amount of facial regard between subject and first confederate, subject's evaluations of the confederates, subject's reactions to the experimental room, and subject's reported comfort in the setting. Those anticipating crowding chose more socially isolated seats, looked at the confederate less, reported more discomfort, liked both confederates less, and perceived the room differently from those not anticipating crowding.

88.   **Baum, Andrew, and Koman, Stuart.** "Differential Response to Anticipated Crowding: Psychological Effects of Social and Spatial Density." *Journal of Personality and Social Psychology* 34 (1976) : 526-536.

Thirty-two male and 32 female undergraduates were told they would be in large or small crowded or uncrowded conditions. Half the subjects were told to expect a structured session. The subject was first alone in a room. At preset intervals two confederates entered the room. From observation the subject's seat position, verbal behavior, and facial regard were noted. Subjects also filled out forms evaluating the room, their comfort, and the experimental session. Among the results it was found that subjects awaiting large-group unstructured sessions felt more crowded than those awaiting large-group structured sessions. In general, behavioral responses to anticipated high social density were mediated by expectation of social structure.

89.   **Baüml, Betty J., and Baüml, Franz H.** *A Dictionary of Gestures.* Metuchen, New Jersey: Scarecrow, 1975. 249 pp. Illus.

This dictionary primarily contains culturally transmitted gestures. It does not include sign language or occupationally specific gestures but does include gestures that have been widely assimilated. All descriptions of gestures in the collection come from verifiable sources, so that for a more specific or subtle idea of a given gesture one can refer to the original source in the book's bibliography. The dictionary is organized alphabetically according to the body part(s) primarily involved in executing a gesture, with the significance(s) of different gestures alphabetically listed under each of these headings.

90.   **Baxter, James C., and Rozelle, Richard M.** "Nonverbal Expression as a Function of Crowding during a Simulated Police-Citizen Encounter." *Journal of Personality and Social Psychology* 32 (1975) : 40-54.

Twenty-nine adult men volunteered to participate in a simulated police interview. Two speech measures and several nonverbal indexes (eye behavior, head activity, protective and nonprotective hand and arm behavior, trunk rotation, and foot activity) revealed patterns significantly related to crowding. Implications of the results for interpersonal attribution processes were examined.

91.   **Bayes, Marjorie A.** "Behavioral Cues of Interpersonal Warmth." *Journal of Consulting and Clinical Psychology* 39 (1972) : 333-339.

Eight male and eight female college students were videotaped responding to questions about their home town, family, school and job experience. Eighteen male and

18 female students made global judgments as to the warmth of each interviewee. Among the results it was found that frequency of smiling was the single best predictor of warmth.

92. **Beach, David R., and Sokoloff, Mark J.** "Spatially Dominated Nonverbal Communication of Children: A Methodological Study." *Perceptual and Motor Skills* 38 (1974) : 1303-1310.

The study developed scales and procedures for assessing children's nonverbal behavior, particularly distance, orientation, eye contact, and position variations. Fourteen middle-class children between four and five years of age were videotaped while engaged in free play. Five of the scales proved usable, with three assessed as having acceptable inter-rater reliability. Interesting results suggest that girls may maintain greater interpersonal distance than boys.

93. **Beakel, Nancy G.** "Parental Verbal and Nonverbal Communication and Psychopathology." Ph.D. dissertation, University of California, Los Angeles. 1971. 95 pp. (Order No. 71-582)

94. **Beattie, Geoffrey W.** "Floor Apportionment and Gaze in Conversational Dyads." *British Journal of Social and Clinical Psychology* 17 (1978) : 1-15.

The author discusses Adam Kendon's findings on the functions of gaze in conversation, especially concerning its role in facilitating turn-taking. In the present study, portions of four videotaped interactions were analyzed to see whether extended gaze at the end of a speaking turn reduced the pause between turns. He found on the contrary that utterances ending with extended gaze had significantly longer pauses than those with no gaze. Utterances ending in no gaze were followed by significantly more immediate switches with no pause. The author concluded that there was no evidence for the role of gaze in facilitating speaker-switches. Kendon replies to this paper as well as to the following one by Rutter *et al.* on pp. 23-24 of the same volume.

95. **Beattie, Geoffrey W.** "Sequential Temporal Patterns of Speech and Gaze in Dialogue." *Semiotica* 23 (1978) : 29-52.

An intensive analysis was made of the speech and gaze of five subjects filmed in supervision or seminar discussions. Speech samples of more than 30 seconds were selected at random, and cognitive cycles were identified with respect to speech units. The relationship between the cognitive cycles of speech and the macropatterns of gaze revealed a loosely coordinated system, with the pattern of gaze seeming to reflect the gross temporal structure of the pause/phonation patterns in speech. Gaze was organized with the plans underlying speech and with the speech flow itself in a coordinated system, with gaze found to be more frequent in fluent phases than in the hesitant phases of the cognitive cycles.

96. **Bechtel, Robert.** *Enclosing Behavior.* Stroudsburg, Pennsylvania: Dowden, Hutchinson, and Ross, 1977. Illus.

Concerned with the relation between behavior and architecture, this book includes a synthesis of the known materials in environmental psychology, notes applications, and stresses new approaches to design problems. It is designed as a reference book for environmental planners and thereby cites specific designs and follow-up studies to assist them.

97. **Beck, Henry.** "Ethological Considerations on the Problem of Political Order." *Political Anthropology, An International Quarterly* 1 (1975) : 109-135. Illus.

An essay on the ethological concepts of fixed action patterns, markers and releasers, and their relation to the nature of social order. Using examples of human and primate threat displays "fear-grins," spatial relationships, and aggression/flight patterns, he discusses the concepts of "spatiality," mobility as intentionality, and temporality in higher animal behavior.

98. **Beck, Henry.** "Neuropsychological Servosystems, Consciousness, and the Problem of Embodiment." *Behavioral Science* 21 (1976) : 139-160.

Important to this bibliography is an essay on how recent work on systems theory and in neurophysiology (especially that of K. Pribram) may provide a link between "the psychology of consciousness, the neurophysiology of movement, and the growing body of work on nonverbal communication."

99. **Beck, Steven J., and Ollendick, Thomas H.** "Personal Space, Sex of the Experimenter, and Locus of Control in Normal and Delinquent Adolescents." *Psychological Reports* 38 (1976) : 383-387.

The subjects were 56 male white adolescents, aged 13 to 17, 28 normal and 28 delinquent. The personal space (PS) measure was the distance at which the subject stopped the experimenter as he or she approached from each of four directions. Results indicated that: delinquents and normals were the same on the PS indexes; both groups needed more PS behind than in front; and both groups allowed females closer than males.

100. **Becker, David George.** "Proxemics and Recreational Spatial Behavior in Yellowstone National Park Campgrounds." Ph.D. dissertation, University of Illinois at Urbana-Champaign. 1977. 180 pp. (Order No. 7803934)

A model of spatial behavior is constructed from factors such as territoriality, change of environment by campers, and socio-economic background of campers.

101. **Becker, Franklin D.** "Study of Spatial Markers." *Journal of Personality and Social Psychology* 26 (1973) : 439-455.

Observers in a large university library wanted to determine the effect of markers (signs of use or occupancy) on seating behavior at tables. In the first experiment the choice of seating and the duration one remained at a library table were less affected for marked tables than occupied tables. In a second study, using photographs and a questionnaire, no subject said they would sit at a marked location.

102. **Beckwith, Leila.** "Relationships between Infants' Social Behavior and the Mothers' Behavior." *Child Development* 43 (1972) : 397-411.

During two visits of one hour each, 24 mothers were observed and scored for frequency and type of verbal and physical contacts with their adopted infants (age eight months to 11 months). Times the mother ignored approaches or crying of the infant, and her "permissiveness" and "restrictiveness" were also rated. Infants were observed and scored on frequencies of social behavior: ignoring, approaches, and responses to mother. The mothers also responded to the Parental Attitude Response Inventory and answered a questionnaire on the social experiences of their infants. The infants were rated on the Rheingold Social Responsiveness Scale. Intercorrelation of measures showed that mothers who showed strong tendency to make contact had infants who showed less self-stimulatory behavior and tended to ignore the mother more. If mothers were more interfering or ignoring, infants had less social play with mother and were more responsive to a stranger. Boys were significantly more responsive to a stranger on the Rheingold Scale than girls.

103. **Beebe, Beatrice.** "Micro-Timing in Mother-Infant Communication." In *Nonverbal Communication Today: Current Research,* edited by M.R. Key. The Hague: Mouton, forthcoming. Illus.

A very clear and useful discussion of the method of microanalysis and of several case studies of mother-infant pairs. The author reviews recent findings on the early capabilities of the infant and on the split-second reactivity observed in maternal and infant behavior. The case studies deal with the spectrum of engagement/disengagement behaviors available to the infant in interaction, the relation of maternal microrhythms to infant engagement, and the synchronization of maternal and infant behaviors in coactive and noncoactive ways. The author concludes with a consideration of the importance of temporal factors in mother-infant communication.

104. **Beebe, Beatrice, and Gerstman, Louis J.** "The 'Packaging' of Maternal Stimulation in Relation to Infant Facial-Visual Engagement." *Merrill-Palmer Quarterly*, in press. Illus.

Approximately two minutes of a mother-infant interaction involving rhythmic hand games were microanalyzed. Mother's and infant's behaviors were coded frame by frame using ordinal engagement scales, each point of which represented a specific combination of orientation, visual attention, and facial expressions. The mother's hand movements varied according to five modes: three measures of rhythmic hand-swings on a horizontal plane (full-out, half-out, and short-out games), transitions, and hand pauses. Analysis of the way in which mother's and infant's level of engagement varied in relation to mother's hand games showed that mother's facial-visual engagement and rhythmic hand movements systematically covaried as a "package"; not all variations were functionally significant for the infant, however. The infant's engagement did not significantly differ between full-out and half-out games, while mother's engagement did. On the other hand, the difference between half-out games and transitions was significant for the infant, while mother's facial-visual engagement remained constant. The significance of maternal rhythms for the infant is discussed.

105. **Beebe, Beatrice, and Stern, Daniel N.** "Engagement-Disengagement and Early Object Experiences." In *Communicative Structures and Psychic Structures*, edited by N. Freedman and S. Grand, pp. 35-55. New York: Plenum Press, 1977. Illus.

The range of behaviors open to the infant to modulate or regulate social stimulation is discussed as an engagement-disengagement spectrum. Gradations on the spectrum were operationalized using five criteria: visual perception of the mother (foveal, peripheral, or none); head orientation in the horizontal plane (center vis-a-vis to beyond 90° from center); reactivity to the mother (micromomentary, inhibition of responsivity, or unrelated); direction of movement (approach, withdrawal, or neither); and facial expressiveness (positive, negative, or neutral). Using these criteria, the gradations of the spectrum are: "facing and looking," "side looking," "visual checking," "dodging," "inhibition of responsivity," "fuss-cry," and "turn to environment." The middle range of the spectrum is illustrated by a discussion of one mother-infant interaction.

106. **Beebe, Beatrice; Stern, Daniel; and Jaffe, Joseph.** "The Kinesic Rhythm of Mother-Infant Interactions." In *Of Speech and Time: Temporal Speech Patterns in Interpersonal Contexts,* edited by A.W. Siegman and S. Feldstein, pp. 23-24. Hillsdale, New Jersey: Lawrence Erlbaum, 1979.

The article describes an investigation of the temporal patterning of a kinesic interaction between mother and four month old infant through frame-by-frame film analysis. Coaction, or simultaneous behavior, was found to predominate, with the infant responding to the mother's behavior in well below reaction time. The noncoactive kinesic episodes showed a rhythmic matching of action and pause that parallels the structure of adult conversation. Comparison with previous results on vocalization revealed the similar nature of vocal and kinesic interaction in infancy and crucial importance of timing in early mother-infant interaction.

107. **Beebe, Steven A.** "Eye Contact: A Nonverbal Determinant of Speaker Credibility." *The Speech Teacher* 23 (1974) : 21-25.

o   College students were exposed to a live public speaking situation in which only the amount of eye contact varied: 46 of them in condition one, no eye contact; 48 in condition two, moderate (50 percent) eye contact, and 42 in condition three, high (90 percent) eye contact. They rated the speaker on 15 semantic differential scales factor-analyzed to yield three factors related to speaker credibility: qualification, dynamism and honesty. The analysis of variance on the qualification factor showed that the speaker was perceived to be significantly more credible in the moderate and high eye contact condition than in the no eye contact condition. On the honesty factor, the speaker was perceived to be significantly more credible in the high eye contact condition than in the moderate or no eye contact conditions. There were no significant differences on the dynamism factor of speaker credibility.

108. **Beebe, Steven Arnold.** "Effects of Eye Contact, Posture, and Vocal Inflection Upon Comprehension and Credibility." Ph.D. dissertation, University of Missouri. 1976. 162 pp. (Order No. 77048-87)

In this study a speaker delivered a speech while manipulating eye contact, posture and vocal inflection. Ratings of the speech videotapes suggest that specific eye contact patterns may enhance credibility and increase comprehension.

109. **Beels, C. Christian.** "Profile: Albert E. Scheflen." *The Kinesis Report: News and Views of Nonverbal Communication* 2 (Fall 1979) : 1-4, 14-15. Illus.

An interview with one of the pioneers in kinesics research, Albert E. Scheflen, who died in the summer of 1980. Scheflen talks about his research philosophy, how his career evolved, and key concepts on his last book, *Levels of Schizophrenia.*

110. **Beier, Ernst G., and Sternberg, Daniel P.** "Subtle Cues Between Newlyweds." *Journal of Communication* 27 (1977) : 92-97.

The authors rated measures of eye contact, touching (both self and other), open and closed body positions, and time talking in order to judge level of marital discord. Interesting correlations and differences in husband and wife behavior and feelings, as well as the subtle cues by which they communicate the quality of their marriage to one another are reported. For example, couples with greater discord sat farther apart, had less eye contact, and showed more self-touch as opposed to other touch, but they talked more.

111. **Beier, Ernst G., and Valens, Evans G.** *People-Reading: How We Control Others, How They Control Us.* New York: Stein and Day, 1975. 283 pp.

Drawing on experience accumulated from their psychotherapy practices, the authors use a communication analysis model to explore the unconscious manipulation of others, both verbal and nonverbal, in parent-child, work, and love relationships.

112. **Bell, Paul; Fisher, Jeffrey; and Loomis, Ross.** *Environmental Psychology.* Philadelphia: W.B. Saunders, 1978. Illus.

The authors begin with a discussion of the nature of environmental psychology and the research methods used to investigate it. Chapter two has to do with how one perceives and evaluates the environment. In the next chapter Bell *et al.* discuss theoretical approaches to environment-behavior relationships. In Chapters four, five, and six the effects of noise, temperature, air pollution, wind, personal space, and crowding are discussed. Next the authors discuss human environmental adaptation. Chapter eight deals with the city. The last two chapters relate to environmental design and conservation.

113. **Bellack, A.S.** "Behavioral Assessment of Social Skills." In *Research and Practice in Social Skills Training,* edited by A.S. Bellack and M. Hersen. New York: Plenum Press, 1979. Illus.

114. **Bellugi, Ursula, and Fischer, Susan.** "A Comparison of Sign Language and Spoken Language." *Cognition: International Journal of Cognitive Psychology* 1 (1972) : 173-200.

Three young adults, hearing children of deaf parents and completely "bilingual" in spoken English and American Sign Language (ASL), told three versions of the same story—in ASL, in spoken English, and simultaneously in both. Excluding pauses, the average number of spoken words per second was twice that of signs when they were performed alone and one-and-a-half times that of signs when performed simultaneously. An analysis of propositions in the stories revealed, however, that the length of time underlying propositions was relatively the same in both modes. The ways in which ASL compensates for the time limitation include the incorporation of location by varying the direction of movement to reflect the spatial layout of what is being discussed. With some verbs movement to or away from the body can mark case or voice. Information about number can be included by using one or two hands or by repetition, manner can be conveyed by varying the size of the movement or its tension, and information about size and shape can be incorporated into a sign by its size or place of performance high or low on the body. Postural shifts and facial expressions also serve grammatical functions in ASL. A shake of the head or frown can negate a sentence, shifting eye movement can mark off a direct quotation, and a question is sometimes marked by raising eyebrows, widening eyes, or by the final position of the hands. Lastly, bodily shifts in narrative can be used to reflect who is being talked about and shifting points of view.

115. **Bendich, Stephen Zachary.** "Sensory Awareness as Self-Discovery: An Exploratory Study." Ph.D. dissertation, New York University. 1973. 471 pp. (Order No. 73-19, 902)

Nineteen university students completed a nine week course in the Selver sensory awareness technique to heighten kinesthetic sensitivity through nonverbal exercises. Certain hypotheses as to the effects of the course were supported on tests administered before and after it, particularly that subjects become more aware of their bodies and that their intellectual self-awareness was enhanced.

116. **Benjamin, Gail R., and Creider, Chet A.** "Social Distinctions in Non-Verbal Behavior." *Semiotica* 14 (1975) : 52-60.

Videotapes of dyads in conversation were shown with only the face of one member visible. Twenty adults and 40 eight and nine year old boys watched 30 second segments of the videotaped conversations and then answered the following questions: "(1) Is this person talking to someone of the same or opposite sex? (2) Is this person talking to someone of the same or different age? (3) Is this person talking to an acquaintance or a non-acquaintance?" The viewing subjects were able to identify the sex and degree of acquaintance of the unseen interactors on the basis of the facial behaviors of the subject they did see. However, only the children guessed age difference incorrectly.

117. **Bennett, Corwin.** *Spaces for People: Human Factors in Design.* Englewood Cliffs, New Jersey: Prentice-Hall, 1977. Illus.

This book is divided into four sections. In the first section the author explores the relation between interior space design and human factors. He attempts to define what specific human needs should be considered in design. Section two relates the way furnishings and space are adapted for human use. In section three the author examines the design of luminous, acoustic, and thermal environments for optimal human use. In section four the author discusses the role of research in design adapted to human needs. He stresses the need for creative problem solving and persuasive appeals to clients.

118. **Benoist, Irving R., and Butcher, James N.** "Nonverbal Cues to Sex-Role Attitudes." *Journal of Research in Personality* 11 (1977) : 431-442.

The 62 undergraduates participating in this study were pretested for grouping into four categories (high-feminine males and females and low-feminine males and females) and then videotaped during a standardized interview. Peer-age judges checked which of 120 adjectives described each student on tape played without sound. Sex role stereotypic attitudes were evidenced in judgments, such as that women were more often seen as affable and unstable and men as dominant and detached. In addition, high-feminine women were seen as submissive, low-feminine women as dominant, and high-feminine men as impulsive, dominant, and socially uneasy.

119. **Benson, Thomas W., and Frandsen, Kenneth D.** "An Orientation to Nonverbal Communication." In *Modules in Speech Communication,* edited by R.L. Applebaum and R.P. Hart, 38 pp. Chicago, Illinois: Science Research Associates, 1976. Illus.

This monograph begins with definitions of nonverbal communication and a section of the science of signs and semiology. There are brief but interesting discussions of some sign systems of nonverbal communication: appearance, voice, face and eyes, gesture, posture and movement, space and touch. The monograph ends with a "case study" of a political poster and exercises in nonverbal analysis.

120. **Benthall, Jonathan, and Polhemus, Ted,** eds. *The Body As A Medium of Expression.* New York: Dutton, 1975. 339 pp.

There are a number of important chapters on body movement in this volume, such as one on finger positions in medieval and ancient art and their symbolic meaning and one dealing with gestural sign language including a paper by Ray L. Birdwhistell. Of particular note is "The Syntaxes of Bodily Communication" by Michael Argyle. In this article, the author points out that there are a number of separate communication systems such as sign language, illustrations during speech, systems to communicate interpersonal attitudes, or systems to express emotions, which all use the same body parts, but which have different properties. For example, gestures of the hand can be used as speech illustrators, but they can also be used to represent interpersonal attitudes by touching or hitting, or they can be used as arbitrary signals as in deaf sign language. Many of those systems can be operating at the same time, thus making nonverbal communication quite complex. The author gives examples of practical applications of research findings that could solve some social and individual problems if we learn to use these systems better.

121. **Bentz, Janet Mills.** "Gender Displays in Portrait Photographs." *Sex Roles: A Journal of Research,* in press.

An examination of 1,296 portrait photographs of high school and university yearbooks showed that females smiled with a significantly greater frequency and expansiveness (broader smiles) than males and "head canted" more than males. The survey did not support a hypothesis that males would face the camera more directly than females.

122. **Berge, Yvonne.** *Vivre son corps: Pour une pedagogie du mouvement.* Paris: Seuil, 1975. 173 pp. Illus.

This book presents the purposes and particulars of movement pedagogy in a growth-oriented, balanced, and creative manner. Concentrating on creative movement classes with young children, it discusses the return to consciousness and activity of the five senses, of spatial and temporal awareness, and of the felt sense of self through movement, as well as the role of the teacher and teaching techniques. The author discusses relaxation, breath, gravity, developmental movement, the relation of central and peripheral musculature and body parts, binary and more complex rhythms, equilibrium, music spatial sense as it relates to the emotions, architecture and nature, choral movement and partaking in a group "organism." While the entire book includes ideas for classroom projects and explorations, the final chapters on pedagogy discuss the physical and psychological self-development of the creative movement teacher in keeping with the issues raised by this book. Written in French.

123. **Berger, Milton M.**, ed. *Videotape Techniques in Psychiatric Training and Treatment,* 2nd edition. New York: Brunner/Mazel, 1978.

124. **Bergman, Eugene.** "Autonomous and Unique Features of American Sign Language." *American Annals of the Deaf* 117 (1972) : 20-24.

Arguments for the linguistic autonomy of ASL are presented through brief analyses of three dimensionality, polarity, and tropes (representations of abstract concepts and relations by specific symbolic gestures), cognitive and conceptual functions of ASL, and parallels with Chinese ideograms. Observations are made on the unique potential of ASL as a tool for the study of communications and its implications about the nature of human language, psychology, and cognition.

125. **Berkson, Gershon, and Becker, James D.** "Expressions and Social Responsiveness of Blind Monkeys." *Journal of Abnormal Psychology* 84 (1975) : 519-523.

Three experiments are reported here involving five sighted and five blind infant macaque monkeys. First, the time it took to identify a randomly placed cage of a sedated or unsedated mother and the percent of time in the proximity of mother by the blind or control infants was measured. Secondly, the preference for and time spent in contact with the sedated or unsedated mother or other female was determined for blind infants. And, finally, the frequency and percentage occurrence of five facial expressions in five categories of social interaction were recorded for four sighted macaques interacting with four blind monkeys in spontaneous activities. Sighted infants were more efficient than blind infants in contacting and maintaining maternal proximity, but blind infants improved in contacting vocalizing (that is, unsedated) mothers, while blind macaque infants showed a nonsignificant preference for mothers. The tendency for subjects to initiate and maintain contact confirmed the importance of tactual cues in establishing primate social affinity. Blind macaque infants showed fewer facial expressions, but, excepting threat faces, they were of normal form. Blind macaque infants did not show a marked decrease in the initiation of social interactions with sighted macaque infants.

126. **Bernick, Niles; Altman, Fred; and Mintz, Daniel L.** "Pupil Responses of Addicts in Treatment to Drug Culture Argot: II. Responses During Verbalization of Visually Printed Words." *Psychonomic Science* 28 (1972) : 81-82.

Words pertaining to control, sex, and drug argot were visually presented to ten former addicts who were asked to verbalize each as it appeared. Stimulus categories did not elicit significantly different mean pupil responses; the authors hypothesize that there may be a correlation between pupil response and degree of commitment to addiction.

127. **Bernstein, Barbara Elaine.** "Body Language in the Classroom." *Journal of Clinical Child Psychology* 6 (1977) : 54.

Anecdotal observations that where the teacher stands and moves in the classroom can signal the teacher's acceptance of a child's anger and overt hostility.

128. **Bernstein, Penny L.** *Theory and Methods in Dance-Movement Therapy.* Dubuque, Iowa: Kendall/Hunt Publishing Co., 1972. 208 pp. Illus.

In a call for a theoretical frame of reference for dance/movement therapy, the author proposes a developmental model. Adaptive and maladaptive modes of functioning in relation to nonverbal communication are discussed in 15 levels of developmental organization. Specific movement descriptions are given for each style of behavior, and dance/movement therapy techniques are outlined. Additional topics include regression, somatization of symbols, the training of a dance/movement therapist, and a comparison chart of Piaget, Gesell, and Labananalysis developmental schemes.

129. **Bernstein, Penny L.** "Pilot Study of the Use of Tension Flow System of Movement Notation in an Ongoing Study of Infants at Risk for Schizophrenic Disorders." *Conference Proceedings of the American Dance Therapy Association* 8 (1973) : 116-125.

Several hypotheses, including that schizophrenic mothers best relate to children in the oral rhythm stage, were tested in a small video research project using Judith Kestenberg's tension flow rhythm analysis. Control and schizophrenic-diagnosed mothers were rated for infant/mother synchrony while bottle feeding and solid food feeding. Results suggested there were also some "at risk" infants in the control group.

130. **Bernstein, Penny L.** "Recapitulation of Ontogeny: A Theoretical Approach in Dance/Movement Therapy." *Conference Proceedings of the American Dance Therapy Association* 8 (1974) : 107-115.

The author presents an introduction to the theory of recapitulation of ontogeny and its relationship to dance/movement therapy. The basic rhythms of movement flow are discussed in relation to adaptive and maladaptive behavior. Some case material is presented.

131. **Bernstein, Penny L.** *Theory and Methods in Dance-Movement Therapy: A Manual for Therapists, Students, and Educators.* Second Edition. Dubuque, Iowa: Kendall/Hunt, 1975. 225 pp. Illus.

The book, written in manual format, spans the field of dance-movement therapy. Theory, techniques, learning, effort/shape movement analysis, body image, touch, and cultural differences in relation to dance therapy are discussed. There are chapters on dance therapy training, case studies, and an appendix containing a developmental chart and several movement diagnostic scales.

132. **Bernstein, Penny L.,** ed. *Eight Theoretical Approaches in Dance Movement Therapy.* Dubuque, Iowa: Kendall/Hunt Publishing Co., 1979. 187 pp. Illus.

The editor has selected eight therapists to present their theoretical approaches to dance/movement therapy. Each discusses the conceptual basis, origins, and applications of her work. Included are the writings of Trudi Schoop, Mary Whitehouse, and Liljan Espenak, as well as the Gestalt, psychoanalytic, Marian Chace, psychodynamic, and transpersonal methods.

133. **Bernstein, Penny, and Cafarelli, Enzo.** "An Electromyographical Validation of the Effort System of Notation." *American Dance Therapy Association Monograph No. 2* (1972) : 78-94. Illus.

In order to test for distinct muscle response patterns in the performance of the Eight Basic Actions of Laban's movement analysis system, an electromyographical study was done on one mover with five trained movement analysts observing for interobserver reliability. The basic actions were performed with both "free" and "bound flow" and each was shown to have distinctive EMG tracings. The observers showed 90 percent accuracy in identifying the actions.

134. **Birdwhistell, Ray L.** "A Kinesic-Linguistic Exercise: The Cigarette Scene." In *Directions in Sociolinguistics: The Ethnography of Communication,* edited by J.J. Gumperz and D. Hymes. New York: Holt, Rinehart and Winston, 1972. Illus.

In this chapter Birdwhistell discusses the instrumental and interactional behavior, kinesic markers, junctures and stress kinemes operating in an 18 second film segment.

135. **Birdwhistell, Ray.** "The Tertiary Sexual Characteristics of Man: A Fundamental in Human Communication." In *Readings in Contemporary Psychology,* edited by R.E. Lana and R.L. Rosnow, pp. 124-129. New York: Holt, Rinehart and Winston, 1972.

Since the average American actually speaks words for only 10 to 11 minutes daily, we estimate (in pseudostatistics) that more than 65 percent of the social meaning conveyed in two-person interaction is carried by totally nonvocal cues. And it seems clear now that communication must be regarded in the broadest sense as a highly structured system of significant symbols from all the sensory-based modalities.

Kinesics is the discipline concerned with the study of all the body motions which are communicative and which may or may not substitute for and/or illustrate, modify, regulate, and adapt speech. Kinesics is concerned with abstracting from the continuous muscular shifts which are characteristic of living physiological systems those groupings of movements which are of significance to the communicational process and thus to the interactional systems of social groups in general.

Ray L. Birdwhistell in "The Language of the Body: The Natural Environment of Words."

136. **Birdwhistell, Ray L.** "The Language of the Body: The Natural Environment of Words." In *Human Communication: Theoretical Explorations,* edited by A. Silverstein, pp. 203-220. Hillsdale, New Jersey: Lawrence Erlbaum, 1974.

A delightfully written sketch of Birdwhistell's orientation, how it emerged from communication theories of the 1930s, 40s, and 50s, and how personal and academic experiences shaped the direction of his thinking. He presents a critique of models and concepts that have influenced communication theory (the dyadic model, dichotomizing, action-reaction sequences, input and feedback, the body-mind dualism, and the primacy of words). He describes some fascinating research which showed how little time per day is spent talking (10 to 11 minutes for the average American), whereas paralinguistics, proxemics, kinesics, and comparable systems from other sensory modalities interrelate to compose the greater part of the communication system. In this chapter there is a transcript of a lecture-demonstration of the body's communication which is as vivid a picture of Birdwhistell in action as is possible from the printed word.

137. **Birdwhistell, Ray L.** "Some Discussion of Ethnography, Theory and Method." In *About Bateson,* edited by J. Brockman, pp. 103-144. New York: Dutton, 1977.

The author discusses discrepancies between methodology and theory and the functioning of a skilled ethnographer. He includes excerpts from a journal written between 1966 and 1968 from which his current research emerged.

138. **Bitti-Ricci, Pio, and Cortesi, Sandro.** *Comportamento Non verbale e Communicazione.* Bologna: Il Mulino, 1977.

Referring to a large number of American and German studies, the author deals with nonverbal elements of interpersonal behavior; nonverbal behavior and early social development; nonverbal behavior and psychological disturbances; and nonverbal research methods. Written in Italian.

139. **Blacking, John,** ed. *The Anthropology of the Body.* London and New York: Academic Press, 1977. 426 pp. Illus.

A collection of papers from a 1975 conference on the Anthropology of the Body, this book includes "Biological and Cultural Contributions to Body and Facial Movement" by Paul Ekman and "To Dance Is Human: Some Psychobiological Bases of an 'Expressive' Form" by Judith Lynne Hanna. Among the other papers dealing with bodily expression and movement are a discussion of medical theories of the relation of psychological states to external appearance, a study of the ritual movements of an Angolan initiation ceremony, and a discussion of the dance notation system of Rudolph Benesh.

140. **Blanck, Peter D.; Zuckerman, Miron; DePaulo, Bella M.; and Rosenthal, Robert.** "Sibling Resemblances in Nonverbal Skill and Style." *Journal of Nonverbal Behavior* 4 (1980) : 219-226.

This study explored the hypothesis that siblings display a tendency for family resemblance in nonverbal decoding skills. Thirty-seven sibling pairs between the ages of nine and 15 were administered the videotaped Nonverbal Discrepancy Test. This audiovisual test assessed decoding accuracy—the extent to which subjects are able to identify affects (positivity and dominance) from face, body, and tone of voice cues; discrepancy accuracy—the extent to which subjects recognize the degree of discrepancy between audio and video cues; and video primacy—the extent to which subjects are more influenced by video (face or body) than by audio cues. Brother-brother pairs showed family resemblances in all three nonverbal indexes, whereas brother-sister pairs displayed family similarity only in discrepancy accuracy. Overall, sibling pairs showed a tendency for family resemblance in nonverbal decoding.

141. **Blass, Thomas; Freedman, Norbert; and Steingart, Irving.** "Body Movement and Verbal Encoding in the Congenitally Blind." *Perceptual and Motor Skills* 39 (1974) : 279-293.

The authors first discuss the role of movement in thought construction and then report a study relating hand movements of ten congenitally blind young adults to linguistic skill. Subjects were filmed performing a five-minute monologue, and movements were categorized as object-focused or body-focused. In contrast to previous research on sighted individuals, blind subjects exhibited almost continuous kinetic activity, and unlike sighted subjects, body-focused finger to hand movements of the blind subjects were significantly related to mean words per complex sentence and "complex portrayal sentences."

142. **Blau, Bette, and Siegel, Elaine.** "Breathing Together: A Preliminary Investigation of an Involuntary Reflex as Adaptation." *American Journal of Dance Therapy* 2 (1978) : 35-42.

Following a discussion of clinical applications of synchronous breathing, the authors present data from their studies concerning the relationship between breathing capacity and psychosis. Thirty-eight psychotic children with a mean age of 10.2 years were compared with a normal control group matched by age, height, and sex. The Forced Vital Capacity (FVC) breathing test and the Oseretsky Test for Motor Proficiency were given to each child. In general, the FVC of the psychotic children was lower and more erratic than that of normal children in the same age range. The psychotic children also tested significantly below normal on motor developmental scales.

143. **Blondis, Marion N., and Jackson, Barbara E.** *Nonverbal Communication with Patients: Back to the Human Touch.* New York: Wiley & Sons, 1977. 108 pp.

Based on the authors' experimental research and their teaching of nonverbal communication skills, this book addresses the dilemma nurses encounter in the dichotomy between technological efficiency and tender patient care. Chapters explicitly discuss pertinent problems encountered with patients throughout the life-cycle and in crisis intervention including problems pertaining to sexual behaviors. A final chapter demystifies concepts of "good" and "bad" patients and discusses the modern patient's hospital experience and growing awareness and the demands to revise the traditional nursing role.

144. **Bloom, Kathleen,** ed. *Prospective Issues in Infancy Research.* Hillsdale, New Jersey: Lawrence Erlbaum Associates, 1981. Approx. 192 pp.

145. **Blubaugh, Jon A., and Pennington, Dorothy L.** *Crossing Difference: Interracial Communication.* Columbus, Ohio: Charles E. Merrill Publishing Co., 1976. 102 pp. Illus.

This lively and well-illustrated text on interracial communication includes the practical as well as conceptual level. Each chapter ends with "Awareness Exercises" to achieve change in attitudes and behavior. Chapter seven deals specifically with crossing nonverbal differences and discusses skin color and physiological features, touch, eye expression, time, space, dress, and objects as variables that impact on communication between races.

146. **Blum, Lucille H.** *Reading Between the Lines: Doctor-Patient Communication.* New York: International Universities Press, 1972. 183 pp.

Written for medical students, this book encourages insight into the patient's verbal and nonverbal communications. The first part of the book presents information on human emotional and physiological development, drawing on psychoanalytic theory and emphasizing infancy, a period which, the author argues, tends to be recalled by the patient's ill-health and dependence on the doctor. The second part explores specific aspects of the physician-patient exchange, including the nonverbal communication of the patient and clues to psychosomatic disorders.

147. **Blurton-Jones, N.G., and Konner, M.J.** "Sex Differences in Behaviour of London and Bushman Children." In *Comparative Ecology and Behaviour of Primates,* edited by R.P. Michael and J.H. Crook, pp. 689-750. London: Academic Press, 1973.

Twenty-three Bushmen and 21 London children age two to six were observed for one hour each during play and their behaviors were recorded according to a large number of facial, gestural, and social categories that were later factor analyzed into clusters. Analysis of the data indicated that boys were significantly higher on measures of aggressive behavior in both cultures. Boys also engaged in more "rough and tumble play" than girls, although the Bushman girls scored much higher than London girls on this measure. In both cultures boys interacted more with other children than with adults, while girls interacted more with adults than with other children. Measures on which there were sex differences for the London children with boys scoring higher than girls but no sex difference among Bushman children include the amounts of vigorous physical activity, sustained directed attention, and social behavior with other children. Among the London children boys preferred to play with boys, but this was not true of the Bushman children. There was a large cultural difference in the amount of interaction with mother.

148. **Blyth, W.A.L.** "Non-Verbal Elements in Education: Some New Perspectives." *British Journal of Educational Studies* 24 (1976) : 109-126. Illus.

This article indicates what some of the nonverbal elements are in education; some ways for the development of these new perspectives; and some suggestions for developing a coherent program of study, practice, and research. A diagram and discussion indicating relationships between verbal and nonverbal elements in education are presented.

149. **Bober, Michael Jr.** "Body Language: The Student-Engineer's Aid to Interviewing." *Journal of Technical Writing and Communication* 5 (1975) : 7-9.

An anecdotal account of how nonverbal communication can be an important part of a job applicant's interview.

150. **Bockner, S.**, ed. *Cultures in Contact.* New York: Pergamon Press, forthcoming.

151. **Boderman, Alvin; Freed, Douglas W.; Kinnucan, Mark T.** "Touch Me, Like Me: Testing an Encounter Group Assumption." *The Journal of Applied Behavioral Science* 8 (1972) : 527-533.

Twenty-one female college students were randomly assigned to a touch or a no-touch condition while interacting with a female confederate during three ESP experiments. The touch condition involved mutual exploration of the face while the eyes were closed. The no-touch condition involved the same interaction without touch. Subjects subsequently rated the accomplice on four dimensions of perceived attractiveness. T-tests revealed that subjects in the touch condition rated the accomplice significantly higher in attractiveness than subjects in the no-touch condition.

152. **Bond, Michael H., and Iwata, Yasuo.** "Proxemics and Observation Anxiety in Japan: Non-Verbal and Cognitive Responses." *Psychologia: An International Journal of Psychology in The Orient* 19 (1976) : 119-126.

The effects of spatial intrusion and of observation anxiety were examined in an interview situation and compared with self-reports, person perception ratings, and nonverbal measures. Sixteen Japanese women were videotaped while being interviewed twice by confederates who were appropriately or intrusively seated. No effects were seen for observation anxiety. In response to close-sitting interviewers, however, the subjects reported a variety of reactions, interpreted as withdrawal, and rated the intrusive interviewers negatively across a number of person perception scales. Subjects displayed longer pauses, fewer glances, and backward leaning postures during intrusion.

153. **Bond, Michael H., and Komai, Hiroshi.** "Targets of Gazing and Eye Contact During Interviews: Effects on Japanese Nonverbal Behavior." *Journal of Personality and Social Psychology* 34 (1976) : 1276-1284.

The authors attempt to distinguish the effects of mutual eye contact versus being a target of another's gaze. Sixteen Japanese male college juniors were interviewed individually by two male graduate students. Both subjects and interviewers were instructed to gaze either at the other's eyes or knees. Torso movement, hand gesture and self-manipulation, proximity, smile, response latency, pause average, and total talking time were noted. Interviewer gazing at the subject's eyes decreased the subject's torso movements, hand gestures, and response latencies; subject gazing at interviewer's eyes increased the subject's hand self-manipulations. Both results were independent of whether or not eye contact was returned.

154. **Bond, Michael H., and Shiraishi, Daisuke.** "The Effect of Body Lean and Status of an Interviewer on the Non-Verbal Behavior of Japanese Interviewees." *International Journal of Psychology* 9 (1974) : 117-128.

Sixteen male and 16 female Japanese university students were interviewed by one of two male graduate students, with status (high or equal) manipulated by interviewer's clothing and description, and with the interviewer either in a forward leaning or backward leaning position. A number of nonverbal dependent variables were measured and were found to be affected by both the status and body lean variables. Female subjects were most affected, particularly by the status variable.

155. **Bonoma, Thomas V., and Felder, Leonard C.** "Nonverbal Communication and Marketing: Toward a Communicational Analysis." *Journal of Marketing Research* 14 (1977) : 169-180.

The major function of nonverbal indicators for marketing applications is seen as the use of unobtrusive nonverbal behaviors as a check on more easily distorted verbal measures of consumption behavior. Three major types of nonverbal behavior are identified and reviewed: the "units of analysis" approach, the "general catalogue" approach, and the "psychological variables" approach. Of these, the psychological variables approach, which deals with the cognitive meaning of nonverbal communications, is considered to have the greatest potential for marketing analysis. A summary of the findings of this approach focusing on the work of Albert Mehrabian is given. The authors suggest the integration of the findings of Mehrabian with the verbal interaction and analysis scheme "Social Influence Rating System" (SIRS) by Bonoma and his colleagues as a step toward a "communication analysis" for understanding marketing transactions.

156. **Booraem, Curtis D., and Flowers, John D.** "Reduction of Anxiety and Personal Space as a Function of Assertion Training with Severely Disturbed Neuropsychiatric Inpatients." *Psychological Reports* 30 (1972) : 923-929.

Seven psychiatric inpatients participating in a 12-session assertion training program were compared with a control group who did not receive assertion training. The experimental group showed significant reduction in personal space and self-reported anxiety, while the control group did not. However, there were pre- and post-treatment differences in the two groups which qualified these results somewhat.

157. **Borden, Richard J., and Homleid, Gorden M.** "Handedness and Lateral Positioning in Heterosexual Couples: Are Men Still Strong-Arming Women?" *Sex Roles* 4 (1978) : 67-73.

In a survey of couples walking along a main university thoroughfare, it was found that females were significantly more often on the preferred (dominant) side of males in same-handedness couples.

158. **Bosmajian, Harg.** *The Rhetoric of Nonverbal Communication: Readings.* Glenview, Illinois: Scott, Foresman, 1971.

159. **Bossley, M.I.** "Privacy and Crowding: A Multidisciplinary Analysis." *Man-Environment Systems* 6 (1976) : 8-19.

Recent models of crowding have stressed the importance of mediating factors in the experience of this subjective state, but the basis of this mediation remains obscure. A multidisciplinary review of the privacy literature suggests two general forms exist. One form appears to have a biological or psychological function, while the other consists of culturally determined factors. The author posits that cultural or subcultural conventions are generally the major influence in the achievement of privacy. The author concludes with a discussion of implications of the present analysis for research into privacy and crowding.

160. **Boucher, Michael L.** "Effect of Seating Distance on Interpersonal Attraction in an Interview Situation." *Journal of Consulting and Clinical Psychology* 38 (1972) : 15-19.

Forty-two schizophrenic and 42 alcoholic inpatient subjects were randomly assigned to either intermediate, far, or close seating positions during interviews. The effect of the seating on attraction to the interviewer was measured by questionnaire responses and by the unobtrusive measure of having the subject pull up a chair after the interview. Schizophrenic subjects were more attracted to the interviewer at intermediate and far distances. On the unobtrusive measure, the alcoholic subjects kept a greater distance in the closer than in the intermediate condition.

161. **Bouissac, Paul A.R.** "What Does the Little Finger Do? An Appraisal of Kinesics." *Semiotica* 6 (1972) : 279-288.

Starting with a review of Ray L. Birdwhistell's *Kinesics and Context,* the author goes on to discuss some of the shortcomings of kinesics research, and suggests a very different way for movement to be assessed in terms of the geometric volume described by the moving part measured through an appropriate device such as in hologrammatic technology.

162. **Bouissac, Paul.** *La mésure des gestes: Prolégomènes à la sémiotique gestuelle.* The Hague: Mouton, 1973. 295 pp. Illus.

Growing out of the author's work on acrobatics and the circus, this book is a search for a means for the scientific description and analysis of dynamic physical activity. Bouissac presents a typology of existing methods, dividing them into "descriptions," based on natural language, and "transcriptions" using systems of notation, either based on language or attempting a scientific analysis through exact measurement. Examples are discussed for each category, dwelling on the methodological presuppostions of each. Within the category of description are early attempts such as that of A. Tuccaro (1599) and P.J. Barthez (1798), as well as acrobats' own descriptions of their acts. Examples of scientific notation include the system of Ray L. Birdwhistell which Bouissac claims is not an objective analysis because the iconic or analogic elements of the code root it in the perceptual or cultural filters of the observer. Of those attempting a scientific measurement of movement E. Muybridge (1901), E.J. Marey (1894), and N. Oseretzky (1931) are discussed. In Part IV Bouissac proposes his own process of measurement, positing the necessary steps for the mathematization of movement to segment the dynamic continuum. The final section deals with the level of combination of units and discusses the problem of meaning within a cybernetic model.

163. **Bouissac, Paul.** *Circus and Culture: A Semiotic Approach.* Bloomington, Indiana: Indiana University Press, 1976. 206 pp. Illus.

This fascinating book is a study of circus acts from a semiotic point of view. Bouissac analyzes circus performances to show how the technical behavior of performers and the zoological components of animal acts are organized along with other subcodes such as costume, music, and language to produce the meaning that the audience perceives. A chapter on "The Performing Horse" deals with the communicative channels between trainer and horse and how these function within the performance. Other chapters deal with the structure of acrobatic acts, juggling and magic acts, and clown performances.

164. **Bovard-Taylor, Alice, and Draganosky, Joseph.** "Using Personal Space to Develop a Working Alliance in Dance Therapy." *American Journal of Dance Therapy* 3 (1979) : 51-59.

Research on proxemics and personal space is summarized, including work done on the relationship between psychopathology and distancing. The use of personal space to establish rapport is highlighted, and clinical applications with reference to cultural or sexual differences are discussed. Therapeutic technique is suggested and a case outline presented.

165. **Braithwaite, Ronald L.** "An Analysis of Proxemics and Self-Disclosing Behavior of Recidivist and Non-Recidivist Adult Social Offenders from Black, Chicano, and White Inmate Populations." Ph.D. dissertation, Michigan State University. 1974. 205 pp. (Order No. 75071-23)

This study investigated self-reported differences in self-disclosure in relation to proxemic distance of three groups of male inmates.

166. **Bramblett, Claud.** *Patterns of Primate Behavior.* Palo Alto, California: Mayfield Publishing, 1976.

167. **Brannigan, Christopher R., and Humphries, David A.** "Human Non-Verbal Behaviour, A Means of Communication." In *Ethological Studies of Child Behaviour,* edited by N. Blurton Jones, pp. 37-64. London: Cambridge University Press, 1972. Illus.

This discussion of the application of ethological methods to the study of human communication cites the need for a careful description of expressive patterns and the natural circumstances in which they occur. The authors describe and illustrate examples of units of facial expression and discuss pitfalls in the description and interpretation of human expressive behavior. Evidence concerning a genetic component in nonverbal behavior is discussed, as well as the application of ethology to psychiatry. The article includes a list of 136 units of nonverbal behavior and their definitions as a contribution to the problem of terminology in nonverbal behavior research.

168. **Brauer, Dorothea V., and DePaulo, Bella M.** "Similarities Between Friends in Their Understanding of Nonverbal Cues." *Journal of Nonverbal Behavior* 5 (1980): 64-68.

Ten pairs of female friends completed a version of the PONS test and a friendship questionnaire. Results showed a marked similarity in decoding of facial cues but not body cues. Additional analyses of nonverbal cue understanding and aspects of the friendship yielded suggested but not significant relationships in facial decoding but not body accuracy.

169. **Brazelton, T. Berry; Koslowksi, Barbara; and Main, Mary.** "The Origins of Reciprocity: The Early Mother-Infant Interaction." In *The Effect of the Infant on Its Caregiver,* edited by M. Lewis and L. Rosenblum, pp. 49-76. New York: John Wiley & Sons, 1974.

An analysis of filmed sequences of mother and infant, and infant and object, recorded weekly from ages four to 20 weeks, showed two different patterns of interaction and expectancy to human and nonhuman stimuli as evidenced in the infant's cycles of attention and inattention. Differences in the mother's sensitivity to the infant's capacity for attention were linked to differences in the interactions over time. The article describes the areas of maternal behavior that influence infant behavior and suggests the role of maternal behavior in the development of the capacity for cognitive acquisitions and self-organization in the infant. The need for rule-learning in the mother-infant relationship especially concerning sensitivity to the infant's capacity for attention, and the interdependency of interaction rhythms were stressed.

170. **Breed, George.** "The Effect of Intimacy: Reciprocity or Retreat?" *British Journal of Social and Clinical Psychology* 11 (1972) : 135-142.

Ninety-six college students interacted with a confederate (female or male) in one of three intimacy conditions differentiated by amount of eye contact, forward body lean, and orientation toward the subject. Periods of eye contact and subject's shoulder orientation, forward lean, and side lean were recorded. Results went contrary to the "intimacy equilibrium" hypothesis and showed that subject's forward leans and eye contact increased as intimacy increased. There was significantly more eye contact with the male confederate than with the female. The male confederate received significantly more forward leans and was directly faced significantly more than the female confederate. Male subjects leaned backward significantly more than females. Female subjects shifted body position significantly more than male subjects, and all subjects shifted position significantly more with the female confederate than with the male.

171. **Breed, George, and Colaiuta, Victoria.** "Looking, Blinking, and Sitting: Nonverbal Dynamics in the Classroom." *Journal of Communication* 24 (1974) : 75-81.

Fifty-two college students' seating choices and their nonverbal behaviors were correlated with their scores on a course midterm and final. Higher test scores were associated with less looking around, less blinking, more looking at the instructor, and more writing time, while different patterns of nonverbal behavior were associated with different seating positions. The highest grades were made by those who could not be characterized as sitting in a specific territory.

172. **Breed, George, and Porter, Maynard.** "Eye Contact, Attitudes, and Attitude Change Among Males." *The Journal of Genetic Psychology* 120 (1972) : 211-217.

Twenty-four male undergraduates talked to a silent confederate partner for about four minutes under one of three role-playing conditions (like, dislike, control). For two of the four minutes the confederate looked constantly into the subject's eye while for the other two minutes he did not. For half of the subjects the confederate began by looking. For the other half he began by not looking. The experimenter recorded the subjects' search for eye contact with the confedrate, and prior to and immediately after the experiment both subjects and confederates described each other on a questionnaire. Among the results it was found that subjects' amount of eye contact with the confederate correlated with positive attitude toward the confederate.

173. **Bremme, Donald W., and Erickson, Frederick.** "Relationships Among Verbal and Nonverbal Classroom Behaviors." *Theory into Practice* 16 (1977) : 153-161.

In a kindergarten/first grade classroom, five videotaped occurrences of "First Circle" (a social occasion occurring each morning) were examined. Analysis of the words spoken, features of the teacher's behavior (4 vocal, 4 nonverbal), and features of the students' behavior (4 vocal, 6 nonverbal) was done for recurring patterns of behavior. Three broad social situations were recurrently enacted within First Circle (teacher's time, students' time, and transition), and particular forms of both verbal and nonverbal behavior defined each form.

174. **Bretherton, Inge, and Ainsworth, Mary D. Salter.** "Responses of One Year Olds to Strangers in a Strange Situation." In *Origins of Fear,* edited by M. Lewis and L. Rosenblum, pp. 131-164. New York: Wiley & Sons, 1974. Illus.

The authors here present a short study examining the behavioral reactions of infants to strangers in an unfamiliar environment. It explores and provides evidence of an interrelationship between four behavioral systems: affiliative, fear/wariness, attachment, and exploratory.

175. **Brislin, Richard W.** "Seating as a Measure of Behavior: You Are Where You Sit." *Topics in Culture Learning* 2 (1974) : 103-118. Illus.

Where people sit is an important index of how they feel about others, as well as how people judge their acceptance or rejection by others. This article reviews studies of what seating behavior means. In addition to an examination of the "who, who with, what doing, when, where, why, and how of seating," the author succinctly reviews those studies dealing with the applied use of seating behavior measures including their cross-cultural applications.

176. **Broekmann, Neil C., and Möller, André T.** "Preferred Seating Position and Distance in Various Situations." *Journal of Counseling Psychology* 20 (1973) : 504-508.

Fifteen white males and 15 white females from South Africa were given the Sixteen Personality Factor Questionnaire and the Personal, Home, Social and Formal Relations Questionnaire. Subjects were shown pictures of various seating arrangements and asked in which of several social settings they would feel most comfortable if seated in that position. Differences were found in preferred seating arrangements for various situations; seating position preferences for home situations differed from all others. Far seating was strongly associated with submissive personality traits while closer seating was associated with aggressive and domineering traits.

177. **Brooks, Jeanne, and Lewis, Michael.** "Attachment Behavior in Thirteen-Month-Old Opposite Sex Twins." *Child Development* 45 (1974) : 243-247.

Thirty-four children, 17 sets of opposite-sex twins, were observed one at a time with their mothers during 15-minute free play sessions. Observers recorded the incidence of the following behaviors: touching mother, looking at mother, pleasant vocalizations to mother, proximity to mother, during unstructured play. Also recorded were toys played with and amount of movement. Girls displayed significantly more attachment behaviors of looking at and proximity to mother, nonsignificantly more touch and vocalization. Boys who were seen after their sisters displayed significantly more touch and proximity behaviors than boys who were seen first. Girls showed significantly more looking behaviors than boys regardless of order seen. There were no differences in toy play or activity level.

178. **Brown, Duane, and Parks, James C.** "Interpreting Nonverbal Behavior, a Key to More Effective Counseling: Review of Literature." *Rehabilitation Counseling Bulletin* 15 (1972) : 176-184.

The author provides a basic literature review on eye contact, gesture, and proxemics and discusses its relevance to the rehabilitation counselor.

179. **Brown, G.A.** "An Exploratory Study of Interaction Amongst British and Immigrant Children." *British Journal of Social and Clinical Psychology* 12 (1973) : 159-162.

Thirty-six British and 37 immigrant children working together in informally structured classrooms were studied. Group members were observed one at a time for five seconds, and nonaggressive verbal, aggressive verbal, nonaggressive bodily, and aggressive bodily contacts were noted. More aggression was shown by the immigrant children towards each other than towards the British children. Differences in verbal contacts seemed to point towards a language barrier.

180. **Brown, Jerram L.** *The Evolution of Behavior.* New York: W.W. Norton, 1975. 761 pp. Illus.

Drawing upon studies by zoologists, evolutionists, geneticists, ecologists, ethologists, and psychologists, this text presents a comparative study of behavior. The answers to questions raised by the comparative study of behavior are sought within the framework of evolutionary biology. Animal communication receives emphatic treatment here. There is an outline of the evolution of territoriality and an analysis of the space around an individual, as well as the patterns and temporal changes in animal dispersion. Reflexes, motor coordination, sensory systems, and orientation of animals are explored. The development of songs and calls — as well as the programming of behavior (with a focus on biological rhythms, attention, and motivation) — receives structured, disciplined analysis.

181.   **Brown, Malcolm.** "The New Body Psychotherapies." *Psychotherapy: Theory, Research, and Practice* 10 (1973) : 98-116.

While exhorting the reader to listen to the wisdom of her or his body, the author discusses the virtues of four body psychotherapies: (1) Gestalt Therapy, as practiced by Fritz Perls; (2) orthodox Reichian Therapy; (3) Lowenian Bio-Energetics; and (4) Janov's Primal Therapy. Each therapy adheres to a principle of natural organismic self-regulation. Each intends to bring the patient's awareness into closer congruence with his or her deeper organismic sensations. The presentation includes a forceful critique of each therapy.

182.   **Brown, Susan Rosensweig.** "Eye Contact As An Indicator of Infant Social Development." Ph.D. dissertation, University of Southern California. 1972. 99 pp. (Order No. 72216-54)

The eye contact behavior of one hundred babies from various well-baby clinics was observed in three-minute periods. Home observations were then made on the 20 infants having highest and lowest amounts of eye contact to assess differences in maternal caretaking.

183.   **Bruchon, Marilou.** "Une modalité expressive de la personnalité: l'expansivité gestuelle." *Bulletin de Psychologie* 26 (1972-73) : 4-21.

In this study, written in French, a correlation was found between extroversion and the use of larger movements in writing and posture and between amplitude in movements in general and emotional stability. The author points to the flaws in the study: how does a subject's experience or love of dance and music, for example, influence the test for amplitude in movements while dancing freely to music? And how far do cultural determinants influence one's way of moving (southern Europeans move more expansively than northern Europeans). She suggests investigating speed of movement or muscle tone in relation to personality.

184.   **Bruchon, Marilou.** "Les mouvements expressifs et la personnalité." *Année Psychologique* 73 (1973) : 311-337.

This article surveys phenomenological, empirical, and structural studies that have tried to relate certain expressive movements to personality and gives examples of each, such as the movement correlates to the anabolic versus catabolic personalities of the Italian school. It also cites a few studies on muscle tonicity and posture as expressive variables. The author concludes that, although two hypotheses on research of this kind, namely that expressive movements are stable and that they are organized in functional units, have been proven by a few structural studies, it would require a combination of all three types to investigate their psychological correlates.

185.   **Bruneau, Thomas J.** "Communicative Silences: Forms and Function." *Journal of Communication* 23 (1973) : 17-46.

The nature of silence is discussed from several vantage points: as a mental con struct, as background for speech signs, as a manifestation of the relationship to subjective time as opposed to artificial time, and as it relates to sensation, perception, and metaphorical movement. Three major forms of silence are defined and described as they relate to some important communication factors: 1) Psycholinguistic Silence, including fast-time and slow-time silence; 2) Interactive Silence; and 3) Sociocultural Silence.

186. **Bruner, Jerome.** "The Ontogenesis of Speech Acts." In *Social Rules and Social Behaviour,* edited by P. Collett. Oxford: Basil Blackwell, 1977. 185 pp.

The author correlates mother-infant nonverbal behaviors (eye contact, following each other's focus, role shifting during play) with signaling and sequencing rules later applicable to the rules of grammar.

187. **Bryan, Tanis H.** "Learning Disabled Children's Comprehension of Nonverbal Communication." *Journal of Learning Disabilities* 10 (1977) : 501-506.

The children's PONS test (Profile of Nonverbal Sensitivity) was administered to 23 learning-disabled (LD) children and a control group. LD children were significantly less accurate than normal children on the PONS. The author discusses the implications of apparent deficit in reading social cues as measured by this test.

188. **Buchanan, Douglas R.; Juhnke, Ralph; and Goldman, Morton.** "Violation of Personal Space as a Function of Sex." *Journal of Social Psychology* 99 (1976) : 187-192.

Subjects were 215 people using the elevators in a large office building. The elevators had floor selection panels at either side of the door. In Experiment I, a female or male confederate stood 12 inches from one of these panels. Subjects tended to avoid intruding on the confederate's personal space. Female subjects were most prone to violate a female's space. In Experiment II, a female and a male confederate stood by each panel respectively, thus forcing subjects to violate personal space. While females showed no significant preference, males more often chose to violate female confederates' space.

189. **Buck, Ross.** "A Test of Nonverbal Receiving Ability: Preliminary Studies." *Human Communication Research* 2 (1976) : 162-171.

The development of a new instrument for measuring the ability to decode affect in others, the Communication of Affect Receiving Ability Test (CARAT), is described. Subjects watch videotapes of "senders" reacting spontaneously to emotionally loaded slides and judge the type of emotional stimulus involved and the degree of pleasant or unpleasant affect experienced by the sender. Preliminary tests showed the instrument to have a moderate degree of internal consistency. Results showed females slightly better in decoding affect than males and business and fine arts majors better than science majors.

190. **Buck, Ross.** "Nonverbal Behavior and the Theory of Emotion: The Facial Feedback Hypothesis." *Journal of Personality and Social Psychology* 38 (1980) : 811-824.

A review of relevant research indicates that only a restricted version of the facial feedback hypothesis has been tested. The hypothesis — that skeletal muscle feedback from facial expressions plays a role in regulating emotional experience and behavior — has not been studied in sufficient detail. The author argues that the studies which appear to support the hypothesis are flawed in certain respects and are unconvincing.

191. **Buck, Ross; Baron, Reuben; Goodman, Nancy; and Shapiro, Beth.** "Unitization of Spontaneous Nonverbal Behavior in the Study of Emotion Communication." *Journal of Personality and Social Psychology* 39 (1980) : 522-529.

Videotapes of spontaneous facial and gestural reactions to affective slides were segmented by observers using an adaptation of Newtson's unitization technique (1976, D. Newtson). The authors conducted experiments using the Newtson procedure to explore three questions: Is it possible for receivers to meaningfully segment spontaneous emotion displays? Do the same type of stimulus variables affect the number of breakpoints? What are the relationships between the number of breakpoints and communication accuracy? Results of their experimentation demonstrated that the unitization technique applied to emotion expression yields reliable patterns of segmentation.

192. **Buck, Ross, and Duffy, R.** "Nonverbal Communication of Affect in Brain-Damaged Patients." *Cortex*, in press.

A slide-viewing technique designed to assess spontaneous nonverbal expressiveness was administered to eight left-hemisphere-damaged (aphasic), ten right-hemisphere-damaged (RHD), nine Parkinson's Disease (PD), and ten nonbrain-damaged (control) male patients. Patients watched affective slides while, unknown to them, their facial/gestural responses were videotaped. Judges rated their reactions. Results indicated that aphasics were more expressive than controls, while RHD and PD patients were less expressive. The possibility that spontaneous nonverbal expressiveness is mediated by the right cerebral hemisphere, with the left hemisphere playing an inhibitory role, was discussed as a tentative hypothesis. (author's abstract)

193. **Buck, Ross W.; Miller, Robert E.; and Caul, William F.** "Sex, Personality and Physiological Variables in the Communication of Affect via Facial Expressions." *Journal of Personality and Social Psychology* 30 (1974) : 587-596.

Thirty-two "senders" were shown 25 emotionally loaded color slides. Unknown to them, their facial expressions were televised to an observer/partner who attempted to judge which slide category the sender was watching. The observer rated how pleasant or unpleasant he thought the sender's reaction was. Among the results it was found that pairs with female senders showed more accurate communication than pairs with male senders. The relationship between accuracy, physiological responsiveness, and personality differences is also discussed.

194. **Buck, Ross W.; Savin, Virginia J.; Miller, Robert E.; and Caul, William F.** "Communication of Affect through Facial Expressions in Humans." *Journal of Personality and Social Psychology* 23 (1972) : 362-371.

Ten observer and sender pairs of female college students and nine observer and sender pairs of male college students participated in this study. Twenty-five color slides representing five categories (sexual, scenic, maternal, disgusting, unusual/ambiguous) were shown to the senders. The observer partner watched the sender's face (without audio) on closed-circuit TV and attempted to judge what category of slide the sender was watching. He or she then rated the sender's emotional experience on a pleasant-unpleasant scale. The results revealed a significant degree of correspondence, particularly among the female pairs. Physiological and personality factors of facial expression are also discussed.

195. **Buckhalt, Joseph A.; Rutherford, Robert B.; and Goldberg, Kay E.** "Verbal and Nonverbal Interaction of Mothers with their Down's Syndrome and Nonretarded Infants." *American Journal of Mental Deficiency* 82 (1978) : 337-343.

In an observational, laboratory-based study, the authors compared verbal and nonverbal interactions between ten mothers and their Down's syndrome infants and ten mothers and their nonretarded infants. Although there was no difference between the groups in mothers' language complexity, mothers of Down's syndrome children spoke at a significantly faster rate. Also Down's syndrome babies smiled and vocalized less, but mothers of the two groups did not significantly differ on the nonverbal interactional behavior observed.

196. **Budd, Richard W., and Ruben, Brent D.**, eds. *Approaches to Human Communication.* New York: Spartan Books, 1972. 464 pp.

Among the many approaches to communication represented in this volume are encounter groups by Richard W. Budd, General System Theory by Brent D. Ruben, nonverbal behavior by Randall P. Harrison, psychology by Ralph V. Exline, and zoology by Hubert Frings.

197. **Bugental, Daphne E.; Love, Leonore R.; and Gianetto, Robert M.** "Perfidious Feminine Faces." *Journal of Personality and Social Psychology* 17 (1971) : 314-318.

Forty families, half with disturbed children and half with normal children, were involved in this study of the verbal and nonverbal (smiling) behavior of parents interacting with their children. Smiles by the fathers were found to accompany positive or approving verbal content, while smiles by the mothers were unrelated to the evaluative content of her speech. There was no relation between the patterns of parental smiling and children's disturbance. The lower-class mothers in this study were found not to smile at all.

198. **Bugental, Daphne E.; Love, Leonore R.; Kaswan, Jacques; and April, Carol.** "Verbal-Nonverbal Conflict in Parental Messages to Normal and Disturbed Children." *Journal of Abnormal Psychology* 77 (1971) : 6-10.

Ten "normal" and ten families with a "disturbed" child were videotaped. Mothers with disturbed children produced a higher percentage of conflicting evaluative messages between channels (verbal, voice tone, kinesics) as compared with the normal family mothers. The evaluative message of fathers of disturbed and normal children did not show this difference.

199. **Bull, P.E., and Brown, R.** "The Role of Postural Change in Dyadic Conversations." *British Journal of Clinical and Social Psychology* 16 (1977) : 29-33.

Scheflen's observations associating postural changes with significant features in the structure of conversation are tested. Some support for Scheflen's work is presented. This work involves an interesting study design and clear presentation of findings.

200. **Bullowa, Margaret**, ed. *Before Speech: The Beginning of Interpersonal Communication.* Cambridge: Cambridge University Press, 1979. 400 pp. Illus.

In this rich and fascinating volume many of the most noted infancy researchers discuss their methods of work and major findings often from a personal point of view. In an introduction the editor discusses precursors and influences of the field of prelinguistic communication, issues and concepts, relevant literature, organizations, conferences, and methods. Mary Catherine Bateson, Patricia F. Chappell and Louis W. Sander, Glyn M. Collis, William S. Condon, M.A.K. Halliday, Kenneth Kaye, John Newson, Colwyn Trevarthen, and E. Tronick, H. Als, and L. Adamson have contributed chapters on varying aspects of structure and development of interaction in infancy. There are discussions of communicative capacities evident in neonatal assessment by T. Berry Brazelton, of communication between blind infants and their mothers by Selma Fraiberg, and of a screening program for communication disorders by Karen Stensland Junker. Derek Ricks has contributed a discussion of early vocal communication in autistic and normal children, E. Richard Sorenson a study of tactile communication in New Guinea, and Frans Plooij a discussion of wild chimpanzee mother-infant play. There is also a chapter on the role of ideologies in child-rearing by Catherine Snow, Akke de Blauw, and Ghislaine van Roosmalen.

201. **Burgoon, Judee K.** "A Communication Model of Personal Space Violations: Explication and an Initial Test." *Human Communication Research* 4 (1978) : 129-142.

The author discusses the Burgoon-Jones model of personal space expectations and their violation as a theoretical system and reports the results of an initial test of the model. Ten primitive terms and 16 constitutive terms together yield the basic axioms of the system, which are combined with a number of assumptions about affiliation, distance and expectations and their violation to generate 13 propositions concerning personal space expectations and the effect of their violation on communication outcomes. The results of an experiment testing five hypotheses on the relationship of distance and positive and negative feedback to recall, attraction, and credibility as communication outcomes provided some support for the model. Positive feedback was found to influence credibility and attraction, and curvilinear relationships were found between distance and communication outcomes for both positive and negative feedback conditions.

202. **Burgoon, Judee.** "Nonverbal Communication Research in the 1970s." In *Communication Yearbook IV,* edited by D. Nimmo. New Brunswick, New Jersey: Transaction Books, forthcoming.

203. **Burgoon, Judee, and Saine, Thomas.** *The Unspoken Dialogue: An Introduction to Nonverbal Communication.* Boston: Houghton Mifflin Company, 1978. Illus.

The authors divide their book into two sections. The first is a discussion of the components of nonverbal communication. Included here are definitions, theoretical approaches, and a discussion of kinesics, haptics, physical appearance, vocalics, chronemics, and artifacts as conveyers of nonverbal messages. Individual, subcultural, and cultural differences are described. Section Two relates to the functions of nonverbal communication. Impression formation, relational messages, communication of affect, regulation of interaction, presentation of self, and manipulation of others are topics considered in this section.

204. **Burns, Jo Ann, and Kintz, B.L.** "Eye Contact While Lying During an Interview." *Bulletin of the Psychonomic Society* 7 (1976) : 87-89.

Twenty college students were interviewed by a male or female confederate. The dependent variable was frequency and duration of eye contact as measured by a stopwatch, measured before and after subjects were asked to lie. Results showed that males looked longer into the female confederates' eyes while lying and the females looked longer into the male confederates' eyes while lying.

205. **Burns, Kenton L., and Beier, Ernst G.** "Significance of Vocal and Visual Channels in the Decoding of Emotional Meaning." *Journal of Communication* 23 (1973) : 118-130.

Six groups of 21 college students each rated several portrayals of seven affective states (angry, sad, happy, seductive, anxious, indifferent, and sarcastic). Each of the six groups rated the portrayals which had been recorded on film under six different conditions; audio/visual, filtered audio/visual, audio, visual, filtered audio, and content. It was found that with visual cues only accuracy declines and that when only audio cues are available accuracy drops still further. However, visual cues provided more information for the decoding of "happy" than combined audio and visual cues.

206. **Burnside, Irene Mortenson.** "Touching is Talking." *American Journal of Nursing* 73 (1973) : 2060-2063. Illus.

The author describes her experiences incorporating the use of touch into sessions designed to increase stimuli for aged patients with organic brain syndrome.

207. **Burroughs, W.; Schultz, W.; and Autrey, S.** "Quality of Argument, Leadership Votes, and Eye Contact in Three-Person Leaderless Groups." *Journal of Social Psychology* 90 (1973) : 89-93.

Thirty female undergraduates participated in the study. Pairs of subjects were placed in a dyad with a confederate. The confederate used either high or low quality arguments in her discussion. Dependent variables were number of leadership votes and eye contact. It was found that high quality arguments elicited more eye contact and more leadership votes.

208. **Burton, Arthur.** "The Presentation of the Face in Psychotherapy." *Psychotherapy: Theory, Research and Practice* 10 (1973) : 301-304.

The author discusses the importance of the face in interpersonal relations. He argues that by judiciously allowing his facial expression to be fully communicative of his "being," the psychotherapist can facilitate the therapeutic process and the ability of the patient to use his face expressively.

209. **Byers, Paul E.** "From Biological Rhythm to Cultural Pattern: A Study of Minimal Units." Ph.D. dissertation, Columbia University. 1972. 128 pp. (Order No. 73-9004)

Speech samples in eight languages including English, Eskimo, Cree, and Bushman were recorded on sound tape, and pen drawings were made of the amplitude of the speech signals at a vastly slowed rate. At this rate speech was seen to be generated in pulses that reflect an underlying biological rhythm. Parallels with body movement were investigated. Analysis of films of Eskimos and rhesus monkeys revealed a common rhythm underlying behavior which matches that of speech.

There are those who think or believe that communicating — even nonverbally — is a matter of exchanging messages and their science is, one way or another, the study of those messages, their creators or originators, and their effects. Many people do very strongly believe that the universe contains causes which have effects. On the other hand, there are those of us who begin with the premise that one of man's most necessary pursuits is getting it together harmoniously with others of his own and other species and that communication is the means by which this is done. We don't study messages. We study, instead, the organization of the communication behavior between or among interactants.

Paul Byers' discussion in *Interaction Rhythms: Periodicity in Communicative Behavior*, edited by M. Davis. New York: Human Sciences Press, forthcoming.

210. **Byers, Paul.** "Biological Rhythms as Information Channels in Interpersonal Communication Behavior." In *Perspectives in Ethology* II, edited by P.P.G. Bateson and H. Klopfer, pp. 135-164. New York: Plenum, 1976.

The author cites evidence for the existence of a universal biological rhythm of ten cycles per second and of a seven-cycle-per-second rhythm in humans which is related to speech. Analyses of filmed interactions of Netsilik Eskimos and of rhesus monkeys reveal a ten-cycle-per-second rhythm underlying body movement. The author links these periodicities to basic brain rhythms that pace and integrate behavior, and discusses communication as the sharing of rhythm states by interactants.

211. **Byers, Paul, and Byers, Happie.** "Nonverbal Communication and the Education of Children." In *Functions of Language in the Classroom,* edited by C. Cazden, V. John, and D. Hymes, pp. 3-31. New York: Teachers College Press, 1972.

Communication as participation in relationship is the theme of this discussion of nonverbal communication and the role of the teacher. The authors argue that the nonverbal aspects of communication are culturally organized and that development in nonverbal communication is necessary for full participation in a culture. A teacher's role is to help a child learn the culture's codes. The analysis of a film of a nursery school class with two white middle-class children, two black children, and a white teacher revealed a mismatch in communication systems between the teacher and the black children. Sharing of nonverbal codes is necessary in order for a child to learn.

212. **Byrne, Donn; Baskett, Glen D.; and Hodges, Louis.** "Behavioral Indicators of Interpersonal Attraction." *Journal of Applied Social Psychology* 1 (1971) : 137-149.

The experiments in this study were designed to test the finding that "physical distance between two individuals is related to degree of acquaintance or positiveness of the relationship between them." Subjects were tested under two conditions: seated in a semicircular arrangement and seated at a card table with confederates who had expressed similar attitudes or dissimilar attitudes to their own. In each experiment the confederates were the same sex as the subject. Among the results, it was found in the semicircular arrangement females preferred sitting beside the confederate who had expressed similar attitudes to their own than to the confederate who had expressed dissimilar attitudes. For males there was no significant relationship. In the card table arrangement males preferred sitting across from the preferred confederate, while females revealed no systematic preference.

213. **Cade, Theo Marshall.** "A Cross Cultural Study of Personal Space in the Family." Ph.D. dissertation, University of Hawaii. 1972. 139 pp. (Order No. 72-31,051)

Two studies, the first involving Hawaiian-Oriental and Caucasian families and the second American, Filipino, and Japanese families, investigated the use of an instrument to measure personal space within the family by manipulating figures representing family members. Both studies yielded similar vertical and horizontal patterns in family member placements, with parents highest, father to the left, daughter to the right, and husband-wife and brother-sister relationships not significantly differentiated.

214. **Caplow-Lindner, Erna; Harpaz, Leah; and Sambert, Sonya.** *Therapeutic Dance/Movement: Expressive Activities for Older Adults.* New York: Human Sciences Press, 1979. 283 pp. Illus.

215. **Carlsoo, Sven.** *How Man Moves: Kinesiological Methods and Studies.* New York: International Publications Service, 1973.

216. **Carr, Suzanne J., and Dabbs, James M. Jr.** "The Effects of Lighting, Distance, and Intimacy of Topic on Verbal and Visual Behavior." *Sociometry* 37 (1974) : 592-600.

Forty female undergraduates took part in two interviews, one involving non-intimate questions and one involving intimate questions. For the intimate interview the subject sat far from or near to the experimenter in a brightly or dimly lit room. In the intimate interview subjects decreased amount of verbal disclosure and number of eye contacts. The interview was seen to be more intimate and less appropriate in the dim and near conditions than the others. Subjects liked the interviewer and the interview better in the near condition. In the dim condition subjects decreased eye contact and increased latency, compared with the bright condition.

217. **Carr, Suzanne J.; Dabbs, James M. Jr.; and Carr, Timothy S.** "Mother-Infant Attachment: The Importance of the Mother's Visual Field." *Child Development* 46 (1975) : 331-338. Illus.

The authors address the importance of mother/child face-to-face contact and the interaction between visual behavior, verbal behavior, and proximity. Nineteen male and five female children, aged 18 to 30 months, were placed in a room. Their mothers spent five minutes in face-to-face contact; turned 180° away from the child; and seated behind a partition. Proximity and child behavior (activity level, talking, crying, time spent within the mother's visual field) were assessed. In the two nonface-to-face conditions children left toys to be within the mother's visual field 50 percent of the time, were more active, looked at her more, talked less, and tended to play closer to her. When the mother was seated behind a partition, the children talked more when they moved farther away.

218. **Cartier, Shirley Virginia.** "The Relationship Between Introversion-Extroversion and the Ability to Assess Nonverbal Behavior Patterns." Ed.D. dissertation, Boston University School of Education. 1972. 159 pp. (Order No. 72-25,424)

Counselors in training were tested with the Eysenck Personality Inventory and placed into one of six groups according to combinations of degree of extroversion-introversion and neuroticism. They rated a film of a counseling session with a semantical differentiated scale based on 40 nonverbal concepts. Scores by the high introverts and high extroverts did not significantly differ.

219. **Cary, Mark S.** "The Role of Gaze in the Initiation of a Conversation." *Social Psychology* 41 (1978) : 269-271.

Experimenters studied videotapes of 80 pairs of unacquainted undergraduates in a waiting room. Almost all dyads shared a mutual look as the second member entered the room. If they looked again after the person closed the door, conversation was likely. In opposite-sex pairs conversation was initiated by the male 72 percent of the time.

220. **Cary, Mark S.** "Comparing Film and Videotape." *Environmental Psychology and Nonverbal Behavior* 3 (1979): 243-247.

This review compares videotape and film to help the researcher choose the one most suited to the specific research problem. The review treats initial costs, running costs, resolution, required light levels, sound, color, processing, and data viewing. Half-inch videotape is the most versatile equipment, especially indoors. A motor-driven 35-mm camera is necessary when extreme resolution is required.

221. **Cary, Mark S.** "Gaze and Facial Display in Pedestrian Passing." *Semiotica* 28 (1979) : 323-326.

Sixty pictures each were taken of a single person or of passing pairs of people where only one person was seen head-on in the picture. The 60 singles pictures were of 30 males and 30 females, and the 60 passing pairs were of 15 each of the four combinations of the sexes. A second set of photos contained sequences of 40 singles and 40 pairs balanced for equal numbers of all sex combinations. People did not freeze their head or gaze position while passing. No instances of tongue-shows, tongue-in-cheek, or lip bites were found. No differences were found between pedestrians walking alone down a street and those about to pass another person. No effects due to sex were found except that cross-sex pairs were more likely to look at each other than were same-sex pairs.

222. **Cary, Mark S., and Rudick-Davis, Dave.** "Judging the Sex of an Unseen Person from Nonverbal Cues." *Sex Roles* 5 (1979) : 355-361.

Raters able to see only one person in videotapes of a dyadic interaction could fairly well guess the sex of the unseen partner when the viewed subject was male (but not when the partner in view was female). However, in a second study, when subjects were not instructed to treat their partners in a sex-stereotyped way as they were in the last condition, raters had difficulty guessing the sex of the unseen partner.

223. Chaikin, Alan L.; Sigler, Edward; and Derlega, Valerian J. "Nonverbal Mediators of Teacher Expectancy Effects." *Journal of Personality and Social Psychology* 30 (1974) : 144-149.

Forty-two undergraduates (half male and half female) tutored one of two male "students" who had been represented as bright, dull, or neither. While tutoring/microteaching, the subjects were unknowingly videotaped. Videotape scoring showed that those with a "bright" student smiled more, leaned forward more, had more direct eye gaze, and nodded their heads up and down more than did those who were in the control condition or those who thought their students were dull. Females smiled more and leaned forward less than males across all conditions.

224. Chaiklin, Harris, ed. *Marian Chace: Her Papers.* Columbia, Maryland: American Dance Therapy Association, 1975. 261 pp.

A collection of the writings of the "mother" of dance therapy, this book contains the majority of her works over a thirty-year period. Biographical material is included, as well as published and unpublished papers. Chace's papers cover such topics as relaxation, social contact, stimulation, and aggression. The edition concludes with panel discussions on rhythm and the meaning of movement and articles about the effects of her dance therapy treatment.

225. Chaiklin, Sharon. "Dance Therapy." In *American Handbook of Psychiatry, Vol. V,* edited by D.X. Freedman and J.E. Dryud, pp. 701-720. New York: Basic Books, 1975.

This article, written for readers unfamiliar with dance therapy or other body-oriented therapies, briefly summarizes the literature, history, and development of the profession and its relationship to psychiatric theory. Separate sections discuss the use of dance therapy with psychotic and neurotic adults and autistic children, with an emphasis on its rehabilitative potential. A last section presents the usefulness of movement observation systems such as Labananalysis.

226. Chapman, Antony J. "Eye Contact, Physical Proximity and Laughter: A Re-Examination of the Equilibrium Model of Social Intimacy." *Social Behavior and Personality* 3 (1975) : 143-155.

Forty boys and 40 girls seven years of age were assigned to same-sex dyads seated at one of two interpersonal distances. One or both members of the dyad listened to humorous material on headphones. Time spent in eye contact with the other child, time spent laughing, and time spent smiling were measured. At the nearer distance there was more eye contact during coaction (both with headphones) than in noncoactive dyads, but no difference at the farther distance. Subjects laughed and smiled more in coactive situations than in noncoactive, and within coactive situations they laughed and smiled more when they sat closer together. In the coactive conditions, the subjects who laughed and smiled most also engaged in the most eye contact. The author discusses his findings as a reversal of Argyle and Dean's equilibrium model of intimacy.

227. Chapple, Eliot D. "Toward a Mathematical Model of Interaction: Some Preliminary Considerations." In *Explorations in Mathematical Anthropology* edited by P. Kay, pp. 141-178. Cambridge, Massachusetts: The MIT Press, 1971.

This chapter begins with a concise summary of Chapple's theoretical framework and system for assessing the individual's basic interaction rhythm and the interrelation of rhythms in two-person interactions. The basic parameters he measures are oscillations of action and inaction of which speaking and silence are one important case. He discusses patterns of double actions in a dyad (interruptions) and patterns of latency of response and termination of interaction. After laying the conceptual groundwork for mathematical equations for the individual's "initial state" rhythms which he regards as deterministic, Chapple discusses cultural constraints, such as spatial distance, on the initial state equations. Interaction of more than two persons requires, according to Chapple, a probabilistic model.

228.   Chapple, Eliot D. *The Biological Foundations of Individuality and Culture.* Huntington, New York: Robert E. Krieger Publishing Co., 1980.

Originally published in 1970 under the title *Culture and Biological Man,* this work is a synthesis of almost 35 years of interaction research. The 1980 edition has a 24-page updating preface elaborating in particular Chapple's argument for adopting the term "Humanics" for the science of interaction. Part I is concerned with the definition of behavior units and measurement of fixed action patterns, circadian rhythms, biological rhythms and personality, and the relation of rhythms of action and inaction to emotion, temperament, and personality. It includes a chapter on the genetic origins of fixed action patterns. Part II focuses on the dimensions of culture that provide constraints on the individual and dyadic interaction rhythms. It includes chapters on constraints of distance, space, sequencing of actions, institutional organization, symbols, and roles on interaction. The final chapters deal with the influence of life crises and rites of passage on interactions and future development of interaction forms. While the topics discussed are quite broad and general, it should be emphasized that this treatise on interaction is based on Chapple's very specific definition and analysis of interaction rhythms.

". . . *there was one universal which seemed to enter into every situation. It was the time duration of events between people, their frequency and the order in which one or another person was expected to initiate or, as we [Chapple and Conrad Arensberg] called it, originate an event. . . . We began with time duration and frequency of events, but to record them found we had to distinguish the actions and inactions between them, beginnings and endings of events themselves being susceptible to alternate explanatory criteria and this was in 1936."*

Eliot D. Chapple from "The Unbounded Reaches of Anthropology as a Research Science and Some Working Hypotheses." Paper presented at the meeting of the American Anthropological Association, 1979.

229.   Chapple, Eliot D., and Lui, Yau-yin. "Populations of Coupled Non-Linear Oscillators in Anthropological Biology Systems."*IEEE International Conference on Cybernetics and Society Proceedings* (1976) : 332-335.

A unique effort to develop a mathematical model for the individual's "action and inaction tempo" in terms of vander Pol-type equations, its extension to dyadic interactions, with a third set of equations for interaction oscillators for groups of more than two. This highly technical paper is notable for its analysis of interaction rhythms in a "hard-science" way.

230.   Chauvin, Rémy. *Ethology: The Biological Study of Animal Behavior.* New York: International Universities Press, 1975. 245 pp. Illus.

Discussion of the building, learning, migration, orientation, mating, and attachment behaviors of animals is followed by a review of animal communication. The book concludes with a chapter on ethological concepts and problems of definition.

231.   Chauvin, Rémy, and Muckensturn-Chauvin, Bernadette. *Behavioral Complexities.* New York: International Universities Press, 1979.

232.   Cheney, Gay, ed. "Dance Therapy Annotated Bibliography." *CORD News* 4 (1972) : 7-56.

This 243-title bibliography contains abstracts on a number of books and articles in the subject area of nonverbal communication.

233. **Cherry, Colin.** *On Human Communication: A Review, A Survey, and A Criticism,* Third Edition. Cambridge, Massachusetts: The MIT Press, 1978. 374 pp. Illus.

The third edition includes a new chapter on the "human-ness" of human communication. Facial expression, gesture, eye movement, and proxemics are described as part of the communication ritual.

234. **Cherulnik, Paul D.** "Sex Differences in the Expression of Emotion in a Structured Social Encounter." *Sex Roles* 5 (1979) : 413-424.

Eighteen male and 18 female college students were videotaped while responding to 10 questions designed to elicit weak or strong affective responses. Raters judged whether there were recognizable facial expressions, and women were found to have more than men and to be judged as having more "happy" and "excited" affects than the men. No sex differences were found in duration or latency of answers or visual behavior.

235. **Chester, Sondra L., and Egolf, Donald B.** "Nonverbal Communication and Aphasia Therapy." *Rehabilitation Literature* 35 (1974) : 231-233.

The various categories of nonverbal communication were listed and described. Five major reasons for recognizing and incorporating the principles and techniques of nonverbal communication into aphasia therapy were listed. A modified version of Flanagan's Critical Incident Technique was used to conduct a preliminary investigation of the interactions (both verbal and nonverbal) of aphasics and others (professionals, family, and so on). Of the 113 critical incidents reported, 91 were judged to be negative and 22 were judged to be positive.

236. **Cheyne, J.A.** "Development of Forms and Functions of Smiling in Preschoolers." *Child Development* 47 (1976) : 820-823.

In this study of 150 preschoolers, smiling frequency, forms (upper, closed, or broad smile), and persons with whom the child interacted were noted during normal play periods. Upper smile frequency increased with older age groups, whereas no change in frequency of closed or broad smiles was found between groups. Upper smiles were used more with same-sex peers, and frequency and forms of boys smiling at girls was markedly similar to that of smiling at teachers.

237. **Cheyne, James A.** "The Effect of Spatial and Interpersonal Variables on the Invasion of Group Controlled Territories." *Sociometry* 35 (1972): 477-489.

In the first study, same and mixed sex pairs stood at a fixed distance either interacting or not interacting in the corridor of a university building. In the second, similar dyads stood conversing at varying interpersonal distances in a shopping mall. Observers recorded the number of times passerby passed through the dyad rather than going around it. Frequency of intrusion varied according to sex of dyad members, activity of the group, and distance apart. Groups standing within Hall's "personal" distance were intruded upon less frequently.

238. **Christensen, Dana; Farino, Amerigo; and Boudreau, Louis.** "Sensitivity to Nonverbal Cues as a Function of Social Competence." *Journal of Nonverbal Behavior* 4 (1980) : 146-156.

The hypothesis that sensitivity to nonverbal messages is an important component of social competence was tested employing 24 female subjects. Subjects were given the task of interviewing a confederate. They were instructed to change the interview topic if the questioning appeared to produce a discomfort in their partner. The confederate displayed a series of nonverbal cues indicating mounting tension while responding to certain questions. Two measures of sensitivity to the cues were obtained: (1) how quickly the subject changed the interview topic in response to the cues, and (2) how many nonverbal cues the subject reported observing. The findings indicated that low-competence subjects reported having observed as many of the nonverbal messages as the high-competence subjects but failed to respond to them. No difference was found between groups for level of anxiety experienced during the interaction.

239. **Christenson, Michael Allen.** "Aspects of Visual Behavior in Relation to Sex of Subject and Expressions of Affect." Ph.D. dissertation, Washington State University. 1973. 39 pp. (Order N. 73-38)

Male and female subjects were videotaped discussion happy, angry, or sad experiences with an interviewer, and the proportion of time spent in eye contact and with eyes downcast was recorded. Subjects of both sexes looked at the interviewer more during discussions of happy and angry experiences than of sad experiences.

240. **Churchill, Don W., and Bryson, Carolyn Q.** "Looking and Approach Behavior of Psychotic and Normal Children as a Function of Adult Attention of Preoccupation." *Comprehensive Psychiatry* 13 (1972) : 171-177. Illus.

Fourteen psychotic (schizophrenic or autistic) institutionalized children were observed during three ten-minute periods in each of three conditions: attentive adult present, preoccupied adult present (seated sideways, working on a puzzle), or no adult present. Although the apparent intent of the play behaviors of the psychotic children differed substantially from that of normals, no difference was noted ingaze behavior of the tendency to keep the adult in sight. Thus this study holds no support for the idea that adult attention creates avoidance behavior in psychotic children.

241. **Ciampa, Bartholomew J.** "Edu-Kinesics: The Non-Verbal Language of the Classroom." *Educational Technology* 12 (1972) : 62.

Teachers should become aware of the effect of their nonverbal communication on their students.

242. **Cicourel, Aaron V.** "Gestural Sign Language and the Study of Non-Verbal Communication." In *The Body As A Medium of Expression,* edited by J. Benthall and T. Polhemus, pp. 195-232. London: Allen Lane, 1975.

The authors contend that the principles that organize visual information and visual imagery for the deaf are not readily available to hearing persons because the structure of gestural sign language is relatively unknown and so is not a good resource for understanding context-sensitive nonverbal information among the hearing. This article focuses on the task of making available a formal normative system for organizing information on nonverbal communication embedded in the deaf sign language. A sign language and its facial and bodily movements can provide a formal language organization comparable to oral-auditory language.

243. **Ciolek, Matthew T.** "Spatial Arrangements in Social Encounters: An Attempt at a Taxonomy." *Man-Environment Systems* 8 (1978) : 52-59.

Comparing existing notation systems for proxemic relationships, the author offers diagrams and notations of two- and three-person group arrangements and provides data on group formation comparisons of three Australian cultures: Australians of Canberra, Enga, and Muragin.

244. **Ciolek, Matthew T.** "Spatial Behavior in Pedestrian Area." *Ekistics* 45(1978): 120-122. Illus.

Based on the author's doctoral research, this is a brief report of pedestrian spatial paths, eight physical and social factors or criteria for them, and pattern interaction in narrow spaces.

245.   **Ciolek, T.M.** "Human Communication Behavior: A Bibliography." *Sign Language Studies* 6 (1975) : 1-64.

A provisional checklist of references to the use of gestures, postures, bodily contact, spacing, orientation, facial expressions, looking behavior, and appearance in the course of face-to-face interactions. Approximately 600 items.

246.   **Ciolek, T.M.; Elzinga, R.H.; and McHoul, A.W.,** eds. "Selected References to Coenetics, the Study of Behavioral Organization of Face-to Face Interactions." *Sign Language Studies* 22 (1979) : 1-74.

This bibliography of 600 items dealing with coenetics, the study of face-to-face interaction, is prefaced by a commentary by Adam Kendon on current issues and trends in the field. Criteria for inclusion in the bibliography were a focus on some aspect of the way in which face-to-face interactions are accomplished, the use of recorded examples of actual events, and a concern with observable, "surface" features of behavior. Some works from neighboring disciplines were included to place the study of coenetics within context, and the bibliography includes an index with 22 subject headings.

247.   **Clark, Virginia P.; Escholz, Paul A.; and Rosa, Alfred F.,** eds. *Language: Introductory Readings,* 2nd edition. New York: St. Martin's Press, 1977. 532 pp. Illus.

This college-level reader has an extensive section on kinesics and proxemics including chapters such as "Space Speaks" by Edward T. Hall, "Learning to Read Gestures" by Gerard I. Nierenberg and Henry H. Calero, and "Communication by Gesture in the Middle East" by Leo Hamalian.

248.   **Clarke, Jack F.** "Some Effects of Nonverbal Activities and Group Discussion on Interpersonal Trust Development in Small Groups." Ph.D. dissertation, Arizona State University. 1971. 156 pp. (Order No. 71-18,955)

The author set out to discover whether a combination of nonverbal activities and group discussion increases interpersonal trust in initial phases of a group. Evidence is presented that it furthers the group's trust no more than does simple discussion.

249.   **Clinkscales, Marcia J. Montgomery.** "Black and White Nonverbal Dyadic Behavior and Attraction." Ph.D. dissertation, University of Denver. 1975.

Thirty pairs of undergraduates males of the same racial background (white/white or black/black) were videotaped for an analysis of their nonverbal behavior and patterns of interpersonal attraction. Among several results the study showed that certain head and facial movements were descriptive of the white pairs in contrast to specific bodily movements (described as orientation and rocking movements), which were characteristic of Black dyads. (from author's abstract)

250.   **Clore, Gerald L.; Wiggins, Nancy Hirschberg; and Itkin, Stuart.** "Gain and Loss in Attraction: Attributions from Nonverbal Behavior." *Journal of Personality and Social Psychology* 31 (1975) : 706-712.

Four videotapes of a "get acquainted" conversation between a role-playing couple were prearranged to convey female warmth or coldness by manipulation of the females' nonverbal behaviors. The tapes were spliced to convey four attraction effects: warm-warm, warm-cold (loss condition), cold-warm (gain condition), and cold-cold. Three hundred thirty-eight subjects viewed one of the four tapes and rated the couple's reaction to each other as well as their own reactions to the female. Additionally, subjects completed attribution ratings of both individuals on such traits as attractiveness, nervousness, warmth, dominance, and confidence. Attraction gain-loss effects were noted only in attributions of the male's attraction to the female and thus were probably due to the attributions of affective responses to the male.

251. Clynes, Manfred. *Sentics: The Touch of Emotions.* New York: Anchor Press/Doubleday, 1977. Illus.

The author defines "sentics" as the study of genetically programmed dynamic forms of emotional expression; the result of brain processes which determine the way we perceive and express emotion. The way he measures these "sentic" forms is disarmingly simple. Subjects are given stimulus words for specific emotions and asked to press a button connected to a computer that measures the pattern of downward and lateral movements. Clynes demonstrates how each emotion has a distinctive curve and rhythm in effect isolating motor rhythm correlates of primary emotions. He explores these sentic forms in movements, tone of voice, perception rates, and even classical music; and discusses implications for therapy and communication.

252. Coates, Brian; Anderson, Elizabeth P.; and Hartup, William W. "Interrelation in the Attachment Behavior of Human Infants." *Developmental Psychology* 6 (1972) : 218-230.

Behaviors such as visual regard, touching, and proximity were examined in 10-, 14-, and 18-month-old infants, particularly in relation to momentary separation from the mother.

253. Cobb, Lynne Seaborg. "Infant Response to Gaze and Face Direction." Ph.D. dissertation, Purdue University. 1979. 151 pp. (Order No. 7926355)

A study of infants' ability to discriminate discrepancies in gaze and face direction using a "habituation/recovery" method.

254. Coger, L., and Pelham, S. "Kinesics Applied to Interpreter's Theatre." *Speech Teacher* 24 (1975) : 91-99.

This article examines some recent research in kinesics and discusses, in particular, findings by Ekman and Friesen on rules of display, Mehrabian on the physical dimensions of emotion, and Scheflen on posture. Applications of the work of these authors by actors and directors of interpreter's theatre are suggested in order to enhance the portrayal of attitudes and emotions with the spoken text.

255. Cohen, Akiba A. "The Communicative Function of Hand Illustrators." *Journal of Communication* 27 (1977): 54-64.

In this exploration of the function of hand illustrators, 144 undergraduates were instructed to give directions to locations that varied in complexity under three conditions: face-to-face, over an intercom, and face-to-face with practice. The number of illustrators was measured and found, as expected, to be greatest in the face-to-face condition. However, results also gave support for an encoding more than a decoding function of illustrators.

256. Cohen, Akiba A., and Harrison, Randall P. "Intentionality in the Use of Hand Illustrators in Face-to-Face Communication Situations." *Journal of Personality and Social Psychology* 28 (1973) : 276-279.

Twenty-four male students in a communications course had the task of giving four sets of directions to a female (supposedly a new secretary). Two sets were given directly (face-to-face), and two sets were given over an intercom. Subjects unknowingly were videotaped throughout, and their hand movements were counted when the hand gestures were judged to be related to what the subject was saying. More hand ilustrators were used in the face-to-face situation than in the intercom situation.

257. Cohen, Bertram D., and Rau, John H. "Nonverbal Technique for Measuring Affect Using Facial Expression Photographs as Stimuli." *Journal of Consulting and Clinical Psychology* 38 (1972) : 449-451.

Fifty hospitalized and 50 nonhospitalized female patients diagnosed as depressives were shown 41 facial expression photographs with two tasks to complete. In the first task patients were asked to complete the sentence "this face looks . . ." with an adjective that best described the "mood," "emotion," or "feeling" portrayed on each face. Then the women were asked to pick from the 41 photographs the picture "that best looks like you feel right now." Among the results it was found that, the more depressed the subject, the more depressive was the picture chosen.

258. **Cohen, Lynn Renee.** "An Inquiry into the Use of Effort/Shape Analysis in the Exploration of Leadership in Small Groups: A Systems View." Ph.D. dissertation, Columbia University. 1975. 290 pp. (Order No. 75-27,391)

Using the Effort/Shape system in the analysis of small groups, it was found that the movement profile of one member mirrored the movement profile of the group as a whole at the time that the person was the most "salient" member of the group. Groups were found to differ in specific effort and shape combinations and in specific relationships between effort and shape qualities. Effort/Shape Analysis is recommended as a precise means of describing group climate or emotional tone.

259. **Cohler, Bertram G.; Grunebaum, Henry U.; Weiss, Justin L.; Gamer, Enid; and Gallant, David H.** "Disturbance of Attention Among Schizophrenic, Depressed, and Well Mothers and their Young Children." *Journal of Child Psychology and Psychiatry* 18 (1977) : 115-135.

The paper reports the findings of a study of the disturbance of attention as measured by the Embedded Figures Test and Continuous Performance Task for a group of 40 psychotic mothers (26 schizophrenic and 14 depressed), a matched group of well mothers, and the children, age five to six, of all the mothers. Schizophrenic mothers did not perform on the EFT as well as the others at a level approaching significance. Controlling for intelligence, there were no significant relationships between mothers and children in any group on the measures of attention. However, the children of psychotically depressed mothers showed the greatest impairment of intelligence and made errors on the EFT significantly more times than the children of schizophrenic or well mothers.

260. **Colaiuta, Victoria Bernadette.** "Effects of Eye Contact on WAIS Performance." Ph.D. dissertation, University of South Dakota. 1973. 32 pp. (Order No. 73275-27)

In this study no significant differences were found between performance on the Wechsler Adult Intelligence Scale and various eye contact patterns established during testing.

261. **Cole, James K.,** ed. *Nebraska Symposium on Motivation 1971.* Lincoln, Nebraska: University of Nebraska Press, 1971. 304 pp.

The book contains three chapters on nonverbal communication. Albert Mehrabian's paper, "Nonverbal Communication," reviews research done on facial and vocal expressions, hand gestures, postures and positions, the relationship between nonverbal and implicit verbal behaviors, and multichannel communication, that is, inconsistent versus consistent messages. The chapter "Visual Interaction: The Glances of Power and Preference" by Ralph Exline describes empirical studies based on the assumption that eye contact is one of the nonverbal processes used to define the power and preference aspects of a relationship. The chapter "Universals and Cultural Differences in Facial Expressions of Emotion" by Paul Ekman presents four experiments with conclusive evidence that there are universal facial expressions of emotion.

262. **Collett, Peter.** "Training Englishmen in the Non-Verbal Behaviour of Arabs: An Experiment on Intercultural Communication." *International Journal of Psychology* 6 (1971) : 209-215.

Ten Arab men and 20 Englishmen participated in the first study. As experimental subjects (ES), ten Englishmen received a training program instructing them in specific Arab nonverbals, while ten control subjects (CS) received unstructured material on the Arab world. Then each Arab met and talked with an ES and a CS. This was videotaped, and an event recorder was used to record specific nonverbal behaviors included within the training program. Afterward, the Arabs made sociometric choices between the CS and ES Englishmen they had met. This experiment was repeated having Englishmen meet CS or ES Englishmen trained in the same way. Significant differences in the Arab experiment were found in interpersonal distance, looking time, and mean length of look. Sociometrically, the Arabs preferred Englishmen who behaved like themselves, but no such distinction was found in the English-English experiment.

263. **Collett, Peter; and Marsh, Peter.** "Patterns of Public Behaviour: Collision Avoidance on a Pedestrian Crossing." *Semiotica* 12 (1974) : 281-299. Illus.

Pedestrians were observed crossing at Oxford Circus in London where, when the light changes, one phalanx of pedestrians is forced to find their way past the other. About four hours of videotapes were examined for collision avoidance behavior. Males and females were significantly different (p < .001) on the "pass index," with males oriented "open" or towards and females "closed" or away from the passer. While most men who were out-of-step performed open passes, most of the women who were out-of-step performed closed passes, (p < .02). More women than men drew one or both of their arms across their bodies when passing another person, (p < .001). Significantly more women than men were carrying something, but the sex difference for arm cross in passing remained, even controlling for this factor. More passers drew one or both arms in front of them when effecting a closed pass. Significantly more women than men crossed themselves when effecting open or neutral passes. The type of pass by women and men was independent of the sex of the person being passed. The type of pass performed by one person was, with the exception of men aged 25-34, unrelated to the age of the other passer.

264. **Collins, O., and Collins, June M.** "Research on the Interaction Problem: A Brief Review." In *Interaction and Social Structure,* edited by O. Collins and J.M. Collins, pp. 38-56. The Hague: Mouton, 1973.

This chapter traces the Chapple-Arensberg Formulation of the interaction process. Eliot D. Chapple and Conrad M. Arensberg had isolated interaction as a field of study that permitted them precise definition of interaction based on observable behavior. A group of researchers advanced their work by supporting the paradigm with empirical data.

265. **Collis, G.M., and Schaffer, H.R.** "Synchronization of Visual Attention in Mother-Infant Pairs." *Journal of Child Psychology and Psychiatry* 16 (1975) : 315-320.

Studying the degree to which mothers visually monitor their baby's gaze, the investigators placed 16 mother-infant pairs in a room and instructed each mother to keep the child on her knee. Visual fixations lasting longer than 0.3 seconds were counted through frame-by-frame film analysis. Infants predominantly gazed at toys which were out of reach, while mothers usually gazed at infants. When both focused on their toys they usually attended to the same one. Mothers tended to focus quickly on what their infants gazed at, a finely timed pattern which, according to the authors, helps them establish synchrony with their infants.

266. **Comer, Ronald J., and Piliavin, Jane A.** "The Effects of Physical Deviance upon Face-to-Face Interaction: The Other Side." *Journal of Personality and Social Psychology* 23 (1972) : 33-39.

Thirty physically handicapped males with disabilities affecting their legs participated in this study of handicapped-normal dyadic interaction. A nonhandicapped confederate wore a leg brace during interviews with half the subjects and appeared normal with the remaining group of handicapped subjects. The results showed that physically handicapped subjects interacting with a normal confederate ended the interaction sooner; portrayed greater motoric inhibitions; showed less smiling behavior; and maintained less eye contact with the confederate. Contrary to prediction, they maintained a greater distance with the handicapped confederate.

267. **Comstock, Tamara.** *New Dimensions in Dance Research: Anthropology and Dance—the American Indians.* New York: CORD, New York University, 1974. 353 pp.

This fine collection of articles includes most of those presented at the Third Conference on Dance Research. The focus of the conference was to gain an understanding of the role of dance in a society and to review anthropological research tools applicable to dance, including field study, linguistic concepts, choreometrics, and kinesics. The conference was scheduled to coincide with the Yaqui Indian holy week and made use of their rituals to expose participants to some of the research techniques being discussed. This volume moves through dance ethnology, dance as a part of the nonverbal and expressive behaviors of a culture, linguistic parallels of dance, and dance as it demonstrates and symbolizes the world-view and myth-ritual complex of a society.

268. **Condon, John C., and Yousef, Fathi S.** *An Introduction to Intercultural Communication.* Indianapolis, Indiana: Bobbs Merrill, 1975. 306 pp.

Among chapters describing cultural differences in rituals, social events, values, languages, and so on, there is a 24-page chapter on nonverbal communication across cultures. It includes discussion of digital versus analogical modes of expression, taboos, "activity orientations," and status differences.

269. **Condon, William S.** "Multiple Response to Sound in Dysfunctional Children." *Journal of Autism and Childhood Schizophrenia* 5 (1975) : 37-56.

Condon reviews his findings on self- and interactional synchrony, the synchronous entrainment of body movement with sound, and then discusses the results of the microanalysis of the movements of 25 dysfunctional children in response to sound. Seventeen of these children were severely dysfunctional (autistic-like, retarded, victims of cerebral palsy, or anoxic at birth), and eight had less severe reading problems. The analysis revealed systematic delays of response varying from one-half to a full second, as if the children were responding to "delayed sound." In one case of retardation the child could synchronize with the movement of others but consistently responded to sound 16 frames late. Condon posits a continuum of severity in what appears to be a perceptual dysfunction that locks the children into an unreal world.

270. **Condon, William S.** "An Analysis of Behavioral Organization." *Sign Language Studies* 13 (1976) : 285-318.

Condon discusses his seminal research from the point of view of the organization of behavior. Units of behavior identified through microanalysis are "forms of order" by which body parts move simultaneously in relation to each other. Examples of self-synchrony and interactional synchrony are discussed.

271. **Condon, William S.** "A Primary Phase in the Organization of Infant Responding Behaviour." In *Studies in Mother-Infant Interaction,* edited by H.R. Schaffer, pp. 153-176. New York: Academic Press, 1977.

The author discusses the microanalysis of behavior as an ethology of "information processing." The ability of the human being to track the structure of incoming sounds as revealed by the synchronization of listener's movement with the sounds has been reported in infants as early as the first day of life. This synchronization of behavior within 50 milleseconds is discussed as an early stage in the discrimination/cognition process. The article includes a discussion of the multiple response to sound and inability to habituate of an infant who had been anoxic at birth.

272. **Condon, William S.** "The Relation of Interactional Synchrony to Cognitive and Emotional Processes." In *The Relationship of Verbal and Nonverbal Communication,* edited by M.R. Key, pp. 49-65. The Hague: Mouton, 1980.

This is a theoretical discussion of the structure of behavior and the nature of human communication revealed by the author's microanalytic study of interaction. "Interactional synchrony," or the synchronization of a listener's movement with the structure of incoming speech, is discussed as the organizational interface of the person with the world. This orderly processing of the order of the world appears to have broken down in autistic-like children whose behavior is marked by asynchrony, multiple entrainment to sound, and multiple orienting responses. Because of the profound participation in another's life that interactional synchrony reveals, the author argues that interaction affects the inner lives of the interactants.

273. **Condon, William S., and Sander, Louis W.** "Neonate Movement is Synchronized with Adult Speech: Interactional Participation and Language Acquisition." *Science* 183 (1974) : 99-101.

The synchronization of neonate movement with the articulated patterns of human speech was observed through the microanalysis of sound films in 16 infants as young as 12 hours of age. Implications for the linguistic/kinesic precursors of language acquisition are discussed.

274. **Conroy, Joseph III, and Sundstrom, Eric.** "Territorial Dominance in a Dyadic Conversation as a Function of Similarity of Opinion." *Journal of Personality and Social Psychology* 35 (1977) : 570-576.

Male subjects with similar or dissimilar opinions worked in dyads on a cooperative task while one partner was a guest in the residence of the other. Results of an analysis of speech patterns from the taped sessions showed that dissimilar pairs talked more, but among similar pairs the visitor talked more. This was also true for instances of simultaneous speech when one member deferred to the other. The findings are interpreted as indications of territorial dominance among dissimilar pairs and of a "hospitality factor" among similar pairs.

275. **Cook, Mark.** "Gaze and Mutual Gaze in Social Encounters." In *Nonverbal Communication: Readings with Commentary.* 2nd edition, edited by S. Weitz, pp. 77-86. New York: Oxford University Press, 1979.

Different methods of recording gaze behavior, typical findings of sex and individual differences in gaze behavior, gaze patterns in psychopathology, the actual unsteadiness of "study" gaze, anthropological and ethological notes on gaze, and studies of when and how long people look are topics covered in this interesting overview of gaze research.

276. **Cook, Mark.** *Perceiving Others: The Psychology of Interpersonal Perception.* New York: Methuen, 1979.

277. **Cook, Mark.** "The Relation Between Gaze and Pausing Examined Afresh." In *Temporal Variables in Speech: Studies in Honour of Freda Goldman-Eisler,* edited by H.W. Dechart and M. Raupach. The Hague: Mouton, forthcoming.

278. **Cook, Mark, and Smith, Jacqueline M.C.** "The Role of Gaze in Impression Formation." *British Journal of Social and Clinical Psychology* 14 (1975) : 19-25.

A study involving 72 male and female university students to determine the effects of three levels of gaze (normal, continuous, averted) and four combinations of sex of interactants (MF, MM, FF, FM) on the subjects' impressions of confederates. Impression formation was measured by subjects' ratings of confederates on semantic differentials and by subjects' free descriptions of confederates in response to certain questions asked by the experimenter. In the continuous gaze condition, female confederates were rated less favorably than males. But in the normal gaze condition they were rated more favorably. Overall, male confederates were rated as more potent than their female counterparts, regardless of gaze. For subjects who mentioned gaze in their free descriptions, confederates were rated lower in potency, like-dislike, and easy to get on with in the averted gaze condition than in the normal gaze condition. Analysis of adjectives used in free description showed confederates to be perceived differently in certainty, fearfulness, and pleasantness according to their gaze behavior.

279. **Cooper, Cary L, and Bowles, David.** "Physical Encounter and Self-Disclosure." *Psychological Reports* 33 (1973) : 451-454.

Two encounter groups in which contact exercises were used were compared to a control encounter group that did not involve these exercises. Physical contact was found to significantly increase self-disclosure after the initial group session.

280. **Coss, Richard G.** "Reflections on the Evil Eye." *Human Behavior* 3 (1974) : 16-22. Illus.

The importance of the symbol of the eye throughout history is examined. The apparent tendencies for prolonged eye contact to intimidate and for gaze aversion to avoid aggression are considered by presenting research on animals and humans.

281. **Costonis, Maureen.** "Case Study of a Puzzling Child: Using the Synchronous Movement Profile as an Evaluation Tool." *Conference Proceedings of the American Dance Therapy Association* 8 (1974) : 162-176.

The author developed a Synchronous Movement Profile to test the abilities of a disturbed child. The test was scored during dance-therapy sessions and showed as high as a 60.5 percent increase in synchronous movement within 10 minutes. The child also achieved a 40 percent decrease in the amount of time necessary to become synchronous. The profile establishes synchrony relative to body part and time units. A sample profile is included.

282. **Costonis, Maureen.** "How I Learned to Wall-Bounce and Love it!" *Conference Proceedings of the American Dance Therapy Association* 9 (1975) : 143-155.

After a brief clinical description of the movement patterns of an atypical child, the author discusses movement observation systems, especially Effort/Shape and Eshkol-Wachmann. The Movement Range Sampler, devised by Constonis and related to the Eshkol-Wachmann system, measures the range of each moving body part and its path in space. A dance-therapy session with the above-mentioned atypical child is rated with the MRS, as well as scored for movement synchrony. The effectiveness of dance therapy in altering bizarre movement patterns for brief periods is noted.

283. **Costonis, Marueen Needham.** *Therapy in Motion.* Urbana, Illinois: University of Illinois Press, 1978. 278 pp.

A collection of readings on dance therapy and nonverbal communication, this book includes several case studies, articles on approaches to dance therapy, discussions of movement and personality, body awareness, and therapeutic change. There are also reprinted articles by Ray Birdwhistell ("The Frames in the Communication Process"), Adam Kendon ("Movement Coordination in Dance Therapy and Conversation"), and Martha Davis ("Movement Characteristics of Hospitalized Psychiatric Patients").

284. **Coutts, Larry M., and Ledden, Maribeth.** "Nonverbal Compensatory Reactions to Changes in Interpersonal Proximity." *Journal of Social Psychology* 102 (1977) : 283-290.

Forty female undergraduates had initial interview sessions followed by a second session in which the interviewer increased, decreased, or maintained the same face-to-face seating distance as in the first session. Subjects looked and smiled at her less when she moved closer. They looked and smiled at her more, leaned forward, and oriented themselves directly towards her when she moved farther away. These compensatory reactions are interpreted as attempts to restore "previous intimacy equilibrium."

285. **Coutts, Larry M. and Schneider, Frank W.** "Visual Behavior in an Unfocused Interaction as a Function of Sex and Distance." *Journal of Experimental Social Psychology* 11 (1975) : 64-77.

This study investigated visual behavior of ten female, ten male, and 20 mixed-sex dyads in an unfocused (waiting room) situation. Results showed that amounts of visual behavior decreased with time and increased with interpersonal distance. Gaze behavior did not significantly vary by the sex of the looker, but females were looked at more than males. Female dyads accounted for more glances than any other type of dyad. Mutual gaze accounted for only 1 percent of interaction time.

286. **Coutts, Larry M., and Schneider, Frank W.** "Affiliative Conflict Theory: An Investigation of the Intimacy Equilibrium and Compensation Hypothesis." *Journal of Personality and Social Psychology* 34 (1976) : 1135-1142.

In this study of dyads discussing thematic apperception test cards, friends exhibited more smiling and mutual gaze than strangers. Notably, when one member reduced looking at her partner as instructed, this did not result in a compensatory increase in the immediacy behaviors of the other. It was concluded that the parameters of behavioral compensation need clarification.

287. **Cozby, Paul C.** "Effects of Density, Activity, and Personality on Environmental Preferences." *Journal of Research in Personality* 7 (1973) : 45-60.

In this study of 74 female undergraduates, results show that the type of activity is a factor in whether high or low density is preferred as well as personal space preferences.

288. **Cranach, Mario von, and Vine, Ian,** eds. *Social Communication and Movement: Studies of Interaction and Expression in Man and Chimpanzee.* New York: Academic Press, 1973. 489 pp. Illus.

This excellent book is a compilation of articles based on presentations at a Working-Group Meeting on Nonverbal Communication sponsored by the European Association of Experimental Social Psychology in 1969. It is an ethological analysis of various forms of nonverbal behavior, as well as a discussion of methodologies and research problems. A. Kendon, J. van Hooff, I. Eibl-Eibesfeldt, I. Vine, and N. Frijada have contributed articles. The topics explored are chimpanzee behavior, deaf-and-blind-born children's expressions, facial-visual signals, pupil dilation, and facial expression. A section on concepts, methods, and strategies includes papers by M. von Cranach, and H. Ellgring.

289. **Crapanzano, Vincent.** "The Hamadsha." In *Scholars, Saints and Sufis* edited by N.R. Keddie, pp. 327-348. Berkeley, California: University of California Press, 1972.

Within a rich and interesting report on the background, beliefs, and practices of the Hamadsha, a Moroccan religious brotherhood, the author describes trance rituals and the movements which accompany them. Certain of the trance rituals done by the men involve self-mutilation with no experience of pain. In some dances women and children may go into trance.

290. **Creider, Chet A.** "Towards a Description of East African Gestures." *Sign Language Studies* 14 (1977) : 1-20.

Facial expression, gestures, and body movements of four Kenyan tribal groups are described in detail and compared to nonverbal expressions in Africa, Latin and North America.

291. **Critchley, MacDonald.** *Silent Language.* London: Butterworth, 1975. 231 pp. Illus.

Gesture as a modality of communication and of self-expression constitutes the principal theme of this engaging book. In this treatment gesture augments, elaborates, intensifies, expands, modifies, maximizes, emphasizes, or in some way alters the reference-function of audible speech. The author explores the neurology of gesture and examines sign language and gestures of primitive and contemporary communities. A survey of gesture in relation to the arts of rhetoric, pantomime, and dance – as well as a section devoted to everyday conversation – rounds out this inclusive work.

292. **Cross, Crispin P.** *Interviewing and Communication in Social Work.* London: Routledge and Kegan Paul, 1974. 176 pp.

This work contains a chapter on nonverbal aspects of the social-work interview including discussion of gaze, facial expression, gesture, proxemics, and paralinguistics.

293. **Crouch, Wayne W.; Frye, Jerry K.; Brindle, Bette; and Wong, Peter C.** "The Syracuse Person Perception Test: A Measure of Responsiveness to Facial and Verbal Cues." In *Graphical Representation of Multivariable Data,* edited by P.C. Wong. New York: Academic Press, 1978.

294. **Cunningham, Michael R.** "Personality and the Structure of the Nonverbal Communication of Emotion." *Journal of Personality* 45 (1977) : 564-584.

In laboratory studies involving videotapes of subjects expressing elation or depression in three different ways, consistency in nonverbal encoding ability was found between voice and face channels (and to a lesser degree body channels) both when subjects were aware and unaware of their expressions. Women subjects showed greater decoding ability. Notably, the ability to encode was negatively correlated with the ability to decode messages. Encoding ability related to measures of extroversion and emotional responsiveness.

295. **Cuny, Xavier.** "Les commandements gestuels: Une expérience avec des ouvriers étrangers débutants." *Bulletin de Psychologie* 26 (1972-73) : 847-852.

The hypothesis of this study, that task-related gestures such as turning a button or pulling a lever can be readily transposable to so-called 'motivated' gestures meant to command others to perform the tasks, was tested with a group of foreign laborers taught gestural commands to signal crane-runway operators. The results show that one can obtain a set of "spontaneous" gestural commands from beginning foreign laborers who have not learned the formal code and that these are related to task-oriented gestures. The authors conclude that codes should not go against this "spontaneous" gesture symbolism. Written in French.

296. **Cupchik, Gerald Chaim.** "Expression and Impression: The Decoding of Nonverbal Affect." Ph.D. dissertation, University of Wisconsin. 1972. 115 pp. (Order No. 73-7184)

Female and male senders were videotaped reacting to four types of affect-evoking slides. Subjects judging the category of slide from the sender's reaction were more accurate in judging gross aspects of affect (negative or positive) than in a more specific task of differentiating between the slides. Females and high-expressive males were more accurate than low-expressive males in the specific judgment among the four slides, and high-expressive subjects were more accurate than low-expressive subjects in all conditions.

297. **Dabbs, James M. Jr.** "Physical Closeness and Negative Feelings." *Psychonomic Science* 23 (1971) : 141-143.

Fifty-six pairs of male subjects argued or talked in a large or very small room. Palmar sweating was measured, as was the subject's attitude toward his partner and their discussion. Results showed that subjects in the small room had generally more negative feelings but tended to suppress them. Arguing aroused more negative feelings than talking did. Subjects were less attentive to the topic when talking than when arguing, and in the small room than in the large room. Palmar sweating decreased the most over time in the small room arguing condition.

298. **Dabbs, James M. Jr.** "Sex, Setting, and Reactions to Crowding on Sidewalks." *American Psychological Association Proceedings* 7 (1972) : 205-206.

Three hundred twenty-one male and 322 female pedestrians were observed in Atlanta, Georgia, just before Christmas. Subjects, standing alone at traffic lights, bus stops, in the open or near a wall, were approached by a stranger who stood close to them. Results showed male experimenters caused more movement than females at bus stops. Female subjects moved more than males at traffic lights.

299. **Dabbs, James M. Jr.; Fuller, James P.H.; and Carr, Timothy S.** "Personal Space When 'Cornered': College Students and Prison Inmates." *American Psychological Association Proceedings* 8 (1973) : 213-214.

Sixty male and female college students and 73 prisoners participated in this study. Both sets of subjects approached or were approached by another subject (in the case of the college students) or by the experimenter (in the case of the prisoners). Subjects stopped or told the person approaching them to stop at a distance comfortable for conversation. Prison inmates maintained greater interpersonal distance than college students. The prisoners also approached the experimenter more closely than they allowed him to approach them. This difference between approaching and being approached was not observed among the college students. All subjects maintained greater distance in the corner than in the center of the room, and this was especially true of the prisoners.

300. **Daniell, Robert J., and Lewis, Philip.** "Stability of Eye Contact and Physical Distance Across a Series of Structured Interviews." *Journal of Consulting and Clinical Psychology* 39 (1972) : 172.

An investigation of the stability of eye contact and physical distance as diagnostic indicators. In a sample of 36 male and female students, half were randomly assigned to be interviewed three times by the same interviewer, and half were assigned to be interviewed by different interviewers. Physical distance and eye contact were observed and measured from behind a one-way mirror. Findings support the stability of eye contact and physical distance as predictors of personality.

301. **Danziger, Kurt.** *Interpersonal Communication.* Elmsford, New York: Pergamon Press, 1975. 238 pp.

The book contains a chapter entitled "Nonverbal Communication" in which the author discusses proxemics, posture, gaze direction, paralanguage, movement, and inconsistency among channels of communication. The author emphasizes that the concepts of channels and codes are of central importance in the process of interpersonal communication.

302. **Daubenmire, M. Jean; Searles, Sharon; and Ashton, Carol.** *Communicative Interaction: Methodology and Analysis.* Columbus, Ohio: The Ohio State University Research Foundation, 1977. 158 pp. Illus.

This is a report of the five-year study of patient-nurse interaction conducted by members of the Ohio State School of Nursing with the participation of computer systems analysts. The authors set out to devise a very complex multivariable recording of verbal and nonverbal interaction in hospital settings. They adapted terminology from various kinesic, proxemic, and movement notation approaches to communication analysis, devising an elaborate coding system for analyzing videotapes that could be computer analyzed. This monograph reviews relevant literature, discusses theoretical issues, and describes the method of data collection and recording procedures and data reduction. The development of the "synchronic notation system," its reliability, and validity are presented. "Synchronology" and a time-process model of human interaction are discussed with particular reference to dyadic communication. The authors define a concept "convergence" and its relation to synchrony and describe specific interaction examples of "eye duration" activity and convergency inactivity patterns.

303. **Daubenmire, M. Jean; Searles, Sharon S.; and Ashton, Carol A.** "A Methodological Framework to Study Nurse-Patient Communication." *Nursing Research* 27 (1978) : 303-310.

The purpose of the authors' research was to develop a methodology for examining the complexity of the interactional processes that occur among nurses and patients in a hospital setting. Extensive videotaped, time-series data of patient-health care personnel interactions involving four patients were collected 16 hours a day from admission to discharge. The communicative interaction patterns among nurses and patients were then examined using the methodologic framework, "synchronology." This approach provides a structure for in-context description and analysis of the complex verbal and nonverbal interaction patterns.

304. **Daubenmire, M. Jean; White, Judith L.; Heinzerling, Kathryn; Ashton, Carol A.; and Searles, Sharon S.** *Synchronics: A Notation System for the Quantitative and Qualitative Description of Presenting Behaviors.* Columbus, Ohio: The Ohio State University Research Foundation, 1977. 217 pp. Illus.

The results of a six-year project on nurse-doctor-patient interaction, this manual presents the coding system for verbal and nonverbal presenting behaviors, what behaviors occur and how. It is designed to transcribe videotape interactions onto 21 channels at few-second intervals of time for later computer analysis. Although based on studies of interactions in hospital recovery and private rooms, it is applicable to a vast range of naturalistic settings and represents one of the most advanced and ambitious attempts to merge ethnographic description with computer systems. The nonverbal descriptors range from proxemic variables to Laban-related terms for describing movement qualities.

305. **D'Augelli, Anthony R.** "Nonverbal Behavior of Helpers in Initial Helping Interactions." *Journal of Counseling Psychology* 21 (1974) : 360-363.

Divided into groups of eight, each of 168 undergraduates participated in a four-minute verbal helping interaction with another group member. Two trained observers tallied helper nonverbal behaviors (smiling, nodding, looking down, and gaze aversion) and scored verbal responses for understanding, emotional honesty, and acceptance. Group participants rated the helper on interpersonal traits. Smiling and nodding were related to observers' ratings of the helpers' interpersonal skills. Smiling related to the participants' perception of the helper as "warm." Nodding related to both judges' and helpees' perceptions of the helper as understanding, warm, accepting, and not set in his/her ways.

306. **Davenport, W.G.; Brooker, Gail; and Munro, Nancy.** "Factors in Social Perception: Seating Position." *Perceptual and Motor Skills* 33 (1971) : 747-752.

Five female college students were photographed five times each occupying different positions at a rectangular table. From these slides, 220 female high school students consistently chose the occupant at the head of the table as having higher ratings of talkativeness, persuasiveness, leadership, self-confidence, friendliness, intelligence. The occupant at the head of the table was also seen as contributing most to the group's discussion.

307. **Davis, Anne.** "Micro-Ecology: Interactional Dimensions of Space." *Journal of Psychiatric Nursing and Mental Health* 10 (1972) : 19-21.

The author discusses the importance of territoriality and personal space in human behavioral patterns and cites some relevant research.

308. **Davis, Flora.** *Inside Intuition: What We Know about Nonverbal Communication.* New York: McGraw-Hill, 1971. 223 pp.

A lively and engaging introduction to the study of nonverbal communication, this book is addressed to the lay reader while reporting the work of the major researchers in the field, often from personal interviews. Topics include gender signals, courting behaviors, body movement, and greeting behaviors, based on interviews with Ray L. Birdwhistell, Albert E. Scheflen, and Adam Kendon; facial expression and eye behavior, based on interviews with Paul Ekman and Ralph Exline; and proxemics, incorporating an interview with Edward T. Hall. "The dance of the hand," posture, communication by smell and touch, and developmental perspectives from the womb through childhood are also treated. William Condon, Paul Byers, and Eliot Chapple have contributed to chapters on the rhythmic dimension of interaction; Martha Davis and Irmgard Bartenieff to a discussion of Effort-Shape analysis and personal dimensions in nonverbal communication; and Erving Goffman to a discussion of behavior and the public order.

309. **Davis, Flora.** *Eloquent Animals: A Study in Animal Communication.* New York: Coward, McCann and Geoghegan, 1978. 223 pp.

Subtitled "How chimps lie, whales sing, and slime molds pass the message along," this popular book on animal communication is readable, scholarly, and interesting. There are chapters on the signing chimps and gorillas, reports of research on insect, bird, and fish communication, whale songs, and dog communication. The book concludes with a chapter on human nonverbal communication and a discussion of the debate on the relationship of animal communication and human language.

310. **Davis, Martha.** *Understanding Body Movement: An Annotated Bibliography* New York: Arno Press, 1972. 190 pp. (Reprinted by Indiana University Press, forthcoming.)

Over 900 annotated books and articles are included in this bibliography of literature on the psychology and anthropology of body movement. The predecessor of the present bibliography, it has an extensive subject index and historical review of nonverbal communication from 1872 to 1971.

311. **Davis, Martha,** adv. ed. *Body Movement: Perspectives in Research Collection.* New York: Arno Press, 1972.

A series of reprints of rare or hard-to-obtain works on the psychology and anthropology of movement, selected for their historical and innovative value. The series includes *Thus Speaks the Body: Attempts Toward a Personalogy from the Point of View of Respiration and Postures* by Bjorn Christiansen (1963); *Behavior Development in Infants* by Evelyn Dewey (1935); *Evolution of Facial Expression,* two accounts by R.J. Andrew and Ernst Huber; *Facial Expressions in Children* with monographs by Ruth W. Washburn, Rene Spitz, and Florence L. Goodenough; *A Psychology of Gesture* by Charlotte Wolff (1948); and *Research Approaches to Movement and Personality* with monographs by Philip Eisenberg, Martti Takala, and Irmgard Bartenieff and Martha Davis.

312. **Davis, Martha,** adv. ed. *Body Movement: Perspectives in Research Collection.* New York: Arno Press, 1975.

Three volumes added to this reprint series in 1975 are anthologies of selected papers. *Anthropological Perspectives of Movement* includes a study of culturally determined gesture styles, an analysis of Navaho movement patterns in work, social, and personal activity, description of 100 common postural patterns, a review of literature on dance and culture, a discussion of proxemics research and notation, and an annotated bibliography. The reprinted works ranging from 1942 to 1963 are by Flora L. Bailey, Edward T. Hall, Francis Hayes, Gordon W. Hewes, Gertrude P. Kurath, and Weston La Barre. The reprinted articles of *Psychoanalytic Perspectives of Movement* span a period from 1921 to 1966 and include: S. Ferenczi, "Psycho-Analytical Observations on Tic"; Sandor Feldman, "The Blessings of the Kohenites"; Ernst Kris, "Laughter as an Expressive Process"; Margaret Mahler, "Tics and Impulsions in Children"; Felix Deutsch, "Analytic Posturology"; Trygve Braatoy, "Psychology vs. Anatomy in the Treatment of 'Arm Neuroses' with Physiotherapy"; Bela Mittlemann, "Psychodynamics of Motility"; and Judith Kestenberg, "Rhythm and Organization in Obsessive-Compulsive Development." *Recognition of Facial Expression* is an anthology of articles ranging from the 1920s to early 1960s. The articles are "The Recognition of Facial Expressions of Emotions" by Arthur Jenness, which is a review of literature on emotion and facial expression; "The Judgment of Facial Expression" by J. Frois-Wittmann; "The Interpretation of Facial Expression in Emotion" by Carney Landis; "The Understanding of Facial Expression of Emotion" by Nico H. Frijda; "Three Dimensions of Emotion" by Harold Schlosberg; and "The Psychology of Expression" by Sylvia Honkavaara, which is a lengthy article including several experimental studies on the perception of emotion.

313. **Davis, Martha.** *Towards Understanding the Intrinsic in Body Movement.* New York: Arno Press, 1975. 132 pp. (Body Movement: Perspectives in Research Series)

This work begins with a review of the kinesic literature, including Darwin, Reich, Scheflen, and Birdwhistell, among others. The author has compiled a detailed glossary of movement terms taken from three notation systems. She then compares sample kinesic descriptions of 17 key researchers in the movement glossary terms. She further discusses the authors' parameter choices, the relationship between a movement and its significance, and proposes ideas for integrating areas of movement research. Included are a complete description of the glossary references and a selected bibliography of notation systems.

314. **Davis, Martha.** *Methods of Perceiving Patterns of Small Group Behavior.* New York: Dance Notation Bureau Press, 1977. 75 pp.

Four observation methods—R. Barker's Psychological Ecology, R. Bales' Interaction Process Analysis, A. Scheflen's Context Analysis, and I. Bartenieff's Effort-Shape Analysis—are discussed in terms of units of behavior, perception of relatedness between group members, patterns of behavior units, and methodological and theoretical aspects. The four methods are then compared by applying each to the same therapeutic interaction in this monograph on problems and possibilities for observing and recording group interaction.

315. **Davis, Martha; Weitz, Shirley; and Culkin, Joseph.** "Sex Differences in Movement Style: A Multivariate Analysis of Naive and Laban-Based Ratings." *American Journal of Dance Therapy* 3 (1980) : 4-11.

Six raters using a Laban-based rating scale assessed movement patterns of pairs of graduate students from videotapes played without sound. A factor analysis yielded six factors: Expressiveness-Animation, Reserved-Friendly, Male-Female Presentation, Status, Self-Touch, and Disengagement. Comparisons of these ratings with "naive" judgments of the same tapes indicated judgments of "Openness" for females were predicted by high ratings on Expressiveness-Animation and low ratings on Disengagement.

316. **Davis, Martha,** ed. *Interaction Rhythms: Periodicity in Communicative Behavior.* New York: Human Sciences Press, forthcoming.

This is a collection of papers on research in face-to-face interaction from microanalyses of mother-infant synchrony to cycles of dyadic conversation recurring over several weeks. Based on the proceedings of the First Annual Research Conference of the Institute for Nonverbal Communication Research in New York City, the volume includes dialogue between participants as well as formal papers. An introduction by Martha Davis, preface by Albert E. Scheflen, and overviews by Paul Byers, Adam Kendon, and Conrad M. Arensberg explore the theoretical issues implicit in the empirical studies presented in this four-part anthology. Part One focuses on microanalyses of behavior such as mother-infant interaction rhythms and has chapters by Eliot D. Chapple, William S. Condon, Beatrice Beebe *et al.*, Daniel Stern, and Judith Duchan. Part Two concentrates on rhythm in paralanguage with presentations by Madeleine Mathiot and Elizabeth Carlock, Joseph Oliva, and an extensive overview of cross-cultural variation of rhythm style by Alan Lomax. Part Three includes papers on the temporal dimension in dyadic conversation, particularly its role in impression formation, by Stanley Feldstein, Cynthia L. Crown, and Aron W. Siegman and Mark Reynolds. Part Four deals with units of interactive behavior lasting several minutes to many hours such as posture-mirroring between professors and students, transactions at a store counter, and conversation during long-term isolation. Its authors include Marianne LaFrance, M. Jean Daubenmire and Sharon Searles, Donald P. Hayes and Loren Cobb, Judson P. Jones and Walburga von Raffler-Engel.

317. **Dean, Larry M.; Willis, Frank N.; and Hewitt, Jay.** "Initial Interaction Distance Among Individuals Equal and Unequal in Military Rank." *Journal of Personality and Social Psychology* 32 (1975) : 294-299.

Interaction distances for 562 pairs in military settings were recorded as conversations commenced. Interactions initiated by subordinates with superiors were characterized by increased distance which varied according to discrepancy in rank. With superior-initiated conversations, initial distance was not significantly different from that taken with peers.

318.   **Deaux, Kay.** *The Behavior of Women and Men.* Monterey, California: Brooks/Cole Publishing Company, 1976. 168 pp. Illus.

This book presents research on behavioral sex differences for the lay reader. Eye contact, facial expression, smiling, touching, proxemic, and approach behaviors are discussed in chapters on communication styles, aggression, and the basis of attraction.

319.   **Deets, Carol Anne.** "Nonverbal Communications of Emotions." Ed.D. dissertation, Indiana University. 1971. 96 pp. (Order No. 72-6701)

Subjects identified emotions and their intensity for six emotions videotaped by four actors, facially, vocally, gesturally, facial-vocally, and gestural-vocally. Among the results it was found that the facial-vocal mode was the most accurate and gestural the least accurate for recognizing emotion, and that the primary emotions are more easily recognizable than the complex emotions.

320.   **DeHavenon, Anna Lou.** "Superordinant Behavior in Urban Homes: A Video Analysis of Request-Compliance and Food Control Behavior in Two Black and Two White Families Living in New York City." Ph.D. dissertation, Columbia University, 1978. 421 pp.

The dissertation defines and demonstrates a materialist approach to the collection and analysis of cross-cultural data using videotape as the primary data base. A distinction is made between materialist or nonsemantic data procedures — whose units are necessarily pancultural and comparative, observer-oriented and defined and verified in terms of their physical properties by more than one observer — and idealist or semantic data procedures, whose units are not defined and verified in terms of their measured physical properties, and whose units may or may not be pancultural and comparative, observer-oriented and defined and verified by more than one observer. Statistical analyses of behavioral observations showed a greater age-ranking of compliance and food behaviors in the black than in the white families. (from the author)

321.   **De Long, Alton J.** "Kinesic Signals at Utterance Boundaries in Preschool Children." *Semiotica* 11 (1974) : 43-73. Illus.

Pairs of four- and five-year-old boys were videotaped discussing the blocks they'd been given. Their behavior was then examined in terms of eight basic movements across eight parts of the body in a search for kinesic signals of the intention to stop talking. Termination of utterances was signaled by a configuration of movement, some of which was mandatory and some of which was optional. The mandatory termination movements were a leftward movement of the head, and a downward shift, which can occur in the head, hands or arms, either individually or in any combination. Three termination-of-utterance positions were found: post-verbally, usually immediately following utterance termination; final word position; and penultimate word position. There was an increase in activity as utterance termination approached. The baseline of rightward movement was deviated from significantly only during the medial segment of pausal utterances. The significant increase in kinesic activity that occurred toward the ends of utterances occurred only in the case of other-directed speech, not in self-directed utterances.

322.   **De Long, Alton J.** "Yielding the Floor: the Kinesic Signals." *Journal of Communication* 27, 2 (1977) : 98-103.

Videotapes were analyzed as to how eight preschool children signal their intent to exchange listener/speaker roles. Eight types of body movement were recorded across eight body parts, with movements of the head down and head and body parts leftward occuring in one of three points: after the last word, on the final word, and on the penultimate word, each point involving a different combination of downward and leftward movement. Additional data analysis revealed that these signals occurred only during other-directed speech, not in the case of self-directed speech.

323. Delph, Edward W. *The Silent Community: Public Homosexual Encounters.* Beverly Hills, California: Sage, 1978.

324. DePaulo, Bella M., and Rosenthal, Robert. "Age Changes in Nonverbal Decoding Skills: Evidence for Increasing Differentiation." *Merrill-Palmer Quarterly* 25 (1979) : 145-150.

Six hundred thirty-two children and adults were administered the PONS (Profile of Nonverbal Sensitivity) to determine if age differences occur in decoding different types of nonverbal communication cues. Sensitivity to nonverbal cues was found to be related to age.

325. DePaulo, Bella M.; Rosenthal, Robert; Eisenstat, Russell A.; Rogers, Peter L.; and Finkelstein, Susan. "Decoding Discrepant Nonverbal Cues." *Journal of Personality and Social Psychology* 36 (1978) : 313-323.

This article reports on the Nonverbal Discrepancy Test, a videotaped test of accuracy in decoding discrepant auditory and visual nonverbal cues. In most of the test items the affects communicated in the audio and visual modalities are discrepant. Results of the test showed that the judgment of subjects was more affected by video than audio cues, and that there was more video primacy for women than for men. Discrepant messages involving the face had more video primacy than those involving bodily cues, as did judgments involving positive affect compared with those involving dominance. In very discrepant messages there was more audio primacy compared with slightly discrepant stimuli.

326. DePaulo, Bella M.; Rosenthal, Robert; Finkelstein, Susan; and Eisenstat, Russell A. "The Development Priority of the Evaluative Dimension in Perceptions of Nonverbal Cues." *Environmental Psychology and Nonverbal Behavior* 3 (1979) : 164-171.

Researchers who have attempted to map the basic structure of broad psychological domains (such as interpersonal behavior) have invariably pointed to the importance of the evaluative dimension. It was predicted that sensitivity to such a salient dimension would develop prior to sensitivity to other important but apparently weaker dimensions, such as dominance-submissiveness. The predicted developmental trend was supported in a study of nonverbal decoding. When judging pairs of emotional cues communicated by the face or body and by the tone of voice, younger subjects, compared to older ones, were more likely to notice discrepancies in the degree of expressed positivity than in the degree of expressed dominance.

327. DePaulo, Bella M.; Zuckerman, Miron; and Rosenthal, Robert. "Humans as Lie Detectors." *Journal of Communication* 30 (1980) : 129-139.

People are able to detect lie telling in others with a better-than-chance probability. Factors affecting detection success include the controllability and spontaneity of the nonverbal cues. Women's superiority at detecting deception through nonverbal cues decreases as the controllability decreases. Persons who test as either socially anxious or self-monitoring are skilled at detecting deception. Persons scoring high on scales rating beliefs in the complexity of human nature and Machiavellian personalities are adept at lying. Any deviation from a contextually normal nonverbal response promotes suspicion of deception.

328. Desor, J.A. "Toward a Psychological Theory of Crowding." *Journal of Personality and Social Psychology* 21 (1972) : 79-83.

Seventy graduate and undergraduate students were given scaled-down rooms and human figures and asked to place as many people as possible in the rooms without overcrowding them. Room area was constant, but architectural features varied according to partitions, linear dimensions, and number of doors. More people were placed in rooms with partitions. In a study varying room size, the mean density of figures placed in the smallest room was greater than in the medium or large room. More people were also placed in rectangular than in square rooms of equal area.

329. Deutsch, Robert, and Auerbach, Carl. "Eye Movement in Perception of Another Person's Looking Behavior." *Perceptual and Motor Skills* 40 (1975) : 475-481.

The first experiment compared accuracy and acuity of nine subjects' perceptions of being looked at when observer's eyes are moving and still. Head orientation affects judgments of gaze. In a second laboratory experiment evidence is presented that the eye movement pattern is taken as an indication of the observer's intention.

330. DeVito, Joseph A. *Communicology: An Introduction to the Study of Communication.* New York: Harper & Row, 1978. 553 pp. Illus.

This college textbook has several brief "units" on nonverbal communication; its metacommunicational, contextual, and "packaged" nature, kinesics (in terms of emblems, illustrators, affect displays, regulators, and so on), proxemics and touch, group formation, and paralanguage.

331. di Carlo, Nicole Scotto "Analyse sémiologique des gestes et mimiques des chanteurs d'opéra." *Semiotica* 9 (1973) : 289-317. Illus.

An investigation of the gestures and facial expressions of different opera singers in analogous situations and whether they use the same gestures as other singers and show recurrences in their own performances. The authors distinguish between communicative gestures, such as an angry frown, and gestures without communicative value, such as raising the eyebrows while emitting a high sound. They categorized singers as those who subordinate theatrics to singing (rated lower) and those who do not (rated higher). The results show that higher-rated singers do not use identical gestures and facial expressions in analogous situations. This disproves that there is a gestural "language" in opera singing that the public can rely on once they understand the code, according to the author.

332. DiCiurcio, Thomas Louis. "Perceived Mental Illnesss As a Function of Body Movement and Context." Ph.D. dissertation, State University of New York at Albany. 1975. 155 pp. (Order No. 75288-80)

It was suggested in this study that "irregular" body movement in an interviewee under certain conditions would lead perceivers to construe that person as mentally ill. To test this 232 perceivers viewed a 10-minute videotape and rated the interviewee on over 40 behavioral items.

333. Dietrich, Lawrence Bernard. "Effects of a Counselor's Race, Sex, and Body Language on Black Clients' Counselor Preference." Ph.D. dissertation, George Washington University. 1977. 163 pp. (Order No. 77-25,535)

In this study of videotaped simulated counseling sessions there is evidence that race and sex are significant factors in preference of counselor, but a counselor's body language may be more powerful.

334. Di Francesco, Gertrude Vilma. "Interaction Distance and Eye Contact in the Counseling Relationship." Ed.D. dissertation, Lehigh University. 1977. 230 pp. (Order No. 78008-34)

Five hundred eighty-four college students rated four videotapes of counseling in teractions. Among the results are evidence that held eye contact is instrumental in conveying positive affect, and verbal and nonverbal messages seemed more congruent if the counselor maintained eye contact while expressing empathy.

335. Dil, Nasim. "Sensitivity of Emotionally Disturbed and Emotionally Non-Disturbed Elementary School Children to Meanings of Facial Expressions." Ph.D. dissertation, Indiana University. 1971. 196 pp. (Order No. 72-6768)

This research explores the relationship between encoding and decoding emotions in groups of normal and disturbed school children. Results showed that children showing disturbed behavior are less accurate in decoding and attribute more negative meanings to photographs of facial expressions.

336. Dil, Nasim. "Kinesics of Affective Instability." *Language Sciences* 1 (1979) : 349-377.

Affective or emotional instability is defined here as imbalanced ways of communicating affects, whether lack of, overexpression, or inappropriately timed or sustained expressions. Following a discussion of kinesics and a theoretical paradigm of affective communication, the author describes three examples of interactions between a father and his mute daughter, and behavior of a "frightened child" and an autistic child.

337. DiMatteo, M. Robin; Friedman, Howard S.; and Taranta, Angelo. "Sensitivity to Bodily Nonverbal Communication as a Factor in Practitioner-Patient Rapport." *Journal of Nonverbal Behavior* 4 (1979) : 18-26.

The relationship between physicians' nonverbal sensitivity and the satisfaction of their patients was tested in two field studies. In the first study, 40 physicians were given a film test of nonverbal sensitivity (the PONS test) and were evaluated by their patients. The second study was a replication using 31 additional physicians. Most noteworthy for research in therapeutic interaction, the present studies contained three methodological advances: (1) the use of actual patients' ratings of satisfaction with treatment, (2) the extension of research from psychological to medical settings, and (3) the use of a standardized test of nonverbal decoding skill. Physicians' skill at reading the emotion conveyed through the nonverbal channel of body movement was found to be significantly correlated with their interpersonal success with patients in the clinical setting.

338. DiMatteo, M. Robin, and Hall, Judith A. "Nonverbal Decoding Skill and Attention to Nonverbal Cues: A Research Note." *Environmental Psychology and Nonverbal Behavior* 3 (1979) : 188-192.

A measure of differential preference for attending to three channels of nonverbal communication was developed, with which scores for differential attention to face, body, and voice tone were generated for 17 college subjects. These scores were correlated with subjects' nonverbal decoding accuracy in the same three channels as measured by a standard test of decoding nonverbal cues. Significant positive relationships between channel preference and accuracy were found for the two video channels; no relationship was found for the audio channel.

339. Dinges, Norman G., and Oetting, Eugene R. "Interaction Distance Anxiety in the Counseling Dyad." *Journal of Counseling Psychology* 19 (1972) : 146-149.

Male and female undergraduates rated anxiety associated with five dyadic interaction distances when told either that the context was a counseling one or given no instruction or "set" as to context. Females showed higher rates of anxiety than males and counseling-set subjects responded with more anxiety than no-set subjects. Anxiety scores across distances indicated that nearer (30 inches) and farther (88 inches) distances received the highest anxiety ratings.

340. **Dittmann, Allen T.** "Development Factors in Conversational Behavior." *The Journal of Communication* 22 (1972) : 404-423.

Studies of listening responses (LRs) such as um's, huh's, and head nods in children are reported. Six children ages six to 12 years and eight subjects from 14 to 35 were videotaped in conversation. There were marked individual differences as well as increases in LRs with age. The social and linguistic functions of LRs are discussed.

341. **Dittmann, Allen T.** *Interpersonal Messages of Emotion.* New York: Springer Publishing Company, 1972. 232 pp.

The book contains chapters on communication theory with a brief overview of the mathematical theory of communication, channels of emotional messages, and research issues. Facial expressions, body movement, psychophysiological responses, kinesics, paralanguage, and language are some of the topics discussed.

342. **Dittmann, Allen T.** "The Body Movement-Speech Rhythm Relationship as a Cue to Speech Encoding." In *Studies in Dyadic Communication,* edited by A.W. Siegman & B. Pope, pp. 135-151. New York: Pergamon Press, 1972.

Dittmann makes the distinction between body movements which he calls "fidgeting" and which are an expression of emotional states, and body movements which occur during and after hesitations or "non-fluencies" in speech. To him these are a manifestation of the encoding process of speech as the speaker is making decisions on how and which of his thoughts he should put into words. Listener responses such as head nods, which also occur at hesitation points in speech, are discussed.

343. **Dittmann, Allen T.** "Style in Conversation." *Semiotica* 9 (1973) : 241-251.

A book review of David Efron's 1941 work on gesture among immigrant Jews and southern Italians in New York, published in a new edition as *Gesture, Race and Culture.*

344. **Ditts, Robert; Grinder, John; Bandler, Richard; Bandler, Leslie C.; and DeLozier, Judith.** *Neuro-Linguistic Programming:* Vol. I, *The Study of the Structure of Subjective Experience.* Cupertino, California: Meta Publications, 1980. 284 pp. Illus.

Within this extensive and rather technical introduction to Neuro-Linguistic Programming, there is an extensive discussion of how various nonverbal behaviors indicate preferred or momentary "representational systems" (various forms of vision, audition, kinesthesis, and olfaction/gustation which in this model are the basic elements on which patterns of behavior are formed). The "accessing cues" discussed are eye movements, breathing patterns, posture, gestures, and tempos of speech and motion. The interpretations given are very detailed and subtle.

345. **Dodd, Carley H.** "Nonverbal Communication Perspectives to Cross-Cultural Communication." In *Perspectives on Cross-Cultural Communication,* by C.H. Dodd, pp. 53-60. Dubuque, Iowa: Kendall/Hunt Publishing Company, 1977.

This brief chapter includes a discussion of cultural variation in kinesics, proxemics, and time, and gives interesting examples of cultural nonverbal miscommunications between Americans and Russians, Latin Americans, and Vietnamese.

346. **Donaghy, William C.** *Our Silent Language: An Introduction to Nonverbal Communication.* Dubuque, Iowa: Gorsuch Scarisbrick Publishers, 1980. 53 pp. Illus.

A good introduction to nonverbal communication, this booklet describes communication within the framework of systems theory as a multichannel process. Each chapter is prefaced by learning objectives to guide study. Chapters deal with nonverbal impression formation, emotional expression, expression of interpersonal attitudes, and conversational behavior. The final chapter suggests techniques for improving sensitivity to nonverbal cues. Revealing photographs complement the text.

347. **Dorch, Edwina, and Fontaine, Gary.** "Rate of Judges' Gaze at Different Types of Witnesses." *Perceptual and Motor Skills* 46 (1978) : 1103-1106.

Two black and two white judges, 52 defendants, 53 civilian witnesses, and 34 police witnesses were involved in this study. The frequency of judges' gaze at witnesses was recorded. Results indicate there was a higher rate of gaze by white judges than black judges; defendants received highest rate of gaze, followed by civilians, then police witnesses; and that black judges looked more at white witnesses, while white judges looked more at black witnesses. Interestingly, there was a positive correlation between rate of gaze at defendant and the fine received if found guilty.

348. **Dosamantes-Alperson, Erma.** "The Creation of Meaning Through Body Movement." In *Clinical Psychology: Issues of the Seventies,* edited by A.I. Rabin, pp. 156-166. East Lansing, Michigan: Michigan State University Press, 1974.

Through a brief historical review of established and humanistic clinical psychological approaches, the author develops the idea of felt and symbolic levels of experience as the underpinnings for verbal self-consciousness. She discusses the role that premature verbal communication can play in inhibiting self-awareness. Focusing on "process-oriented" movement therapists and "authentic movement," she describes the transformation, within the therapeutic context, of an ongoing, continuous flow of energy and incipient body movement to felt-body movement, to imagery, and, finally, to verbal awareness and communication.

349. **Dosamantes-Alperson, Erma.** "The Function of Empirical Methodology on Outcome and Process Studies of Movement Therapy." *Conference Proceedings of the American Dance Therapy Association* 8 (1974) : 86-90.

A brief article on the designing of research verification for dance-movement therapy. On a basic level, a good introduction for clinicians and students.

350. **Dosamantes-Alperson, Erma.** "The Intrapsychic and the Interpersonal in Movement Therapy." *American Journal of Dance Therapy* 3 (1979) : 20-31.

Two modes of experience, receptive and active, are related to muscle tension, movement preferences, and psychological process. Specific movement observations are given for each state, and several clinical examples are cited.

351. **Dougherty, Frank E.; Bartlett, Edmund S.; and Izard, Carroll E.** "Responses of Schizophrenics to Expressions of the Fundamental Emotions." *Journal of Clinical Psychology* 30 (1974) : 243-246.

Thirty-two photographs depicting eight cross-culturally standardized emotional expressions were presented in random order to 54 women, 31 of them hospitalized schizophrenics. Subjects were measured for their ability to classify emotional expressions into *a priori* labeled categories and to recognize emotional expressions in a free response task. Normal subjects made significantly more accurate classification responses than schizophrenics on the categorization task. On the free response task, significant differences occurred primarily due to the schizophrenics' high frequency of use of the enjoyment-joy category.

352. **Doyle, G.A.** "Behavior of Prosimians." In *Behavior of Nonhuman Primates: Modern Research Trends,* edited by A.M. Schrier and F. Stollnitz, pp. 155-353. New York: Academic Press, 1974. Illus.

This exhaustive examination of the behavior of prosimians not only surveys their ecology and general behavior (territory and home range, activity rhythms, sleeping and grooming behavior, ingestive behavior, and locomotion), but it examines the theme of "Senses and Communication" (olfactory communication, vocal communication, visual communication). This in-depth study also includes highly researched sections on their courtship and mating behavior. Additional topics covered include the social groupings, intelligent behavior, and play of prosimians.

353. **Draughon, Margaret.** "Duplication of Facial Expression: Conditions Affecting Task and Possible Clinical Usefulness." *Journal of Personality* 41 (1973) : 140-150.

The experiment examined the process of duplicating facial expressions under two conditions: with the aid of a mirror and without the aid of a mirror. Subjects attempted to duplicate their own and "other" facial expressions under the two conditions from photographs taken of them while talking to an experimenter about drugs. The study confirmed that a person can learn to duplicate facial expressions with the aid of a mirror, that there was a deterioration of duplication in the nonmirror condition, that high-anxious people duplicate better in the nonmirror condition, and that low-anxious people perform better in the mirror condition.

354. **Driscoll, John Burton.** "The Effects of a Teacher's Eye Contact, Gestures, and Voice Intonation on Student Retention of Factual Material." Ph.D. dissertation, University of Southern Mississippi. 1978. 91 pp. (Order No. 79051-19)

In this study of 80 tenth graders listening to a lecturer, results indicated that the students in the "eye contact-gestures-dynamic voice intonation" groups had significantly better retention scores than students in "no eye-contact-no gesture-monotone" voice groups.

355. **Dropsy, Jacques.** *Vivre dans son corps.* Paris: EPI, 1973.

The author describes his methods of therapeutic work to obtain the conscious integration of the psychomotor being. Among a number of topics he analyzes body image and self-knowledge, space and body form, body rhythms, and respiration, and the force and energy of the person. Written in French.

356. **Dubner, Frances S.** "Nonverbal Aspects of Black English." *Southern Speech Communication Journal* 37 (1972) : 361-374.

Citing a lack of communication between blacks and whites in the United States, the author points out the need for an understanding of the nonverbal aspects of black communication patterns. She reviews research from the areas of anthropology, linguistics, sociology, and communication, and presents a chart of the major types of nonverbal behaviors with examples from black culture. These are sign language, such as the Black Power salute; kinesics including eye behavior, self-representation and "style"; iconics; paralinguistics; tactile/cutaneous communication such as handshakes; olfactory and gustatory communication; chronemics; proxemics; and aesthetics.

357. **Duck, Steve,** ed. *Theory and Practice in Interpersonal Attraction.* New York: Academic Press, 1977. 367 pp. Illus.

In addition to numerous references throughout this book to the role of physical appearance in sexual and nonsexual attraction processes, a review of recent literature by Mark Cook entitled "The Social Skills Model of Interpersonal Attraction" explores the integral functions of nonverbal communication in social skills. In particular, the importance of gaze and postural cues for the regulation and maintenance of interactions; paralanguage, proximity, and facial expression for formation of expectations, and nonverbal factors in translation and response are discussed with references to cultural differences. Eye contact is also discussed in Icek Ajzen's essay,

"Information Processing Approaches to Interpersonal Attraction," while aspects of touch as the "proximal receptor" are examined in "Predictability, Power and Vulnerability in Interpersonal Attraction" by Peter Kelvin.

358. **Dudeck, James E.** "Developmental Study of Haptic-Tactual Perceptual Skill Utilization Among Sighted, Partially Sighted and Blind Children." Ph.D. dissertation, George Peabody College for Teachers. 1974. 109 pp. (Order No. 74-29,161)

Fifty-four children (of two age levels: about 7½ years and 11 years and three levels of sightedness: blind, partially sighted, and normally sighted) were given tasks involving haptic discrimination and recognition and tactual discrimination and recognition. A "significant second order interaction effect between age, sightedness, and task difficulty" was found.

359. **Duke, Marshall P., and Mullens, Mary Colleen.** "Preferred Interpersonal Distance as a Function of Locus of Control Orientation in Chronic Schizophrenics, Nonschizophrenics, Patients, and Normals." *Journal of Consulting and Clinical Psychology* 41 (1973) : 230-234.

Forty female mental patients, 20 of whom were schizophrenic, served as subjects. Twenty normal female nonprofessionals served as a control group. Subjects were asked to judge the comfortable distance of hypothetical interactants on the Comfortable Interpersonal Distance Scale. Preferred distance, as measured by this scale, was greatest for schizophrenics, intermediate for nonschizophrenic patients, and least for normals.

360. **Duke, Marshall P., and Nowicki, Stephen Jr.** "A New Measure and Social Learning Model for Interpersonal Distance." *Journal of Experimental Research in Personality* 6 (1972) : 119-132.

This article reviews previous concepts of personal space and interpersonal distance and analyzes existing measurement methods. Finding a lack of theoretical basis for prediction and understanding, the authors present a new method of measurement, the Comfortable Interpersonal Distance scale. Reliability, validity, and derivative studies are discussed.

361. **Duke, Marshall, and Wilson, Jan.** "A Note on the Measurement of Interpersonal Distance in Preschool Children." *Journal of Genetic Psychology* 123 (1973): 361-362.

This study discusses the viability of an adapted version of Duke and Nowicki's (1972) Comfortable Interpersonal Distance Scale (CID) for use with preschoolers. CID involves a replica of a round room with doors. The child is to imagine standing in the center and being approached by various people who are to be "stopped" at the distance the child prefers.

362. **Dulicai, Dianne.** "Nonverbal Assessment of Family Systems: A Preliminary Study." *International Journal of Arts in Psychotherapy* 4 (1977) : 55-62.

A diagnostic scale utilizing effort/shape analysis of movement was devised to analyze the nonverbal interactions of two groups of four families over an 18-month period. The two groups were divided between those families who had never sought treatment and families who had sought help for only one member. The data were rated in two ways. Nonverbal behaviors such as "gesture blocked" or "bonding-behavior-parent" were scored numerically, and how these behaviors affect the family system was subjected to a pattern analysis. The results confirmed the hypothesis that the two groups scored differently and that conflictual messages and disturbed functioning can be detected through assessment of nonverbal behaviors and their "deviations."

363. Duncan, Starkey D. Jr. "Interaction During Speakng Turns in Dyadic, Face-to-Face Conversations." In *Organization of Behavior in Face-to-Face Interaction,* edited by A. Kendon, R. Harris, and M.R. Key, pp. 199-213. The Hague: Mouton, 1975.

Examples from two 19-minute segments of dyadic conversations are used to illustrate the author's approach to segmenting behavioral units in terms of "speaking-turn interacting units" and speaker and listener turn-taking, and continuation signals and listener "back-channel" behavior.

364. Duncan, Starkey Jr.; Brunner, Lawrence J.; and Fiske, Donald W. "Strategy Signals in Face-to-Face Interaction." *Journal of Personality and Social Psychology* 37 (1979) : 301-313.

The notion of a "strategy signal" is introduced and defined as an action that is not an interaction organization signal, has an effect on the probability of occurrence of a subsequent action, is consistent across participants, and causes an effect which is one of legitimate alternatives rather than invariable. Eight dyadic conversations were observed and provided the basis for a discussion of speaker head direction, smiling, and speaker turn cues as strategy signals.

365. Duncan, Starkey Jr.; and Fiske, Donald W. *Face-to-Face Interaction: Research, Methods, and Theory.* Hillsdale, New Jersey: Lawrence Erlbaum Associates, 1977. 361 pp.

One of the most complex and detailed volumes on the vicissitudes of systematically assessing conversational behavior, this work includes an excellent overview of face-to-face interaction research and discussion of the problems of definition, coding, and reliable analysis. Careful description of the authors' project on interaction assessment, the variables coded, and method of data analysis are accompanied by reports of individual and sex differences in brief interactions and specific patterns, such as turn-taking, back-channel, and smile and gaze behaviors. Interestingly, in the research project used as illustration there were few correlations between extensive self-descriptive scores and the conversational acts. Chapters devoted to transcriptions of interaction, the "turn system," the "dynamics of interaction," and "interaction strategy" reflect the authors' early research interests and their meticulous approach to method and metatheory.

366. Dunham, Randall B. and Herman, Jeanne B. "Development of a Female Faces Scale for Measuring Job Satisfaction." *Journal of Applied Psychology* 60 (1975) : 629-631. Illus.

The Kunin Faces Scale of male faces portraying different degrees of happiness is used to obtain nonverbal responses to job satisfaction inquiries. An equivalent scale using female faces was developed and tested by correlating verbal responses. Analysis of the response of 103 employees revealed no correlation differences between subjects using same or opposite sex faces scales.

367. Dunkell, Samuel. *Sleep Positions: The Night Language of the Body.* New York: New American Library (Signet) 1977. 216 pp. Illus.

A psychotherapist's analysis of the psychological significance of various sleeping positions and position relationships between partners. A popularized account written in an informal tone, it includes analysis of common and exotic positions and the details of smaller body part positions.

368. Dunning, Gail B. "The Identification and Measurement of Nonverbal Communication in the Counseling Interview." Ed.D. dissertation, University of Nebraska. 1971. 104 pp. (Order No. 72-15,978)

Counseling students were trained in the use of an instrument to identify and measure their own nonverbal behaviors. Results showed that they could learn to use this instrument accurately in a short period of time, but that its use did not significantly affect their nonverbal behavior when compared with a control group.

369. **Dychtwald, Ken.** *Body-Mind.* New York: Harcourt Brace Jovanovich, 1978. 298 pp. Illus.

The author attempts a definite and simple system of "body-mind reading and diagnosis" which draws on yoga and on the work of Reich, Lowen, Schutz, Rolf, Feldenkrais, Perls, Keleman, and Prestera. Throughout the book the author focuses on the emotional and psychological patterns underlying given body configurations. Chapters sequentially deal with different body parts (feet and legs, pelvis, abdominal region and lower back, chest cavity, shoulders and arms, neck, throat and jaw, face and head) in considerable detail. For example, a section on the eyes ranges from discussion of eye shape and placement, to iris and sclera diagnoses. Drawings illustrate integrated as well as problematic postures and conditions of body parts.

370. **Dye, Joan Carol.** "The Use of Body Movement to Facilitate Second-Language Learning for Secondary School Students: Listening and Speaking." Ph.D. dissertation, New York University. 1977. 440 pp. (Order No. 78030-49)

Research to develop a teacher's guide for using body movement to enrich second-language learning is reported.

371. **Eakins, Barbara Westbrook, and Eakins, R. Gene.** *Sex Differences in Human Communication.* Boston, Massachusetts: Houghton Mifflin, 1978. 217 pp. Illus.

An excellent college textbook which is replete with documented examples of the subtleties of sex differences in everyday interactions. Following a discussion of theories of the origins and causes of sex differences, the authors detail the linguistic differences in male and female speakers, turn-taking, timing and paralinguistic variations, voice tone and amplitude differences, and the power of labels, titles, and certain terms to delineate gender. They stress the cultural bases of gender communication differences and the status and power issues implicit in the behavior. There is an extensive chapter on sex differences in nonverbal communication, particularly eye contact, facial expression, posture, gesture, touch, and proxemics. They conclude with suggestions for changing sexist communication patterns.

372. **Eberts, E.H., and Lepper, Mark R.** "Individual Consistency in the Proxemic Behavior of Pre-School Children." *Journal of Personality and Social Psychology* 32 (1975) : 841-849.

Preschool children's proxemic behavior was explored in two experiments. A study of the relation of eye contact and success or failure on a task to the interaction distance children kept with an adult experimenter showed that increase in experimenter eye contact significantly increased the interaction distance, while task success or failure did not affect it. Children approached female experimenters more closely than male experimenters. Subjects' spatial behavior was observed one month later during "free-play." The results showed that interaction distances were quite consistent across situations in interactions with both adults and children.

373. **Eco, Umberto.** "Bibliographica Semiotica." *VS: Quaderni di Studi Semiotica* 8/9 (1974) : Special issue (in Italian).

374. **Eco, Umberto.** *A Theory of Semiotics.* Bloomington, Indiana: Indiana University Press, 1976. 354 pp.

The author describes this work as an exploration of the theoretical possibility of a general semiotic theory to account for all types of signs and includes within the semiotic field the research areas of zoosemiotics, tactile communication, kinesics, and proxemics. Eco discusses the case of nonintentional signs such as certain gestures and body movements, which raise the possibility of intention and thus deception. The relation of nonverbal gestures to deictic verbal signs is discussed, and a compositional analysis of kinesic pointers is given. The question of the semantic content of gestures is addressed as well as the existence and structure of semiotic systems not based on language.

375. **Edney, Julian J.** "Human Territoriality." *Psychological Bulletin* 81 (1974) : 959-975.

This article is a review of the somewhat disjointed literature on human territoriality. It summarizes the theory and discusses definitions of the term and field of study. Various approaches and methodologies are evaluated. More recent experiments have focused on the relationship of dominance and aggressiveness with territoriality, territoriality in different age groups and settings, behaviors such as marking one's own territory, individual and group territoriality, and placement of self or objects to enhance defense.

376. **Edney, Julian J., and Jordan-Edney, Nancy L.** "Territorial Spacing on a Beach." *Sociometry* 37 (1974) : 92-104.

One hundred ten groups of people on a large beach were used as subjects. Interviewers approached the groups and asked a series of questions, including how they would assess the size and shape of their territory. The group's size and sex composition were noted. Results showed group territories did not increase with group size, but space per person tended to decrease with group size. Females claimed significantly smaller territories than males. All-male groups estimated the capacity of the beach to be larger than did other groups. There was a significant relationship between group density and respondents' occupational background for same-sex groups.

377. **Edney, Julian J.; Walker, Carol A.; and Jordan, Nancy L.** "Is There Reactance in Personal Space?" *The Journal of Social Psychology* 100 (1976) : 207-217.

Two studies were conducted to investigate the relationship between the psychological factors of "security," "freedom," and "control" as they relate to people's reactions to the close proximity of others. Results indicate that the amount of personal space claimed by an individual is not necessarily related to the amount of space available. Further findings suggest that the underlying variable in determining personal spacing is more likely to be "control" than "freedom."

378. **Edwards, David J. A.** "The Determinants of the Symmetry or Asymmetry of Social Orientation Schemata." *Journal of Experimental Social Psychology* 9 (1973) : 542-550.

Thirty male subjects were asked to place two male dolls to represent interactions in which levels of eye contact were expected to be symmetrical or asymmetrical. Results showed that asymmetrical interactions resulted in wider angles of orientation and the interactor seeking more eye contact was placed more directly facing the other figure.

379. **Efran, Michael G., and Cheyne, James A.** "Shared Space: The Co-operative Control of Spatial Areas by Two Interacting Individuals." *Canadian Journal of Behavioural Science* 5 (1973) : 201-210. Illus.

One thousand two hundred fifty-six males and females on three different university campuses made up the subject sample. The authors examined the possibility that individuals can cooperatively control the space around themselves by varying their physical proximity to each other. In three separate experiments, confederates engaged in conversation in a public hall and varied the distances between themselves.

The number of persons walking around or between them was recorded. When in closer proximity to each other at "personal distances," a significantly smaller number of people passed between the confederates than when interacting from farther apart at "social distances."

380. **Efran, Michael G., and Cheyne, J. Allan.** "Affective Concomitants of the Invasion of Shared Space: Behavioral, Physiological, and Verbal Indicators." *Journal of Personality and Social Psychology* 29 (1974) : 219-226.

Thirty-nine male Canadian students were subjects for the experiment. Dependent measures were the subject's heart rate, expressive behavior rated from a videotape, and a self-report mood scale. Subjects were required to walk through a corridor between two conversants, past two conversants but not between them, or down a corridor in which confederates were replaced by inanimate objects. Subjects in the intrusion condition displayed more agonistic facial responses (frequency and duration of head and gaze down, eyes closed, eyes partially closed, and negative mouth gestures) and less positive mood ratings.

381. **Efron, David.** *Gesture, Race and Culture.* The Hague: Mouton, 1972. 226 pp. Illus.

Originally published in 1942, this book describes a naturalistic study of the gestures of Southern Italians and Eastern Jews in New York City. The author concludes that gestural behavior is related to sociopsychological factors. The appendix includes a dictionary with pictures of gestures. There is an introduction to this edition by Paul Ekman.

382. **Eggen, Paul Duane.** "A Comparison of Student Affect and Kinesic Behavior." Ph.D. dissertation, Oregon State University. 1972. 215 pp. (Order No. 72276-26)

One hundred eighty-one junior high and high school students were involved in this exploration of relationships between their nonverbal behaviors and attitudes toward their teacher and class.

383. **Ehrlichman, Howard; Weiner, Susan L.; and Baker, A. Harvey.** "Effects of Verbal and Spatial Questions on Initial Gaze Shifts." *Neuropsychologia* 12 (1974) : 265-277. Illus.

This three-part study was designed to replicate K. Kocel and M. Kinsbourne's experimental results correlating question type with direction of gaze shift. Using both camera and face-to-face encounters, two groups of adults answered original verbal, spatial, and neutral questions. The third group answered 40 of K. Kocel and M. Kinsbourne's questions and 40 designed by the authors. Gaze shifts were scored one-to 12 (using a clockface scheme for direction of gaze) or noted as no contact (premature gaze shift), head down, head turn, closed eye, or stare. Spatial questions produced stares in all but the face-to-face encounter. Verbal questions produced more downward shifts in all conditions; however, this tendency was not seen specifically with Kocel and Kinsbourne's verbal questions. Question type had no effect on direction of *lateral* gaze shift. Contradictions between these and previous test results may be due to subject variables or differences in verbal questions, but they indicate that gaze shift is not directly attributable to lateralization of hemispheric activity.

384. **Eibl-Eibesfeldt, Irenäus.** *Love and Hate: On the Natural History of Behaviour Patterns.* Trans. by Geoffrey Strachan. London: Methuen, 1971. 263 pp. Illus.

This clear and fascinating book describes the biological basis of sociability and aggression from an ethologist's point of view. The author discusses the basic concepts of ethology and the comparative method and reports findings on inherited motor patterns in animals and humans (facial expressions, eye and body movements, dominance behaviors) from studies of blind-born children and cross-cultural comparisons, and on innate recognition schemes and learning dispositions. Universal and cultural manifestations of aggression are discussed as well as its biological advantages. Most interesting, however, are the author's views on the biological bases of bonding and altruism, such as the infant schema as an innate releasing mechanism. The mother-child relationship is called the nucleus of the human community, and animal and cross-cultural examples are furnished to show that the behavioral patterns used to establish or strengthen social bonds and to keep groups together are borrowed from this relationship, including kissing, rubbing, embracing, grooming, and feeding. Greetings and festivals as social mechanisms are also discussed.

385. **Eibl-Eibesfeldt, Irenäus.** "Les universaux du comportement et leur genèse." In *L'unité de l'homme: invariants biologiques et universaux culturels,* ed. by E. Morin and M. Piatelli-Palmarini, pp. 233-245. Paris: Seuil, 1974.

The author reviews his position on the learned versus innate issue and gives examples of innate philogenetic behavior in man by presenting the results of his studies of facial expressions of deaf and blind-born children, as well as his cross-cultural study of the universality of the "eye-brow lash" greeting behavior. Written in French.

386. **Eisenberg, Abne M., and Smith, Ralph R.** *Nonverbal Communication.* Indianapolis, Indiana; Bobbs Merrill, 1975. 133 pp. Illus.

A textbook in the publisher's speech communication series which surveys definitions, judgment of facial expression, the social function of nonverbal communication, and cross-cultural studies. It ends with a fairly extensive chapter of exercises in nonverbal communication.

387. **Eisler, Richard M.; Hersen, Michel; and Agras, W.S.** "Videotape: A Method for the Controlled Observation of Nonverbal Interpersonal Behavior." *Behavior Therapy* 4 (1973) : 420-425.

Smiling and looking behavior of six married couples was noted by four observers during live observation, observation via a TV monitor, and videotape analysis. Interrater reliabilities for each system were more than 93 percent, justifying the use of videotape in assessing such behaviors.

The field's become a fad. Too many investigators who are in too great a rush. . . . Most of what I see now in the journals is very trivial. There's not the tradition of being a naturalist, of describing behavior carefully, of taking nature at its full complexity and working with that.

Paul Ekman quoted in an interview by Randall Harrison for *The Kinesis Report* 3 (Fall 1980) : 4.

388. **Ekman, Paul,** ed. *Darwin and Facial Expression.* New York:Academic Press, 1973. 273 pp. Illus.

An excellent book on facial expressions commemorating the centennial of Darwin's classic work, *The Expression of the Emotions in Man and Animals.* Each of the authors points out that, while modern methods of collecting data have shown Darwin to have made some faulty observations and deductions, research findings over the past hundred years tend to substantiate his original hypothesis. Each chapter presents Darwin's ideas on the topic along with a critical integration of current findings. The chapter "Facial Expressions of Emotions in Non-human Primates" by Suzanne Chevalier-Skolnikoff elaborates on and confirms Darwin's concept that human facial expressions evolved from those of man's non-human primate ancestors. She takes into account advances in genetics and neurophysiology in her discussion on how the evolution of facial musculature and the nervous system is related to variations in facial expressions across different species. The chapter "Facial Expressions of Infants and Children" by William R. Charlesworth and Mary Anne Kreutzer presents a survey of studies on feral, institutionalized, and blind children which supports Darwin's hypothesis that facial expressions are in part the result of innate factors. Evidence for the universality of some facial expressions in the human species is discussed in the chapter "Cross-Cultural Studies of Facial Expressions" by Paul Ekman. Each of the authors stresses the interplay between innate and environmental factors. The chapter "Darwin and the Representative Expression of Reality" deals eloquently with Darwin's contributions to the history of ideas.

389. **Ekman, Paul.** "Movements with Precise Meanings." *Journal of Communication* 26 (1976) : 14-26.

This article discusses "emblems," as opposed to gesture "illustrators," which have a direct verbal translation whose precise meaning is known and used deliberately to communicate with a specific person or group. Focusing on those which involve tools or bodily activities, the author examines differences in emblems among cultures, categories and iconicity of emblems, syntax within a string of emblems, age differences, and emblem appropriateness. Facial expressions of emotion were found to be universal among cultures, although emblems incorporating these expressions may vary by culture.

390. **Ekman, Paul.** "Facial Signs: Facts, Fantasies, and Possibilities." In *Sight, Sound and Sense.*, edited by T. Sebeok, pp. 125-156. Bloomington, Indiana: Indiana University Press, 1978.

Distinguishing between static (structural), slow (occurring with age), rapid (momentary facial movements), and artificial (for example, glasses, cosmetics) sign vehicles for facial information. Ekman discusses the relation of the first three to determining personal identity, kinship, race and gender, temperament and personality, and beauty and sexual attractiveness. He also discusses these distinctions in terms of judging intelligence, emotion, mood, and the function of rapid facial movements as emblems, adaptors, illustrators, and regulators. He concludes with a brief discussion of how the face reflects age and previous emotional life.

391. **Ekman, Paul.** *The Face of Man: Expressions of Universal Emotions in a New Guinea Village.* New York: Garland STPM Press, 1980. Illus.

A collection of candid photographs of spontaneous facial expressions taken by Ekman is presented with captions explaining the context of each picture. There is an introductory chapter on his field research of universal facial expressions and a concluding chapter reviewing studies of facial expression in literate and preliterate cultures. (from publisher's information)

392. **Ekman, Paul; Brattensani, Karen A.; O'Sullivan, Maureen; and Friesen, Wallace V.** "Does Image Size Affect Judgments of the Face?" *Journal of Nonverbal Behavior* 4 (1979) : 57-61.

Whether the video-image of the face was larger than life or about one-fifth life size made no difference in observers' judgments of emotions, attitudes, and personality traits.

393. **Ekman, Paul, and Friesen, Wallace V.** "Measuring Facial Movement." *Environmental Psychology and Nonverbal Behavior* 1 (1976) : 56-75.

A procedure has been developed for measuring visibly different facial movements. The Facial Action Code was derived from an analysis of the anatomical basis of facial movement. The method can be used to describe any facial movement (observed in photographs, motion picture film or videotape) in terms of anatomically based action units. The development of the method is explained, contrasting it to other methods of measuring facial behavior. An example of how facial behavior is measured is provided, and ideas about research applications are discussed.

394. **Ekman, Paul, and Friesen, Wallace V.** *The Facial Action Coding System (FACS).* Palo Alto, California: Consulting Psychologists Press, 1978. Illus.

Based on seven years of research, FACS is a method for objective description of facial movement. Measurement units are based on the anatomy of facial action. The authors have made available an "Investigator's Guide to the FACS," an instructional manual, film cartridges demonstrating facial actions, practice materials, scoring sheets, computer programs for coder reliability checks, and a final test of scoring ability as part of a package to be applied to sophisticated studies of facial expression.

395. **Ekman, Paul; Friesen, Wallace V.; and Ellsworth, Phoebe.** *Emotion in The Human Face: Guidelines for Research and an Integration of Findings.* New York: Pergamon Press, 1972. Illus.

An examination of the adult human face and emotion. In attempting to clarify conceptual terminology such as emotion, accuracy, generality, the authors articulate the complexities involved in researching this phenomenon. Two research approaches are compared: a component study (". . . whether a certain position or movement of the subject's face is related to some measure of the subject's emotional state") and a judgment study (whether observers who judge a subject's face can agree about the subject's emotion or can distinguish between facial behaviors emitted under different emotional states or circumstances). Methodological considerations and techniques for measuring facial behavior are reviewed, and guidelines are provided for future studies. The authors integrate findings from different experiments selecting seven major questions to resolve, such as what emotional categories can observers judge from facial behavior, can judgments of emotion from facial behavior be accurate, and what are the similarities and differences in facial behavior across cultures? The authors point out that, although many past experiments were either inadequate, utilized defective mehodology, or were misinterpreted, there remains considerable evidence that the face does not provide information regarding emotion. New questions are asked, such as whether there are particular facial behaviors which are not specific to any one emotion, but which may provide information about matters other than emotion, and is there a special class of facial behaviors which function as regulators to manage the back-and-forth flow of interaction during conversation.

396. **Ekman, Paul; Friesen, Wallace V.; O'Sullivan, Maureen; and Scherer, Klaus.** "Relative Importance of Face, Body, and Speech in Judgments of Personality and Affect." *Journal of Personality and Social Psychology* 38 (1980) : 270-277.

Three experiments were conducted to test the hypothesis that the relative contribution of a channel (face, body, or speech) would depend on variables such as the attributed being judged or the type of social situation in which the behavior had occurred. The results from all three experiments show that no single channel predominates in judging other people. The study reveals the complexity of the phenomena in judging another person's emotional state, attitude, or personality.

397. **Ekman, Paul, and Oster, Harriet.** "Facial Expressions of Emotion." *Annual Review of Psychology* 30 (1979) : 527-554.

This literature review on facial expressions of emotions covers studies that have been made since 1970. Examining what has been discovered and listing some unasked or unanswered questions, the authors review studies which indicate the relevance of facial expression to research in developmental psychology, person perception, theories of emotion, and the neurophysiology of emotion.

398. Ekman, Paul, and Scherer, Klaus, eds. *Handbook of Methods in Nonverbal Behavior Research.* Cambridge: Cambridge University Press, forthcoming.

This is the proceedings of a 1979 Advanced Study Institute sponsored by NATO in London. Participants in this symposium included Adam Kendon, Erving Goffman, Robert Rosenthal, Mario von Cranach, Ralph Exline, and Howard Rosenfeld, J.R.M. van Hooff, Heiner Ellgring, and Candace West. Also presenting were P. Garrigues and Hubert Montagner, Rolf Kuschel, Jerry Boucher, P. Ricci-Bitti, and Harald Wallbott. (from pre-publication information)

399. Ellgring, Heiner. "Nonverbal Communication: A Review of Research in Germany." *The German Journal of Psychology,* forthcoming.

In this very useful summary of German nonverbal communication literature of the 1960s and 1970s, Ellgring cites the major influences on this research as *Ausdruckspsychologie* (psychology of expression), ethology, and Anglo-American research. He discusses the theoretical approaches in current German research, emphasizing the expression and impression functions of nonverbal behavior, in the fields of psychology, ethology, and psychobiology, conversation analysis and linguistics. Research in the specific areas of facial expression, gaze, gesture and posture, speech and voice, and odor is discussed in terms of description, measurement, coding, and observer accuracy. Approaches to "multimodal analysis" and developmental perspectives in mother-infant research are described. Applications of research, teaching and research in universities, and future trends are also included. There is an extensive bibliography of works written in German.

400. Ellgring, J.H., and Cranach, Mario von. "Processes of Learning in the Recognition of Eye-Signals." *European Journal of Social Psychology* 2 (1972) : 33-43.

The experiment reported here supports the need for pretraining observers of nonverbal communication, specifically those studying gaze behavior. It was found that the accuracy with which observers judged direction of gaze was very poor and improved substantially when they were given feedback. The improvement was independent of visual acuity, and no correlation was found between observer accuracy and such personality characteristics as extraversion or neuroticism.

401. Ellsworth, Phoebe C. "The Meaningful Look." *Semiotica* 24 (1978) : 341-351.

This review of *Gaze and Mutual Gaze* by Michael Argyle and Mark Cook (Cambridge University Press, 1976) specifies the theoretical ideas the reviewer considers are shared by most researchers of gaze behavior. In so doing, she suggests a theoretical basis for organizing the existing data on gaze and simplifies the theory. A discussion further elaborating the distinction between gaze as a channel and as a signal is included.

402. Ellsworth, Phoebe, and Carlsmith, J. Merrill. "Eye Contact and Gaze Aversion in an Aggressive Encounter." *Journal of Personality and Social Psychology* 28 (1973) : 280-292.

Sixty-one male students participated in this study. The subjects, angered or not angered by a confederate, were allowed to deliver shocks to the confederate who looked at the subject, looked away, or varied gaze behavior in a random sequence. Comparing the subjects who interacted with a confederate who consistently either looked at them or looked away, the angered subjects shocked their victims less if the victim looked at them. Subjects interacting with a confederate who varied his behavior randomly, however, gave more shocks to the victim when he looked at them than when he did not.

403. **Ellsworth, Phoebe; Carlsmith, J. Merrill; and Henson, Alexander.** "The Stare as a Stimulus to Flight in Human Subjects: A Series of Field Experiments." *Journal of Personality and Social Psychology* 21 (1972) : 302-311.

In a series of five experiments, 451 car drivers and pedestrians were used as subjects. Subjects were stared at or not stared at by experimenters at stop lights. Experimenters were either motorcycle riders pulling up next to subjects in cars, pedestrians staring into subjects' cars, or pedestrians staring at pedestrians. Results showed that staring caused either pedestrians or cars to move more quickly away from the crosswalk.

404. **Ellsworth, Phoebe, and Langer, Ellen.** "Staring and Approach: An Interpretation of the Stare as a Nonspecific Activator." *Journal of Personality and Social Psychology* 31 (1976) : 117-122.

Sixty unaccompanied female shoppers were confronted by a confederate who gave either a clear or an ambiguous story about needing help from them. This confederate either engaged the subject in eye contact or looked down. Observers rated the response of the subject with regard to helping the victim (confederate). There was no main effect for staring, *per se*, but more help was elicited with the clear story when the victim stared than with the ambiguous one.

405. **Ellsworth, Phoebe C., and Ludwig, Linda M.** "Visual Behavior in Social Interaction." *Journal of Communication* 22 (1972) : 375-403.

The authors examine visual behavior from several aspects and review research on individual differences, sex differences, and personality differences, observer awareness of visual behavior, and its regulatory and information-seeking functions. The influence of visual behavior in interaction and its use as a source of attribution in relation to interpersonal attraction and involvement are also considered. The authors conclude with speculations about future research in the area.

406. **Ellsworth, Phoebe, and Ross, Lee.** "Intimacy in Response to Direct Gaze." *Journal of Experimental Social Psychology* 11 (1975) : 592-613.

One hundred male and 120 female undergraduate subjects were paired with a same-sex confederate. They experienced one of four experimental conditions (the confederate-listener responded either with continuous gaze, direct gaze contingent upon intimate statements, aversive gaze, and aversive gaze contingent upon intimate statements) as the subjects told personally revealing monologues. Direct gaze prompted intimacy among females and reticence among males. Gaze avoidance had opposite effects. Positive feelings, liking for the listener, and task satisfaction were reported by the females in the direct gaze condition.

407. **Elman, Donald.** "Eye Contact, Interest, and Arousal." Ph.D. dissertation, Columbia University. 1973. 120 p. (Order No. 73266-04)

Two laboratory experiments using 64 male undergraduate subjects were performed in order to test hypotheses about the determinants of eye contact and psychological consequences of receiving different amounts of gaze.

408. **Elman, Donald; Schulte, Duane C.; and Bukoff, Allen.** "Effects of Facial Expression and Stare Duration on Walking Speed: Two Field Experiments." *Environmental Psychology and Nonverbal Behavior* 2 (1977) : 93-99.

Two field experiments investigated the generality of the stare-escape phenomenon for pedestrians. Experiment 1, conducted at a traffic intersection, failed to replicate a previous finding that being stared at leads to faster walking speed. One hypothesis that could explain this failure is that the relatively short staring times used in Experiment 1 were insufficient for subjects to attribute a threatening meaning to the stare. In Experiment 2, conducted at a library elevator, duration of staring was systematically varied—either two seconds or more than 15 seconds. Consistent with the attribution time hypothesis, subjects increased walking speed after a long stare but decreased it after a short stare. In both experiments a smile coupled with a stare appeared to neutralize the effects of a stare alone.

409. Elzinga, Rob H. "Nonverbal Communication: Body Accessibility Among Japanese." *Psychologia* 18 (1975) : 205-211.

In this study of physical accessibility among the Japanese, a translation of Jourard's body-contact questionnaire was administered to 175 Japanese students, 143 females and 32 males. Analysis of the data supported the cross-cultural applicability of the instrument. Japanese females were found to be touched more in all relationships than males. When the results were compared with those of Jourard for American subjects, they showed a striking contrast in physical accessibility between opposite-sex friends; the Japanese data showed relatively little physical contact in heterosexual relationships, while the American data revealed physical contact in such relationships to be two-to three-times that of other relationships.

410. Emde, Robert N.; Gaensbauer, Theodore; and Harmon, Robert J. *Emotional Expression in Infancy. A Biobehavioral Study.* Psychological Issues, Monograph 37. New York: International Universities Press, 1976. 198 pp.

In a section entitled "The Development of Emotional Expressions," the authors discuss research on infant affects, the development of social smiling, stranger and separation distress, fussiness, and crying as part of a "biological message system." They explore how these expressions differentiate into increasing levels of complexity.

411. Engebretson, Darold E. "Human Territorial Behavior: The Role of Interaction Distance in Therapeutic Interventions." *American Journal of Orthopsychiatry* 43 (1973) : 108-116.

The author encourages therapists to attend to their patients' proxemic behavior. He reviews human and nonhuman territorial actions and goes on to describe how attention to and manipulation of distancing can facilitate therapy.

412. Erickson, Frederick. "Review of 'Context Analysis of a Family Interview' Film by Christian Beels and Jane Ferber, produced by Jacques Van Vlack and Ray Birdwhistell." *American Anthropologist* 76 (1974) : 731-732.

This is a review of two reels of film illustrating the "natural history" method for "context analysis" developed by Ray Birdwhistell and Albert Scheflen. The first reel contains the data, a family therapy interview, while the second reel contains a visual introduction to context analysis, using this therapy film and the postures of the adults in it as illustrating how context analysis is done.

413. Erickson, Frederick. "Gatekeeping and the Melting Pot: Interaction in Counseling Encounters." *Harvard Educational Review* 45 (1975) : 44-70.

Interviews involving 25 male students and four male counselors were videotaped and analyzed. Two counselors were white and two were black. After the interview the counselor and the student separately viewed and commented on the videotape of their encounter. Three variables were studied: social identity, outcomes of the interviews, and the interactional characters of the interviews, measured by the Overall Behavior Symmetry Coefficient and the Rhythmic Symmetry Code. Among the results it was found that students sharing the same ethnic background with the counselor tended to receive more special help than students of differing backgrounds; the warmest encounters occurred when high co-membership was established; and several scoring methods showed significant differences for those pairs establishing some co-membership.

414. Erickson, Frederick. "One Function of Proxemic Shifts in Face-to-Face Interaction." In *Organization of Behavior in Face-to-Face Interaction,* edited by A. Kendon, R.M. Harris, and M.R. Key, pp. 175-187. The Hague: Mouton Publishers, 1975.

A sample of 26 ten-minute films of junior college counseling interviews (involving two white and two black counselors and 22 students) was studied. Results showed that proxemic shifts were the best predictors of new segments of the data. These interaction segments were also identified by changes in speech style and content and interaction style, suggesting that proxemic shifts may function as situational shift indicators.

415. Erickson, Frederick. "Gatekeeping Encounters: A Social Selection Process." In *Anthropology and the Public Interest: Fieldwork and Theory,* edited by P.R. Sanday, pp. 111-145. New York: Academic Press, 1976.

Eighty-two instances of face-to-face interaction of white, Latin, and black subjects were carefully studied. Six hundred minutes of film were coded for speech behavior (including linguistic and paralinguistic phenomena), nonverbal behavior (including gaze direction and involvement, proxemic phenomena, and kinesic rhythm), and hierarchical ordering of segments of speaking/listening behavior using "etic" and "emic" codes for segmentation, with special focus on the "uncomfortable moments" of the interactions. An asymmetry segments code, a rhythmic asymmetry code, and measures of affect and special help were also developed to assess the "uncomfortable moments." The asymmetry segments code showed a clear relationship between ethnicity and the "match" between speaker-listener behavior. An even closer relationship was found between the speaking-listening ratio and the social category of "pan-ethnicity." For everything except rhythmic asymmetry, pan-ethnicity explained more of the variance in the data than did ethnicity. Co-membership (a shared social bond other than ethnicity) explained more variance than did ethnicity or pan-ethnicity. The rhythmic asymmetry code was more closely related to ethnicity than to pan-ethnicity or co-membership. Differences in communication style may be overridden or overlooked under some conditions of co-membership.

416. Erickson, Frederick. "Talking Down: Some Cultural Sources of Miscommunication in Interracial Interviews." In *Nonverbal Behavior: Applications and Cultural Implications,* edited by A. Wolfgang, pp. 99-126. New York: Academic Press, 1979.

The author examined "LRRMs" (listening response-relevant moments) occurring during seven films of school counseling interviews and two of job interviews. In addition to locating each LRRM and each LR (listening response), a speech transcript and the counselor's nonverbal behavior were also recorded. It became apparent that more active listening behavior occurred at some points than others, and these moments were examined more closely. Results indicated differing listening responses for the blacks and the whites in the interviews, with one person apparently not responding appropriately to the other's LRRM or LR. A social and cognitive model was proposed for making a point within a conversation, and implications for policy, practice, and training were suggested.

417. Erickson, Frederick, and Shultz, Jeffrey. "When is a Context? Some Issues and Methods in the Analysis of Social Competence." *The Quarterly Newsletter of the Institute for Comparative Human Development* 1 (1977) : 5-10.

After a literature review of the study of contexts, the research methodology the authors used for studying contextualization cues is described. Using, for example, film or videotape of shifts in classroom participation structure, they first view each reel and make notes of approximate locations of occasions and transitions between occasions. They then search the corpus of tapes for analogous occasions, attending mainly to the junctures between parts rather than to the parts themselves. Then they locate and identify the differences in participation structure across the junctures, attending primarily to the participation structures ahead of the junctures. They then attempt an initial test of the validity of the model and try to establish the generalizability of the single case analysis by searching the corpus of tapes for analogous instances of the kind of occasion they have investigated.

418. **Eschbach, Achim,** ed. *Zeichen-Text-Bedeutung: Bibliographie zu Theorie und Praxis der Semiotik.* Munich: Wilhelm Fink Verlag, 1974. 508 pp.

This bibliography on the theory and practice of semiotics includes a section on "Nonverbal Communication" with 377 items, many of them non-English titles or rare historical references. Also of special interest are section 1.6, on applied semiotics and part 5.0, on interdisciplinary areas of semiotics.

419. **Eschbach, Achim, and Rader, Wendelin.** *Semiotik-Bibliographie I.* Frankfurt am Main: Syndikat, 1976. 221 pp.

This bibliography of references in semiotics is a sequel to Eschbach's 1974 bibliography *Zeichen-Text-Bedeutung* and contains 4,000 references to monographs, articles, reviews, and unpublished papers appearing between 1965 and June, 1976. There are 12 chapters dealing with various areas in semiotics. Chapter 8 is on nonverbal communication and contains 306 items, among them many non-English titles. Other chapters deal with film, art, the history of semiotics, and "socio-semiotics." The final chapter of miscellaneous titles contains references on animal communication. There is an introduction in English as well as in German and French.

420. **Eshkol, Noa; Shoshoni, Michael; and Dagan, Mooky.** *Movement Notations: A Comparative Study of Labanotation (Kinetography Laban) and Eshkol-Wachman Movement Notation.* Holon, Israel: The Movement Notation Society, 1979. 34 pp. Illus.

This is a technical but very clear and well illustrated monograph on the similarities and differences in these two principal movement notation systems. The staffs, body part notations, spatial recording, steps and frames of reference, and methods of noting time are paralleled and compared.

421. **Esser, Aristide H.,** ed. *Behavior and Environment: The Use of Space by Animals and Men.* New York: Plenum Press, 1971. 411 pp. Illus.

This book is the text of all papers and edited discussions at the five-session symposium on "The Use of Space by Animals and Men" sponsored by the Animal Behavior Society in December 1968. Session one is entitled "Territoriality and Dominance" and contains papers by A.H. Esser, F. Fischer, and P. Leyhausen. Session two on "Space and Contact Behavior" includes contributions by G. McBride, J.L. Brereton, and A. Watson and R. Moss. "Population Density and Crowding" is covered in papers by D.E. Davis, K. Myers, C.S. Hale, R. Mykytowycz, R.L. Hughes, and H.F. Ellenberger. M. von Cranach, I. Eibl-Eibesfeldt, and E.T. Hall have contributed to a session on "Orientation and Communication," and a fifth session on "Communal Behavior and the Environment" includes papers by V.C. Wynne-Edwards, R. Sommer, and I. Altman.

422. **Evans, Gary W.** "Personal Space: Research Review and Bibliography." *Man-Environment Systems* 3 (1973) : 203-215.

Personal space can be distinguished from territory in that territory is relatively stationary, visibly bounded, and can be maintained by aggressive behavior. Personal space, on the other hand, is portable, invisibly bounded, and person-centered. This paper presents an extensive bibliography of personal space research and summarizes major findings and methodological aspects of the topic.

423. Evans, Gary W., and Eichelman, William. "Preliminary Models of Conceptual Linkages Among Proxemic Variables." *Environment and Behavior* 8 (1976) : 87-116.

Stress, information overload, and micro-macro models of proxemic behavior are each analyzed critically. A research strategy derived from a functional perspective is presented.

424. Evans, Gary W., and Howard, Roger B. "Personal Space," *Psychological Bulletin* 80 (1973) : 334-344.

This article is a summary of relevant research and major findings on personal space. The authors examine work from clinical psychology, demographic studies, cross-cultural studies, and familiarity and affinity studies. Methodological problems are considered, the authors citing a lack of experimental controls contributing to a lack of consistency in findings. They recommend increased use of multivariate techniques and propose a theory of the nature of the personal space construct.

425. Exline, Ralph. "Visual Interaction: The Glances of Power and Preference." In *Nebraska Symposium on Motivation,* edited by J.K. Cole, pp. 163-206. Lincoln: University of Nebraska Press, 1971. Illus.

The foundation of this series of experimental studies is that eye contact is one of the bases for establishing relationships. In several studies the author examines the relationship between visual interaction and comfort, competition, sex, need for affiliation, power differences, and perceptions of another's potency. He focuses on the role of visual interaction in affiliative and dominance relationships.

426. Exline, Ralph V., and Fehr, B.J. "Applications of Semiosis to the Study of Visual Interaction." In *Nonverbal Behavior and Communication,* edited by A.W. Siegman and S. Feldstein, pp. 117-157. Hillsdale, New Jersey: Lawrence Erlbaum Associates, 1978.

This overview of mutual gaze and visual behavior research is organized into the validity and reliability of measurements of gaze direction, duration and frequency, the "syntactics of eye engagement," and relationship between visual signs and other behavioral signs, the meanings of various gaze patterns, gaze as an independent variable and its effects on the respondent (for example, effects of a confederate's staring), and gaze as a message about the interactants' relationship.

427. Fast, Julius. *The Body Language of Sex, Power and Aggression.* New York: M. Evans and Company, 1977. 192 pp.

Nonverbal communication of attractiveness, power, and aggression is discussed through a question-answer format with occasional references to research studies in this popularized account.

428. Feld, Steve, and Williams, Carroll. "Toward a Researchable Film Language." *Studies in the Anthropology of Visual Communications* 2 (1975) : 25-32. Illus.

The authors of this provocative position paper argue against the "locked off camera" of traditional social science research and for "researchable film observation" that takes the researchers' objectives and perceptions into account.

429. Feldenkrais, Moshe. *Awareness Through Movement: Health Exercises for Personal Growth.* New York: Harper & Row, 1972. 173 pp. Illus.

This is a basic primer on Feldenkrais' ideas and techniques. The first section of this book is theoretical, while the second outlines 12 lessons of fundamental exercises involving the whole body and its essential activities. The chapters on theory discuss self-image and self-education, correction of movements as the best means of self-improvement, awareness and human development, and how and where to start. The following 12 lessons, introduced by a few practical observations and illustrating specific points from the Feldenkrais system and techniques cover posture, movement, self-image, spatial relationship, eye movement, thinking, and breathing.

430. **Feldman, Michael, and Thayer, Stephen.** "A Comparison of Three Measures of Nonverbal Decoding Ability." *Journal of Social Psychology,* in press.

The authors compared test results from two measures of nonverbal decoding behavior — the Profile of Nonverbal Sensitivity (PONS) and Beier's test. The results of these two tests were then compared with the results of one empathy measure, the Affective Sensitivity Scale, Form D (AFSS). The results of the study, in which 60 subjects participated, reveal no significant positive relationship between the PONS test and Beier's test. The study also showed no significant positive correlation between each test of nonverbal decoding ability and the empathy test.

431. **Feldman, Robert S.** "Nonverbal Disclosure of Teacher Deception and Interpersonal Affect." *Journal of Educational Psychology* 68 (1976) : 807-816. Illus.

To determine the role of nonverbal cues in revealing the truthfulness of a teacher's remarks (deception) or the teacher's real feelings about a student (leakage), the following study was created. Thirty-two undergraduates taught a confederate a lesson, overheard her evaluation, administered a test which the confederate completed with 100 percent accuracy, and administered a final test on which the confederate performed either well or poorly. Teachers were told to always praise the confederate's responses, manipulating the deception variable. Teacher evaluations were manipulated to produce teacher like or dislike of the confederate. Lastly, the final test was performed with the teacher present or behind a one-way screen. Thirty-seven undergraduate judges viewed silent films of the teacher administering the last test and rated "how pleased the teacher was with the student." Nonverbal behavior was found to discriminate lying from truthful behavior. Underlying affect was only leaked when teachers were giving truthful praise. Lastly, teachers showed more "pleasure" with students when in private. No differences were found whether judges viewed the face or the whole body.

432. **Feldman, Robert S., and White, John B.** "Detecting Deception in Children." *Journal of Communication* 30 (1980) : 121-139.

This study, involving 74 children between the ages of five and 12, examined children's ability to conceal a lie and adults' ability to detect verbal dissembling from the children's facial and body cues. Verbal deception was discerned slightly more from the body movements of older girls than from those of younger girls. However, judges were significantly more accurate in determining deception in older boys via facial expression than in younger boys. Findings suggest that rate of facial and body disclosure are inversely related to each other and that they develop in opposite directions for boys and girls. Also girls are better at pretending they dislike something they actually like, while boys are better at pretending to like something they actually dislike.

433. **Felker, Donald W.** "Social Stereotyping of Male and Female Body Types with Differing Facial Expressions by Elementary School Age Boys and Girls." *The Journal of Psychology* 82 (1972) : 151-154.

First, third, and fifth graders were shown male and female silhouettes of ectomorph, mesomorph, endomorph body types. One of each had a "smiling face" while the other had a "frowning face." Subjects were asked questions about the different body forms. Among the results it was found that for both boy and girl subjects across grades the endomorph body type received the greater number of negative responses. The smiling silhouette received the more favorable adjectives.

434. **Finkelstein, Jonathan C.** "Experimenter Expectancy Effects." *Journal of Communication* 26 (1976) : 31-38.

The author discusses recent research on nonverbal communication. He covers research indicating nonverbal behaviors that may influence experiments: the impact on subjects of the mood and atmosphere determined by the experimenter, why subjects rate neutral photos as affectively loaded, and paralinguistic analyses of experimenter directions.

435. **Firestone, Ira J.** "Reconciling Verbal and Nonverbal Models of Dyadic Communication." *Environmental Psychology and Nonverbal Behavior* 2 (1977) : 30-44.

This paper examines two distinct theoretical descriptions of dyadic communication, the distance-equilibrium and reciprocity formulations, and shows that they carry divergent implications for changes that can occur in interpersonal relations. A review of relevant studies reveals ample support of each model. Reciprocity effects, first identified in disclosure research, also obtain for nonverbal aspects of interaction. Similarly, compensation effects initially discovered for nonverbal research also apply to disclosure. Several suggestions are considered toward reconciling these theories by delimiting their spheres of applicability. These include the mediating role of attraction, the tempo and perception of control over distance change, and initial differences in the level of verbal and nonverbal variables.

436. **Firestone, Marsha Larrie.** "Farewell Behavior: A Descriptive Analysis of Nonverbal Farewell Behavior." Ph.D. dissertation, Columbia University. 1972. 232 pp.

The analysis of farewell behaviors following a dinner party revealed two different periods of behavior: farewell interactions and farewell displays. Forty-two specific nonverbal behaviors were identified in the analysis with their functions. Couples were found to perform the same eight-behavior routine, and individuals performed a three-step display. A dictionary with photographs of the behaviors is included in the text.

437. **Firth, Raymond.** "Bodily Symbols of Greeting and Parting." In *Symbols— Public and Private,* edited by R. Firth, pp. 299-327. London: George Allen and Unwin, Ltd., 1973.

The handshake, kiss, and use of clothing accessories are included in the discussion of proxemics, facial expression, gestures of the whole body, hand, and arm used in greeting behavior.

438. **Fischer, Hal.** *Gay Semiotics.* San Francisco: NFS Press, 1978. Illus.

439. **Fischer, Kenneth Charles.** "An Inquiry Into the Supremacy of Eye Contact in Social Likeability Decisions." Ph.D. dissertation, Washington State University. 1972. 45 pp. (Order No. 72312-70)

The thesis of this study is that, contrary to assumption, trained subjects are not able to control other verbal/nonverbal cues while manipulating eye contact but that these cues vary with eye direction.

440. **Fischer, Susan D.** "Unsound Research on Soundless Language." *Semiotica* 25 (1979) : 359-378.

8# r

This is a review of *Developmental Features of Visual Communication* by B. Th. M. Tervoot (Amsterdam: North Holland, 1975). This reviewer found almost everything to be wrong with Tervoot's study, and proceeded to enumerate mistakes in Tervoot's study of deaf students learning English or Dutch in schools that did not permit the use of sign language in the classroom.

441. **Fisher, Jeffrey David.** "Situation-Specific Variables as Determinants of Perceived Environmental Aesthetic Quality and Perceived Crowdedness." *Journal of Research in Personality* 8 (1974) : 177-188.

One hundred and twenty-nine college students interacted with an attitudinally similar or dissimilar confederate at one of four distances. Subjects in the similar condition perceived the environment significantly more favorably and perceived themselves to be significantly less crowded at two of the distance conditions than subjects interacting with a dissimilar confederate. Subjects interacting with similar confederates were also significantly more attracted to them than subjects in the dissimilar condition. There were no sex differences except on an unobtrusive measure of attraction—female subjects sat closer to female confederates than male subjects to male confederates.

442. **Fisher, Jeffrey D., and Byrne, Donn.** "Too Close for Comfort: Sex Differences in Response to Invasions of Personal Space." *Journal of Personality and Social Psychology* 32 (1975) : 15-21.

Subjects had their personal space "invaded" by a female or male confederate from one of three directions. Regardless of the invader's sex, males responded most negatively when a stranger sat across from them and females responded most negatively when a stranger sat next to them. Observation revealed females set up barriers against invasion from the side, while males set up barriers against face-to-face invasions.

443. **Fitzgerald, Thomas P., and Clark, Richard M.** "The Use of Body Language to Evaluate Staff Training Presentations." *Improving Human Performance Quarterly* 7 (1978) : 326-336.

Forty-one reading specialists and administrators participating in a staff development program responded to semantic differential items evaluating the session, attitudes, and personality of the presenter, with a subset of nine participants' responses rated via photographic and body language assessments during the program. The semantic differential and body language measures of evaluations of the sessions were significantly related.

444. **Fleshman, Bob, and Carey, Diane,** eds. *Bibliographical Anthology of Theatrical Movement,* revised. Metuchen, New Jersey: Scarecrow Press, forthcoming.

This is to be a collection of essays with basic bibliographies on various areas of movement relevant to those working in theater, dance, and related movement forms. Written by experts in the given areas under discussion, it includes sections on mime, the actor in space, historical styles of movement, movement for actor training, performance in non-Western cultures, movement notations, nonverbal communication, and the anthropology of human movement.

445. **Florio, Susan, and Shultz, Jeffrey.** "Social Competence at Home and at School." *Theory Into Practice* 18 (1979) : 234-243.

The authors attempted a direct comparison of children's school life and home life in an effort to better understand the different ways of participating and interacting at home and at school. Because direct comparison proved troublesome, the authors observed those ways of interacting at home and at school which seemed comparable in terms of style. For example, the authors compared the interactions of mealtimes at home and the interactions of teacher-directed group lessons. Videotaped instances of each event revealed important functional similarities between them. These insights should facilitate the integration of home and school experiences.

446. Foa, Uriel G.; Foa, Edna B.; and Schwarz, Larry M. "Nonverbal Communication: Toward Syntax, by Way of Semantics." *Resources in Education*, in press.

Departing from the traditional search for syntactical rules which govern nonverbal communication, this study considers the semantic and syntactical issues within a unified framework. The authors examined the hypothesis that a combination of nonverbal signals is sufficient for a unique determination of meaning. A review of the existing literature with regard to the channels of distance, looking, and carriage seems to support the hypothesis. Implications for its cross-cultural validity are briefly discussed.

447. Fogel, Alan Dale. "Gaze, Face and Voice in the Development of Mother-Infant Face-to-Face Interaction." Ph.D. dissertation, University of Chicago. 1976 (Not available from University Microfilms)

One infant/mother pair was videotaped ten times during a seven-week observation period in this study of the relationship of the mother's behavior, particularly to the infant's "cyclic" activity.

448. Forgas, Joseph P. "The Effects of Behavioural and Cultural Expectation Cues on the Perception of Social Episodes." *European Journal of Social Psychology* 8 (1978) : 203-213.

Two groups of 24 subjects, students and their wives, viewed two couples' realistic interactions (previously designated as intimate/nonintimate nonverbally and as intimate/nonintimate episodically). The videotapes were viewed in a mixed design, and subjects within each group were given randomly varied written episodic descriptions, so that subjects never rated the same couple more than once. Each group then rated both information sources separately. The nonverbal cues overwhelmingly influenced the judgments and definitions of the encounter, while the episode descriptions significantly affected the judgments of discordant encounters.

449. Forsdale, Louis. *Nonverbal Communication.* New York: Harcourt Brace Jovanovich, Inc., 1974. 162 pp. Illus.

This is a lively and personal introduction to the study of nonverbal communication enhanced by many photographs and illustrations. Seeking to encourage an awareness of communication in action, the author deals with topics such as tactile communication, body movement, facial expression, and space, exploring cultural differences, and making connections with animal communication. Included are dialogues with the psychiatrist and researcher Albert Scheflen and with the dancer Edward Villella. The volume ends with a series of observational problems.

450. Forsdale, Louis. *Perspectives on Communication.* Reading, Massachusetts: Addison-Wesley, 1981. Illus.

In this wide-ranging and original introduction to the study of communication, the author discusses several definitions and models of communication, expanding on an understanding of communication within a systems framework. Nonverbal aspects of communication are touched on throughout this book, in chapters on the history of communication, the cultural context of communication, brain laterality, communication codes, and animal communication. Chapter eight deals specifically with nonverbal communication, discussing touch, odor, posture, eye pupil size, time, and the relationship of nonverbal and verbal communication. The final chapter offers examples and strategies for learning to observe communication in operation. "Ponderings and Projects" and "Books You Will Enjoy" follow each chapter. Striking photographs by the author and Lynn Forsdale complement the text. An instructor's manual is also available.

451. **Frances, Susan J.** "Sex Differences in Nonverbal Behavior." *Sex Roles* 5 (1979) : 519-535.

Eighty-eight dyads involved in seven-minute conversation were videotaped, each person being paired with a stranger of the same sex and one of the opposite sex. Various measures of speaking turn, back channel (listening) behavior, paralanguage, laughing and smiling, gaze behaviors, postural shifts, gesticulating versus self-adaptor hand movements and foot movements were made. Sex of the subject but not sex of the partner had a significant effect, although sex of subject × sex of partner was related to number of talk turns. The numerous sex differences found are discussed and interpreted.

452. **Frankel, A. Steven, and Barrett, James.** "Variations in Personal Space as a Function of Authoritarianism, Self-Esteem, and Racial Characteristics of a Stimulus Situation." *Journal of Consulting and Clinical Psychology* 37 (1971) : 95-98.

Forty white American males participated in the study. It was hypothesized that, when approached by white or black males, subjects high in authoritarianism and low in self-esteem would maintain the greatest personal space, and even greater distances in relation to the black confederates' approach. The hypotheses were supported.

453. **Franklin, Sheila Beth.** "Movement Therapy and Selected Measures of Body Image in the Trainable Mentally Retarded." *American Journal of Dance Therapy* 3 (1979) : 43-50.

Twenty-two trainable, mentally retarded youth with mean age 15 years, ten months were given Cratty and Sams' Body Image Screening Test and a Draw a Person Test before and after ten weeks of movement therapy or physical education. Body image was significantly improved post-movement therapy. No significant changes on the DAP for either intervention were noted.

454. **Fraser, J.T.** *et al.*, eds. *Study of Time, Vols. I, II, and III*: Conference of the International Society of the Study of Time. New York: Springer Verlag, 1972, 1975, 1978.

455. **Freedman, Jonathan L.** *Crowding and Behavior.* New York: The Viking Press, 1975. 177 pp.

The author maintains and defends the proposition that crowding does not have negative effects on people. Crowding can have good and bad effects, depending on the situation. Freedman supplies the background for this statement and notes its implications. In ten chapters, the author defines crowding, notes its naturalistic occurrence, examines crowding research, poses a density-related theory of crowding , and addresses design-related questions.

456. **Freedman, Jonathan L.; Levy, Alan S.; Buchanan, Roberta Welte; and Price, Judy.** "Crowding and Human Aggressiveness." *Journal of Experimental Social Psychology* 8 (1972) : 528-548.

The effects of crowding on aggressiveness were investigated in two experiments in which same-sex and mixed-sex groups of high school students were placed in small or large rooms for several hours. In experiment I, a labyrinth game was used to test competition and cooperation. All-female groups were more cooperative in small rooms, whereas all-male groups were more competitive in small rooms. In experiment II, a prisoner's dilemma game was conducted. All-female groups were more lenient, while all-male groups were more severe in the small room than in the large room. In addition, females were more positive with each other in the small room and males in the large room. Mixed-sex groups were not affected by room size.

457.   **Freedman, Norbert.** "Hands, Words, and Mind: On the Structuralization of Body Movements During Discourse and the Capacity for Verbal Representation." In *Communicative Structures and Psychic Structures,* edited by N. Freedman and S. Grand, pp. 109-132. New York and London: Plenum Press, 1977. Illus.

This article discusses the use of body movement for self-regulation and monitoring. Freedman illustrates with examples from psychoanalysis how kinesic behaviors can represent externalized communication regulatory factors. He particularly notes the intraindividual function of motoric behavior.

458.   **Freedman, Norbert, and Grand, Stanley,** ed. *Communicative Structures and Psychic Structures — A Psychoanalytic Interpretation of Communication.* New York and London: Plenum Press, 1977. 465 pp. Illus.

Designed as a dialogue between researcher and clinician, this collection of articles is the proceedings of the Conference on Research Concerning the Psychoanalytic Interpretation of Communication held at Downstate Medical Center in 1976. The six sections cover research and interpretations following the development of communication structures from early object experiences to the psychoanalytic experience for adults. Included are several important studies in nonverbal communication, such as data supporting sensori-motor origins in mother/infant dialogue and three studies of recorded communication samples during the development from basic to symbolic verbal dialogue. There are recorded communication samples defining the variability of language construction with clinical states. The impact of the unconscious on communication is discussed with documentation from laboratory sources. Finally, the psychoanalytic situation is examined — both the motoric phenomena involved in the transition from unconscious to conscious, and the measuring of the process through word frequency, representation, and interaction of thematic material. Chapter authors focusing on movement include Louis W. Sander, Beatrice Beebe and Daniel N. Stern, Allen T. Dittmann, Stanley Grand, George F. Mahl., Louis A. Gottschalk and Regina L. Uliana, and Sebastiano Santostefano.

459.   **Freedman, Norbert; O'Hanlon, James; Oltman, Phillip; and Witkin, Herman A.** "The Imprint of Psychological Differentiation on Kinetic Behavior in Varying Communicative Contexts." *Journal of Abnormal Psychology* 79 (1972) : 239-258.

The "object- and body-focused" hand movements of 12 female students tested as field-independent (F-I) and 12 as field-dependent (F-D) were observed from videotaped interviews in which they spoke with a "cold" then a "warm" interviewer or vice versa. A third condition involved a five-minute "warm-up" interchange with a "warm" doctor that was videotaped. During cold and warm interviews F-D subjects engaged in more hand-to-hand body-focused movements, while during wary interchange, they had more "motor primacy"-type object-focused gestures. Certain body-focused (body touching, not hand-to-hand) movements did not correlate with psychological differentiation, but with negative interpersonal contact (the cold condition). The authors conclude that certain hand movements as they assess them are governed by cognitive style, while others may reflect the unverbalized experiences of the relationship in this rich and complex paper.

460. **Freedman, Norbert, and Steingart, Irving.** "Kinesic Internalization and Language Construction." *Psychoanalysis and Contemporary Science* 4 (1975) : 355-403.

One of several articles by the authors on the relationship of verbal communication and object- and body-focused movement. Using a normal test population, they explore how "kinesic internalization" relates to cognitive processing.

461. **French, Patrice.** "Kinesics in Communication: Black and White." *Language Sciences* 28 (1973) : 13-16.

In Experiment I the subjects were fourth-grade students from two southern schools, one primarily black, one primarily white. A "Series I film" was made of students individually pantomiming gestures listed on stimulus cards. In "Series II films" students individually acted out (without vocalization or mouthing) their own choice of message. Black students' films were labeled BI and BII, white students' films WI and WII. Each film was shown to all students who then guessed the meaning of each item. Both classes did poorer on the WI film, with the black class doing the poorest; both classes scored highest on the BII film. In Experiment II both black and white adults and undergraduates were shown the four films produced in Experiment I and guessed the meaning of each item. Adults showed a pattern similar to the children's decoding of the gestures, although they were less accurate.

462. **French, Patrice L., and von Raffler-Engel, Walburga.** "The Kinesics of Bilingualism." In *Social Aspects of Language Contact,* edited by W. Mackay. Quebec: Laval University Press, forthcoming.

463. **French, Russell L.** "Nonverbal Patterns in Youth Culture." *Educational Leadership* April (1978) : NP.

Written in a lively anecdotal style, this article describes the influence of the kinesics of the black culture on white adolescents, citing relevant research and making a plea for better understanding of these nonverbal patterns among educators.

464. **Fretz, Bruce R.; Corn, Roger; Tuemmler, Janet M.; and Bellet, William.** "Counselor Nonverbal Behaviors and Client Evaluations." *Journal of Counseling Psychology* 26 (1979) : 304-311.

This article reports the findings of three studies on the effect of eye contact, body orientation, and body lean on client evaluation of counselor attractiveness and facilitativeness. In Study I, 104 female college students rated ten-minute videotapes of counselors in one of two nonverbal conditions: high levels (90-100 percent) of eye contact, forward trunk lean, and direct body orientation; and low levels (less than 40 percent) of the same nonverbal behaviors. For both male and female counselors, subjects rated counselors in the high condition significantly higher on measures of attractiveness and facilitativeness. In the second study, a videotape was made of counselors expressing low verbal empathy to investigate whether the nonverbal conditions would then be still more significant in evaluation of the counselor. Results confirmed those of Study I, but the low verbal empathy did not exaggerate the effect of the high and low nonverbal levels. In Study III, student volunteers interacted in real counseling situations with counselors in the same conditions of high and low levels of nonverbal behaviors. In this case, no significant differences were obtained on ratings of counselor attractiveness and facilitativeness.

465. **Fried, Matthew L., and DeFrazio, Victor J.** "Territoriality and Boundary Conflicts in the Subway." *Psychiatry: Journal for the Study of Interpersonal Processes* 37 (1974) : 47-59.

Observations by the authors suggest that individuals on crowded New York City subways use the avoidance of eye contact and verbal interaction as a means of creating distance. Examination of riders' seating and standing patterns indicates that passengers will choose a standing area, with clear boundaries, over a seat on a crowded bench. Passengers' awareness of the usual patterns of density seems to determine their immediate selection of seat or standing area, with their goal being to preserve the maximum personal space and territory.

466. **Friedman, Howard S.** "The Interactive Effects of Facial Expressions of Emotion and Verbal Messages on Perceptions of Affective Meaning." *Journal of Experimental Social Psychology* 15 (1979) : 453-469.

Photographs of teacher-confederates' faces in expressions of happy, surprised, angry, or sad were shown with various written sentences. Students judged the "episodes" for sincerity, positivity, and dominance. A number of "cue combinations" affected perceptions in interesting ways. For example, "perceived sincerity" was related to consistency in "positivity" but not "dominant" cues.

467. **Friedman, Howard S.** "Nonverbal Communication Between Patients and Medical Practitioners." *Journal of Social Issues* 35 (1979) : 82-99.

This is a general discussion of the topic that draws on research in touch, gaze, facial expression, paralanguage, and so on, and its relevance to patient-medical personnel interaction.

468. **Friedman, Howard S.; DiMatteo, M. Robin; and Mertz, Timothy L.** "Nonverbal Communication on Television News: The Facial Expression of Broadcasters during Coverage of a Presidential Election Campaign." *Personality and Social Psychology Bulletin* 6 (1980) : 427-435.

The authors conducted a nonverbal content analysis of the news anchorpersons' facial expressions, which demonstrated significant differences in perceived "positivity" as they related stories on the 1976 presidential candidates (for example, Walter Cronkite's facial expressions were perceived to indicate a more favorable attitude toward Carter than Ford).

469. **Friedman, Howard S.; DiMatteo, M. Robin; and Taranta, Angelo.** "A Study of the Relationship Between Individual Differences in Nonverbal Expressiveness and Factors of Personality and Social Interaction." *Journal of Research in Personality* 14 (1980) : 351-364.

A two-part study of physicians' individual expressive behavior as recorded in manner of voice tone and facial and body movement while saying three clinical-type remarks and in a brief greeting of the patient. Several correlations between independent judges (high school students for the voice tone, undergraduates for the voice and body behavior, and for the "likeability" of the greeting), actual patients of the physicians, and personality assessments completed by the physician-subjects are reported. Notable among them is evidence that degree of physician's expressiveness correlates with likeability of his or her greeting style and data supporting a relationship between expressive ability and certain personality traits.

470. **Friedman, Howard S.; Prince, Louise M.; Riggio, Ronald E.; and DiMatteo, M. Robin.** "Understanding and Assessing Nonverbal Expressiveness: The Affective Communication Test." *Journal of Personality and Social Psychology* 39 (1980) : 333-351.

The development, testing, reliability, and first validity measures of a self-report test, ACT (The Affective Communication Test), is described. This test has 13 items such as "at small parties I am the center of attention," "my laugh is soft and subdued," and "I usually have a neutral facial expression." Preliminary studies of degree of expressiveness and occupation, sex differences, extroversion and neuroticism, personality measures, social desirability, and other measures are reported.

471. **Friedman, Howard S.; Riggio, Ronald E.; and Segall, Daniel O.** "Personality and the Enactment of Emotion." *Journal of Nonverbal Behavior* 5 (1980) : 35-48.

The meaning of personality traits for social interaction was investigated by exploring the personality correlates of abilities to pose emotions. This framework focuses on individual differences in socio-emotional skills. Thirty-one males and 37 females were videotaped while attempting to communicate seven basic emotions nonverbally (that is, using standard content communications), and sending success was measured by showing edited videotapes to judges. Hypothesized relationships between "acting" ability and scores on the Jackson Personality Research Form and the Eysenck Personality Inventory were then examined. The findings were seen to have implications for predicting individual strengths and weaknesses in social interaction as a function of certain personality traits and for understanding person perception.

472. **Friedman, Lynn A.,** ed. *On the Other Hand: New Persepctives on American Sign Language.* New York: Academic Press, 1977. 245 pp.

This vigorous treatment of the American Sign Language (ASL) challenges the layman's view that language is basically writing and the linguist's view that language is basically speech. From the opening chapter (a phonemic analysis of the four articulatory parameters) to the book's conclusion (a discussion of eye contact and eye movement as turn-taking regulators in discourse), the work presents a multifaceted but integrated look at ASL. Presentation of data such as that which supports the claim that ASL lacks grammatical subordination elucidates the distinction between language itself and the modality in which it is manifested. The argument for a linguistically significant level of visual imagery in the grammar of ASL is well developed.

473. **Fries, Margaret E.** "Longitudinal Study: Prenatal Period to Parenthood." *Journal of American Psychoanalytic Association* 25 (1975) : 115-140.

A longitudinal study investigating the role of constitution and environment on personality development. Specific activities were observed in four longitudinal cases from birth to seven years. Early neonate activity in the following two areas was observed in the first ten to 12 days of life: congenital activity type (assessed as active, moderately active, quiet, hyperactive, or hypoactive) and activity pattern. The development of the four children in light of their particular congenital activity type and activity pattern was studied. Preliminary findings suggest that sensorimotor reactivity is a constitutional factor which persists through life. It was found to play an important role in forming the initial mother-infant relationship.

474. **Friesen, Wallace Verne.** "Cultural Differences in Facial Expressions in a Social Situation: An Experimental Test of the Concept of Display Rules." Ph.D. dissertation, University of California, San Francisco. 1972. 101 pp. (Order No. 73-3651)

The facial behaviors of Japanese and American subjects interacting with members of their own cultures were videotaped after the subjects viewed a negative affect-arousing film. A first hypothesis that Japanese more than Americans would display positive affect was confirmed only in the second part of the interview; there was a consistent trend for the Americans to display more negative affect than the Japanese, as a second hypothesis had predicted.

475. **Friesen, Wallace V.; Ekman, Paul; and Wallbott, Harald.** "Measuring Hand Movements." *Journal of Nonverbal Behavior* 4 (1979) : 97-112.

Hand movements were classified into speech illustrators, body manipulators, and actions that convey precise symbolic information. The behavioral code noted whether the action involved the left, right, or both hands, and the manipulator code also included the part of the body manipulated. The application of this code to videotapes of conversations provided data to examine a number of methodological issues. Reliability was inspected in a number of ways; each showed high intercoder agreement. Little redundancy was found among the various hand measures, although scores for the frequency of an activity and for the duration of an activity were highly intercorrelated for most classes of hand actions. An economical method for coding hand activity was compared with the standard, more time-consuming method. Similar results were obtained, although the economical method appeared to be more vulnerable to measurement error.

476. **Frieze, Irene H., and Ramsey, Sheila J.** "Nonverbal Maintenance of Traditional Sex Roles." *Journal of Social Issues* 32 (1976) : 133-141.

The authors discuss patterns of territoriality, personal space, touching, body posture, eye contact, and paralanguage as nonverbal cues which reflect status relationships and maintain sex-role stereotypes.

477. **Frings, Hubert, and Frings, Mabel.** *Animal Communication.* Second edition, revised and enlarged. Norman: University of Oklahoma Press, 1977. 207 pp. Illus.

This revised and enlarged edition of the authors' 1964 book contains a final chapter which reviews the literature since that date. A clear introduction to animal communication for the nonspecialist, it covers among other types of signals, the tactile and visual signals animals use for species identification, social cooperation, courtship, and care of the young.

478. **Frisch, James E., and Zedeck, Sheldon.** "Status, Interest, and Proximity as Factors in Interaction and Communication Channels." *The Journal of Psychology* 82 (1972) : 259-267.

The study investigated the influence of and interaction between: physical proximity; status; and perceived similarity of interests. A sample of 57 graduate students made self-reports on these variables on two separate occasions. Findings indicate that students had more contact with individuals perceived to be of equal status and to have similar interests, rather than with persons who were within close physical proximity.

479. **Fristoe, Macalyne, and Lloyd, Lyle L.** "Manual Communication for the Retarded and Others with Severe Communication Impairment: A Resource List." *Mental Retardation* (1977) : 18-21.

This article provides a resource list of nonverbal communication systems which are used or can be used by those persons with severe communication impairment. While most of the references pertain to teaching American Sign Language (ASL) or pedagogical sign systems, some listings include more general reference material about the use of nonspeech communication systems. Approximately 60 listings are included.

480. **Fromme, Donald Karl, and Beam, Donna Clegg.** "Dominance and Sex Differences in Nonverbal Responses to Differential Eye Contact." *Journal of Research in Personality* 8 (1974) : 76-87.

Sixteen male and 16 female college students divided into high and low dominance groups approached a confederate (male or female) who gazed continuously either at the floor or at the subject's eyes. Subjects were told to approach the confederate to the point at which they felt most comfortable. High-dominant subjects decreased their distance and low-dominant subjects increased their distance to the confederate with high eye contact. In the high eye contact condition males decreased their personal space and females increased their personal space. Similarly, in the high eye contact condition males increased their approach rate and females decreased their approach rate. On the average males maintained more eye contact than females. Positive attitudes toward the confederate were associated with high eye contact for all but low-dominant males.

481. **Fromme, Donald K., and Schmidt, Carol K.** "Affective Role Enactment and Expressive Behavior." *Journal of Personality and Social Psychology* 24 (1972) : 413-419.

Sixteen male college students participated in an experiment to determine if the enactment of affective roles (fear, anger, sorrow, and neutral) resulted in different patterns of personal space, eye contact, and rate of approach. The subjects were instructed to approach an experimental assistant, a white male wearing sunglasses, and to enact one each of the four affects. Several of the hypotheses were confirmed. Subjects maintained greatest distance while expressing fear. Greater personal space was kept for sorrow than for anger. It was also found that sorrow elicited significantly less eye contact and a tendency toward slower movements.

482. **Fry, Anna M., and Willis, Frank N.** "Invasion of Personal Space as a Function of the Age of the Invader." *Psychological Record* 21 (1971) : 385-389.

Sixty female and 60 male adults waiting in lines at a movie served as subjects. Children ages five, eight, and ten invaded the adult's personal space, while observers recorded their reactions. The five-year-old invaders received a positive reaction (smiling, talking), eight-year-olds received no observable reaction, and ten-year-olds received a negative reaction (moving or leaning away, excessive motor behavior).

483. **Fry, Rick, and Smith, Gene F.** "The Effects of Feedback and Eye Contact on Performance of a Digit-Coding Task." *Journal of Social Psychology* 96 (1975) : 145-146.

In this study of experimenter expectancy effects, 48 male subjects performed a digit-coding task. Results show that those receiving high eye contact from the tester correctly encoded more digits than the others.

484. **Frye, Jerry K.** *FIND: Frye's Index to Nonverbal Data.* Duluth, Minnesota: University of Minnesota, 1980. 344 pp.

This is a bibliography of 4,072 titles in nonverbal communication drawn from the last hundred years but primarily covering 1950 to the present. Arranged alphabetically by author, the titles are subject-indexed according to categories such as culture, deception, development, dyadic interactions, emotions, facial, environment, paralanguage, personality, and physical appearance. A very useful reference produced by the author at the University of Minnesota Computer Center, it is updated annually, and one can obtain a customized search from the data base.

485. **Fugita, Stephen S.** "Effects of Anxiety and Approval on Visual Interaction." *Journal of Personality and Social Psychology* 29 (1974) : 586-592.

Seventy-two male students experienced different levels of social anxiety by talking with a higher or lower status, approving or disapproving confederate. Subjects looked more at the approving confederate but only in the high status condition. Subjects speaking to the lower status confederate maintained an equal amount of eye contact, regardless of condition. With the approving confederate, subjects lengthened the duration of their glances over time, while they reduced the number of glances at the nonapproving confederate over time.

486. **Fugita, Stephen; Wenley, Kenneth; and Hillery, Joseph.** "Black-White Differences in Nonverbal Behavior in an Interview Setting." *Journal of Applied Social Psychology* 4 (1974) : 343-350.

Twenty black and 20 white female college students were interviewed by either a white or black college age male in an employment interview setting. Analysis of duration of eye contact, number of eye contacts, speech duration, and speech latency indicated that white subjects tended to maintain more visual interaction with both white and black interviewers than did black subjects. Black interviewers were visually interacted with less and were given shorter glances than white interviewers. Speech latency was related only to the type of question asked, while analysis of speech duration yielded no significant relationship. The authors attribute the speech latency results to anxiety produced by the racist nature of particular interview questions.

487. **Fujita, Byron N.; Harper, Robert G.; and Wiens, Arthur N.** "Encoding-Decoding and Nonverbal Emotional Messages: Sex Differences in Spontaneous and Enacted Expressions." *Journal of Nonverbal Behavior* 4 (1980) : 131-145.

Male and female encoding-decoding of spontaneous and enacted nonverbal affective behavior was evaluated using the Buck (1977) slide-viewing paradigm. The eliciting stimuli were carefully selected and evaluated to insure a comparable emotional impact on both sexes, and all subjects received the same decoding task. Consistent with previous research, females were superior decoders overall. Also as predicted, females were superior encoders, principally when reacting spontaneously to the slides. Given no evidence of differential affective arousal, this sex difference for spontaneous encoding is interpreted to reflect differences in male-female display rules. Contrary to several previous findings spontaneous and enacted encoding measures were not strongly related, especially for males, where display rules may modify their spontaneous and enacted expressive behavior in comparison to females.

488. **Furth, Hans G.** *Deafness and Learning: A Psychosocial Approach.* Belmont, California: Wadsworth Publishing Co., 1973. 127 pp.

Within this important work on deafness, there is discussion of thinking and congitive development in deaf children and thinking without language which relates to questions of the role of nonverbal patterns in cognition.

489. **Galard, Jean.** "Pour une poétique de la conduite." *Semiotica* 10 (1974) : 351-368.

Arguing that linguistic constructs for the study of the language can be applied to gestural behavior, the author posits that gesture is to behavior what the figure of speech is to discourse.

490. **Gale, Anthony; Lucas, Bonnie; Nissim, Ruth; and Harpham, Brian.** "Some EEG Correlates of Face-to-Face Contact." *British Journal of Social and Clinical Psychology* 11 (1972) : 326-332.

The EEG of 12 male undergraduates paired with a male experimenter was measured for three conditions of gaze. The experimenter either smiled at the subject, looked at the subject without smiling, or averted his/her eyes. Among the results it was found that the averted eye condition yielded higher EEG amplitudes than the other two conditions.

491. **Galin, Daniel, and Ornstein, Robert.** "Individual Differences in Cognitive Style—I. Reflective Eye Movements." *Neuropsychologia* 12 (1974) : 367-376.

Eighteen lawyers and 17 ceramicists, groups chosen for their inferred differences in verbal and spatial abilities, were given a series of performance tests and then asked 60 questions: 20 demanding verbal, logical, or arithmetic reasoning, 20 requiring spatial ability, and 20 neutral or allowing either type of answer. The direction of their first eye movement was then recorded. For direction of eye movement, lateral and vertical movements were analyzed separately, revealing significant differences between groups only in vertical movements, with ceramicists showing more upward and significantly fewer downward movements. When analyzed according to question type, there were more downward movements on verbal questions than on spatial, and significantly more stares (no movement) on spatial. Although there were no significant differences in lateral movements with this group, a modified version of the questions given to a nonspecialized group showed significant differences in lateral movements, with more rightward movements on verbal tasks than on spatial.

492. **Gallahue, David L.; Werner, Peter H.; Luedke, George C.** *A Conceptual Approach to Moving and Learning* New York: John Wiley and Sons, 1975. 423 pp. Illus.

Written for preschool and elementary teachers, this book details motor development and describes movement in relation to cognitive, affective, and perceptual-motor skills. Concepts behind the integration of movement into language arts, math, science, social studies, music and art curricula are explored through examples.

493. **Gallois, Cynthia, and Markel, Norman.** "Turn Taking: Social Personality and Conversation Style." *Journal of Personality and Social Psychology* 31 (1975) : 1134-1140.

Temporal aspects of turn-taking behavior in speech transactions were analyzed in relation to the phase of conversation and to the language spoken by 13 bilingual, Cuban college students in conversations with Spanish-speaking and English-speaking friends. Results indicated that the duration of speech and frequency of speech acts per turn were greater in English than in Spanish conversations, while Spanish conversations showed longer average switching pauses. Variations in turn-taking behaviors, when correlated to the opening, middle, and end of the conversation were the same in Spanish and English. The authors propose that this constancy of variation from phase to phase may be a useful gauge for examining the social psychology of conversational interactions by reflecting situational factors or traits involving role, social personality, and cultural norms.

494. **Galloway, Charles M.** "Analysis of Theories and Research in Nonverbal Communication." *Journal of the Association for the Study of Perception* 6 (1971) : 1-21.

The purpose of this overview of nonverbal communication is to help educate teachers about nonverbal communication and its use in the classroom. Many different aspects are covered, including research problems and nonverbal training and skill development for classroom teachers.

495. **Galloway, Charles M.** "The Challenge of Nonverbal Research." *Theory into Practice* 1 (1971) : 310-314.

Educational research needs to include nonverbal communication research. Problems in analyzing nonverbal data relate to questions of: when to look, what to look for, and how to observe. The nonverbal behavior research challenge is the collection of data showing that nonverbal cues provide crucial information unobtainable solely from the observation of verbal behavior.

496. **Galloway, Charles M.** "Nonverbal Teacher Behaviors: A Critique." *American Educational Research Journal* 11 (1974) : 305-306.

This critique of Woolfolk and Woolfolk's 1974 study suggested a hierarchy for arranging the various combinations of verbal/nonverbal behaviors as being positive/negative, so that the surprising experimental results could be explained. The researching of nonverbal teacher influences was praised.

497. **Galloway, Charles M.** "Nonverbal." *Theory Into Practice* 16 (1977) : 129-219.

Charles Galloway has studied and lectured about nonverbal communication in the classroom for two decades. This is the second issue of the education journal he edits, *Theory Into Practice*, devoted to nonverbal communication. It includes a wide range of articles on classroom nonverbal interaction, teacher nonverbal behavior, classroom space, movement and cognition, and teaching nonverbal expressive skills. Among the many authors represented are Truman Whitfield, Russell L. French, Barbara M. Grant, Dorothy Grant Hennings, Paul Byers, Laurence B. Rosenfeld, Aaron Wolfgang, and Edward T. Hall and Mildred Reed Hall.

498. **Galloway, Charles M.** "Teaching and Nonverbal Behavior." In *Nonverbal Behavior: Applications and Cultural Implications,* edited by A. Wolfgang, pp. 197-207. New York: Academic Press, 1979.

Nonverbal behavior within a classroom setting is discussed, including three dimensions of teacher activity that have been witnessed: institutional, task, and personal behaviors of the teachers. A promising approach to the recording of nonverbal behaviors is suggested, that is, recording nonverbal acts in narrative descriptions. Galloway then lists ten dimensions of encouraging-restricting models of nonverbal behavior.

499. **Gardin, Hershel; Kaplan, Kalman J.; Firestone, Ira J.; and Cowan, Gloria A.** "Proxemic Effects on Cooperation, Attitude, and Approach-Avoidance in a Prisoner's Dilemma Game." *Journal of Personality and Social Psychology* 27 (1973) : 13-18.

Ten pairs of students played the Prisoner's Dilemma game seated side by side or across the table from each other . They were allowed eye contact with partners or had it blocked. The experimenters wanted to determine the impact of different seating and eye contact patterns on cooperation and attitude. Side-by-side seating yielded more positive cooperation and attitudes when eye contact was blocked. When eye contact was available, positive outcomes for cooperation, attitude, and approach-avoidance were associated with the across-the-table position.

500. **Gardiner, Harry.** "The Use of Human Figure Drawings to Assess a Cultural Value: Smiling in Thailand." *Journal of Psychology* 80 (1972) : 203-204.

One thousand forty three drawings of men and women by Thai boys and girls aged nine to 11 supported the hypothesis that "children draw human figures with smiling faces in proportion to the degree in which smiling is socially approved or culturally valued."

501. **Gardiner, Richard Andrew.** "Nonverbal Communication Between Blacks and Whites in a School Setting." Ph.D. dissertation, The University of Florida. 1972. 71 pp. (Order No. 73-559)

Black teachers and white teachers were videotaped giving the same verbal instructions, and the videotapes were shown to black and white ninth and tenth grade students, either with or without sound, or with sound only and no picture. Students rated teachers of their own race more positively, and black students rated teachers of both races without sound significantly more positively than white students.

502. **Gardner, Rick M.; Beltramo, Janelle S.; and Krinsky, R.** "Pupillary Changes during Encoding, Storage and Retrieval of Information." *Perceptual and Motor Skills* 41 (1975) : 951-955.

Six undergraduates were asked to repeat seven-digit numbers after 0, 5, and 10 second pause intervals. Measurement of pupillary size was made each second. Dilation occurred during stimulus presentation and initial reporting; constriction occurred during the retention pause. Thus dilation appears to be related to encoding and retrieval and constriction with rehearsal of one's response.

503.   **Garfield., Charles A.** *Rediscovery of the Body: A Psychosomatic View of Life and Death.* New York: Dell Publishing Co., 1977. Illus.

This collection of articles and papers by authors from many disciplines was designed as a reader's guide to the wisdom of the body and the psychosomatic wholeness which, the editor states, gives human life its meaning in the face of death. A section on Western disciplines includes chapters on Reich, therapeutic breathing techniques,rolfing, transpersonal psychology, and a case study using rolfing, guided imagery, and group encounter. The section on Eastern disciplines includes chapters on Transcendental Meditation and Aikido, as well as four chapters on yoga. A final section on the death of the body includes articles on the experience of dying; a theory of disease based on anthropological observation; the traditional idea of sudden death due to stress; psychical and mystical perspectives on death, dying and "beyond"; and one ego functioning, fear of death, and altered states of con¼ sciousness.

504.   **Gartner, Jane E.L.** "A Study of Verbal, Vocal, and Visual Communication." Ph.D. dissertation, Columbia University. 1972. 127 pp. (Order No. 72-28,041)

Interactions involving four young married couples were presented to observers in four conditions: sound videotape, videotape without sound, audiotape, and transcript. Comparison of the kind and amount of information conveyed in the different modes showed that the visual mode differed from the other three in conveying more affective information, but less overall information and factual information, and less about personal traits apart from emotional and interpersonal ones.

505.   **Geis, F., and Viksne, V.** "Touching: Physical Contact and Level of Arousal." *American Psychological Association Annual Convention Proceedings* 7 (1972) : 179-180.

Opposite-sex pairs of students agreed to participate in a study in which they gave each other back rubs "to relax between experimental sequences." A control group did individual relaxation exercises. Results show that after the relaxation phases touch-condition subjects showed a decrease and no-touch-condition subjects showed an increase in active sweat glands.

506.   **Geisen, James Martin.** "Effects of Eye Contact, Attitude Agreement, and Presentation Mode on Impressions and Persuasion." Ph.D. dissertation, Kent State University. 1973. 136 pp. (Order No. 74073-15)

This study employed a "videophone" technique to investigate the effects of degree of eye contact, "agreement-disagreement" of an interactant, presentation mode (live or prerecorded), and sex of interactant on impressions and persuasion.

507.   **Geizer, Ronald Stanley.** "Interaction Context and the Perception of Non-verbal Dyadic Communication Systems." Ph.D. dissertation, The Ohio State University. 1971. 146 pp. (Order No. 72-15,209)

Students receiving different information about the roles of the interactants viewed three videotaped sequences from an actual physician-patient interview. It was found that nonverbal cues provided information about status or roles, that subjects' prior assumptions about the context influence evaluations given to nonverbal cues, and that subjects can evaluate dynamic nonverbal communication accurately.

508.   **Geller, Jesse D.** "The Body, Expressive Movement, and Physical Contact in Psychotherapy." In *The Power of Human Imagination,* edited by J. Senger and K. Pope, pp. 347-377. New York: Plenum Press, 1979.

From a review of some basic assumptions of body movement therapies such as bioenergetics and dance therapy, the author discusses the overemphasis on words, content, and language in psychoanalytic psychotherapy, the search for meaning and movement as psychologically expressive, and some basic contrasts between the movement therapies and psychoanalytic therapy, such as in style of therapist authority. Final sections deal with the meaning of touch in movement therapies and in psychoanalytic therapy and changing notions of countertransference. (from pre-publication manuscript)

509. **Gendlin, Eugene T.** *Focusing.* New York: Everest House, 1978.

510. **Genthner, Robert, and Moughan, James.** "Introverts' and Extroverts' Response to Nonverbal Attending Behavior." *Journal of Counseling Psychology* 24 (1977) : 144-146.

Twenty-six introverts and 26 extroverts, selected from groups of male college students through the Eysenck Personality Questionnaire, were required to tell a listener about a recent dream. Half of each group spoke to an intensely attending listener (forward leaning), while the other half spoke to a listener who maintained an upright posture. The participants then rated the listeners by use of a semantic differential-like scale. Results indicated that extroverts were more threatened by the upright posture than introverts; introverts were not threatened by either posture. Both groups viewed the forward leaning listener as more attentive, and introverts generally gave the listeners more favorable ratings.

511. **Gergerian, Edmund, and Ermiane, René.** *Atlas of Facial Expressions/Album des expressions du visage.* Paris: La Pensée Universelle, 1978. 216 pp. Illus.

Written in French in the front and English in the back, this book contains the HANEST (Head and Neck Expression Scoring Technique) with about 200 photos illustrating the expressions scored. Various facial muscles are used to identify the expressions to be scored. This technique was used with psychiatric patients to describe the movements of chronically depressed, hypomanic, and paranoid schizophrenic patients, with the technique enabling differentiation of over 100 hypomanic patients originally diagnosed as paranoid schizophrenics.

512. **Gerhardt, Lydia A.** *Moving and Knowing: The Young Child Orients Himself in Space.* Englewood Cliffs, New Jersey: Prentice-Hall, 1973. 202 pp. Illus.

The author discusses the importance of movement in space in the development of perception, imagery, and thought. Examples of classroom activities with three to six year olds are followed by a chapter on designing a curriculum integrating movement. An annotated bibliography is included.

513. **Gilbert, Anne Green.** *Teaching the Three R's through Movement Experience: A Handbook for Teachers.* Minneapolis, Minnesota: Burgess Publishing Co., 1977. 297 pp. Illus.

Based on the premise that incorporation of movement experiences into the elementary school classroom can increase motivation, learning, and stimulate growth in all realms, this book is designed as a guide for teachers to create their own programs. Presentation of basic concepts underlying development of movement experiences is followed by a description of numerous activities designed to facilitate learning in the language arts, mathematics, science, social studies, and art.

514. **Gilman, Sander L.,** ed. *The Face of Madness: Hugh W. Diamond and the Origin of Psychiatric Photography.* New York: Brunner/Mazel, 1976. 111 pp. Illus.

The book includes a 1856 paper by the first psychiatric photographer, Hugh W.

Diamond, "On the Application of Photography to the Physiognomic and Mental Phenomena of Insanity" and 54 photographs of the insane taken by Diamond and illustrations made from them. Diamond believed that the photograph captured the external symptoms of mental derangement. The case studies by the psychiatrist John Conolly (1858) that accompany 17 of the photographs demonstrate how posture, use of hands, and eye movement, as well as facial expression, were used in the diagnosis of the insane.

515. **Ginsburg, Harvey L.** "Altruism in Children: the Significance of Nonverbal Behavior." *Journal of Communication* 27 (1977) : 82-86.

This study was motivated by observations that termination of aggression between male elementary school children is primarily influenced by nonverbal cues of submission by the child under attack and that the intervention of a third child to stop the aggression tends to occur when the aggressor doesn't heed the appeasement cues. Videotapes made during a six-month period support these observations and reveal specific appeasement displays such as kneeling, bowing head, slumping shoulders, prostration, or shoe tying. In a later phase of the study third and fourth grade children saw the videotapes and were asked to predict and explain aid-giving interventions by a third child. Results show that the children were able to correctly predict if a given fight would end in aid giving or by itself; however, they were unable to verbalize the reasons for their judgments.

516. **Ginsburg, Harvey J.; Pollman, Vicki A.; and Wauson, Mitzi S.** "An Ethological Analysis of Nonverbal Inhibitors of Aggressive Behavior in Male Elementary School Children." *Developmental Psychology* 13 (1977) : 417-418.

Approximately thirty eight to 12 year old boys were observed during 24 play periods. Instances of aggressive behavior were videotaped. Analysis of the height and posture of the child under attack before cessation of the encounter showed that in most cases the child made himself smaller, a pattern interpreted as a pervasive human way to inhibit aggressive behavior.

517. **Ginsburg, Harvey J.; Pollman, Vicki A.; Wauson, Mitzi S.; and Hope, Marti L.** "Variation of Aggressive Interaction among Male Elementary School Children as a Function of Changes in Spatial Density." *Environmental Psychology and Nonverbal Behavior* 2 (1977) : 67-75.

The behavior of children was monitored during unstructured playground activity in areas of differing size. The frequency of fighting increased significantly in the smaller area, although the aggressive episodes were of briefer duration. In addition, the style of aggression differed significantly between the two conditions. Fighting in the smaller area typically involved more than two children. The results are considered in the context of Hediger's critical distance hypothesis.

518. **Gitter, A. George; Black, Harvey; and Fishman, Janet E.** "Effect of Race, Nonverbal Communication and Verbal Communication of Perception of Leadership." *Sociology and Social Research* 60 (1975) : 46-57.

Eight films of similar monologues were made by varying nonverbal cues (leader and follower characterizations), verbal cues (strong and weak language), and race (the white actor could also appear black by use of makeup and a wig.) One hundred fifty-one white students each viewed one film and rated the actor on leadership traits. Nonverbal cues were more important than verbal cues in determining perception of leadership. More leadership qualities were attributed by female observers.

519. **Gitter, A. George; Black, Harvey; and Goldman, Arthur.** "Role of Nonverbal Communication in the Perception of Leadership." *Perceptual and Motor Skills* 40 (1975) : 463-466.

To convey superior and subordinate positions two films were made of an actor delivering the same monologue twice—in one he protrayed Clark Gable doing it, and in the other Wally Cox. One hundred seven undergraduates, divided into six groups, were presented with a complete film, a silent film, or heard a soundtrack. Half of the students witnessed the "superior position" delivery, the remaining the subordinate delivery. They then rated the actor on leadership qualities. Leadership qualities were attributed more frequently to the actor in the superior position across all modes of presentation, indicating that nonverbal cues are among those very important in impression formation.

520. **Gitter, A.G.; Black, H.; and Mostofsky, D.** "Race and Sex in the Communication of Emotion." *Journal of Social Psychology* 88 (1972) : 273-276.

This study involved 48 undergraduates (24 black men and women, 24 white men and women) and examined the effects of race and sex in both decoding and encoding. Photos were taken of 20 actors as each expressed seven emotions. Each subject was presented with 35 photos in random order and asked to identify the emotion represented. Results showed black subjects perceived emotion more accurately than white subjects; the nature of the emotion and the sex of the expressor also affected perception.

521. **Gitter, George A.; Mostofsky, David; and Guichard, M.** "Some Parameters in the Perception of Gaze." *Journal of Social Psychology* 88 (1972) : 115-121.

Ten photographs depicting two white females (designated 1p and 2p) were shown to 200 undergraduates who were asked to evaluate direction of gaze, focus of gaze, and type of emotion expressed. All students were asked to evaluate 1p for the above attributes. Half the subjects were then asked to judge if 2p was looking at 1p. Among the results it was found that the presence of a second person affected the perceived direction of gaze and expression of emotion that the subjects perceived in the first person.

522. **Givens, David B.** "Shoulder Shrugging: A Densely Communicative Expressive Behavior." *Semiotica* 19 (1977) : 13-28.

Six ten-minute conversations were videotaped of all possible pairs of four students, with a verbal transcript and 105 nonlinguistic units assessed for each. Analysis focused on the 105 behavioral units, classified as: dominant-like, submssive-like, affiliative, or aversive cues, with the shoulder-shrugging complex of actions being the most closely studied.

523. **Givens, David B.** "Contrasting Nonverbal Styles of Mother-Child Interaction: Examples from a Study of Child Abuse." *Semiotica* 24 (1978) : 33-47.

Videotapes of 14 mothers playing with their two- to 2½-year-old youngsters, with half physically abusive mothers and half controls, were studied with a checklist of nonverbal behaviors. The nonverbal presentations and repertoires of the physically abusive mothers differed considerably from those of the nonabusive (control) mothers.

524. **Givens, David B.** "Greeting a Stranger: Some Commonly Used Nonverbal Signals of Aversiveness." *Semiotica* 22 (1978) : 351-367.

Fifty encounters between strangers, in each of three places—the Seattle Public Market, a popular Seattle Irish bar, and on the Unversity of Washingon campus—were studied. For only one person in the encounter detailed behavioral units were recorded of only those facial expressions, body movements, and gaze patterns that were performed subsequent to the contact-phase and that were terminated once the unfocused interaction was stopped. In 137 of 150 cases of unfocused interaction various combinations of the following activities were observed: lip-compression, lip-bite, tongue-show, tongue-in-cheek; downward, lateral, and maximal-lateral gaze avoidance; hand-to-face, hand-to-hand, hand-to-body, and hand-behind-head automanipulations; and postures involving flexion and adduction of the upper limbs, with these behaviors intitiated during the contact-phase and terminated abruptly after social contact with the stranger stopped.

525. Gladney, Karen, and Barker, Larry. "The Effects of Tactile History on Attitudes Toward and Frequency of Touching Behavior." *Sign Language Studies* 24 (1979) : 231-252.

This study measures the relationship between the individual's tactile history and two current patterns: the frequency of and attitude toward touching in public. Subjects who came from high-touch-oriented familes had more positive attitudes to touching in public than those from moderate-touch-families who in turn had more positive attitudes to touching in public than low-touch families.

526. Gladstein, Gerald A. "Nonverbal Communication and Counseling/Psychotherapy: A Review." *Counseling Psychologist* 4 (1974) : 34-57. Illus.

One hundred fifteen references involving nonverbal communication and the helping process were reviewed and arranged alphabetically within a comparison/evaluation chart. Five findings about nonverbal communication that could be useful for the counselor/therapist were listed and discussed. Nonverbal communication origins, functions, significance, and the procedures and criteria used in evaluating articles for this review were discussed; and models, strategies, and methods were suggested for further research.

527. Glaserfeld, Ernst von. "Sign, Communication, and Language." *Journal of Human Evolution* 3 (1974) : 465-474.

Noting the vagueness and confusion in the animal behavior literature with regard to the phenomenon of communication, an attempt is made to define "sign" and "communication" from the point of view of cybernetics, drawing also on Susanne Langer's philosophy of symbols. In accord with developments in feedback theory, the cyberneticist's concept of purpose makes possible a viable classification of signs as well as the discrimination of communication from other types of interaction.

528. Goffman, Erving. *Frame Analysis.* New York: Harper & Row, 1974. 586 pp.

This entertaining and well written discussion of the frameworks used in Western society to make sense of events contains much implicit description of body movement, gestures, and facial expression in its analysis of the process of keying frameworks, as in play and ritual, and fabricating frameworks, as in deception and dramatic performance. A chapter on "out-of-frame activity" discusses "directional," "disattended," and "concealment" tracks where nonverbal behaviors may function for a variety of purposes.

529. Goffman, Erving. *Gender Advertisements.* New York: Harper & Row, 1976. 84 pp. Illus.

This fascinating analysis of gender roles particularly as displayed in advertising photographs begins with an introduction by Vivian Gornick and a complex analysis of "Gender Display" and of the sociology of pictures by Goffman. The greater part of the monograph is devoted to examples of "gender commercials," hundreds of photos organized by themes such as display of rank through relative size, gender roles in the family, the "unseriousness' and "childlike" demeanor of the woman, and "licensed withdrawal" as a female role display.

530. Goldberg, Gale, and Mayerberg, Cathleen Kubiniec. "Emotional Reactions of Students to Nonverbal Teacher Behavior." *The Journal of Experimental Education* 42 (1973) : 29-32. Illus.

One hundred twenty black and white students from second and sixth grades of an urban elementary school participated in this study. The same, previously unknown, white teacher taught students a lesson, holding verbal behavior constant while varying her nonverbal behavior to be either positive, neutral, or negative. Students evaluated the teacher using a semantic differential. The "neutral" teacher was evaluated most positively by black second graders while white second graders and all sixth graders tended to evaluate most positively the "positive" teacher.

531. Goldberg, M., and Wellens, A. "A Comparison of Nonverbal Compensatory Behavior Within Direct, Face-to-Face and Television Mediated Interviews." *Journal of Applied Social Psychology* 9 (1979) : 250-260.

Gaze and smiling behaviors of 32 male subjects were related to the intimacy level of conversation topics in direct face-to-face and interactive television (IATV) interviews. Statistical analysis of the results supported predictions based on affiliative-conflict theory. Only one difference, an increase of gaze behavior during IATV interviews, was observed in comparison to the face-to-face interviews.

532. Goldstein, James Michael. "Effects of Duration of Eye Contact on Information Retention and Liking in Mixed- and Same-Sex Dyads." Ph.D. dissertation, Catholic University of America. 1977. 89 pp. (Order No. 77145-85)

144 male and female undergraduates interacted with a confederate who varied amount of eye contact to investigate how this affects liking for the confederate and the subject's retention of what is said.

533. Goldstein, Melvin A.; Kilroy, M. Catherine; and Van de Voort, David. "Gaze as a Function of Conversation and Degree of Love." *The Journal of Psychology* 92 (1976) : 227-234.

Three-minute interactions between nine "strong love" couples and ten unacquainted pairs were videotaped and scored for gaze (individual, mutual, and gaze without conversation), conversation time, mutual gaze with conversation and mutual focus. Significant differences were noted in all scores except mutual gaze during conversation, indicating that lovers tend to both talk to and gaze at each other more than strangers. Additionally, the authors comment on the economy, reliability, and accuracy of videotape to record eye contact behaviors.

534. Goldwater, Bram C. "Psychological Significance of Pupillary Movements." *Psychological Bulletin* 77 (1972) : 340-355.

This literature review covers psychological investigation using pupillary dilation, the light reflex, and spontaneous fluctuations in pupil size as dependent variables. It discusses the evidence for the effectiveness of the pupil as a research index of autonomic activity, as well as methodological problems and areas for further research. Pupillary movements are discussed with respect to affect, emotions, and attitudes; sensory stimulation and muscular activity; mental activity and attention; classical conditioning of pupillary responses.

535. Gorlitz, Dietmar, ed. *Perspectives on Attribution Research and Theory.* Cambridge, Massachusetts: Ballinger, 1981.

This anthology is edited by a psychologist experienced in nonverbal communication research and development of attributional processes in the nonverbal area. Of note here is the chapter "Attribution, Dimensionality, and Measurement: How You Measure is What You Get" by Seigfried Streufert and Susan C. Streufert. (from publisher's information)

536. **Gottheil, Edward; Thornton, Charles C.; and Exline, Ralph V.** "Appropriate and Background Affect in Facial Displays of Emotion: Comparison of Normal and Schizophrenic Males." *Archives of General Psychiatry* 33 (1976) : 565-568.

A black-and-white head-and-shoulder photograph was taken of 16 normal and 16 schizophrenic men in each of five different posed emotions (happiness, sadness, fear, surprise, anger). Six normal male raters matched the photographs with the appropriate emotion word printed on separate index cards. The mean number of correct judgments by all raters for all 32 subjects ranged from a low of 41 percent correct for the "fear" poses to a high of 90 percent correct for the "happy" poses. The hypothesis that schizophrenic men are poorer expressers of emotions than are normal men was not supported for all poses combined.

537. **Gottlieb, Jay; Gampel, Dorothy H.; and Budoff, Milton.** "Classroom Behavior of Retarded Children Before and After Integration into Regular Classes." *Journal of Special Education* 9 (1975) : 307-315.

Twenty-two educable mentally retarded (EMR) children between the ages of 103 and 157 months were assigned to two conditions: half were integrated into regular classes and half attended segregated EMR classes. The subjects were observed three times: at the beginning of the study when all attended special classes, during November of the school year in which they were assigned to the new classes, and again in May. Using a time-sampling method, observers coded the subjects' behavior according to 12 categories including attention, restlessness, self-stimulation, uncoordinated motor response, and aggressive behavior towards peers. Data on an additional 110 subjects obtained using similar procedures in previous studies had been submitted to a factor analysis that yielded three factors accounting for the variance: prosocial behavior, verbally hostile behavior, and physically hostile behavior. Analysis of the data from the present study showed that integrated and segregated subjects differed significantly only on prosocial behavior at the third observation, with the integrated subjects scoring significantly higher on this factor. Comparison with data on a nonretarded sample showed the integrated EMR children at the third observation to be engaged in higher incidences of prosocial behaviors and fewer physically aggressive behaviors, but more verbally aggressive behaviors than the nonretarded referent group.

538. **Gottman, John M.** *Marital Interaction: Experimental Investigations.* New York: Academic Press, 1979.

Reporting on his seminal work on systematic analysis of dyadic interactions, the author elaborates on the reliability, validity, generalizability, and clinical value of the "Couples Interaction Scoring System," a major section of which involves nonverbal decoding.

539. **Gottman, John; Markman, Howard; and Notarius, Cliff.** "The Topography of Marital Conflict: A Sequential Analysis of Verbal and Nonverbal Behavior." *Journal of Marriage and the Family* 39 (1977) : 461-477. Illus.

Five distressed and five nondistressed young married couples were videotaped while discussing a current marital problem. Conversation was coded for content; voice tone, facial, and body behaviors were coded for positive or negative affect. Nondistressed couples were discriminated by positive content codes and used positive nonverbal codes during lags throughout the conversation. Distressed couples were discriminated by negative nonverbal codes and were apt to use positive nonverbal codes during lags at the beginning of the conversation.

540. **Gottschalk, Louis A., and Uliana, Regina L.** "A Study of the Relationship of Nonverbal to Verbal Behavior: Effect of Lip Caressing on Hope and Oral

References as Expressed in the Content of Speech." *Comprehensive Psychiatry* 1 (1976) : 135-152.

Twenty male and female students gave four five-minute speech samples. Each five-minute period was accompanied by either hand-position A (hands at one's side) or B (one hand caressing one's lips). The speech concerned any interesting or dramatic life experience. Speech samples were tape recorded. Each subject then completed several questionnaires. Subjects spoke significantly fewer words when they caressed their lips. There were more verbal references during lip caressing to frequency of the content category of "not willing to be recipient of good fortune or God's blessings." Correlations between hope scores and social assets score were .42 during hand position A and .29 during position B.

541. **Graham, Jean Ann, and Argyle, Michael.** "A Cross-Cultural Study of the Communication of Extra-Verbal Meaning by Gestures." *International Journal of Psychology* 10 (1975) : 57-67. Illus.

English and Italian students described two-dimensional shapes of high or low verbal codability to members of their own culture who attempted to draw the shapes from their descriptions. They were to speak either with or without gestures. Both the English and Italians performed significantly better when gestures were allowed and when the shapes were of high codability. The English speakers performed significantly better overall than the Italians, but this was mainly due to their performance of high codability items. The use of hand gestures improved performance significantly more on low codability items than on high codability items. The performance of the Italians improved significantly more than that of the English when they were permitted to gesture.

542. **Graham, Jean Ann, and Heywood, Simon.** "The Effects of Elimination of Hand Gestures and of Verbal Codability on Speech Performance." *European Journal of Social Psychology* 5 (1975) : 189-195.

Five male college students were asked to describe line drawings, some easy to describe (high verbal codability) and some not (low verbal codability) with and without restriction of hand gestures. The effect of gesture on semantic content and patterning of speech was evaluated. Descriptions of low encodability drawings showed a greater mean pause length and more words, phrases, spatial relations phrases and demonstratives. Elimination of hand gestures increased the use of verbal demonstratives, spatial relations phrases, and pause during speaking time. Inhibition of gestures during description of drawings with low encodability increased the number of hesitations.

543. **Grand, Stanley; Marcos, Luis; Freedman, Norbert; and Barroso, Felix.** "Relation of Psychopathology and Bilingualism to Kinesic Aspects of Interview Behavior in Schizophrenia." *Journal of Abnormal Psychology* 86 (1977) : 492-500.

Ten bilingual schizophrenic patients were interviewed in their native and second languages and their hand movements were scored from videotapes. In this examination of the role and function of kinesics as an index of communicative stress, the results support the hypothesis that kinesic behavior as coded here with this population is related to cognitive and language-processing dysfunction.

544. **Grant, Barbara M.** "Body Language in an 'Open' Elementary School." *Education* 93 (1973) : 209-210.

The teachers' and students' body movements were observed and videotaped in K-5 multi-unit "open" schools. While the same sorts of movements were observed in both open and self-contained classrooms, the following were observed in the "open" schools: children roam over a larger area; children tend to move in more relaxed and natural ways; students use specific unique motions when using the materials, equipment, and devices within their environment; students tend to be more mobile; teachers' activities also tend to be more mobile; and teachers' postures tend to be more informal.

545. Grant, Barbara M., and Hennings, Dorothy Grant. *The Teacher Moves: An Analysis of Non-Verbal Activity.* New York: Teachers College Press, 1971. 133 pp. Illus.

Analysis of the verbalizations and physical motions of five elementary school teachers from videotape describes teachers' movements as personal or as instructional (conducting, acting or "wielding"). A description of teaching styles is followed by a chapter on improving the way a teacher moves.

546. Grant, E.C. "Non-verbal Communication in the Mentally Ill." In *Non-Verbal Communication,* edited by R.A. Hinde, pp. 349-358. Cambridge: Cambridge University Press, 1972.

The author discusses some results of the application of ethological techniques to the study of nonverbal communication in the mentally ill. Studies have found that the behavioral units used and the situations in which they are used do not differ for mentally ill and normal individuals. The ability to recognize and respond to the nonverbal cues of others may, however, be impaired in the mentally ill. These individuals may also differ from normal individuals in showing a bias towards one particular kind of behavior, a rigidification of behavior, and a restriction of behavioral repertoire. The author also describes some examples of dominance hierarchies and territorial behavior among mental patients.

547. Graves, James R., and Robinson, John D. II. "Proxemic Behavior as a Function of Inconsistent Verbal and Nonverbal Messages." *Journal of Counseling Psychology* 23 (1976) : 333-338.

Eighty college students role-played a standard counseling situation with a confederate whose nonverbal behaviors (eye contact, orientation, trunk lean, and leg orientation) and level of verbal empathy were consistently positive or negative or inconsistent (positive nonverbal with negative verbal or negative nonverbal with positive verbal). The inconsistent conditions resulted in greater interpersonal distance than the consistent conditions. Positive verbal behavior paired with negative nonverbal behavior produced the greatest distance. Counselors also received higher ratings of genuineness in the consistent conditions.

548. Gray, Sandra Lee. "Eye Contact as a Function of Sex, Race, and Interpersonal Needs." Ph.D. dissertation, Case Western Reserve University. 1971. 46 pp. (Order No. 71228-05)

Ninety-nine white college freshman talked to either a black or white male interviewer during a low-stress interview. The amount of time the subject looked at the interviewer was recorded in order to determine how it is affected by need for affiliation, dominance, sex of subject, and race of interviewer.

549. Green, Jerald R. "A Focus Report: Kinesics in the Foreign-Language Classroom." *Foreign Language Annals* 5 (1971) : 62-68.

In this article addressed primarily to foreign-language teachers, the author discusses the history of the cultural study of gestures in foreign-language classes and notes the need for comprehensive cross-cultural gesture inventories. He presents the basic dialogue found in most language texts as an ideal place for the integration of culturally appropriate nonverbal behaviors and discusses the materials available for the foreign-language teacher, most of which deal with pedagogical applications of French or Spanish kinesic patterns.

550. **Greenbaum, Paul, and Rosenfeld, Howard M.** "Patterns of Avoidance in Response to Interpersonal Staring and Proximity: Effects of Bystanders on Drivers at a Traffic Intersection." *Journal of Personality and Social Psychology* 36 (1978) : 575-587.

A male confederate seated at one of eight distances from a curb (0-12 meters) turned and stared at drivers approaching a red light. The stopping position, gaze behavior, verbalization, speed and latency of 846 drivers' departures were measured. Forty-five percent of drivers stopped their cars in positions which avoided eye contact with the confederate (avoidant drivers). Up to 3.5 meters distance nonavoidant drivers tended to gaze and verbalize. Among silent drivers, decreased driver gaze and increased departure speed were found at all distances. Females exhibited more avoidance behaviors than males.

551. **Greenbaum, Paul E., and Rosenfeld, Howard M.** "Varieties of Touching in Greetings: Sequential Structure and Sex-Related Differences." *Journal of Nonverbal Behavior* 5 (1980) : 13-25.

The functional significance of structural and sex-related differences in greeting behavior was analyzed through systematic observation of naturally-occurring contact greetings. Subjects were 152 greeting dyads, composed of airline travelers and their greeters. Greeting sequences were found to contain one or more of seven discrete types of behavioral components. Type of greeting varied with location in sequence and sex-composition of dyad. The handshake, mutual-lip kiss, and face kiss occurred early in greeting sequences, whereas hand to upper body was the characteristic terminating act. Male-male dyads typically engaged in a brief, mutual handshake. In contrast, female-female and cross-sex dyads displayed relatively longer contacts, composed of mutual-lip kisses, mutual-face contacts, embraces, and hand-to-upper-body touches.

552. **Greenberg, Carl I., and Firestone, Ira J.** "Compensatory Responses to Crowding: Effects of Personal Space Intrusion and Privacy Reduction." *Journal of Personality and Social Psychology* 35 (1977) : 637-644.

One hundred twenty-eight male students assigned to an interview experienced spatial intrusion, surveillance by other students or no surveillance, and sat in a corner seat location or a center seat location. Intrusion and surveillance each produced greater degrees of felt crowding than no intrusion and no surveillance. The experimenters concluded that intrusion is the more potent determiner of felt crowding.

553. **Greene, Les R.** "Body Image Boundaries and Small Group Seating Arrangements." *Journal of Consulting and Clinical Psychology* 44 (1976) : 244-249.

It way hypothesized that more body image "boundary-indefinite" than "boundary-definite" subjects would prefer more peripheral seats in a group. A study of 40 male and 16 female undergraduates pretested on the body image boundary variable confirmed the predicted tendency towards greater defensive distancing by boundary-indefinite participants.

554. **Greenfield, Patricia Marks, and Smith, Joshua H.** *The Structure of Communication in Early Language Development.* New York: Academic Press, 1976. 238 pp.

This study of early language acquisition looked at the development of single-word utterances in two children. The authors focused on how children combine words with nonverbal cues such as gesture, looking, and intonation in systematic ways that are related to the structure of language. The role of dialogue in the development of language is also stressed.

555. **Greenfield, Sarah Curtice.** "Notation Systems for Transcribing Verbal and Nonverbal Behavior in Adult Education Research: Linguistics (Phonetics and Phonemics), Paralinguistics, Proxemics, the Microanalysis of Organized Flow of Behavior, Haptics, Dance Notations, and Kinesics." Ph.D. dissertation, Arizona State University. 1975. 500 pp.

An extensive investigation which included examination and description of notation systems for transcribing human communicative behavior, particularly in an adult education research context, is presented. Seven multidisciplinary research projects utliizing two or more of these notation systems are described.

556. **Greenfield, Sarah C.** "Navajo-Anglo Nonverbal Communication." *Journal of the Arizona Communication and Theater Association* 10 (1979) : 1-3.

This anecdotal record describes some of the author's experiences as an Anglo counselor for Navajo seventh and eighth grade students. Observations include the Navajos' avoidance of eye contact and a description of the Navajo handshake, both of which are compared with Edward Hall's descriptions of these during the early 1930s.

557. **Greenspan, Stephen; Barenboim, Carl; and Chandler, Michael J.** "Empathy and Pseudo-Empathy: The Affective Judgments of First and Third Graders." *Journal of Genetic Psychology* 129 (1976) : 77-88.

Eighty first and third graders were presented with two videotaped interactions. Half viewed an unambiguous tape and half viewed a similar but ambiguous interaction in which the character's nonverbal affective response was incongruent with the situation. As predicted, both groups were similar in empathetic response to the actor in the unambiguous tape. However, first grade subjects relied on simplistic inference strategies based on only one of the incongruous cues, while third grade subjects recognized and expressed difficulty in resolving the ambiguities. These age differences are discussed within a Piagetian framework.

558. **Greer, Rachel Dean.** "The Effects of a Program of Total Body Movement Upon the Educable Mentally Retarded Child's Ability to Understand Selected Geometric Forms." Ed.D. dissertation, Northwestern State University of Louisiana. 1972. 200 pp.

A program including activities such as movement of the whole body through space, contact skills, balance skills, and bilateral skills was designed to test the program's effects on the ability of the educable mentally retarded child to understand certain geometric forms.

559. **Grieve, D.W.; Miller, D.I.; Mitchelson, D.; Paul, J.P.; and Smith, A.J.** *Techniques for the Analysis of Human Movement.* London: Lepus Books, 1975. 177 pp. Illus.

The techniques reviewed include photographic, computer simulation, EMG, and use of dynamometers. Available equipment, methods of analysis, advantages and disadvantages of each technique are presented in detail.

560. **Griffard, Charles David.** "An Adaptation of the Linguistic-Kinesics Research Model to College Classroom Interaction Analysis." Ph.D. dissertation, University of Pittsburgh. 1971. 165 pp. (Order No. 71261-64)

Microanalysis of a 16-mm film of two college classes was done, measuring the number of students sharing movement with the teacher every one second. Consistent relationships were noted between teacher and student nonverbal behavior and the verbal context in which the posture was shared.

561.   **Griffin, Jeanne Gemmil.** "The Effect of Self-Disclosure on Seating Position, Related Differences in Eye Contact, and Promise of Feedback." Ph.D dissertation, Templé University. 1978. 153 pp. (Order No. 78122-08)

562.   **Griffitt, William; May, James; and Veitch, Russell.** "Sexual Stimulation and Interpersonal Behavior: Heterosexual Evaluative Responses, Visual Behavior, and Physical Proximity." *Journal of Personality and Social Psychology* 30 (1974) : 367-377.

In one of two studies reported here 27 male and 25 female subjects experienced (reading) erotica-produced sexual arousal and were then placed in the company of a male and female confederate. Their visual interaction and seating choices (next to a male or female) were noted. Subjects of both sexes attended visually more to opposite sex than same-sex confederates. Sexually aroused subjects who responded negatively to sexual stimulation physically avoided heterosexual persons in seating choice. Those who responded positively to sex stimulation looked more at opposite-sex confederates.

563.   **Grossnickle, William F.; Lao, Rosina C.; Martoccia, C.T.; Range, Donna C.; and Walters, Frances C.** "Complexity of Effects of Personal Space." *Psychological Reports* 36 (1975) : 237-238.

In two studies (one a replication of the other), 360 subjects of both sexes listened to a female speaker at various distances (far, intermediate, and close). Subjects' attitude change on the topic and attitudes toward the speaker were measured. Neither study found a relationship between distance of a speaker and her persuasive impact. In one study subjects felt that the close distance made them nervous. In the other, subjects perceived the speaker to be most sincere at the intermediate distance.

564.   **Grove, Cornelius Lee.** "Nonverbal Behavior, Cross-Cultural Contact, and the Urban Classroom Teacher." *Equal Opportunity Review* (February 1976). New York: ERIC Clearinghouse on Urban Education. 5 pp.

This short paper reviews the literature on nonverbal communication and cultural differences for the urban educator. Studies of differences in spatial assumptions between linguistic groups and sources of interracial misunderstanding are cited, as well as research for cross-cultural differences in eye contact, smiling, and spatial preferences. Directions for teachers and further readings are suggested.

565.   **Guardo, Carol J.** "Personal Space, Sex Differences, and Interpersonal Attraction." *The Journal of Psychology* 92 (1976) : 9-14.

Fifty sixth graders placed cutouts of figures representing themselves near drawings of same-sex peers described as having one of 14 attractive or unattractive qualities. All children tended to place figures closer to peers described as outgoing, happy-go-lucky, intelligent, and forthright and farther away from those described as emotionally labile and expedient. Boys were significantly more drawn toward vigorous and assertive peers, and distanced from apprehensive and labile peers. Girls were drawn toward the tender-minded and distanced from the phlegmatic.

566.   **Guardo, Carol J., and Meisels, Murray.** "Factor Structure of Children's Personal Space Schemata." *Child Development* 42 (1971) : 1307-1312.

Four hundred thirty-one children in grades three to ten were categorized into four sex and age groups. Subjects were asked to manipulate a silhouette figure representing the self in relation to printed figures described as friends, strangers, and liked, disliked, or feared persons, and the results were factor analyzed. Females had consistent spatial schemata across age groups, the schemata being more rigid for older girls. Males showed more development of schemata with age. Females were found to have a schema for patterning interactions with strangers, while males did not. Females also tended to have spatial patterns based on the emotional tone of the interaction, while males tended to base their spatial behavior on the sex of the interactant.

567. Guilmet, George M. "Instructor Reaction to Verbal and Nonverbal-Visual Styles: An Example of Navajo and Caucasian Children." *Anthropology and Education Quarterly* 10 (1979) : 254-266.

Thirteen Navajo and seven Caucasian preschool and day-care students in an urban setting were studied. Using a technique created for this study, observations were made of the subjects and their instructors, including distance from student and talk/non-talk between subjects and instructors. Instructors were more often nearer and talking to the Caucasian students than the Navajo students. Caucasian students were more often attended to than were the Navajo students, and an evaluation program was discussed to offset the instructors' differentially attending to the two groups.

568. Gunning, Susan Volwiler, and Holmes, Thomas H. "Dance Therapy with Psychotic Children." *Archives of General Psychiatry* 28 (1975) : 707-713.

The results of continuous evaluation and observation of strengths and disturbances in the movement repertoires of psychotic children ages three to 12 are reported. Each child received two years of dance therapy. The Volwiler Body Movement Analysis scale (VBMA, developed to evaluate the effect of the therapy) provided a quantitative assessment of 19 aspects of body movement. The data indicate that the psychotic children were significantly different from the control group of children in most categories of body movment. Scale assessment at the end of dance therapy treatment indicated that most of the disordered body-movement patterns had improved.

569. Guthrie, R. Dale. *Body Hot Spots: The Anatomy of Social Organs and Behavior.* New York: Van Nostrand Reinhold Co., 1976. 240 pp. Illus.

This book correlates changes in appearance with the evolution of human behavior. For example, bearded faces are discussed in relation to menacing behavior, use of the eyes are described in relation to menacing behavior, use of the eyes are described in relation to emotion, and the sex differences in postures are reviewed.

570. Guttentag, Marcia. "Negro-White Differences in Children's Movement." *Perceptual and Motor Skills* 35 (1972) : 435-436.

An observational study of the amount and variety of spontaneous gross movement in black and white four year olds. There was a greater amount and variety of movement among the black children.

571. Haase, Richard F., and Markey, Martin J. "A Methodological Note on the Study of Personal Space." *Journal of Consulting and Clinical Psychology* 40 (1973) : 122-125.

Four common proxemic methodologies were compared in a study with 28 male and eight female students. Live participation, observation of live actors, felt-board placement, and judgment of photographs were the methods examined. Results indicate that live observations and felt-board techniques were more accurate representations of subject's actual spatial behavior than photograph judgments.

572. Haase, Richard F., and Tepper, Donald T. Jr. "Nonverbal Components of Empathetic Communication." *Journal of Counseling Psychology* 19 (1972) : 417-424.

Fifty-two subjects took the role of client or counselor to participate in this study of the communication of empathy in the counseling dyad. Five factors in 48 different combinations were performed by the counselors: eye contact (eye contact-no eye contact), trunk lean (forward-backward), body orientation (direct-rotated), distance (36-72 inches), and levels of verbal empathy (high-low-medium). The 26 counselors were then shown a videotape of these interactions and asked to judge each combination as to degree of empathy communicated. Among the results it was found that maintaining eye contact, forward trunk lean, close distance, and medium or high-rated verbal empathy all independently produced higher levels of judged empathy. It was also found that the nonverbal components produced slightly more than twice as much variance in the judged level of empathy than the verbal message.

573.   **Hackney, Harold.** "Facial Gestures and Subject Expression of Feelings." *Journal of Counseling Psychology* 21 (1974) : 173-178.

The experiment was designed to test the effects of four levels of nonverbal behavior—no expression, head nod, smile, and head nod and smile combination—by a male and female experimenter on 72 female subjects in a quasi-interview setting. Among the results it was found that subjects had greater amounts of feeling and self-reference affect responses for all but the "no expression" condition with the female experimenter but not the male experimenter.

574.   **Haft-Pomrock, Yael.** "Chirology as a Self-Creating Mirror." *Confinia Psychiatrica* 21 (1978) : 51-57. Illus.

Chirology is based on the assumption that the structure of the hand and the inter-relations and correspondences of the components—palms, fingers, elevation of the hands—are basically connected with psychic structures and with the nervous system. Research has found that the formation, tonus, and expression of the hand and its lines reflect personality.

575.   **Hager, Joseph C., and Ekman, Paul.** "Long-Distance Transmission of Facial Affect Signals." *Ethology and Socobiology* 1 (1979) : 77-82.

This study examined the distance at which certain facial expressions can transmit affect messages. Photographs of facial expressions which represented six affects were shown to 49 observers who composed four groups, 30, 35, 40, and 45 meters away from the photographs. The results indicated that every observer was able to label the expressions accurately, although accuracy declined as distance increased.

576.   **Hahn, M.E., and Simmel, E.C.,** eds. *Communicative Behavior and Evolution.* New York: Academic Press, 1976. 176 pp. Illus.

In the chapter "Concerning the Evolution of Nonverbal Communication in Man" by T.K. Pitcairn and I. Eibl-Eibesfeldt, examples cited include early infant grasping and self-protective behavior, gaze fixation of blind children, and the similarity of facial expression between deaf-blind and normal children. Similar greeting behaviors of adults, infants, and chimpanzees are noted through photographs. The human smile is discussed in relation to the chimpanzee play face and bare-teeth, open-mouth grimace. Other chapters consider evolution, behavior and language, genetics and communication, the evolution of communicative patterns in animals and of learned language in chimpanzees.

577.   **Haith, Marshall M.** "The Forgotten Message of the Infant Smile." *Merrill-Palmer Quarterly* 18 (1972) : 321-322.

Reacting to an emphasis in the literature on the external aspects of infant smiling (for example, effect of others, smiling as a triggered response), the author argues for consideration of the smile as a reflection of the infant's internal (affective as well as cognitive) state.

578. **Hall, Edward T.** "Mental Health Research and Out-of-Awareness Cultural Systems." In *Cultural Illness and Health: Essays in Human Adaptation,* edited by L. Nader and T.W. Maretzki, pp. 97-103. Washington, D.C.: American Anthropological Association, 1973.

At this conference of psychiatrists and anthropologists meeting to discuss anthropological contributions to the field of mental health, Hall focuses on cultural communication problems that anthropologists already have examined and found to be relevant, concentrating on those findings concerned with nonverbal communications of space, proxemics, and building construction.

Interviewer: Your work on proxemics has generated a great deal of research on people's use of space in the last ten years. Are there trends in this research that surprise you?

Hall: In some ways. It's not disappointing, but I hoped people would do more with my work as a whole system. What they've done is taken little bits and pieces of it. It means that proxemics has become fragmented, and actually it is a system and it all fits together. It is possible, of course, to take the little pieces and work with them. Personal distance can be studied itself or how people handle architectural spaces, or you can take all the sensory stuff and work with that. But you are still left with fragments and a coherent system has been linearized. As soon as you linearize, of course, it goes off in one direction.

Edward T. Hall quoted in interview by Martha Davis for *Kinesis* 1 (1978) : 10.

579. **Hall, Edward T.** *Handbook for Proxemic Research.* Washington, D.C.: The Society for the Anthropology of Visual Communication, 1974. 124 pp. Illus.

Handbook for Proxemic Research is exactly that: a how-to-do-it book for conducting proxemic research. Included are the coding manuals and statistical analysis methods necessary for using this revised proxetic notation with a computer, plus computer programs (PROX and DATAGRF) specifically designed for proxemic computer analysis. Background and theory about proxemic research are also included. Several studies are described. One found that photographers from the same ethnic group were more reliable at photographing the significant interactional changes taking place. A pilot study was conducted using proxetic notation of photographs of three groups: working class blacks, Latins, and North European whites. Group comparisons on individual variables found several proxetic variables to be statistically significant. Analysis of total scores indicated that the blacks were significantly more involved than either Latins or whites in the particular context in which they were observed. If only one variable were selected for indicating overall involvement, for the blacks it would be kinesthetics, for whites it would be eye behavior, and, if anything could serve for Latins, kinesthetics would be the choice. Proxetic notation was also applied to motion picture analysis; results of how one rater decoded two films with similar situations and subjects are presented. Another pilot study involved one black and one white encoding the same data. Results indicated similarities on coding ten of the 18 variables, but the remaining eight did show differences in the perception and coding by the two raters.

580. **Hall, Edward T.** *Beyond Culture.* Garden City, New York: Anchor Press/Doubleday, 1977. 298 pp.

Beyond Culture is concerned with culture as a human extension system that can be evolved much faster than the body. Significant portions of such extension systems still function out of awareness, making awareness and change very difficult. Hall defines an action frame as the sequence of events, while action chains are cultural transactions with the inanimate environment and/or other extension systems; other living things; and/or intrapsychic transactions involving various parts of one's psyche. Situational frames are the materials and contexts within which these actions occur. These structural features of cultures direct the organization of each person's psyche, thus having a profound effect upon everything, including, for example, the ways people behave and organize their lives, and how they think and look at things. Monochronic versus polychronic use of time is an example of how cultures differ, while high-context versus low-context is another example of cultural differences in structuring and valuing of interactions and communication. How one learns, as well as what one learns, is also culturally determined. This learning is our way of evolving to ensure the survival of the individual, the culture, and the species. Eventually, humans must begin to try to transcend both obvious overt culture and the more important unconscious culture.

581. Hall, Edward T., and Hall, Mildred Reed. "Nonverbal Communication for Educators." *Theory into Practice* 16 (1977) : 141-144.

The authors argue that, if a teacher is prejudiced, this must be made explicit and taken into account, known, and accepted on both sides. They underline the higher status of "WASPs." There are great advantages in the interethnic situation to working and thinking in contextual terms (because the teacher may not know what stimulus to apply in many cases). Nonverbal behavior can be correctly interpreted by knowing the meaning in the context of the person's own culture. Signals of how one is clued in and listening differ in different cultures. Proxemics vary. Discipline is handled differently by different ethnic groups; and attitudes toward competition also vary widely from one culture to another.

582. Hall, Judith A. "Gender Effects in Decoding Nonverbal Cues." *Psychological Bulletin* 85 (1978) : 845-857.

The results of 75 studies addressing the question of gender differences in ability to decode nonverbal cues of emotion for face, body, or vocal cues (alone or in combination) are reviewed. The research is summarized according to direction of effects, effect sizes, and significance levels. The studies were coded according to year, sample size, age of judges, sex, and age of stimulus person(s), and the channel of communication and medium. Among the results the studies showed a clear female advantage and that the effect size was significantly greater for visual-plus-auditory studies than for a single modality.

583. Halverson, Charles F., Jr., and Waldron, Mary F. "The Relation of Mechanically Recorded Activity Level to Varieties of Preschool Play Behavior." *Child Development* 44 (1973) : 678-681.

Activity data of 33 boys and 25 girls age 2½ years were recorded over five weeks in three ways: by an individually worn activity recorder device; observations of time spent and frequencies of behaviors; and daily ratings by two teachers on an 11-point scale on social, emotional, and play dimensions. Observed activity data and teachers' ratings were significantly related to activity recorder data. Boys' activity level was more consistent indoors and outdoors than girls'. Boys were more active than girls outdoors. Other data suggest boys' activity levels were more affected by playing in groups.

584. Hamilton, Marshall L. "Imitation of Facial Expression of Emotion." *Journal of Psychology* 80 (1972) : 345-350.

Fifty-four nursery school children were tested under three conditions for their ability to imitate facial expressions of emotions. In condition A the children viewed slides of an adult female posing nine emotional expressions. An observer determined which of the nine expressions the child's face was showing. In condition B the child was instructed to pick out a face "just like the one the lady made" from a set of drawings. In condition C the children were asked to imitate a series of behaviors done by the model who was also in the slides (touching her nose, clapping hands). Among the results it was found that the children imitated facial expressions at above chance levels in all conditions.

585. **Hamilton, Marshall L.** "Imitative Behavior and Expressive Ability in Facial Expression of Emotion." *Developmental Psychology* 8 (1973) : 138.

Twenty-four nursery school, second- and fifth-grade children participated in this experiment which found that the ability to recognize and imitate facial expressions of emotion improves with age while the level of spontaneous imitation does not increase with age.

586. **Hanna, Judith Lynne.** "African Dance: Some Implications for Dance Therapy." *American Journal of Dance Therapy* 2 (1978) : 3-15. Illus.

The latent and explicit functions of dance, particularly that of the Ubakala, are outlined. Hanna proposes three ways in which dance-plays function therapeutically: anticipatory psychic management—a kind of preparation or education; alternative catharsis-tension release; and paradox mediation-balancing opposites. She presents a semantic grid designed to help understand Ubakala dance-plays and applicable to the therapeutic process in which dance is the mode of communication.

587. **Hanna, Judith Lynne.** "Movements Towards Understanding Humans through the Anthropological Study of Dance." *Current Anthropology* 20 (1979) : 313-339.

This paper offers a summary of the field and a communication model for the study of dance within the discipline of anthropology. It presents a theoretical orientation to dance which integrates textual and contextual approaches and symbolic interaction. With modification, the model is applicable to the study of other forms of performance, for example, ritual and play.

588. **Hanna, Judith Lynne.** *The Anthropology of Dance: A Selected Bibliography.* (Distributors: Seattle: R.L. Shep; Amsterdam: GeNabrink; Toronto: Theatrebooks; New York: Dance Mart; Oakland: Dance Etc.) 1979.

A selected bibliography with sections such as communication and semiotics, movement notation and analytic units, structural analysis of dance, politics and dance, and other topics.

589. **Hanna, Judith Lynne.** *To Dance Is Human.* Austin and London: University of Texas Press, 1979. 327 pp. Illus.

The purpose of this major work is "To generate theory and insights into dance as human thought and action and to stimulate dance research." The author uses a communication model of dance to discuss the intrinsic and extrinsic meanings of dance. Recurrent themes include a search for psychobiological and social functions and the interrelation of psyche/soma/society/environment. The text is illustrated with several models of dance analysis, and the appendix consists of a chart of Dance Movement Data Categories and a sample profile from the Ubakala culture. In a concluding chapter, dance research potentials and the application of theory are discussed. A lengthy reference section and extensive index follow.

590. **Hanna, Judith Lynne.** "Toward Semantic Analysis of Movement Behavior: Concepts and Problems." *Semiotica* 25 (1979) : 77-119.

The author presents a semantic analysis of movement and a semantic grid for conveying meaning in movement as a tool for data collection and analysis applicable to a variety of structured movement activities.

591. **Hanna, Judith Lynne.** "African Dance Research: Past, Present, and Future" *Africana Journal* 11 (1980) : 33-51.

A very comprehensive overview of research on African dance in terms of its part in culture and society. Topics covered include attempts at dance description, dance structure apart from context, literature which overgeneralizes and ignores regional variation, and directions for the future. It has an extensive bibliography. (from prepublication draft)

592. **Hanna, Judith Lynne.** "Dance." In *Encyclopedic Dictionary of Semiotics,* edited by T.A. Sebeok. Bloomington, Indiana: Indiana University Press, forthcoming.

What dance is, how its meaning(s) can be analyzed, dance devices for conveying and encapsulating meaning, the syntactics of dance, and types of structural analysis of dance are described in this very concise and condensed essay. It includes a lengthy bibliography. (from prepublication draft)

593. **Hanna, Judith Lynne.** *Like Me, Meddle Me: Life in a Desegregated School.* Urbana, Illinois: University of Illinois Press, forthcoming.

This book presents children's perceptions of life in a desegregated school. Four pairs of contrastive threads weave through the story: black/white, working class/middle class, neighbor/stranger, and child/adult. Children's reflections and the researcher's observations identify "meddlin'"—meaning verbal and nonverbal aggression—as the key catalyst and instrument of social dissonance among groups in the school. Low-income neighborhood black children were found to engage in greater and more intense "meddlin'" than others, with deleterious results for integration efforts. The patterns of "meddlin'" are described within evolutionary and historical perspectives. Consequences and prescriptive strategies are suggested. (abstract by the author)

594. **Hanna, Judith Lynne.** "Public Social Policy and the Children's World: Implications of Ethnographic Research for Desegregated Schooling." In *Doing the Ethnography of Schooling: Educational Anthropology in Action,* edited by G.D. Spindler. New York: Holt, Rinehart and Winston, forthcoming.

Within this excellent report of children's accounts of their school experience and the author's observations of aggression and racial tension within a desegregated grade school, there is a section on the behavior of aggression or "meddlin'" displayed in various parts of the school. The styles and contexts of fighting are elaborately described with numerous examples such as spontaneous dances of rebellion, provocative facial expressions, types of walk. Six causes of "meddlin'" are discussed. There is a section on the vicissitudes of such field work and the importance of observing the nonverbal level. The author concludes with an extensive discussion of the implications of the study for education and social policy.

595. **Hansen, Judith Friedman.** "Proxemics and the Interpretive Process in Human Communication." *Semiotica* 17 (1976) : 165-179.

Beginning as a book review of Edward Hall's *Handbook for Proxemic Research,* the major portion of this article was concerned primarily with theoretical bases underlying some of Hall's assumptions.

596. **Hansen, Judith Friedman.** "The Proxemics of Danish Daily Life." *Studies in the Anthropology of Visual Communication* 3 (1976) : 52-62. Illus.

Arguing for a holistic analysis of proxemic behavior involving cultural definitions, attitudes, values, and behavioral strategies, the author first examines key Danish concepts and values and shows how they are reflected in the spatial and physical layout of homes and public areas and how they affect behavior. Proxemic relations are then illustrated in a description of a social gathering in the home. Formation of interaction clusters, placement of lights, eye contact, tactile contact, and orientation to the interaction are among the dimensions discussed. Photographs and a cartoon illustrate the text.

597. **Hardee, Betty B.** "Interpersonal Distance, Eye Contact, and Stigmatization: A Test of the Equilibrium Model." Ph.D. dissertation, Johns Hopkins University. 1976. 78 pp. (Order No. 76229-20)

The effects of handicaps and of potential for eye contact on spatial invasions and other nonverbal behavior were investigated in two field experiments.

598. **Hargadine, Martha P.** "Development and Criticism of a Measurement Instrument for Scope of Movement." *Conference Proceedings of the American Dance Therapy Association* 8 (1974) : 152-161.

To determine the relationship between self-actualization and scope of movement, 24 students, aged 17 to 54, with less than two years of dance, were observed. The scope of movement was defined as total amount of different movement patterns. No significant relationship was found between Movement Scope Check List scores and Shostrom's Personality Orientation Inventory. The author questions the general "expansion of movement vocabulary" as a therapeutic goal. The MSCL is included in an appendix.

599. **Hargadine, Martha P.** "Agreement of Independent Estimates of Movement Synchrony from One-Time Observations." *Conference Proceedings of the American Dance Therapy Association* 9 (1975) : 156-163.

Thirty students from university dance classes viewed a videotape of paired students attempting to achieve movement synchrony and rated them on overall synchrony and specific aspects of synchrony. Correlation was low to insignificant on five ratings.

600. **Harper, Lawrence V. and Sanders, Karen M.** "Preschool Children's Use of Space: Sex Differences in Outdoor Play." *Developmental Psychology* 11 (1975) : 119.

Sixty-four three- to five-year-old children were observed during 35-50 minute play periods. Each child was observed at least 30 times. Both indoor and outdoor play space was available to the children. Boys spent more time outdoors and used a greater variety of play spaces. Girls tended to play at craft tables and kitchens, while boys tended to play in the sand, on tractors, climbing structures, and in the equipment shed.

601. **Harper, Robert; Wiens, Arthur; and Matarazzo, Joseph.** *Nonverbal Communication: The State of the Art.* New York: John Wiley and Sons, 1978. 355 pp.

This book covers much of the literature on nonverbal communication and organizes it in such a way as to overview the field, map out domains and promising areas of research, and provide an up-to-date summary into which new findings can be integrated. The authors group the research into the realms of paralanguage, facial expressions, kinesics, eye and visual behavior, and proxemics and discuss each of these areas in detail.

602. **Harper, Robert G.; Wiens, Arthur N.; and Matarazzo, Joseph D.** "The Relationship Between Encoding-Decoding of Visual Nonverbal Emotional Cues." *Semiotica* 28 (1979) : 171-192.

Twenty-one adult males were unobtrusively videotaped while watching emotion-arousing slides previously selected as being the best elicitors of four emotions (happy, interest, sad, or injury). A videotape was prepared illustrating each of the four emotions, and segments were selected to include two high, two medium, and two low expressive encoding subjects. Decoding subjects were the same people approximately two weeks later. They watched two hour-long videotapes to identify the emotions. Subjects also completed personality questionnaires and other measures during both the encoding and decoding phases. Encoding ability was measured by the number of eliciting stimuli (that is, slide categories) correctly identified by a specially designated group of observers who viewed the encoding subjects' videotaped emotional reactions to the slides. Decoding ability was measured by the number of emotion-arousing categories correctly identified from watching the taped subjects' nonverbal reactions to the slides. No relationship was found between encoding and decoding skills.

603. Harris, Bruce; Luginbuhl, James E.R.; and Fishbein, Jill E. "Density and Personal Space in a Field Setting." *Social Psychology* 41 (1978) : 350-353.

Two male and two female experimenters invaded the personal space of 189 male and female shoppers at a large shopping mall under conditions of high and low density. Male shoppers were more likely to react to the spatial intrusion under conditions of low density but only by a male invader. Although invaded subjects reacted with various types of body movements, there were no observed instances of subjects changing their facial expressions.

604. Harris, Joanna G. "Movement Observation in Context." *American Journal of Dance Therapy* 2 (1978) : 8-9.

This brief article presents a chart of considerations for movement observation. The observation topics are divided into general context and specific movement themes, and a sample observation is given.

605. Harris, Joanna G., and Beers, Judy, eds. *Bibliography on Dance Therapy 1974: Books/Articles/Films.* Columbia, Maryland: American Dance Therapy Association, 1974. 67 pp.

This compact bibliography has arranged titles on dance therapy by topic. The topics include the theory, practice, and research of dance therapy; nonverbal communication (emotion and expressive movement); body image; and group dynamics.

606. Harrison, Michael H. "Eye Contact, Attribution and Aggression: Situational Determinants of Aggressive Behavior and Person Perception." Ph.D. dissertation, University of Pennsylvania. 1974. 93 pp. (Order No. 75027-35)

Gazing and staring were experimentally investigated to examine whether victims emit nonverbal messages which may either inhibit or provoke further aggression.

607. Harrison, Randall P. "Nonverbal Communication." In *Handbook of Communication* edited by I. de Sola Pool, W. Schramm, F.W. Frey, N. Maccoby, and E.B. Parker, pp. 93-115. Chicago: Rand-McNally, 1973.

This article presents an overview of research into nonverbal communication as of 1973. The author begins by classifying nonverbal signs according to performance codes, artifactual codes, mediational codes, and contextual codes. Research into nonverbal communication is put into historical perspective by a discussion of early landmark studies. The work of Ray Birdwhistell is discussed as typifying the anthropological-linguistic tradition in recent research, and the work of Paul Ekman as exemplifying the psychological tradition. The article also contains a summary of research findings, especially on facial expression, but also on eye and head behavior, posture, spacing, gesture, and touch. The author ends with a discussion of future trends in the field, including the increasing influence of ethology, the development of more sophisticated recording technology, and increased application of research findings in educational and therapeutic fields. The article includes a bibliography of over 250 items.

608. **Harrison, Randall P.** *Beyond Words: An Introduction to Nonverbal Communication.* Englewood Cliffs, New Jersey: Prentice-Hall, 1974. 210 pp. Illus.

Explanation of a systems approach to the understanding of communication is followed by descriptions of performance codes, paralinguistics, facial expressions, proxemics, and gesture behavior. Each chapter begins and ends with questions designed to provoke further discussion and thought in this college-level textbook.

609. **Harrison, Randall P.** "The Face in Face-to-Face Interaction." In *Explorations in Interpersonal Communication,* edited by G. Miller, pp. 217-235. Beverly Hills, California: Sage Publications, 1976. Illus.

To illustrate facial codes the author describes a study where subjects matched adjectives with pictographs differing in the eyebrow angle, openness of eye and shape of mouth. Cultural and personal display rules are considered in a discussion of interpersonal implications.

610. **Harrison, Randall.** "Profile: Paul Ekman." *The Kinesis Report: News and Views of Nonverbal Communication* 3 (Winter 1980) : 1-4.

An interview with psychologist Paul Ekman, in which he recalls details of his long career in research of facial expression and nonverbal behavior, his views on research methodology, the current state of the art, and what is needed for good future research.

611. **Harrison, Randall.** *The Nonverbal Dimension of Human Communication.* Englewood Cliffs, New Jersey: Prentice-Hall, in press.

Designed as a text for upper-level college courses, the book offers an integrative "theory" of nonverbal communication. It covers standard interpersonal topics (facial expression, gesture, body movement) plus intrapersonal topics (right brain/left brain, mental imagery), and mass media and intercultural topics (by the author).

612. **Harrison, Randall P.; Cohen, Akiba A.; Crouch, Wayne W.; Genova, B.K.L.; and Steinberg, Mark.** "The Nonverbal Communication Literature." *Journal of Communication* 22 (1972) : 460-476.

This article reviews early literature on nonverbal communication, then concentrates on the upsurge of writing done from 1970 to 1972. It gives a good idea of the trends and context of this literature and discusses the popular literature, new editions of old pioneers in the field, textbooks, and recent research on facial expression.

613. **Harrison, Randall P., and Knapp, Mark L.** "Toward An Understanding of Nonverbal Communication Systems." *Journal of Communication* 22 (1972) : 339-352.

An historical and theoretical overview of some current trends and research developments in nonverbal communication.

614. **Hartemink, B.G.** "Trainen van vaardigheid in het nonverbaal communiceren." In *Nederlands Tijdschrift voor de Psychologie en haar Grensgebieden* 28 (1973) : 37-50.

Suggestions for a training program to develop or change nonverbal repertoire. Written in Dutch.

615. **Harter, Susan; Shultz, Thomas R.; and Blum, Barbara.** "Smiling in Children as a Function of Their Sense of Mastery." *Journal of Experimental Child Psychology* 12 (1971) : 396-404.

Twenty-one four-year-olds and 20 eight-year-olds were given parts of the Peabody Picture Vocabulary Test in two 15-minute sessions. In the first session difficulty levels of each question were established for each child. In the second session magnitude of smiling (zero, slight or full smile, and laugh) was recorded. Children were asked to answer every question and were not informed of the correctness of their answers. The eight-year-olds were later queried as to which answers were guesses. Children smiled more when giving correct answers, except when guessing. No relationship between the magnitude of the smile and difficulty level of the question was found. This may be due to the limited range of difficulty or the nonproblem-solving nature of the PPVT.

616. Hatfield, John D., and Gatewood, Robert D. "Nonverbal Cues in the Selection Interview." *The Personnel Administrator* (1978) : 30, 35-37.

The authors draw on research findings to show that the nonverbal factors that can greatly affect the selection decision are in reality influenced by social, cultural, and personal dimensions that may not be related to job performance. They discuss eye contact, appearance, touch behavior, and proxemics, and the variables that affect them. Interviewers are urged to make the factors influencing their impressions explicit and to consider if their assessments are in fact warranted.

617. Haviland, Jeanette M. "Sex-Related Pragmatics in Infants' Nonverbal Communication." *Journal of Communication* 27 (1977) : 80-84.

Sixty undergraduates viewed ten videotapes of infants ages eight to 15 months and were asked to note the sex of the infant; the other 30 students were given answer sheets with the sex noted correctly or incorrectly. Female infants' emotions were coded as joy twice as often as males; male infants' emotions were coded as fear, anger, or distress twice as often as females. Emotions of infants who were incorrectly labeled the opposite sex tended to be coded in accordance with differences for that (incorrect) sex.

618. Havis, Andrew Lee. "Alternatives for Breaking the 'Discipline Barrier' in Our Schools." *Education* 96 (1975) : 124-128.

Among other responses to misbehavior in the classroom, the author discusses the effectiveness of a slowing down of the tempo of the teacher's movements and the use of gesture for giving directions to young children.

619. Hayano, David M. "Communicative Competency Among Poker Players." *Journal of Communication* 30 (1980) : 113-120.

This fascinating article describes poker game communicative behavior ranging from gaze to verbal and gestural behavior. It describes amateur behaviors, individual styles, and the refinement of deception by professionals. It ranks communicative competency into three categories such that encoding precedes decoding skill: body, facial, and limb management and control of leakage of information; encoding and the ability to disguise and distort levels and channels of communication; and abilities in decoding and reading others and their hidden cards.

620. Hayduk, Leslie Alec. "Personal Space: An Evaluative and Orienting Overview." *Psychological Bulletin* 85 (1978) : 117-134.

This article delineates and defines the personal space construct and discusses personal space theories and measurement techniques. The author concludes that the stop-distance method is best for experimental studies and the unobtrusive techniques are best for naturalistic studies. If only the strongest measurement methods are considered, then age, physical or psychological situation, stigmatizing conditions, psychological disorders, flight from intrusion, and cultural appropriateness are primary factors producing spatial differences.

621. **Hayes, Charles S., and Koch, Richard.** "Interpersonal Distance Behavior of Mentally Retarded and Nonretarded Children." *American Journal of Mental Deficiency* 82 (1977) : 207-209.

In this article the authors compared interpersonal distance choice behavior of 60 mildly retarded children and 60 nonretarded children to a male adult stranger. They found that interpersonal distances of retarded children were generally different from those of nonretarded children. However, further analysis indicated that, when the adult approached the child (in contrast to when the child approached the adult), the retarded children preferred greater distances.

622. **Hayes, Merwyn A.** "Nonverbal Communication: Expression without Words." In *Readings in Interpersonal and Organizational Communication,* Second Edition, edited by R.C. Huseman, C.M. Logue, and D.I. Freshley, pp. 25-39. Boston, Massachusetts: Holbrook Press, 1973.

The author presents a detailed description of proxemics, paralanguage, and kinesics patterns in this overview of nonverbal communication.

623. **Heckel, Robert V.** "Leadership and Voluntary Seating Choice." *Psychological Reports* 32 (1973) : 141-142.

A naturalistic study of 55 mental health professionals attending a week-long workshop showed a slight tendency for participants who were perceived by the group as leaders to sit at the heads of tables during mealtimes.

624. **Heidi, Gloria.** "These Gestures Shout that You're Getting Old." *New Woman.* (1976) : 53-59.

Directed toward the lay audience, this article states that attractiveness and youthfulness can be projected by modification of breathing, clothing, eye contact, facial expression, gesture, posture, and gait, and gives suggestions for how to do so.

625. **Heimann, Robert A., and Heimann, Hope M.** "Nonverbal Communication and Counselor Education." *Comparative Group Studies* 3 (1972) : 443-460.

The authors review studies on the impact of special training programs for sensitizing counselors to nonverbal communication and discuss what is indicated for the establishment of such programs.

626. **Heimstra, Norman, and McFarling, Leslie.** *Environmental Psychology,* 2nd Edition. Monterey, California: Brooks/Cole Publishing Company, 1978. 210 pp. Illus.

In this overview of the field of environmental psychology, the authors first define and delimit the scope of this field and various research methods employed. The next several chapters of the book examine actual environments and their effect on humans. They discuss rooms, housing, buildings, social institutions, and cities. Finally, they explore the relation between behavior and the physical-natural environment.

627. **Henderson, L.F., and Lyons, D.J.** "Sexual Differences in Human Crowd Motion." *Nature* 240 (1972) : 353-355.

An earlier analysis of the speed and density of individuals in crowds led to the hypothesis that males and females act like different populations within the same crowd. This hypothesis was investigated and supported in the present study. The researchers also found that for pedestrians on a crosswalk the distribution for females was significantly skewed compared to males, interpreted to mean that motorists can more easily disturb the walk of females than of males.

628. Henley, Nancy M. *Body Politics: Power, Sex and Nonverbal Communication.* Englewood Cliffs, New Jersey: Prentice-Hall, 1977. 214 pp. Illus.

The author discusses how nonverbal behaviors are used to wield power, maintain the *status quo*, dominate minority group and women, and to establish either an equal or unequal interpersonal relationship. Using a systems approach, the author divides the book into nine areas of study: space, time, environment, elements of language, dimensions of demeanor, touch, body movement, eye contact, and facial expressions.

629. Henley, Nancy M. "Gender Hype." *Women's Studies International Quarterly* 3 (1980) : NP.

This is a review of Erving Goffman's *Gender Advertisements*, which deals with the "cultural assumptions about the nature of the sexes" as reflected in advertisements. The reviewer, a feminist researcher experienced in the study of sexual "body politics," summarized key aspects of Goffman's theoretical essay and picture analysis and expresses much regard for Goffman's monograph. However, she takes issue with some of Goffman's treatise and argues that his understanding of women's experiences stops short, and she strongly disagrees with his analyses of the interbalance of sex roles as part of the maintenance of social order rather than as destructive social control. (from pre-publication manuscript)

630. Henley, Nancy M., and Thorne, Barrie, eds. *Language and Sex: Difference and Dominance.* Rowley, Massachusetts: Newbury House Publishers, 1975. 311 pp.

This book contains a chapter by Nancy Henley on verbal and nonverbal behaviors which maintain the power structure, particularly with regard to the dominance of woman. Lexicon, syntax, intonation, patterns of language, demeanor, space, touch and eye contact are among the behaviors discussed. The book also contains an extensive annotated bibliography on sex differences in language and nonverbal communication.

631. Hennings, Dorothy Grant. *Smiles, Nods and Pauses: Activities to Enrich Children's Communication Skills.* New York: Citation Press, 1974. 232 pp.

A practical handbook on nonverbal communication development for preschool and elementary school teachers, this book is a source of enrichment activities that aid the development of the child's expressive and interpretive use of posture, gesture, and paralanguage. It offers a "guide and a plea" for teachers to include nonverbal communication in the language arts curriculum. In addition to sections on pantomime and dramatic play, numerous references are included to suitable scenarios, seating arrangements, accompanying music, stories, poems, games and skits, and films. This book also includes methods for teaching observation and interpretation of nonverbal communication; ideas and motivational aids help to integrate nonverbal training into the standard curriculum and a documented argument for reluctant administrators.

632. Hersen, Michel; Miller, Peter M.; and Eisler, Richard M. "Interaction between Alcoholics and Their Wives: A Descriptive Analysis of Verbal and Nonverbal Behavior." *Journal of Studies on Alcohol* 34 (1973) : 516-520.

During four brief periods of conversation about alcoholism and unrelated topics, wives tended to look at their alcoholic husbands more when discussing alcoholism, while husbands looked at their wives more when discussing unrelated topics.

633. Hersov, Lionel A., and Shaffer, David, ed. *Aggression and Anti-Social Behavior in Childhood and Adolescence.* Elmsford, New York: Pergamon Press, 1978. 171 pp.

Written by scientists in a variety of disciplines, the chapters address such general issues as provocation of aggression and persistent aggression, the correlation between televised or filmed violence and aggressive behavior, and whether aggression is a reflection of character or environment. Articles include: "Sadism and Paranoia: Cruelty as Collective and Individual Response," "Relationship Between EEG Abnormality and Aggressive and Anti-Social Behavior," "Styles of Hostility and Social Interactions at Nursery, at School, and at Home," "Experiments on the Reactions of Juvenile Delinquents to Filmed Violence," "The Family Backgrounds of Aggressive Youth," "Family, Area, and School Influence on the Genesis of Conduct Disorders," "Behavioral Treatment of Children and Adolescents with Conduct Disorders," and "The Effectiveness of Residential Treatment for Delinquents."

634. **Heshka, Stanley, and Nelson, Yona.** "Interpersonal Speaking Distance as a Function of Age, Sex and Relationship.' *Sociometry* 35 (1972) : 491-498.

Fifty-seven dyads in London were photographed out-of-doors during spontaneous interactions. Male-male dyads maintained similar distances whether or not they were acquainted. Females interacting with a stranger of either sex stood farther apart than male-male dyads. During nonstranger interaction female-female dyads maintained the closest distance, male-male the intermediate, and female-male the farthest distance from each other. Distances increased with age up to 40 years and diminished thereafter.

635. **Heslin, Richard and Boss, Diane.** "Nonverbal Intimacy in Arrival and Departure at an Airport." *Personality and Social Psychology Bulletin* 6 (1980) : 248-252.

Using pretested observation forms that measured 27 variables (including types of touch, sex and age of the traveler and those seeing them off or greeting them, proximity and amount of touching),. 103 encounters were rated. The results indicated that males initiated touch more than females and that older people initiated touch more than younger people. The findings also indicated that there was a greater "touch intimacy" between relatives and those in emotionally arousing situations.

636. **Hess, Eckhard H.** "Pupillometrics: A Method of Studying Mental, Emotional, and Sensory Processes." In *Handbook of Psychophysiology,* edited by N.S. Greenfield and R.A. Sternbach, pp. 491-531. New York: Holt, Rinehart and Winston, 1972.

"Pupillometrics" encompasses the effects of psychological influences, especially negative and positive affect states, perceptual processes, and mental activity, on the size of the eye pupil. This chapter deals in detail with some of the many psychological variables that can be reflected in pupil responses. The technology of pupillometrics is discussed as extremely important for valid conclusions about psychological processes. The chapter includes information on the historical background and neuro-anatomical bases of the "psychopupil" response.

637. **Hess, Eckhard.** *The Tell-Tale Eye.* New York: Van Nostrand Reinhold Company, 1975. Illus.

This book summarizes Hess' and others' research on the study of human pupil dilation. The book begins with a history of pupillometric research, and the conclusions reached by researchers in pupillometry are detailed. Pupil response is an indicator of interest, attitude change, and other mental processes. Hess includes a chapter on the effective use of pupillometry with other physiological measures and a chapter on the pupil and advertising. He concludes with a look at future research areas.

638. **Hess, Eckhard H., and Goodwin, Elizabeth.** "The Present State of Pupillometrics." In *Pupillary Dynamics and Behavior,* edited by M.P. Janisse, pp. 209-248. New York: Plenum Press, 1974. Illus.

This is an extensive review of the literature since 1960 with emphasis on pupillometric assessment of psychological reactions to stimuli and factors causing pupil constriction.

639. **Hess, Valerie L, and Pick, Anne D.** "Discrimination of Schematic Faces by Nursery School Children." *Child Development* 45 (1974) : 1151-1154.

Forty nursery school children participated in this study to determine whether some facial features affect the children's ability to discriminate faces more than others. Among the results it was found that pairs of faces with different eyes were identified with greater accuracy than pairs of faces with different mouths, suggesting they are a most important source of information for perception of faces.

640. **Heston, Judee K.** "Effects of Personal Space Invasion and Anomia on Anxiety, Nonperson Orientation, and Source Credibility." *The Central States Speech Journal* 25 (1974) : 19-27.

Three hundred ten college students comprised the total sample. Fourteen male and 14 female of these were high scoring on an alienation-anomia scale. Another 14 males and females were low scoring on the same inventory. Subjects were classified as normals and anomics and placed in a personal space invasion or noninvasion condition. A male experimenter was used in all conditions. Anxiety and nonperson orientation of subjects were measured after the invasion. Analysis failed to confirm hypotheses that anomics exhibit less situational anxiety when their space is invaded, that invasion of space increases situational anxiety in general, that anomics have a higher level of nonperson orientation in invasion conditions, and that invasion of personal space increases nonperson orientation. It was confirmed that anomics have a higher level of nonperson orientation and that invasion decreases the perceived sociability of the invader.

641. **Hetherington, E. Mavis.** "Effects of Father Absence on Personality Development of Adolescent Daughters." *Developmental Psychology* 7 (1972) : 313-326.

This study examined the effect of father absence due to divorce or death on 72 lower and lower-middle class, first born, adolescent white girls. The effects of father absence were most apparent in the daughter's interaction with males. Results showed that daughters of divorcees manifested proximity and attention-seeking from males, and nonverbal communication behaviors associated with openness and responsiveness with males, such as forward lean, arm and leg openness, eye contact, and smiles. Daughters of widows manifested inhibition on these measures in interaction with males. Early separation from fathers had a greater effect on daughter's behavior than late separation.

642. **Hewes, Gordon W.** "Primate Communication and the Gestural Origin of Language." *Current Anthropology* 14 (1973) : 5-24.

The author provides evidence for the theory of a gestural origin of language by referring to the adaptive need for language, the involuntary emotional primate calls, the persistence of gesture during verbalization today, and the behavior of chimpanzees when using sign language. The article is followed by 15 discussants' essays and an author's reply.

643. **Hewes, Gordon W.** "Gesture Language in Culture Contact." *Sign Language Studies* 4 (1974) : 1-34.

This article draws on the accounts of early voyagers and travellers showing how much communication is possible between different language cultures. It takes issue with recent anthropological opinion that speaking via signs is not a universally efficient means of human communication.

644. **Hiat, Alice Biernoff.** "Explorations in Personal Space." Ph.D. dissertation, University of New Mexico. 1971. 128 pp. (Order No. 71-15,459)

This study of personal space preferences found personal space to be a highly reliable measure and consistent for individuals. Distance was also found to be smaller with friends than with strangers, with an inanimate object than a person, and with a neutral object than one arousing negative affect.

645. **Hicks, Carl F.** "An Experimental Approach to Determine the Effect of a Group Leader's Programmed Nonverbal Facial Behavior Upon Group Members' Perception of the Leader." Ph.D. dissertation, University of Arkansas. 1972. 186 pp. (Order No. 72-10,185)

The effect of selected nonverbal facial expressions of the group leader in a decision-making group was examined. It was concluded that negative nonverbal facial expressions caused subjects to perceive the leader as having a significantly less favorable attitude toward them. This perception was irrespective of the length of time the negative expressions were maintained by the leader.

646. **Hill, Sir Dennis.** "Nonverbal Behaviour in Mental Illness." *British Journal of Psychiatry* 124 (1974) : 221-230. Illus.

The author distinguishes pathological forms of nonverbal behavior into those accompanying severe inhibitory states, partial inhibitory states, and disinhibitory states. Factors contributing to these behaviors and the effect of phenothiazine medication on the nonverbal behavior of chronic schizophrenics are discussed.

647. **Hillabrant, Walter John.** "Locomotion and Gaze Direction As Determinants of Judgements Concerning Persons Engaged in Face-to-Face Interaction." Ph.D. dissertation, University of California, Riverside. 1972. 68 pp. (Order No. 73156-35)

Videotapes were made of eight short dyadic encounters. The locomotor activity and gaze direction/aversion of the dyad was experimentally manipulated. Raters judged the locomoting person as more dominant than the stationary member and the "gaze-directing" person as both more dominant and attractive than the "gaze-averting" member.

648. **Hinchliffe, Mary; Hooper, Douglas; Roberts, F. John; and Vaughan, Pamela W.** "A Study of the Interaction Between Depressed Patients and Their Spouses." *British Journal of Psychiatry* 126 (1975) : 164-172.

Ten depressed psychiatric patients and 11 surgical control patients were videotaped in interaction with their spouses during a free discussion period. The depressed patients were also analyzed in interaction with a stranger and then again with their spouses several months later after discharge. The nonverbal dimensions analyzed were frequency of body- and object-focused hand movements and total time spent in postural congruency. Slower-speaking depressed patients were found to have significantly fewer object-focused movements than controls, but they also showed a significant increase at the time of the follow-up when the number of their object-focused movements became more symmetrical with their spouses. Rates of body-focused movements between spouses also became more symmetrical over time. Fast-speakers became more posturally congruent with their spouses over time, resembling the control couples at the time of the follow-up.

649. **Hinchliffe, Mary K.; Lancashire, Meredith; and Roberts, F.J.** "A Study of Eye-Contact Changes in Depressed and Recovered Psychiatric Patients." *The British Journal of Psychiatry* 119 (1971) : 213-215.

A sample of 16 patients diagnosed as having depression were observed in interview situations for length of speech and eye-contact patterns and changes. Sixteen controls were observed for the same behaviors. The interviewer was monitored for possible social reinforcement behavior. Controls exhibited significantly greater frequencies and length of eye-contact than did depressed patients.

650. **Hinde, Robert A.**, ed. *Non-Verbal Communication.* Cambridge: Cambridge University Press, 1972. 443 pp. Illus.

Based on several years of meetings and discussions by the members of an interdisiplinary Royal Society study group on nonverbal communication, this important volume contains papers by the participants linked by introductions, comments, and an epilogue by the editor. The first part deals with the nature of communication and the relations between verbal and nonverbal communication. It contains a formal analysis of communicative processes by D.M. MacKay, a comparison of vocal communication in animals and humans by W.H. Thorpe, and a discussion of human language by John Lyons. Part two is devoted to signaling systems in animals and contains a paper by J.M. Cullen on principles of animal communication, articles by W.H. Thorpe on communication among the lower vertebrates and invertebrates and on vocal communication in birds, and a paper by R. J. Andrew on information in mammalian displays. The final section on nonverbal communication in humans includes a study of the phylogeny of laughter and smiling by J.A.R.A.M. van Hooff, a discussion of nonverbal communication in human social interaction by Michael Argyle, and a review of research on nonverbal communication in children by N.G. Blurton Jones. Cultural factors in nonverbal behavior are discussed in papers by I. Eibl-Eibesfeldt on similarities and differences between cultures in expressive movements and by Edmund Leach on the importance of the cultural context for nonverbal communication. E.C. Grant has contributed a chapter on nonverbal communication in the mentally ill. The final two papers of the book are a discussion of the nonverbal aspects of theatrical performance by Jonathan Miller and an analysis of action and expression in Western art by E.H. Gombrich.

651. **Hittelman, Joan H.** "Adult-Neonate Mutual Gaze As a Function of the Infant's Sex and Adult Stimulation: Implications for the Mother-Infant Interaction." Ph.D. dissertation, Columbia University. 1975. 91 pp. (Order No. 76127-45)

A study of mutual gaze during the infant's awake-alert-inactive state in relation to the sex of the infant and the quality of her/his involvement with a female experimenter is reported. Significant differences were not found between gender and frequency of mutual gaze, but infant gestation correlated with mutual gaze, suggesting it is to an extent a measure of maturation.

652. **Hobson, G.N.; Strongman, K.T.; Bull, D.; and Craig, G.** "Anxiety and Gaze Averson in Dyadic Encounters."; *British Journal of Social and Clinical Psychology* 12 (1973) : 122-129.

In study 1, six English subjects of each sex were assigned to each of three conditions: a situation where anxiety was induced by verbal negative reinforcement, a condition in which performance was positively reinforced, and a control group. In study 2 eight male students were placed in a high anxiety group and eight in a low. Gaze behavior was studied and found to be unaffected by induced anxiety.

653. **Hocking, John E., and Leathers, Dale.** "Nonverbal Indicators of Deception: A New Theoretical Perspective." *Communication Monographs* 47 (1980) : 119-131.

As part of a test of a theory of nonverbal behavior during deception, 19 male and four female undergraduates were filmed in two separate sequences of deceptive and honest behavior. Four observers coded subjects' behaviors into four general areas: body movement, facial expression, paralanguage, and eye contact. Results show that behavior differences for liars and truth-tellers in body movement variables approach significance, but this is not the case for facial expression. Deceivers exhibit greater vocal nervousness and fewer foot movements. The duration of deceiver's eye contact was significantly shorter than truth-tellers.

654. Hockings, Paul, ed. *Principles of Visual Anthropology.* The Hague: Mouton, 1975. 521 pp. Illus.

This important collection of papers written in connection with the International Conference on Visual Anthropology in 1973 contains many articles dealing with film and videotape in anthropological research and teaching. "The History of Ethnographic Film" by Emilie de Brigard covers key films, filmmakers, and technical developments in the study of movement and behavior, and does "The Camera and Man" by Jean Rouch. John Collier, Jr. has contributed a paper on "Photography and Visual Anthropology" and Alan Lomax a study of "Audiovisual Tools for the Analysis of Culture Style." Papers specifically on kinesics and proxemics research are "Filming Body Behavior" by J.H. Prost, "A Photographic Method for the Recording and Evaluation of Cross-Cultural Proxemic Interaction Patterns" by Shawn E. Scherer, and "Proxemic Research: A Check on the Validity of Its Techniques" by Robert F. Forston.

655. Hoffer, Bates, and St. Clair, Robert. *Developmental Kinesics: The Emerging Paradigm.* Baltimore, Maryland: University Park Press, forthcoming.

656. Holahan, Charles. "Seating Patterns and Patient Behavior in an Experimental Dayroom." *Journal of Abnormal Psychology* 80 (1972) : 115-124.

One hundred twenty male psychiatric patients participated in this study of the effect of seating arrangements on patient interaction. Patients were seated in chairs arranged sociofugally, sociopetally, in a mixed pattern, or in a free pattern determined by individual subjects. Sociopetal and mixed patterns produced more conversation and other verbal interaction and more conversations between three or more people. An unexpected finding was that the free setting resulted in much less social interaction than the sociopetal and mixed settings.

657. Hoogerman, Dennis. "An Extended Test of Argyle's Equilibrium Model: A Reevaluation of Mutual Eye Contact." Ph.D. dissertation, State University of New York at Buffalo. 1973. 71 pp. (Order No. 74044-05)

The author extended Michael Argyle's equilibrium model to cover friend as well as stranger relationships, and he conceived a mutual eye avoidance as a form of symmetrical interaction equivalent of mutual eye contact.

658. Hore, Terry, and Paget, Neil S. *Nonverbal Behavior: A Selected Annotated Bibliography.* Victoria, Australia: Australian Council for Educational Research, 1975. 164 pp.

This 686-title bibliography is divided into experimental studies and descriptive studies which are annotated, and dissertations, foreign (non-English) articles, and additional references which are not annotated. Most titles are from the 1960s and early 1970s. The experimental studies are reported in terms of question, sample, dependent and independent variables, design, and results. Some special bibliographies are described as good for further reference.

659. Horvath, Frank S. "Verbal and Nonverbal Clues to Truth and Deception during Polygraph Examinations." *Journal of Police Science and Administration* 1 (1973) : 138-152.

Routine administration of polygraph recordings includes a pretest session where the interviewer notes subjects' verbal and nonverbal responses to 14 questions. One hundred completed interview sheets were reviewed by 10 examiners. Verbal and nonverbal notations were categorized as typical of a truthteller's response (genuinely friendly, good eye contact, relaxed, and so on) or a liar's response (evasive answers, poor eye contact, nervous facial movements, and so on). Ninety-four percent of the interviews classified as truthtelling were of subjects later found to be innocent by the polygraph; 82 percent of those classified as liars were found to be guilty.

660. Howard, Pierce Johnson. "Nonverbal Communication of Teacher Expectations." Ph.D. dissertation, University of North Carolina at Chapel Hill. 1972. 135 pp. (Order No. 73-4838)

Twenty white female teachers were videotaped interviewing "a high- and then a low-ability white male student." Judges rated the tapes according to A. Mehrabian-type observations, but a factor analysis of the results did not correspond to Mehrabian's, and clear differences in teacher behavior toward each student were not found.

661. Huggins, W.H., and Entwisle, Doris, eds. *Iconic Communication: An Annotated Bibliography.* Baltimore, Maryland: Johns Hopkins University Press, 1974. 171 pp. Illus.

Although the editors dismiss body movement as "incapable of expressing precise structural relationships," this annotated bibliography on communication through images has an interesting section on facial mnemonics and the study of the parameters used in perceiving information in the face.

662. Hunt, Valerie V. "Neuromuscular Organization in Emotional States." *Conference Proceedings of the American Dance Therapy Association* 7 (1973) : 16-41.

The author summarizes her own and other's research into human expenditure of energy. She has found in one study that highly anxious people use more energy in the distal muscles than "low anxious" people who concentrate muscle usage in proximal groupings. The discussion continues with a review of paranormal energy use, including psychics, healers, and acupuncture.

663. Hurt, H. Thoms; Scott, Michael D.; and McCrosky, James C. *Communication in the Classroom.* Reading, Massachusetts: Addison-Wesley, 1978. Illus.

This work has an illustrated chapter on nonverbal communication in the classroom which briefly surveys personal space and seating arrangements, touch norms, body movement, time, and paralinguistics and their impact on communication in the classroom.

664. Hutt, S.J., and Hutt, Corrine. *Direct Observation and Measurement of Behavior.* Springfield, Illinois: Charles C. Thomas, 1978.

665. Ickes, William, and Barnes, Richard D. "Boys and Girls Together — and Alienated: On Enacting Stereotyped Sex Roles in Mixed-Sex Dyads." *Journal of Personality and Social Psychology* 36 (1978) : 669-683.

In a controlled situation, four types of male-female dyads were studied in an effort to determine the effects of sex-role orientation on the initial interactions of 43 mixed-sex dyads. the composition of the dyads was based on the sex-role identification of its members: androgynous, stereotypically male, or stereotypically female. The measures used included observation of nonverbal interaction and behavior. The results showed greater interpersonal incompatibility and stress for dyads in which each member manifested stereotypical sex-role behaviors.

666. Ickes, William; Schermer, Brian; and Steeno, Jeff. "Sex and Sex-Role Influences in Same-Sex Dyads." *Social Psychology Quarterly* 42 (1979) : 373-385.

In this paper the "androgynous" individual is described as one who exhibits both male (instrumental) and female (expressive) interactional behavior. One hundred twenty-six undergraduates previously determined to have sex typed (ST) or androgynous (A) interactive behavior were paired into same sex dyads and covertly videotaped during spontaneous interaction. Then they were asked to complete questionnaires concerning their feelings about the interaction. The videotape was coded for static behaviors (who sat and talked first, proximity, body orientation, body posture) and dynamic behaviors (gaze behavior, gesture, and facial expressions). Androgynous dyads of both sexes had the most involving and satisfying interactions. Female ST-ST dyadic interactions were more socially expressive and affiliative, but the least satisfying. Androgynous subjects in ST-A dyads exhibited sex-typed behavior making ST-A interactions no different from those of ST-ST dyads. The authors conclude that satisfaction with interactive involvement is dependent upon the extent to which one's expressive needs have been met. They suggest that androgynous behavior allows truly voluntary interaction because it does not depend upon another's type of participation.

667. Ikegami, Yoshihiko. "A Stratification Analysis of the Hand Gestures in Indian Classical Dancing." *Semiotica* 4 (1971) : 365-391. Illus.

The fundamental unit of the classical dancing of India is the *Karana* or 'single posture,' made up of certain types of prescribed bodily position, gait, and hand gestures. There are 31 types of single hand gesture and 27 types of gestures by both hands. In this article these hand gestures are analyzed according to position of the fingers, degree of bending, space between the fingers, and contact with the thumb. Each hand gesture is then transcribed using these descriptive features. Double hand gestures are analyzed and transcribed by types of single hand gestures involved and the relative positions of the two hands. Using a structural linguistics model the hand gesture communicational system is then described in terms of strata or hierarchically related levels, together with the relationships of the strata and co-occurrence restrictions. Meanings of the hand gestures are also examined.

668. Imada, Andrew S., and Hakel, Milton D. "Influence of Nonverbal Communication and Rater Proximity on Impressions and Decisions in Simulated Employment Interviews." *Journal of Applied Psychology* 62 (1977) : 295-300.

In this study of 72 female subjects who participated as interviewees or observers, results indicate that nonverbal communication had a signficant effect on interview impressions and subsequent discussions. Self-report measures suggest that involvement differs as a function of rater's proximity.

669. Ing, Dean Charles. "Proxemics Simulation: A Validation Study of Observer Error." Ph.D. dissertation, University of Oregon. 1974. 137 pp. (Order No. 74265-40)

In this study trios of university subjects estimated the distance and orientation of two moving mannikins. Observer sex, viewing angle, effects of repeated observations, and mannikin "closure" speed were factors examined.

670. Ingham, Roger. "Preferences for Seating Arrangements in Two Countries." *International Journal of Psychology* 9 (1974) : 105-115.

An English sample of 83 males and 62 females and a Swedish sample of 67 males and 89 females were given a questionnaire with a diagram indicating possible seating choices. Subjects indicated which seating arrangement they would select in each of a number of situations. Swedish subjects chose more face-to-face seating arrangements than did the English subjects. For the English, the most frequently chosen arrangement in a low-intimacy condition was opposite; in medium intimacy it was a right angle, and for high intimacy it was adjacent. For Swedish subjects, the predominant choice for both the low- and medium-intimacy conditions was facing, while for high intimacy conditions adjacent was preferred most.

671. Insel, Paul M., and Lindgren, Henry. *Too Close for Comfort: The Psychology of Crowding.* Englewood Cliffs, New Jersey: Prentice-Hall, 1978. 180 pp.

This book is an examination of crowding from the social ecologist's point of view. The authors examine the relationship between crowding and physical and psychological health, stressing the need for human privacy. In nine chapters they discuss and define crowding, its relation to territoriality and personal space, individual differences in crowding, urban stress and the social cost of crowding, and the health-aggression-crowding relationship.

672. Ittelson, William H.; Proshansky, Harold M.; Rivlin, Leanne G.; and Winkel, Gary H. *An Introduction to Environmental Psychology.* New York, Holt, Rinehart and Winston, 1974. 406 pp. Illus.

The authors present a general discussion of environmental psychology, historical aspects, theories and guiding assumptions with regard to this topic. The relation between perception and environment, social-environmental issues, individual development and the environment, and research methods are examined. The authors also look at the city as an unnatural habit. Final chapters in the book are devoted to perception and use of the natural environment and innovations in environmental design.

673. Izard, Carroll E. *Human Emotions.* New York: Plenum Press, 1977. 495 pp. Illus.

The book begins with a definition of emotion, descriptions of the different theories of emotions (including the "differential emotions theory"), and principles and methods behind the psychology of emotion. Emotions are discussed in relation to the face, touch, arousal, consciousness, and drives. Separate chapters are devoted to the emotions of interest-excitement, joy, surprise-startle, distress, anger, fear, shame, and guilt.

674. Izard, Carroll E. "Facial Expression, Emotion, and Motivation." In *Nonverbal Behavior: Applications and Cultural Implications,* edited by A. Wolfgang, pp. 31-49. New York: Academic Press, 1979.

This overview of research on facial expression and emotion explores such topics as physiological studies of affect, emotions as the "primary motivational system," developmental studies, and emotion control and psychotherapy. Focusing particularly on the work of the author and his colleagues, there is reference to specific instruments such as Izard's "Differential Emotions Scale" and "Emotion Attitude Questionnaire."

675. Izard, C.E.; Huebner, R.R.; Risser, D.; McGinnes, G.C.; and Dougherty, L.M. "The Young Infant's Ability to Produce Discrete Emotion Expressions." *Developmental Psychology* 16 (1980) : 132-140.

Five studies involving description of infant facial expressions are described. Undergraduates and female health service professionals described videotaped expressions similarly to classifications derived from the Facial Expression Scoring Manual (FESM); correlations improved after subject training using FESM descriptors. An objective, theoretically structured, anatomically based method — Maximal Discrimination Facial Movement Coding System — is described and used to code facial expressons with 87 percent agreement with FESM. The authors conclude that infant facial expressions are socially valid indicators of affect.

676. **Jackson, Joseph D.** "The Relationship Between he Development of Gestural Imagery and the Development of Graphic Imagery." *Child Development* 45 (1974) : 432-438.

This article reports on a test of whether children's development of symbolic gestural abilities conforms to Piaget's stages of imaging. Forty-five children age five (preoperational), age eight (transitional), or age 11 (operational) participated. They were given graphic tasks (static, kinetic, and tranformational) and gestural tasks (static, with and without an object of action, and kinetic/transformational, with and without an object of action). The results only supported the hypothesized developmental sequence of symbolic gestural abilities: failure to imitate, use of body part to represent, then symbolic representation. A stage-like development of graphic abilities or a simultaneous development of gestural and graphic stages was not supported. A supplementary test of five and eight year olds on gestural tasks (with an object of action but with object not present) showed both groups to be better with the cue absent, so the link of this condition to operational stages was not supported.

677. **Jacobs, Theodore J.** "Posture, Gesture and Movement in the Analyst: Cues to Interpretation and Countertransference." *Journal of the American Psychoanalytical Association* 21 (1973) : 77-92.

Following a brief review of interest in nonverbal communication in the psychoanalytic tradition, research and clinical examples illustrating the nonverbal factor in the analytic setting are discussed. The author posits that the analyst, by tuning into his or her kinetic responses to a client, obtains clues to understanding the client's unconscious communications as well as to countertransference feelings previously undetected.

678. **Jaffe, Joseph; Stern, Daniel N.; and Peery, J. Craig.** " 'Conversational' Coupling of Gaze Behavior in Prelinguistic Human Development." *Journal of Psycholinguistic Research* 2 (1973) : 321-329.

Six four month old infants were observed during free play with their mothers and with several experimenters. Dyadic gazing was coded on an Esterline-Angus event recorder as one of four states: neither looking, infant looking, adult looking, and both looking at one another. This dyadic communication was then compared with adult conversation. The results indicated a Markov chain structure (a stochastic process which moves through a finite number of states) is applicable to both systems with regard to the temporal sequence of the four states. In other words, mathematical regularities in the gross temporal pattern of infant-adult gaze behavior are identical to those found in adult verbal conversations. Such regularities suggest some universal property of human communication that predates the onset of speech.

679. **Jakobson, Roman.** "Motor Signs for 'Yes' and 'No.' " *Language in Society* 1 (1972) : 91-96.

Three different pairs or systems of head and facial motions habitually used in Europe for expression of agreement or approval and dissent or disagreement are described, analyzed, and compared. The systems are distinguished as those of general Europe, of Bulgaria, and of Greece and Southern Italy.

680. **James, John Andrew.** "Social Dominance and Eye Contact." Ph.D. dissertation, University of Missouri-Columbia. 1973. 152 pp. (Order No. 74185-54)

Contrary to prediction, in this study of 80 male undergraduates no relationship between amount of eye contact and "dominance" was supported.

681. **Jancovic, Merry Ann; Devoe, Shannon; and Wiener, Martin.** "Age-Related Changes in Hand and Arm Movements as Nonverbal Communication: Some Conceptualizations and an Empirical Exploration." *Child Development* 46 (1975) : 922-928.

Children and adolescents aged four to 18 viewed a cartoon and were videotaped during subsequent questioning. Subjects' hand/arm gestures as they spoke were identified by two judges as deictic (simplest), pantomimic, semantic modifying or relational (most complex). Comparison across age groups revealed more hand-arm gestures of greater complexity used at increasing ages.

682. **Janisse, Michel Pierre.** "Pupil Size and Affect: A Critical Review of the Literature Since 1960." *The Canadian Psychologist* 14 (1973) : 311-329.

An attempt is made to review all of the relevant research since 1960 on the relationship between pupil size and positive and negative affect. It is judged that Eckhardt Hess' notion of pupil dilation with pleasant stimuli and constriction with unpleasant stimuli is not substantially supported by the literature. The most consistent finding related greater dilation to increases in the intensity of stimulation, whether positive or negative. The author proposes that results of pupillometry studies may be artifactual due to contrast effects of the visual stimuli.

683. **Janisse, Michel P.** *Pupillometry: The Psychology of the Pupillary Response.* London: John Wiley and Sons, 1977. 204 pp. Illus.

In this summary of the research done on pupillometry, the author cites results of studies and notes other fruitful lines of research. He reviews the research of Eckhard Hess and the studies of pupil dilation, patterns in relation to sexual arousal, attitudes and anxiety, thinking and mental effort, individual differences, and abnormal behavior.

684. **Janisse, Michel Pierre, and Peavler, W. Scott.** "Pupillary Response Today: Emotion in the Eye." *Psychology Today* 7 (1974) : 60-63. Illus.

This article critiques Eckhard Hess' thesis that the size of a person's pupils varies according to his or her psychological state. The authors trace Hess' general method and list some of the criticisms that subsequent pupil studies and researchers from other disciplines have made. When possible confounding factors are controlled, the evidence fails to support the theory that unpleasant stimuli make the pupils contract. However, there is evidence that emotions and mental effort can increase pupil size.

685. **Jaspars, J.M.F., and Duijker, H.C.J.,** eds. "Niet-verbale communicatje." Special issue of *Nederlands Tijdschrift voor de Psychologie en haar Grensgebieden* 28 (1973).

This special issue of articles written in Dutch includes an overview of research in nonverbal communication by J.M.F. Jaspars, P.G. Saager, and T. van den Oever, and a discussion of determinants of nonverbal communicative behavior by H.C.J. Duijker. Jaspars has also contributed an article on eye contact and cognitive equilibrium and with A.C.C. van den Oever, F.W.A. Boeckhorst, H.W. an den Borne, C. den Hartog, and H.L.A. Theunissen an article on observing eye contact. There is also a discussion of a method for the three-dimensional recording of movements by H.J.G. Kempen.

686. **Jellison, Jerald M., and Ickes, William J.** "The Power of the Glance: Desire to See and Be Seen in Cooperative and Competitive Situations." *Journal of Experimental Social Psychology* 10 (1974) : 444-450.

Forty-eight male undergraduates were told that they would be either cooperating or competing with another person in a game and that they would interview their partner or be interviewed. Interviewers could choose to see their partner through a one-way mirror first; interviewees could choose to be seen or not. Perception was allowed in all cases except interviewees who expected a competitive game.

687. **Jensen, Marvin D.** "Using the Q-sort to Identify Nonverbal Perception." *Communication Education* 28 (1979) : 150-152.

A description of how to devise and administer a Q-sort to students so they may compare and discuss perceptions of each other, which are likely to be based largely on nonverbal communication.

688. **Jensen, Marvin D.** "Brain Specialization Research and the Teaching of Nonverbal Communication." *Iowa Journal of Speech Communication* 12 (1980) : 19-27.

Taking a "connectionist" position as to brain laterality (that some functions are laterally localized but somewhat represented in the other hemisphere), the author discusses the importance of stressing nonlinear, impressionistic, complex aspects of nonverbal communication when teaching the subject to secondary and college level students.

689. **Johnson, David.** "Some Diagnostic Applications of Drama Therapy." In *Drama in Therapy*, vol. 2, edited by R. Courtney and G. Schattner. New York: Drama Book Specialists, forthcoming.

Drama therapy—the name for the group of therapeutic approaches which utilize in a significant way the nonverbal and symbolic media of creative drama and dramatic role-playing—can prove useful in diagnosis. This chapter, in addition to examining the limitations of drama as a diagnostic tool and presenting the general characteristics of role-playing, explores how the ability to play is an important aspect of our personality structure; on which reflects cognitive and emotional dimensions of our experience. (from prepublication draft)

690. **Johnson, David, and Sandel, Susan.** "Structural Analysis of Group Movement Sessions: Preliminary Research." *American Journal of Dance Therapy* 1 (1977) : 32-36. Illus.

The authors developed the Structural Analysis of Movement Sessions (SAMS) in response to a need for a method for studying dance and drama therapy sessions. The SAMS assesses sessions according to three main dimensions of group activity: task, space, and role, which consist of some 46 structures. These are defined, and two therapy groups are analyzed.

o691. **Johnson, Harold G.; Ekman, Paul; and Friesen, Wallace V.** "Communicative Body Movements: American Emblems." *Semiotica* 15 (1975) : 335-353.

Emblems are movement patterns so precise that a glossary for each action and message can be written. This article does so for several American emblems. "WASP" males were videotaped enacting the emblems they knew for a list of verbal messages. Three groups of different male and female informants viewed the action pattern performances on videotape of a single person. Decoding subjects made four decisions after viewing each motor pattern: the message conveyed; one to seven rating of their certainty of the message conveyed; a Natural Usage versus Artificial Usage decision; and one to seven rating of their certainty of their Natural-Artificial Usage score. The results are presented in four tables listing verified emblems, probable emblems, and two levels of ambiguous emblems.

692. **Johnson, Kenneth R.** "Black Kinesics—Some Non-Verbal Communication Patterns in the Black Culture." *The Florida F L Reporter* 9(Spring/Fall) : 17-20, 57.

Several black kinesic patterns were described: rolling the eyes, reluctance to look another person directly in the eye, avoiding eye contact, the limp stance of young black males, the "black walk," the "pimp strut," the stationary "pimp strut" stance, the way males punctuate laughter, the "rapping stance" of young black males, turning their backs on each other, greeting with one hand cupped over the genitals, and the black female position placing one hand on hip. Some were contrasted with white nonverbal behavior. It was hypothesized that some of these black kinesics are similar to or derived from black African movement patterns.

693.   **Jones, Frank Pierce.** *Body Awareness in Action: A Study of the Alexander Technique.* New York: Schocken, 1976. 171 pp. Illus.

The book, considered one of the best on the subject, ranges in approach from an autobiographical account of the author's experience—first as a student of F.M. Alexander and later as a teacher of the technique—to a theory of the mechanisms underlying the sense of kinesthetic lightness, an important goal of the technique. It describes Alexander's discoveries and the development of his ideas, as well as how they have been received by opponents and advocates alike.

694.   **Jones, N. Blurton.** "Criteria for Use in Describing Facial Expressions of Children." *Human Biology* 43 (1971) : 365-413. Illus.

Fifty-two components of facial expressions in children are described as well as the inter-observer reliability for scoring them.

695.   **Jones, N. Blurton,** ed. *Ethological Studies of Child Behavior.* Cambridge: Cambridge University Press, 1972. 400 pp. Illus.

This volume is divided into studies of child-child interactions and mother-child interactions and begins with a discussion by the editor of the characteristics of ethology relevant to the study of human behavior. Christopher R. Brannigan and David A. Humphries have contributed a discussion of nonverbal behaviors in communication including definitions of 136 units. Studies of child-child interactions include "Patterns of Play and Social Interaction in Pre-School Children" by Peter K. Smith and Kevin Connolly, "Categories of Child-Child Interaction'; by N. Blurton Jones, "Aspects of Social Development in Nursery School Children, with Emphasis on Introduction to the Group" by W.C. McGrew, and "Reactions of Pre-School Children to a Strange Observer" by Kevin Connolly and Peter K. Smith.

Research on mother-child interactions is represented by a discussion of the aims, methods, and results of an observational study of mother-infant interaction by M.P.M. Richards and Judith F. Bernal, a study of attachment behavior out of doors by J.W. Anderson, and a study of separation and greeting behaviors of mothers and children by N. Blurton Jones and Gill M. Leach. Also included are "A Comparison of the Social Behaviour of Some Normal and Problem Children" by Gill M. Leach, "Aspects of the Developmental Ethology of a Foraging People" on Bushman infants by M.J. Konner, "Comparative Aspects of Mother-Child Contact" by N. Blurton Jones, and "The Evolution and Ontogeny of Hand Function" by Kevin Connolly and John Elliott.

696.   **Jones, Stanley E., and Aiello, John R.** "Proxemic Behavior of Black and White First-, Third-, and Fifth-Grade Children." *Journal of Personality and Social Psychology* 25 (1973) : 21-27.

The subjects were 192 children from two New York City elementary schools comprised of lower-class blacks and middle-class whites. The children were paired and asked to converse on a particular subject. An observer recorded interpersonal distance and the axis of body orientation. Results showed that particularly in earlier grades blacks face one another less directly than whites, and up to the fifth grade blacks also stood closer than whites, after which time the difference disappeared.

697.   **Jordan, I. King, and Battison, Robbin.** "A Referential Communication Experiment with Foreign Sign Language." *Sign Language Studies* 10 (1976) : 69-80.

The authors present evidence that deaf signers understand their own sign language far better than foreign sign languages, which is contrary to the common conception of signing as a universal language.

698. **Jurich, Anthony P., and Jurich, Julie A.** "Correlations Among Nonverbal Expressions of Anxiety." *Psychological Reports* 34 (1974) : 199-204.

Forty female college students were each interviewed by a male experimenter who asked questions regarding premarital sex attitudes. Prior to and immediately after the interview a finger sweat index test was taken to determine the subject's level of anxiety. Immediately following the interview, subjects rated their anxiety level on a scale from one to ten. The nonverbal responses of the subjects during the interview were videotaped and rated by pairs of judges. Among the results it was found that the rater's global rating and the finger sweat print highly correlated with each other. However, the subject's assessment of her own level of anxiety was not highly correlated with anxiety as measured from, for example, percentage of eye contact, number of times touching head, and postural shifts.

699. **Kachur, Donald S., and Sweet, Bruce W.** "Nonverbal Discipline." *School and Community* 60 (1974) : 31.

Nonverbal behaviors that teachers can use to control behavior in the classroom are listed and briefly discussed.

700. **Kagan, Jerome.** *Change and Continuity in Infancy.* New York: John Wiley & Sons, 1971. 298 pp. Illus.

This important work reports the results of a two-year longitudinal study of 180 infants assessed at ages four, eight, 13, and 27 months. The purpose of the study was to examine the development of cognitive structures, the stability of individual differences in cognitive organization, and sex and class differences in relation to these. Of specific interest to the researcher in body movement are the chapters on fixation time, tempo of play, and smiling, irritability, and activity. There is also a brief discussion of the coding of motor activity and postural changes done on a small group of the subjects.

701. **Kahn, Arnold, and McGaughey, Timothy A.** "Distance and Liking: When Moving Close Produces Increased Liking." *Sociometry* 40 (1977) : 138-144.

Eighty-eight college students took part in this study of the effect of interpersonal distance, nonverbal friendliness, and sex of the interactant upon subjects' evaluations. Results showed that the near condition resulted in increased liking but only in opposite-sex and not in same-sex pairs.

702. **Kalish, Beth.** "Developmental Studies Using the Behavior Rating Instrument for Autistic and Other Atypical Children (BRIAAC)." *Conference Proceedings of the American Dance Therapy Association* 9 (1975) : 131-136.

This brief article outlines the results of a study designed to validate the Behavior Rating Instrument for Autistic and Other Atypical Children (BRIAAC) as a developmental scale. Two hundred children, ages one to five, were measured by the BRIAAC. Preliminary data show that the BRIAAC will differentiate between normal developmental levels.

703. **Kalish, Beth Isaacs.** "Body Movement Scale for Autistic and Other Atypical Children: An Exploratory Study Using a Normal Group and an Atypical Group." Ph.D. dissertation, Bryn Mawr College. 1976. 248 pp. (Order No. 77065-24)

One hundred ninety-five normal children and 75 autistic children were scored according to movement, vocalization, and psychosexual scales in this study. The development of a new scale for assessing movement behavior of atypical children is presented.

704. **Kaplan, Kalman J.** "Structure and Processing in Interpersonal 'Distancing.'" *Environmental Psychology and Nonverbal Behavior* 1 (1977) : 104-121.

The present paper focuses on who-why-where-when-how-what-whom structural model of interpersonal "distancing." The term "distancing" denotes either approach or avoidance movement along an "intimacy-immediacy" dimension. This dimension itself is defined as an integration across proxemic, kinesic, paralinguistic, and linguistic interpersonal modalities. Parallels are drawn between the concepts of "intimacy" disequilibrim and cognitive dissonance; the latter deals with attitude-behavior discrepancies and the former with attraction-approach discrepancies. A compensatory model is expanded across partners and sensory modalities, and the concept of "intimacy overload" is offered as a clarifying tool for the "social refractoriness" and "information overload" explanations appearing in various aspects of the literature.

705. **Kaplan, Robert Alan.** "The Effects of Manipulating Nonverbal Behaviors of Interviewers on the Nonverbal Behavior of Interviewees." Ph.D dissertation, Michigan State University. 1971. 143 pp. (Order No. 72-8712)

College students interacted with confederate interviewers who were trained to manipulate movements in four body areas (head and neck, hands and arms, legs and feet, and body and postural shifts) at specific times during the interview. Subjects' head and hand movements were found to vary across time periods although not as predicted. Measures of affiliation were not related to the nonverbal variables, but females were significantly more positive on measures of affiliation than males.

706. **Karabenick, Stuart A., and Meisels, Murray.** "Effects of Performance Evaluation on Interpersonal Distance." *Journal of Personality* 40 (1972) : 275-286.

Ninety-nine male undergraduates were divided according to measures of their strength to approach success, and motive to avoid failure. Each received either positive or negative feedback after a task. They were also approached by a confederate. Results showed interpersonal distance was affected by the type of feedback received; smaller distances were associated with positive feedback. Subjects having less anxiety approached their dyad partners more closely.

707. **Karger, Kenneth Jay.** "The Relationship of Nonverbal Counselor Behavior to Client and Rater Perceptions of Empathy." Ph.D. dissertation, University of Wisconsin. 1974. 82 pp. (Order No. 74-19,921)

Twenty-four female clients and male counselors-in-training were videotaped in initial interviews. Client's evaluations and judges ratings of the counselors' body orientation and lean indicated a possible relationship between body orientation and evaluations of empathy.

708. **Kauffman, Lynn E.** "Tacesics, The Study of Touch: A Model for Proxemic Analysis." *Semiotica* 4 (1971) : 149-161.

The focus of this paper is on modes of tactile (touching) contact and on the study of tactile proxemes, coining the term for such study "tacesics." A tacesic model is suggested, with the probability of success based on the measurement of entropy in the situation. This model was successfully tested in two contextual settings: with 16 graduate students in communications seminar focusing on sensitivity awareness; and with the audience while the author presented her paper on the tacesic model at an annual meeting of the Southwestern Anthropological Association.

709. **Kavner, Richard S., and Dusky, Lorraine.** *Total Vision.* New York: A&W Publishers Inc., 1978. 264 pp. Illus.

Written for both lay and professional audiences, this book is an introduction to vision therapy and behavior optometry. It includes discussion of relationships between vision styles and personality, cognitive and developmental factors in eye coordination and vision, and posture and eye coordination. There is an extensively illustrated section on visual "games" or exercises to be done to expand one's visual repertoire.

710. **Kawamura, Y.** "Psychological Background of Body Language." *Journal of Dental Research* 55 (1976) : D181.

This is an abstract of a study aimed at sensitizing dentists to the nonverbal behaviors of the client who cannot talk while dental work is being performed. Facial expression and increase of muscle tension, eye, neck, hand, foot, and body movements are discussed.

711. **Kazdin, Alan E., and Klock, Joan.** "The Effect of Nonverbal Teacher Approval on Student Attentive Behavior." *Journal of Applied Behavior Analysis* 6 (1973) : 643-654.

After collecting baseline data with a class of 12 retarded children, the teacher maintained her baseline level of verbal approval while increasing her use of contingent nonverbal approval (that is, smiles and physical contact). Eleven of 12 students increased their attentive behavior during the nonverbal approval phase.

712. **Kealiinonomoku, Joann Wheeler.** "Theory and Methods for an Anthropological Study of Dance." Ph.D. dissertation, Indiana University. 1976. 383 pp. (Order No. 76-21,511)

Elaborating a theory of "ethnochoreology," or the anthropology of dance, the author describes dance as a species specific phenomenon by which societies can resolve needs. The mechanisms of genetics, environment, conditioning, and biorhythms are examined in this study, and the author cites play theory, homeostasis, psychology of body image, circadian and other biorhythms, interaction anthropology, and the role of exterior and interior senses as specific influences on her analysis. Methods are presented to illustrate the applied analysis of dance and to suggest ways of developing the theories.

713. **Keenan, A., and Wedderburn, A.A.I.** "Effects of the Nonverbal Behaviour of Interviewers on Candidates' Impressions." *Journal of Occupational Psychology* 48 (1975) : 129-132.

Twenty-two male and two female subjects were interviewed by persons using approval behaviors (smiling, nodding, eye contact) or disapproval behaviors (frown, head shaking, avoidance of eye contact). After being interviewed in each condition subjects completed a questionnaire comparing the two interviewers. Interviewers with approving nonverbal behaviors were seen as friendlier, were liked more, and made the subjects feel more at ease. Disapproving interviewers were perceived to be more nervous. No significant differences were found in either the amount of subjects' talking or subsequent subject ratings of their own performance at the interview.

714. **Keiser, George J., and Altman, Irwin.** "Relationship of Nonverbal Behavior to the Social Penetration Process." *Human Communication Research* 2 (1976) : 146-161. Illus.

Two pairs of actresses role-played either good friends or casual acquaintances in conversations on superficial and intimate topics. Each pair had three three-minute conversations on different topics for each condition. Videotapes were scored on 24 nonverbal behaviors (including arm, leg, head and eye movements, body lean, verbalizations, and facial expressions). Two or more behaviors in a one-second interval occurring at least five times were designated a pattern. Good friends discussing superficial topics exhibited relaxed behavior; casual acquaintances discussing intimate topics showed tense behavior. "Core patterns" (those found in at least 15 percent of the patterns) defined the interaction atmosphere. The authors conclude with a discussion of the validity of using role-playing in research.

715. **Keith, L. Thomas; Tornatsky, Louis G.; and Pettigrew, L. Eudora.** "An Analysis of Verbal and Nonverbal Classroom Teaching Behaviors." *The Journal of Experimental Education* 42 (1974) : 30-38.

Forty-three teacher-interns in kindergarten through sixth grade classrooms were videotaped at least twice using a time sampling procedure. A behavioral instrument for measuring both verbal and nonverbal teacher-learner classroom behaviors was developed, and this was used to categorize teaching subjects' and students' verbal and nonverbal behaviors. Cluster analysis indicated that the teacher-interns' approval tended to be nonverbally, passively expressed (for example, smiling), while disapproval tended to be verbally, explicitly expressed.

716. **Kelley, David L.** "Toward a Coherent Language of Movement." *Semiotica* 24 (1978) : 177-180.

This is a book review of Noel W. Schutz, Jr.'s 36-page monograph *Kinesiology: The Articulation of Movement* (Lisse: The Peter de Ridder Press, 1976). In this book, the sites of movement are given names consistent with traditional kinesiological and medical terminology, but new movement names are adopted for the segments (joints), while the spatial characteristics of body movements are classified according to a triplanar reference system. This then is extended to a notation system for movement.

717. **Kelly, Francis Donovan.** "Nonverbal Communication in the Counseling and Psychotherapeutic Interaction: An Investigation of the Differential Effect of Selected Therapist Proxemic Variables on Client Attitude." Ed.D. dissertation, University of Massachusetts. 1971. 212 pp. (Order No. 72-4045)

In this study videotapes of five therapists were judged by 60 male subjects with varying psychological disorders. The study concluded that, to the client, different therapist proxemic cues convey positive or negative affect.

718. **Kelly, Francis.** "Communicational Significance of Therapist Proxemic Cues." *Journal of Consulting and Clinical Psychology* 39 (1972) : 345.

Sixty males representing a diversity of client subgroups, from acute paranoid schizophrenics to college students with personal or school-related problems, rated 72 pictures showing all possible combinations of variations in distance, eye contact, posture, trunk lean, and body orientation. The most favorable client responses were associated with closer distance, eye contact, forward leaning, and face-to-face orientation by the therapist.

719. **Kelly, Joseph Richard.** "Visually Perceived Nonverbal Behaviors of Teachers and their Relationship to Affective Responses of Students." Ed.D. dissertation, Oregon State University. 1973. 143 pp. (Order No. 73-12,864)

Thirty teachers were videotaped teaching their classes, and these were shown without sound to 879 seventh to ninth grade students. Students' scores on a semantic differential and their records of the teacher's characteristics indicated, among other results, that students liked teachers who smiled often, boys liked teachers who gestured more, and girls preferred "teachers who seldom manipulated objects while teaching."

720. **Kendall, Philip C.; Deardoff, P.A.; Finch, A.J. Jr.; and Graham, Lewis.** "Proxemics, Locus of Control, Anxiety, and Type of Movement in Emotionally

Disturbed and Normal Boys." *Journal of Abnormal Child Psychology* 4 (1976) : 9-16.

An investigation of the interpersonal distancing needs of normal and emotionally disturbed boys was conducted. A sample of 20 elementary school boys and 20 emotionally disturbed boys were given: the Nowicki-Strickland Locus of Control Scale for Children; the State-Trait Anxiety Inventory for Children; the Subject Movement Index (SMI); and the Experimenter Movement Index (EMI). Findings indicate that emotionally disturbed boys require significantly more personal space. Further results suggest that neither anxiety nor locus of control account for the differences in spatial requirements between the two groups.

721. **Kendon, Adam.** "How People Interact." In *The Book of Family Therapy*, edited by A. Ferber, M. Mendelsohn, and A. Napier, pp. 351-386. New York: Science House, 1972.

A very clear and useful summary of research on the role of visible behavior in interaction. The author discusses the varieties of visible behavior under the aspects of appearance, proximation, and kinesis. The role of spatial arrangement, orientation, gaze, and posture in the regulation of conversation is addressed, as well as the regulation of utterance exchanges through orientation, gaze, and movement synchrony. The relation of changes in body position to units of the individual's performance is also discussed.

722. **Kendon, Adam.** "Gesticulation, Speech, and the Gesture Theory of Language Origins." *Sign Language Studies* 9 (1975) : 349-373.

Kendon discusses Gordon Hewes' hypothesis that language developed in prehistory from gesture in the light of his own research on the relationship of gesticulation to speech. This research has shown that not only do gesture and speech share a common rhythmic organization but that gesture is related to the semantic content of speech. Gestures often begin before the related speech, are completed even if the speech is hesitant or interrupted, and reflect the theme or central idea of the utterance. This is taken as evidence that gesture is integral to the act of uttering and that gesture and speech are alternate channels in the encoding of ideas, providing support for a reportive function of gesture at an earlier stage of human development.

723. **Kendon, Adam.** "Some Functions of the Face in a Kissing Round." *Semiotica* 15 (1975) : 299-334.

This is an intitial attempt to explore the function of the face in the organization of interaction. The author describes the analysis of a four-minute film of a man and woman kissing in a public park. A repertoire of nine classes of facial patterns is identified for the female. The role of these facial patterns in maintaining, regulating, and modifying the phases of interaction is analyzed. Specifically, a change in the interaction appears to be signaled by a "pre-enactment" of the new behavior which allows the partner to respond and makes the change a joint achievement. This research suggests that females possess more differentiated facial expressions than males. A comparison with couples observed in similar settings suggests that females share a repertoire of facial patterns that function in similar ways as in the interaction described above.

724. **Kendon, Adam.** *Studies in the Behavior of Face-to-Face Interaction.* Lisse, Netherlands: Peter de Ridder Press, 1977. 260 pp.

A collection of key papers by an important researcher of human interaction, this volume contains Kendon's seminal papers on the organization of interaction, "Some Functions of Gaze Direction in Social Interaction" (1967) and "Movement Coordination in Social Interaction" (1970). Other chapters include a review of R.L. Birdwhistell's *Kinesics and Context* (1972), "Some Functions of the Face in a Kissing Round" (1975), and "A Description of Some Human Greetings" (1973) with Andrew Ferber. Also included is a new paper, "The F-formation System: Spatial Orientational Relations in Face-to-Face Interaction," and an appendix on techniques of film analysis.

725. **Kendon, Adam.** "Some Theoretical and Methodological Aspects of the Use of Film in the Study of Social Interaction." In *Emerging Strategies in Social Psychological Research,* edited by G.P. Ginsburg, pp. 67-91. New York: Wiley, 1979.

This is a clear and useful account of the historical background, theoretical assumptions, and methodological procedures of the context analysis of social interaction. There is a discussion of Albert Scheflen's formulation of the procedures of context analysis with reference to recent developments in other disciplines, such as conversation analysis, that are similar in outlook. Practical matters dealing with the making of films are addressed and an overview of findings from research using this approach is presented.

726. **Kendon, Adam.** "The Sign Language of the Women of Yuendumu: A Preliminary Report on the Structure of Warlpiri Sign Language." *Sign Language Studies* 27 (1980) : 101-113.

This article, along with a series of articles on the sign langue of the Enga Province of Papua New Guinea forthcoming in *Semiotica*, represents an extension of Kendon's interest in gesture into the area of sign language. The Warlpiri sign language reported here is an "alternative sign language," one used by people who also have available spoken language; its analysis may clarify how the medium of expression affects the development of a linguistic code.

727. **Kendon, Adam.** "Geography of Gesture." *Semiotica,* forthcoming.

This extended discussion of gesture centered on Desmond Morris et al.'s *Gestures: Their Origins and Distributions* begins with a history of the study of gesture. Focusing on the type of gestures called "emblems," Kendon discusses the methods used by the authors in their study and the meanings of the emblems they identified in relation to the properties of gesture as an expressive medium. He expands upon the topics of the geographical distribution, diffusion and history of emblems and discusses the processes by which gestures originate.

728. **Kendon, Adam.** "Semiotics and Nonverbal Communication." In *The Encyclopedic Dictionary of Semiotics,* T.A. Sebeok, Editor-in-Chief. Bloomington, Indiana: Indiana University Press, and London: Macmillan, forthcoming.

In this overview of nonverbal communication, Kendon discusses the origin and inadequacies of the term "nonverbal communication," and the psychological, structural and ethological approaches to nonverbal communication research. The bulk of the article is a survey of findings on the visible aspects of interaction: appearance, behavioral style, spatial organization, posture, turn-taking and the regulation of interaction, the face, direction of gaze, touch, and gesture.

729. **Kendon, Adam, and Ferber, Andrew.** "A Description of Some Human Greetings." In *Comparative Ecology and Behaviour of Primates,* edited by R.P. Michael and J.H. Crook, pp. 591-668. London: Academic Press, 1973. Illus.

Ninety-two greeting sequences were analyzed to reveal a common structure underlying them. The general phases and specific behaviors that characterize them are: sighting and initiation of approach, marked by eye contact, head movements, smiling, and synchronization of movement; distance salutation characterized by head toss, head lower, nod, or wave; head dip sometimes noted on the part of one interactant; approach, marked by facial orientation, "body cross" (one or both arms crossing upper part of body), and grooming; final approach, accompanied by smiling, distinctive headset, and "palm presentation"; and close salutation with or without body contact. The authors note conflicting findings on cultural differences and universals in greetings and suggest that there is a difference in function between close and distance salutations.

730. **Kendon, Adam; Harris, Richard M.; and Key, Mary Ritchie,** eds. *Organization of Behavior in Face-to-Face Interaction.* The Hague: Mouton, 1975. 509 pp. Illus.

This landmark book is a collection of papers presented and discussed at a research conference on face-to-face interaction reported to the IX International Congress of Anthropological and Ethnological Sciences in 1973. The introduction by Adam Kendon describes the history of approaches to the study of interaction and the main topics of the conference. Among the 25 articles are theoretical perspectives including Harvey B. Sarles on an ethological approach to human communicaton and Albert Scheflen on models and epistemologies in the study of interaction, and methodological studies by Margaret Bullowa on the synchronization of behavior in mother-infant interactions, Siegfried Frey on tonic effects in interaction, and Henry W. Seaford, Jr. on dialects of facial expression. Studies of the organization of behavior in social encounters include Albert Scheflen on micro-territories in interaction, Frederick Erickson on proxemic shifts, and articles by Norman Markel and Starkey Duncan, Jr. on conversation analysis. Articles on the relationship of body movement and language include Walburga von Raffler-Engel on the correlation of gestures and verbalization in first language acquisition, William C. Stokoe, Jr. on sign language; and A.A. Leontiev on psycholinguistics; new developments in paralinguistics are discussed in papers by Richard M. Harris and David Rubinstein; Philip Lieberman; and Fernando Poyatos. Ian Vine has contributed a paper on the spatial regulation of interaction, and Glen McBride a study of the control of behavior in interaction. Cultural differences in interaction are discussed in papers by Dean C. Barnlund on communicative styles in Japan and the United States and Alan Lomax on culture-style factors in face-to-face interaction. The volume concludes with postscripts by Don Handelman and Frederick Erickson.

731. **Kern, James Lewis.** "An Analysis of the Effects of Physical Distance and Sex of the Counselor on Client Response in the Counseling Situation." Ph.D. dissertation, University of Wyoming. 1971. 125 pp. (Order No. 71-13,035)

Undergraduates viewed one of three counselor pairs in a session with counselors seated about three, six, or 12 feet from the client. Effects of seating distance but not sex of counselor significantly related to the scale scores of semantic differential. However, some interaction effects of counselor sex x distance are reported.

732. **Kern, Stephen.** *A Cultural History of the Human Body.* Indianapolis, New York: The Bobbs-Merrill Co., 1975. 307 pp. Illus.

The body influences our social existence and oftentimes is a source of anxiety and pain. Since the mid-nineteenth century, the author argues, Western men and women have gradually approached an acceptance and understanding of their corporeality. In addition to outlining the dissolution of restrictive sexual morality in the Victorian era, the author traces developments in fashion and art and their relation to the "liberation" of the body. He also recounts theories on the bodily determinants of gender roles and family relations.

733. **Kestenberg, Judith S.** *Children and Parents: Psychoanalytic Studies in Development.* New York: Jason Aronson, 1975. 496 pp.

This noted child analyst has pursued the study of movement patterns in infants and children for over 25 years. In this volume on her psychoanalytic writing, there are several chapters devoted to the special perspective on movement, personality, and development developed by Kestenberg and her associates. "Development of the Young Child as Expressed through Bodily Movement," coauthored by J. Kestenberg, H. Marcus, E. Robbins, J. Berlowe, and A. Buelte, discusses the mechanisms of "self-regulation" in the infant in terms of movement rhythms of "tension flow" and "shape flow," and psychosexual stages as evidenced in motor rhythms; "The Development of the Young Child from Birth through Latency, as Seen through Bodily Movements, II" and "Rhythmic Patterns in Motility," coauthored by J. Kestenberg and E. Robbins, follows this line of research into adolescence with analysis of bodily attitudes fluctuating and consolidations of movement rhythms and their developmental correlates.

734. **Kestenberg, Judith S.** "Ego Organization in Obsessive-Compulsive Development: A Study of the Rat Man, Based on Interpretation of Movement Patterns." In *Freud and His Patients,* Volume 2, edited by M. Kanzer and J. Glenn, pp. 144-179. New York: Jason Aronson, 1980.

The author sets out to reconstruct the "ego organization" defenses and identification of this famous patient who came to be called the "Rat Man" from Freud's description of his movements and "action-thoughts." This is done within the author's formulation of movement patterns specific to particular drives and developmental stages. While it is technical psychoanalytic writing, tables at the end with movement terms and their interpretation help clarify the concepts used.

735. **Kestenberg, Judith S., and Marcus, Hershey.** "Hypothetical Monosex and Bisexuality: A Psychoanalytic Interpretation of Sex Differences As They Reveal Themselves in Movement Patterns of Men and Women." In *Psychosexual Imperatives,* edited by N.M. Colemna and J. Ikenberry, pp. 146-181. New York: Human Sciences Press, 1979.

Making a distinction in analytic notions of "active" and "passive" in terms of attitudes toward reality, to forms of relating, and to "aims of drives," the authors present movement correlates of these. Adapting R. Laban and W. Lamb's concepts for movement description, they discuss what is "aggressive, active, and male" and what is "sexual, passive, and female" and a "monosexual model" of what is "pure femaleness" and "pure maleness," although "both men and women use all patterns of movement in countless combinations."

736. **Kestenberg, Judith S., with Sossin, K. Mark.** *The Role of Movement Patterns in Development.* Vol. 2, Epilogue and Glossary. New York: Dance Notation Press, 1979. 164 pp.

This volume continues the report of three children followed from infancy to 20 years of age, particularly the development of their movement patterns in relation to personality and to significant relationships. It is also a concise treatise on the author's method of analyzing movement rhythm, particularly the "tension flow" and "shape flow" measures of rhythmic fluctuation. Developmental stages from infancy through adolescence are conceptualized within a psychoanalytic framework and individual movement styles assessed through a complex Movement Profile utilizing concepts of Laban's effort-shape analysis. Interaction between mother and child is discussed in terms of compatible and clashing rhythms and movement style preferences. There are chapters on notation of these rhythms, recording, scoring, and constructing Movement Profiles, and a very thorough glossary of terms for the movement and developmental analyses.

737. **Key, Mary Ritchie.** "Review of Garrick Mallery, *Sign Language Among North American Indians: Compared with that Among Other Peoples and Deaf Mutes* (Reprinted in *Approaches to Semiotica* 14)." *Linguistics* 132 (1974) : 116-123.

This book review of the reprinted version of Mallery's classic work contains many references to other articles on various sign languages.

738. **Key, Mary Ritchie.** *Male-Female Language: With a Comprehensive Bibliography.* Metuchen, New Jersey: Scarecrow Press, 1975. 190 pp.

In a chapter entitled "Non-Verbal Extra-Linguistic Messages" the author reviews a portion of research on paralinguistic and kinesic differences between males and females. Cross-cultural differences in nonverbal behavior between the sexes are also discussed. The bibliography in the book deals primarily with linguistic behavior but does include some references to kinesic literature.

739. **Key, Mary Ritchie.** *Paralanguage and Kinesics.* Metuchen, New Jersey: Scarecrow Press, 1975. 246 pp.

Part one of this book is a detailed discussion of human nonverbal behavior including definitions, a theoretical model, and an overview of the general field. It has a discussion of paralanguage, kinesics, senses, silence, contexts, and dialects. Part two contains an extensive bibliography.

740. **Key, Mary Ritchie.** *Nonverbal Communication: A Research Guide and Bibliography.* Metuchen, New Jersey: The Scarecrow Press, 1977. 439 pp.

In the first part the author provides a literature review and background material on nonverbal communication to help conceptualize the field and appreciate its research methods. The author addresses many topics including the nature of communication, acquisition of communication, notation systems of nonverbal behavior, elements of nonverbal behavior, and dialects. Part two of the book is a detailed bibliography of nonverbal communication.

741. **Key, Mary Ritchie,** ed. *The Relationship of Verbal and Nonverbal Communication.* The Hague: Mouton, 1980. 388 pp. Illus.

Authors from three continents have contributed articles that describe research in language and nonverbal communication in cross-cultural ways. Speech acts and nonverbal acts, as two modes of communication, are inextricably related. They are seen as organizers of social systems. Linguistic concepts can be applied to nonverbal acts. Rhythm and timing, for example, combine the force and range of vocalizations and movement to make up the suprasegmental of human interaction. Among the authors represented in this volume are William S. Condon, Willett Kempton, Carolyn Leonard-Dolan, Thomas J. Bruneau, Starkey Duncan Jr., Howard M. Rosenfeld, Margaret Hancks, Adam Kendon, Edward S. Tronick, Heidelise Als, and T. Berry Brazelton. (from pre-publication notice by the editor)

742. **Key, Mary Ritchie,** ed. *Nonverbal Communication Today: Current Research.* The Hague: Mouton, Illus. Forthcoming.

This work is a compliation of recent research in all areas of nonverbal communication. The book is divided into six general sections. Section one is entitled "Overall Considerations of Human Beings Interacting in Their World" and is authored by Mary Key. A second section by V. Sonnenfeld relates to ecological and artifactual patterning. Section three related to physiological and social aspects of interaction. Section four deals with expressive and linguistic aspects of nonverbal behavior. The origins and development of communicative behavior are the concerns of section five. Theoretical modeling of communicative behavior is explored in section six. Authors contributing chapters related to kinesics include Betty A. Edwards, Howard S. Friedman, Glendon Schubert, Michael Argyle, Jean A. Graham and Marge Kreckel, Nico H. Frijda, Fernando Poyatos, Beatrice Beebe, Kenneth H. Abrams, Sheila J. White, Jaan Valsiner and Juri Allik. Special topics covered include eye pupil to eye pupil interaction, nonverbal communication as political behavior, behavioral elements of social and work situations, micro-timing in mother-infant communication, children's facial movement and parents' understanding of it, and nonverbal antecedents to language function. (information from the author)

743. **Kiesler, Donald J.** "An Interpersonal Communication Analysis of Relationship in Psychotherapy." *Psychiatry* 42 (1979) : 299-311.

The author's approach to psychotherapy views abnormal behavior as that which elicits an aversive reaction from the communication partner. The goal of the therapist is to uncover the aberrant message given, bring it to the patient's attention, and restore normal communication. He states that nonverbal behaviors play an important role in the communication process and need to be carefully looked at.

744. **Kimura, Doreen.** "Manual Activity During Speaking—I. Right-Handers." *Neuropsychologia* 11 (1973) : 45-50.

The hand movements of 12 male and 12 female right-handers were recorded for five minutes in each of three conditions: speaking, performing a silent verbal task, and performing a silent nonverbal task. Analysis of the frequency of self-touching and free (nonself-touching) movements revealed significantly more movement during speaking than in nonspeaking conditions. Free movements almost never occurred without speech and nearly always involved the right hand. Self-touching movements were performed equally by the right and left hand. During the silent verbal task self-touching movements were more often performed by the left hand than the right, but during the silent nonverbal task the right hand was more often involved. In a further test to investigate movement during vocalization, the movements of 24 subjects were recorded during five minutes of humming and five minutes of speaking. The occurrence of free movements during humming was negligible. In a final test for cerebral lateralization of speech functions, it was found that the laterality of free movements was significantly related to the cerebral hemisphere that controls speech.

745. **Kimura, Doreen.** "Manual Activity During Speaking—II. Lefthanders." *Neuropsychologia* 11 (1973) : 51-55.

The hand movements of 18 left-handers, 17 right-handers, and nine ambidextrous subjects were recorded during speaking. Subjects were also given a hand preference test and a dichotic words test to determine cerebral dominance for speech. Results for left-handed and ambidextrous subjects were combined. There was a significant difference between the total number of movements made by right-handers with left speech laterality and left-handers with right speech laterality but not between right- and left-handers who both had left speech laterality. Ther were significantly more free (nonself-touching) movements made by left-handers than right-handers, with no difference between the two left-handed groups. The results supported previous evidence that speech is more bilaterally organized in left-handers than in right-handers.

746. **King, Nancy R.** *A Movement Approach to Acting.* Englewood Cliffs, New Jersey: Prentice-Hall, 1981. 300 pp. Illus.

This book offers a series of exercises for acting students to explore nonverbal communication and group dynamics. There are sections on fundamentals of alignment, breathing, and movement warm-ups, "physicalizing a script," "unarmed stage combat," and the like, plus illustrative references to specific plays. (from publisher's information)

747. **Kinsbourne, Marcel.** "Eye and Head Turning Indicates Cerebral Lateralization." *Science* 176 (1972) : 539-541.

It was hypothesized that the direction in which people look while thinking reflects cerebral lateralization. In a study of 40 undergraduates, results showed that right-handed subjects turned eyes and head to the right with verbal problems and to the left and up with nonverbal and spatial problems.

748. **Kinsbourne, Marcel.** "Direction of Gaze and Distribution of Cerebral Thought Processes." *Neuropsychologica* 12 (1974) : 279-281.

A review of the pertinent literature—Kocel *et al.*, Hiscock, and Berman *et al.*—concludes that during verbal thought subjects look right, while during spatial thought they look up and to the left. This effect is weakened or abolished if subjects are asked to hold central fixation, if they are confronted by an experimenter or by the sound of his voice, or if they are set to respond other than straight ahead. The phenomenon is considered a useful index of "cerebral lateralization of cognitive function."

749. **Kiritz, S.** "Hand Movement and Clinical Ratings at Admission and Discharge for Hospitalized Psychiatric Patients." Ph.D. dissertation, University of California, San Francisco. 1971. 100 pp. (Order No. 73-3669)

This study examined in particular the effects of depression, anxiety, and hostility on hand movements ("illustrators" and "adaptors") of 32 female psychiatric inpatients. Results indicated that depression reduced illustrator hand movements, anxiety increased self-touch (adaptors), and that hostility increased the amount of scratching and picking adaptor hand movements.

750. **Kirk, Lorraine, and Burton, Michael.** "Physical versus Semantic Classification of Non-Verbal Forms: A Cross-Cultural Experiment." *Semiotica* 17 (1976) : 315-337.

This study tested two alternative hypotheses: that classification of emblems (a specific nonverbal behavior that could be interchanged with equivalent verbal form) would focus on visual/anatomical criteria; and that classification of emblems would focus on semantic/verbal critieria. Verbal and kinesic versions of the emblems were administered to groups of Kikuyu and Maasai. The results support the hypothesis that people use the same criteria for classifying the nonverbal emblems as they use for classifying the verbal labels.

751. **Klaus, Marshall H.; Jerauld, Richard; Kreger, Nancy C.; McAlpine, Willie; Steffa, Meredith; and Kennell, John H.** "Maternal Attachment: The Importance of the First Postpartum Days." *New England Journal of Medicine* 286 (1972) : 460-463.

Traditionally bottle-feeding mothers are allowed brief contact with their newborns shortly after birth, within six to 12 hours after birth, and 20 to 30 minute visits every four hours. In this study 14 mothers were additionally allowed one hour within the first three hours and five extra hours each afternoon during the first three days after delivery. To evaluate possible differences in behavior, control and extended-contact, mothers were interviewed, observed during an examination, and filmed while feeding the infant one month after delivery. Orientation, body contact, and fondling were among the 25 activities that were scored. During the examination the extended contact mothers were more hesitant to leave the infant, usually stood, watched, and exhibited soothing behavior. No significant difference in gaze behavior or caretaker activities were noted during feeding, but extended contact mothers fondled and used "en face" orientation more frequently. The authors suggested this early postnatal time may affect the attachment of the mother to the child.

752. Kleck, Robert E.; Vaughan, Robert C.; Cartwright-Smith; Jeffrey E.; Vaughan, Katherine B.; Colby, Carl Z.; and Lanzetta, John T. "Effects of Being Observed on Expressive, Subjective, and Physiological Responses to Painful Stimuli." *Journal of Personality and Social Psychology* 34 (1976) : 1211-1218.

A first experiment found that nonverbal expressive responses to shock decreased when the 20 male subjects were observed, accompanied by a general decrease in self-report and autonomic responses to painful stimuli. The experiment was replicated with 40 male undergraduates, and the sex of the observer was found to have no effect on the expressive, subject, and autonomic measures of arousal.

753. Kleinfeld, J.S. "Effects of Nonverbally Communicated Personal Warmth on the Intelligence Test Performance of Indian and Eskimo Adolescents." *The Journal of Social Psychology* 91 (1973) : 149-150.

After being given a baseline WAIS, 15 Athabascan Indian and Eskimo students were randomly assigned to be retested by a black male on two subtests in a nonverbally warm or nonverbally cold manner. On both subtests, in the nonverbally warm condition most students gained points, while in the nonverbally cold condition several lost points, some stayed the same, and only one gained points.

754. Kleinfeld, J.S. "Effects of Nonverbal Warmth on the Learning of Eskimo and White Students." *The Journal of Social Psychology* 92 (1974) : 3-9.

Twenty Eskimo and 20 white ninth graders were instructed by a white female teacher in a nonverbally warm manner, then a nonverbally neutral manner, or the reverse sequence. Eskimos asked significantly more questions in the warm-neutral sequence, while no effects were found for whites. Eskimo males learned significantly more in the warm-neutral sequence, but white males did not. White males learned significantly more in the neutral-warm sequence. Among females, significantly more learning took place only in the neutral-warm sequence. Only females showed significant effects on question answering in the neutral-warm sequence.

755. Kleinke, Chris L. *First Impressions: The Psychology of Encountering Others.* Englewood Cliffs, New Jersey: Prentice-Hall, 1975. 137 pp.

Within this text on impression-formation, the author discusses those nonverbal elements, such as attractiveness, gaze, distance paralanguage, and body language which contribute to a person's first impressions of another.

756. Kleinke, Chris L. "Compliance to Requests Made by Gazing and Touching Experimenters in Field Settings." *Journal of Experimental Social Psychology* 13 (1977) : 218-223.

In the first experiment, a female experimenter approached men leaving a phone booth where a dime had been left. While she asked each man if he had found a dime, she used a low or high rate of direct gaze and touched or did not touch the subject. In the second experiment, a female experimenter approached both men and women in a middle-class shopping mall and asked if she could borrow a dime. Results show no relationship in the first study between the person's estimated age and compliance; compliance was greater under touch and high gaze conditions. In the second experiment, men responded more often than women.

757. Kleinke, Chris L. "Interaction Between Gaze and Legitimacy of Request on Compliance in a Field Setting." *Journal of Nonverbal Behavior* 5 (1980) : 3-12.

It was hypothesized that experimenter gaze would lead to increased compliance with a legitimate request and decreased compliance with an illegitimate request. Subjects (95 males, 73 females) in Experiment 1 gave more dimes for a phone call to gazing rather than nongazing female experimenters. Experimenter gaze did not influence dimes given by subjects for a candy bar. Experiment 2 replicated Experiment 1 with a different legitimacy manipulation and with an additional treatment including both gaze and touch. A significant interaction showed that subjects 56 males, 58 females) gave more dimes for a legitimate request (phone call) when they received gaze alone or gaze and touch from a female experimenter. Subjects gave more dimes for an illegitimate request (buying gum) when the experimenter did not gaze at or touch them.

758. **Kleinke, Chris L.; Bustos, Armando A.; Meeker, Frederick B.; and Staneski, Richard.** Effects of Self-Attributed and Other Attributed Gaze on Interpersonal Evaluations Between Males and Females." *Journal of Experimental Social Psychology* 9 (1973) : 154-163.

Thirty male-female pairs of undergraduates were left alone for ten minutes to talk about anything they wished. The experimenter returned and gave the subjects false feedback about the amount of gaze that had occurred between them during that time. Subjects then evaluated each other on a rating scale. Among the results it was found that male subjects rated their female partners least favorably when they thought that their gaze toward the female was high and most favorably when they thought that their gaze towards the female was low. The opposite pattern was found for the women. They gave a positive rating to male partners when told that their gaze had been high and a less favorable rating to those male partners whom they thought they had gazed at less.

759. **Kleinke, Chris L.; Desautels, Marilynn S.; and Knapp, Barbara E.** "Adult Gaze and Affective and Visual Responses of Preschool Children." *Journal of Genetic Psychology* 131 (1977) : 321-322.

Forty-eight children between the ages of three and five participated in this study. Female experimenters gazed either 80 percent or 20 percent of the time at the child while playing a five-minute word game. Girls were found to gaze at the experimenter more than boys, and all subjects gazed more at experimenters with a high rate of gaze. Boys liked experimenters better when the rate of gaze was low, while the opposite was true for girls.

760. **Kleinke, Chris L.; Meeker, Frederick B.; and La Fong, Carl.** "Effects of Gaze, Touch, and Use of Name on Evaluation of 'Engaged' Couples." *Journal of Research in Personality* 7 (1974) : 368-373.

Videotapes were made of six actors playing the roles of engaged couples in an "interview." Actors varied their behavior in terms of gaze-no-gaze, touch-no-touch, and using each other's names or not. The tapes were shown to undergraduates who were asked to evaluate the couples on such adjectives as "phoney," "relaxed," and so on. Results show most favorably received couples gazed and touched and did not use each others' names as much as those less favorably rated. The results are discussed in terms of equilibrium theory and research on interpersonal attraction.

761. **Kleinke, Chris L.; Staneski, Richard A.; and Berger, Dale E.** "Evaluation of an Interviewer as a Function of Interviewer Gaze, Reinforcement of Subject Gaze, and Interviewer Attractiveness." *Journal of Personality and Social Psychology* 31 (1975) : 115-122.

The amount of gaze by female interviewers was manipulated in interviews with 54 male college students. When subjects returned the gaze, they were reinforced with green light feedback, receiving red light feedback when averting gaze for more than six seconds. Subjects in a control condition received red and green lights at random.

The attitude of the experimental subjects to the interviewer was not affected, although their gaze increased slightly. Interviewers in the no-gaze condition received the most negative reactions from subjects. Attractiveness of the interviewer did not affect the subjects' reactions in the nongazing condition.

762. **Kleinpaul, Rudolf.** *Sprache ohne Worte: Idee einer allgemeiner Wissenschaft der Sprache.* The Hague: Mouton, 1972.

Number 17 of the Approaches to Semiotics Series, this is a reprint of an original 1888 work in German on "language without words."

763. **Klima, Edward S., and Bellugi, Ursula,** ed. *The Signs of Language.* Cambridge, Massachusetts: Harvard University Press, 1979. 417 pp. Illus.

This collection of papers reports on research carried out at the Salk Institute for Biological Studies concerning the properties of American Sign Langage (ASL) as a language system. Part 1 deals with the iconic and arbitrary aspects of gestural signs. Following Stokoe, the authors discuss lexical signs as the simultaneous occurrence of particular values of the three parameters of hand configuration, place of articulation, and movement. Part 2 reports studies of the functional reality of these sublexical parameters. Of special interest is "A Feature Analysis of Handshapes," a distinctive feature analysis for ASL hand configurations analogous to the analysis of phonemes for spoken language. Part 3 discusses the discovery of grammatical processes in ASL and the structured use of space and movement that they exhibit.

764. **Knapp, Mark L.** *Nonverbal Communication in Human Interaction.* Second Edition. New York: Holt, Rinehart and Winston, 1978. 428 pp. Illus.

This second edition of Knapp's textbook provides an in depth report of many aspects of nonverbal communication research. Child development, personality, and territoriality are some of the many topics discussed. The book also includes a selected bibliography at the end of every chapter as well as any photographs, charts, and diagrams. An instructor's manual revised by Mary Wieman accompanies the text.

765. **Knapp, Mark L.** *Social Intercourse: From Greeting to Goodbye.* Boston, Massachusetts: Allyn and Bacon, 1978.

766. **Knapp, Mark L.** *Essentials of Nonverbal Communication.* New York: Holt, Rinehart & Winston, 1980.

767. **Knight, David L.; Langmeyer, Daniel; and Lundgren, David C.** "Eye Contact, Diatance, and Affiliation: The Role of Observer Bias." *Sociometry* 36 (1973) : 390–401. Illus.

The role of observerbias in identification of eye contact was investigated. In one experiment two observers, at a constant distance from the dyad, noted the time spent of two, five, and eight feet. The amount of recorded eye contact increased with distance. The confederate in the second experiment made minor gaze adjustments, looking at an ear or shoulder during the conversation. Analysis of 36 observers in 18 dyadic trials revealed substantial overrecording of eye contact at all distances. The use of video for analysis of eye contact is proposed.

768. **Knight, Philip H. and Bair, Carolyn K.** "Degree of Client Comfort as a Function of Dyadic Interaction Distance." *Journal of Psychology* 23 (1976) : 13–16.

Twenty-seven college students interacted with male counselors at one of three interpersonal distances (18, 30, or 48 inches). Responses on semantic differential scales indicated significant differences in reported comfort at the three distances, with subjects at 30 inches reporting the greatest comfort and those at 18 inches the least comfort.

769. **Knott, Gladys P.** "Nonverbal Communication During Early Childhood." *Theory Into Practice* 18 (1979): 226–244.

This article is an overview and synthesis of the major contribution so nonverbal communication to the study of childhood and child development. Using E.Moerk's model of nonverbal communication (where nonverbal communication is a precursor to auditory verbal behavior), the author discusses three functions of nonverbal communication in young children (substituting, complimenting, and supporting), the relationship between verbal and nonverbal behavior in children, the gestural behavior of young children, and some nonverbal communication deficiencies in young children and their implications.

770. **Knowles, Eric S.** "Boundaries Around Social Space: Dyadic Responses to an Invader." *Environment and Behavior* 4 (1972) : 437–445.

Seventy-two adult dyads were observed that contained equal numbers of same-and mixed-sex pairs. An experimenter purposefully walked between approaching natural dyads. It was felt that the integitry of the dyad would be maintained, especially for opposite-sex combinations. Results showed that a significant number of dyads moved to maintain their integrity from invasion, and this was more true for the male-female dyads than for the same-sex combinations, and least true for male-male dyads.

771. **Knowles, Eric S.** "Boundaries Around Group Interaction: The Effect of Group Size and Member Status on Boundary Permeability." *Journal of Personality and Social Psychology* 26 (1973) : 327–331.

Experimenters observed groups of two or four interacting people and "control groups" of two or four wastebaskets that were positioned in the center of a university hallway. Results showed that fewer subjects walked through high-status than low-status groups; fewer subjects penetrated the four-person than the two-person groups; and arrangements of wastebaskets were walked through more than interacting groups.

772. **Knowles, Eric S.** "Convergent Validity of Personal Space Measures: Consistent Results with Low Intercorrelations." *Journal of Nonverbal Behavior* 4 (1980) : 240–248.

Low correlations among personal space measures have been used as evidence against their convergent validity. This argument is analyzed and found limited to personality trait assumptions. Convergent validity more generally concerns whether findings from one measure generalize to other measures. In the present study 91 subjects completed three measures (a disguised interaction distance, figure placement distances, and the Comfortable Interpersonal Distance Scale) under different conditions of subject sex, sex of the other person, and acquaintance with the other person. The three measures showed an average intercorrelation of r =.034, but consistent significant effects of acquaintance. These findings demonstrate that convergence of findings may be obtained even when measures are not highly correlated.

773. **Knowles, Eric; Kreuser, Barbara; Haas, Susan; Hyde, Michael; and Schuchart, Guy.** "Group Size and the Extension of Social Space Boundaries." *Journal of Personality and Social Psychology* 33 (1976) : 647–654.

In the first of two experiments, pedestrians in a university hallway were observed passing a bench that was either empty, occupied by one person, or occupied by interacting groups of two, three, or four people. Passer-by walked farther from individuals than from an empty bench and farther from groups than from individuals. In the second experiment, 20 college students were given ten drawings of a hallway with an alcove containing one, two four six,eight people, or no one. The groups were arranged in either a closed circle or facing into the hall. The subjects were asked to trace an imaginary pathway they would take past each arrangement. The deflections increased with the group size, supporting the authors' hypoyhesis of a social space boundary around interacting groups.

774. **Knust, Albrecht.** *a Dictionary of Kinetography Laban (Labanotation).* Vol. I; *Text.* Vol.II; *Examples.* Estover, Plymouth, England: MacDonald and Evans, 1979. 420pp. and 162 pp. Illus.

These two volumes present the notation originally developed by Rudolf Laban with the text of volume I organized by categories such as "direction signs," "support," "floor pattern," and so on and volume II presenting the respective symbols illustrating notations of these categories.

775. **Kocel, Katherine; Galin, David; Ornstein, Robert; and Merrin, Edward L.** "Lateral Eye Movement and Cognitive Mode." *Psychonomic Science* 27 (1972) : 223–224.

Verbally oriented questions are presumed to trigger the left brain hemisphere whereas spatially oriented questions the right hemisphere. To investigate a possible correlation between hemispheric activity and lateral gaze shifts, 16 males and 13 females were videotaped when asked 20 verbal and 20 spatial questions. The first eye movement during or following a question was scored as either a right or left shift. Both types of questions were found to elicit lateral eye movements. Individual tendencies toward left or right gaze shifting were noted and were strongly augmented by the type of question posed.

776. **Kochman, Thomas.** *Rappin' and Stylin' Out: Communication in Urban Black America.* Urbana, Illinois: University of Illinois Press, 1972. 424 pp. Illus.

A volume intended to identify some of the communicative and behavioral norms of urban black America, this collection of essays includes selections on nonverbal, verbal, and expressive role behaviors. The five articles dealing with nonverbal communication include discussions of time-related etiquette; "giving skin," highly personalized gretting touches; postures; styles of walking; hair and clothing; black folk music; the aesthetics of black music, particularly jazz, and the response characterictics of black audiences. Additional information concerning role specific modes of nonverbal communication are included in the selections on the street youth or "gowster" and the preacher, while the definition and etymology of many terms dealing with nonverbal behavior in the urban black dialect are included in the selections of the kinetic elements in black American English and African elements in American English.

777. **Koivumaki, Juidth H.** "Body Language Taught Here." *Journal of Communication* 25 (1975) : 26-30.

This short review of contemporary popular books on nonverbal communication presents the pros and cons of individual books and discusses why their dissemination may be unfit. Specific examples of body language and its representation in these books are used throughout and explain how, in the author's opinion, they may be misleading.

778. **Koltai, Judith.** "An Experimental Study in the Reading of Movement Expression: Description, Observation, and Interpretation." *American Dance Therapy Association Monograph No. 2* (1972) : 13-34.

Ninety college students observed four one-minute scenes acted by two male actors portraying anger, fear, sorrow, and joy without vocalization and with clurred facial features. Subjects were asked to observe emotion, postural and gestural movements. The Semantic Differential Method of rating in terms of evaluation, potency, and activity was used. A high rate of consistency between observers was found in all categories, and there were no statictical difference between male and female observers.

779.   **Konecni, Vladimir J.; Libuser, Lynn; Morton, Houston; and Ebbesen, Ebbe B.** "Effects of a Violation of Personal Space on Escape and Helping Responses." *Journal of Experimental Social Psychology* 11 (1975) : 288-299

In a series of four field experiments of relation of personal space invasion to helping behavior was studied. Subjects were pedestrians waiting to cross a street. In the first experiment the experimenters stood at varying distances from subjects while they were waiting to cross the street. Results showed that the closer an experimenter stood, the faster the subject crossed the street. In the following experiments subjects had their personal space violated a short or long priod of time and then had the opportunity to return to the violator a low value of high value object that the violator dropped. The short invasion of space decreased the frequency of return of the low valued object. Victims of the longer invasion of space helped significantly less, regardless of the value of the object

780.   **Koneya, Mele, and Barbour, Alton.** *Louder Than Words: Non-Verbal Communication.* Columbus, Ohio: Charles E. Merrill, 1976.

781.   **Korner, Anneliese F.** "Sex Differences in Newborns with Special Reference to Differences in the Organization of Oral Behavior." *Journal of Child Psychology and Psychiatry* 14 (1973) : 19-29.

In this article the author reviews research on sex differences in newborns. Research findings point to come innate sex differences in tactile sensitivity, photic receptivity, type of spontaneous discharge behaviors, and frequency of reflex smiles and rhythmic mouthing. Also discussed are the results of an analysis of hand-mouth contact made from 1000 feet of film on each of 32 newborns, 17 males and 15 females. Data analysis of the frequences of hand approaching the mouth movements and mouth approaching the hand movements showed that females engage in significantly more mouth-to-hand approaches than males.

782.   **Korner, Anneliese F., and Thoman, Evelyn B.** "The Relative Efficacy of Contact and Vestibular-Proprioceptive Stimulation in Soothing Noenates." *Child Development* 43 (1972) : 443-453.

Forty full-term breast- or bottlefed newborns were given six common ways of being soothed, for example, being lifted from an examining table and put on the shoulder, or cradled horizontally. Results showed being ehld upright (vestibular-proprioceptive) stimulation had the greatest soothing effect both during and after intervention. Also, breast-fed infants cried significantly more after intervention, perhaps because they were hungrier. Individual differences in soothability were found.

783.   **Krail, Kristina A., and Leventhal, Gloria.** "The Sex Variable in the Intrusion of Personal Space." *Sociometry* 39 (1976) : 170-173.

Eighteen female and 18 male subjects seated at tables in a library were observed as a male or female confederate invaded their peraonal space by sitting across from or next to the subject, or sitting next to the subject and reading the subject's book. There was a significant decrease in the latency of response as the immediacy of the intruder increased, and in all conditions the male intruder elicited a reaction in a shorter period of time than the female intruder. Shorter latency of response occurred in same-sex intruders.

784. **Krames, Lester; Pliner, Patricia; and Alloway, Thomas,** eds. *Aggression, Dominance, and Individual Spacing: Advances in the Study of Communication and Affect,* Vol. 4. New York: Plenum Press, 1978. 173 pp. Illus.

The volume is composed of eight articles on aggression, dominance, and spacing and their role in the communication of affect. The acticles relate to nonverbal human communication are J. Freedman's review of crowding research, R. Abramovitch and F. Strayer's discussion of preschool social organization, and J. Cheyne's discussion of communication, affect, and social behavior. Other volumes in this series of note here include*Nonverbal Communication*edited by L. Krames, P. Pliner and T. Alloway and *Nonverbal Communication of Aggression* edited by P. Pliner, L. Krames, and T. Alloway.

785. **Krause, Rainer.** "Non verbales interaktives Verhalten von Stotterern und ihren Gesprächspartnern." *Schweizerische Zeitschrift für Psychologie und ihre Anwendungen* 37 (1978) : 177-201. Illus.

Pairs of stutterers interacting with fluent speakers were filmed in greeting situations and political discussions. It was found that in the political discussion context stutterers occupy more floor time and produce less "back-channel" behavior than fluent speakers. However, in the greeting context a control group of pairs of fluent speakers showed more interruptive speech than dyads including stutterers. There are descriptions of the back-channel behavior (smiles, headnods, head tilts toward the stutterer) observed in fluent speakers conversing with stutterers. Written in German.

786. **Krauss, Robert M.; Garlock, Connie M.; Beicker, Peter D.; and McMahon, Lee E.** "The Role of Audible and Visible Back-Channel Responses in Interpersonal Communication." *Journal of Personality and Social Psychology* 35 (1977) : 523-529. Illus.

A total of 48 pairs of student volunteers worked cooperatively on a communication task. Half the dyads communicated over a normal audio channel; the remainder communicated over a channel with one second audio delay. Half of the subjects could see their partners on an undelayed video image; the remainder of the subjects had no visual access. Encoding efficiency was greater in the no-delay than in the delay conditions, but the deleterious effects of delay were mitigated by visual access.

787. **Kraut, Robert E.** "Verbal and Nonverbal Cues in the Perception of Lying." *Journal of Personality and Social Psychology* 36 (1978) : 380-391.

These two experiments examine strategies observers use to detect lying in self-presentation. In experiment I male college students lied or told the truth in simulated job interviews. Forty-one observers were moderately accurate in their judgments. Plausability was found to be the best cue to truth-telling. Hesitation, inconsistency, postural shifts, smiling, and grooming were used in judgments of lying. A second experiment explored the effects of the manipulation of verbal content and silence on judgments of lying.

788. **Kravitz, Harvey, and Boehm, John J.** "Rhythmic Habit Patterns in Infancy: Their Sequence, Age of Onset and Frequency." *Child Development* 42 (1971) : 399-413.

In part one, the onset of hand-to-mouth sucking in normal infants and infants with low Apgar scores and perinatal disease was examined. The abnormal newborns showed significant delay in hand sucking. In part two, older infants were observed for the sequence, age of onset, and frequency of other common rhythmic habit patterns, such as fact kicking, lip sucking, arm biting, body rocking, toe sucking, head rolling and banging, and teeth grinding. Infants with Doan's syndrome and cerebral palsy show a marked delay in onset of these common rhythmic habits. Rhythmic habit patterns may help in the early diagnosis of developmental retardation.

789. **Krieger, Dolores.** "Therapeutic Touch: The Imprimatur of Nursing." *American Journal of Nursing* 75 (1975) : 784-787. Illus.

An experimental group of 16 nurses practiced treatment by therapeutic touch while caring for their patients; the control group of 16 gave nursing care without using therapeutic touch. Each nurse worked on two patients. Following treatment by therapeutic touch the mean hemoglobin values of the patients in the experimental group changed significantly from their pretest value, while no significant difference between the pre- and the post-test hemoglobin values was seen in patients cared for by the control group of nurses.

790. **Kristeva, Julia; Rey-Debove, Josette; and Umiker, Donna Jean,** eds. *Essays in Semiotics.* The Hague: Mouton, 1971.639 pp.

The wide-ranging collection of papers in English and French deals with the theory of semiotics and its application in several fields, among them linguistics, anthropology, and the arts. Of special note is the paper by Albert E. Scheflen, "Psychoanalytic Terms and Some Problems of Semiotics," on the problem of the generalizability of psychoanalytic concepts and their relationship as words to the behaviors they refer to. Kinesics is represented by "La sémiotique non linguistique" by Henri Hécaen and "Kinesics: Inter- and Intra-Channel Communication Research" by Ray L. Birdwhistell. Thomas A. Sebeok has contributed "On Chemical Signs" dealing with communication by smell, and Glen McBride in "On the Evolution of Human Language" suggests that developments in animal communication, nonverbal communication, and the study of language give clues to the way in which language originally developed.

791. **Kumin, Libby, and Lazar, Martin.** "gestural Communication in Preschool Children." *Perceptual and Motor Skills* 38 (1974) : 708-710

Fifty-six nursery school children were asked to encode and decode a specific nonverbal behavior, the emblem. The 30 emblems employed had such verbal equivalents as "hello" and "quiet." Moreover the emblems conveyed a range of verbal equivalents, from the simple to the complex. Four year olds were able to encode significantly more emblems than three year olds and correctly identified the more complex emblems.

792. **Kurtz, J.** "Nonverbal Norm Setting and Territorial Defense." Ph.D. dissertation, University of Delaware. 1975. 94 pp. (Order No. 75-20,554.)

Subjects were found to spatially avoid a staring confederate when given an "intrusive" rather than a "waiting" set.

793. **Kurtz, P. David; Harrison, Michael; Neisworth, John T.; and Jones, Russell T.** "Influence of 'Mentally Retarded' Label on Teacher's Nonverbal Behavior Toward Pre-School Children." *American Journal of Mental Deficiency* 82 (1977) : 204-206.

Twelve teachers were assigned to either an experimental or a control child. Although none of the children was handicapped, the experimental group children were labeled mentally retarded. After reading a description of the child's developmental status, the teacher read her or him a story. Results show that teachers showed less social distance by increased forward body lean with experimental retarded children.

794. **Kurtz, Richard M.** "Body Attitude and Self Esteem." *Proceedings of the 79th Annual Convention of the American Psychological Association* 6 (1971) : 467-468.

Twenty male and 20 female undergraduates were administered a group form of the Body Attitude Scale and the Ziller Self-Esteem Scale. High-esteem males see their bodies as more potent than low-esteem males, and high-esteem females see their bodies as less potent than low-esteem females.

795. **Kurtz, Ron, and Pretera, Hector.** *The Body Reveals.* New York: Bantam Books, 1977. 162 pp. Illus.

This is an introduction to what body structure, posture, and physiognomy can reveal about a person's character and "way of being" inm the world. Basic concepts such as energy, gravity, and grounding are clarified. Analyses of specific people's bodies, including the authors', are presented as illustrations. The final chapter discusses body-oriented therapies: Rolfing, Bioenergetics and Reichian therapy, Aston patterning, and the Alexander and Feldenkrais techniques.

796. **Kuschel, Rolf.** "The Silent Inventor: The Creation of a Sign Language by the Only Deaf-Mute on a Polynesian Island." *Sign Language Studies* 3 (1973) : 1-28. Illus.

This is a case study of the only deaf-mute, Kangobai, known to have lived on the Polynesian island, Renell. The gestures discussed are divided into gestures decipherable by members of other cultures; by members of Kangobai's culture only; and by only a few selected members of Kangobai's culture. Research methods to avoid ethnocentrism are discussed.

797. **Kushner, Richard I., and Forsyth, G. Algred.** "Judgment of Emotion in Human Face Stimuli: An Individual Differences Analysis." *Journal of General Psychology* 96 (1977) : 301-312. Illus.

"Face-pair photos were created by dividing photographs into four facial areas (horizontal strips including forehead, eyes, nose,and mouth and chin), and mixing the strips to form two composite faces for each subject, one using elements from "angry" and "neutral" expression photos and the other using elements from "pleased" and "neutral" expression photos. Eighty of these face-pairs were judged by 100 undergraduates. Analysis of the differential use of face regions in distinguishing between angry and pleased facial expressions yielded five subgroups of judges.

798. **Kutner, David H. Jr.** "Overcrowding: Human Responses to Density and Visual Exposure." *Human Relations* 26 (1973) : 31-50.

One hundred twenty males participated in a test of the hypothesis that visual over exposure to others, not distance *per se,* causes anxiety in overcrowded settings. Several measures of anxiety were taken while subjects faced each other or not in groups of varying size at near or far distances. Group size, intyerpersonal distance, and visual exposure had no discernable effect on subject' task performance or self-reported anxiety. However, subjects in the face-to-face condition increased their number of protective body positions over time.

799. **Laban, Rudolf.** *The Language of Movement: A Guidebook to Choreutics,* edited by L. Ullmann. Boston, Plays: 1974. 214 pp. Illus.

This work is a guidebook to choreutics, which the author describes as the study of the various forms of harmonised movement. "Choreutics" is a term adapted from the Greek word for the logic or science of circles. The author treats it as a kind of "grammar and syntax" of the language of movement, dealing not only with the spatial patterning of movement as a "harmonic" study but also with its mental and emotional content. He introduces choreutics as the exploration through analysis and moving of the lines, forms, and actions of the body in the "kinesphere" and offers the reader many illustrations to explain the principles of choreutics. There are also drawings and examples presented with Labanotation, the dance/movement notation which Rudolf Laban invented.

800. **Laban, Rudolf, and Ullman, Lisa,** eds. *The Language of Movement: A Guidebook to Choreutics.* Boston: Plays, 1974. 214 pp. Illus.

"Choreosophis" is a term for the study of the phenomena of circles existing in nature and in human movement. "Choreography," and "Choreutics" form the three main branches of "Choeosophy." In addition to an investigation of the principles of orientation in space, choreosophy embraces such concerns as "kinesphere" (personal space), the natural sequences and scales in space which one's movements follow, and the "trace-forms" which the body creates in movement.

801. **La Barbera, J.D.; Izard, C.E.; Vietze, P.; and Parisi, S.A.** "Four- and Six-Month-Old Infants' Visual Responses to Joy, Anger, and Neutral Expressions." *Child Development* 47 (1976) : 535-538.

While sitting on their mothers' laps 12 four-month-old and 12 six-month-old infants viewed slides of joyous, angry, and neutral facial expressions. Observers recorded the duration of time infants spent gazing at each face. Four-month-olds gazed longer in general than six-month-olds, and all infants gazed longer at joyous expressions.

802. **LaCross, Michael B.** "Nonverbal Behavior and Perceived Counselor Attractiveness and Persuasiveness." *Journal of Counseling Psychology* 22 (1975) : 563-566.

Two male and two female counseling graduate students were trained to depict affiliative and nonaffiliative behaviors based on six nonverbal categories (smiles, positive head nods, gesticulations, eye contact, shoulder orientation, and body lean). Twenty male and 20 female college students viewed videotaped depictions of affiliative or nonaffiliative behaviors by the counselors in simulated counseling sessions and rated them on levels of perceived attractiveness and persuasiveness. Analysis of variance procedures revealed that, regardless of sex of subjects or counselors, subjects perceived "affiliative counselors" as significantly more attractive and persuasive than counselors not exhibiting affiliative behavior. High correlations between attractiveness and persuasiveness suggested that the functions may be related to one another on a more general level.

803. **LaFrance, Marianne.** "Nonverbal Synchrony and Rapport: Analysis by the Cross-Lag Panel Technique." *Social Psychology Quarterly* 42 (1979) : 66-70.

Fourteen college classes were videotaped during the first week of a six-week session and 13 during the last week. Verbal rapport was measured by the students using 15 bipolar scales. Posture was coded from the videotape by two trained observers using a system categorizing 9 torso positions and 16 arm positions. Postural synchrony and rapport were positively correlated over both sets of tapings. The cross-lag difference was not significant but showed a tendency for postural synchrony to be influential in establishing rapport.

804. **LaFrance, Marianne, and Mayo, Clara.** "Racial Differences in Gaze Behavior During Conversation: Two Systematic Observational Studies." *Journal of Personality and Social Psychology* 33 (1976) : 547-552.

In the first study a black graduate student is recorded on 16 mm film talking for ten minutes to a white corporate executive and then to a black institutional worker. The second naturalistic study involving 63 black dyads and 63 white dyads produced the same results as the first. Black listeners gazed less at the face of the speaker than white listeners.

805. **LaFrance, Marianne, and Mayo, Clara.** *Moving Bodies: Nonverbal Communication in Social Relationships.* Monterey, California: Brooks/Cole, 1978.

The author's primary thesis is that nonverbal communication is influenced by the context and environment in which it occurs. The book is organized into three main sections dealing with the nonverbal cues of emotional expression, personality, and psychopathology; attraction, aggression, status, and influence factors in interaction; and sex differences, cultural and cross-cultural patterns, child development, and the relationship between verbal and nonverbal modes of expression. In each section relevant research is reviewed in this textbook.

806. **LaFrance, Marianne, and Mayo, Clara.** "On the Acquisition of Nonverbal Communication: A Review." *Merrill-Palmer Quarterly* 24 (1978) : 213-228.

The authors review research on the development of nonverbal behaviors which enable a child to understand and be understood by those around him/her. "Emotional communication," "interpersonal interaction," and "conversational competence" are the topics discussed.

807. **LaFrance, Marianne, and Polit, D.** "Sex Differences in Reaction to Spatial Invasion." *Journal of Social Psychology* 102 (1977) : 59-60.

An experiment on differential reactions to spatial invasion between 60 male and 60 female college students seated alone at a library table. A "standard invasion condition" (where an invader did not speak) and an "invasion saliency condition" (where the invader asks whether the seat next to the person is taken) were used. A control group that had no "attempted invasion" was observed and their departure times noted. Females departed more quickly than did males, particularly when the invasion saliency condition was used.

808. **Laird, James.** "Self Attribution of Emotion: the Effects of Expressive Behavior on the Quality of Emotional Experience." *Journal of Personality and Social Psychology* 29 (1974) : 475-486.

Seventy-seven undergraduates induced to smile or frown reported feeling more angry when frowning and more happy when smiling. In a second study subjects viewing cartoons while smiling reported them to be funnier than those viewed while frowning.

809. **Lalljee, Mansur.** "The Role of Gaze in the Expression of Emotion." *Australian Journal of Psychology* 30 (1978) : 59-67.

This article relates the semantic dimensions of emotions to the physical expression of the direction of gaze. The author stresses the continuity between the nonverbal behavior involved in emotional expression and that involved in other aspects of social interaction.

810. **Lamb, Michael E.** "Interactions Between Eight-Month-Old Children and Their Fathers and Mothers." In *The Role of the Father in Child Development* by M.E. Lamb, pp. 307-327. New York: John Wiley and Sons, 1976. Illus.

Twenty infants were observed in the home environment in the presence of mother, father, and observer, once at age seven months and once at eight months. Physical contact, play, and other infant behaviors (smiling, fussing, reaching, touching, and so on) were coded. Attachment behaviors were found to be directed toward both mother and father; affiliative behaviors were directed toward fathers. Infants responded more positively to fathers' idiosyncratic play. Mothers held infants more than fathers, primarily in caretaking activities, as distinct from fathers' holding of infants during play.

811. **Lamb, Warren.** "Universal Movement Indicators of Stress." *American Journal of Dance Therapy* 2 (1978) : 27-31. Illus.

Using effort/shape movement analysis as a frame of reference, the author discusses factors which indicate stress on a movement level. He emphasizes the importance of studying movement, as opposed to fixed positions. "Locked" postural movements due to extreme concentration, or lack of movement, in the various effort/shape categories are considered a major indication of stress here.

812. **Lamb, Warren, and Watson, Elizabeth.** *Body Code: The Meaning of Movement.* London: Routledge & Kegan Paul, 1979. 190 pp. Illus.

The major subject of this book is what the authors call Posture-Gesture Merging (PGM), the ability to transfer a movement from one part of the body to the whole or vice-versa. Lamb and Watson state that, without merging, there is no spontaneity of genuine expression and, further, that the pattern in which PGMs take place is revealing of one's personality. The authors describe the concepts of shape (the forms that movements trace in space) and effort (the dynamic qualities of movement) and conclude with a theory of the three-stage action scheme, in which an action is made up of attention, intention, and commitment stages. From this they derive their categories for three major types of personalities: the communicator, the presenter, and the operator.

813. **Lamedica, Domenico.** "Gesti di Saluto e di Commiato nel Patrimonio Espressivo Calabrese." Atti del 16° Congresso Della Società di Linguistica Italiana. *Linguistica e Antropologia.* Forthcoming.

Kinesics and proxemics annotations on greeting gestures in the countryside and cities of Calabria. Written in Italian with theoretical introduction and statistical notes. (from the author)

814. **Lamedica, Domenico.** "Variazioni fra Due Sistemi Gestuali Regionali Italiani: DeJorio e Pitré." *Annáli dell' Istituto di Filosofia dell' Università della Calabria,* in press.

An examination of the differences between two regional gestural systems, of Sicily and Campania in Italy, based on descriptions in a text by DeJorio written in 1832 on Neapolitan gestures and one written in 1883 by Pitré on Palermo gestures. (from the author)

815. **Lange, Roderyk.** *The Nature of Dance: An Anthropological Perspective.* New York: International Publication Service, 1976. 142 pp. Illus.

This volume stresses an historical as well as anthropological approach to dance in human culture. It begins by tracing the history of dance in Western civilization, and then goes on to discuss rhythm and movement as underlying all forms of human creative expression. In a chapter on dance as a spiritual activity, the author discusses evidence associating dance to the earliest traces of human spirituality. Cultural comparisons referred to throughout the book are demonstrated in photographs and highlighted in the final chapters.

816. **Langer, Ellen J.; Fiske, Susan; Taylor, Shelley E.; and Chanowitz, Benzion.** "Stigma, Staring, and Discomfort: A Novel-Stimulus Hypothesis." *Journal of Experimental Social Psychology* 12 (1976) : 451-463.

In experiment one the first 15 males and 15 females who stopped to look at an exhibit consisting of three photographs (one physically normal woman, one pregnant woman, and one woman with an elaborate leg brace) comprised the subject population. An observer unobtrusively recorded the amount of time the subject spent staring at each photo. There was a significant main effect for stimulus novelty. Females spent more time staring than males. In experiment two photographs were used (a normal man and a hunchbacked man). Subjects either viewed the photographs alone or in the presence of a confederate who briefly stared at the subject after he or she began looking at the photographs. Being observed had a significant effect on staring. In experiment three 72 college students interacted with a crippled, pregnant, or normal woman. Half of the subjects were first given a chance to observe their partners beforehand. The results indicated that reduction in novelty resulted in reduced avoidance.

817.   **Lanigan, Richard L.** "A Semiotic Metatheory of Human Communication." *Semiotica* 27 (1979) : 293-305.

A metatheory construction of communication is discussed in terms of certain theory construction rules belonging respectively to semiology, social systems theory, communication theory, and existential phenomenology, combining them into a metatheory construction that would be by nature and function *human*. The analysis deals with six topics: the coding function; the nature of coding; human communication as best accounted for by social systems theory, not information theory; metatheory having only functional models in the social world; the ecosystem model and the phenomenological model; and the prolegomena for communication theory and praxis that are human in nature. Saussure's *langue* and *parole* are also discussed.

818.   **Lasher, Margot D.** "The Pause in the Moving Structure of Dance." *Semiotica* 22 (1978) : 107-126. Illus.

The perception of dance involves a complex relationship between the visual and kinesthetic perceptual systems of both the audience and the dancer. A structural description of two units of the dance (the step and the phrase) is given in terms of units of motion between points of rest and apparent rest.

819.   **Lassen, Carol L.** "Effect of Proximity on Anxiety and Communication in the Initial Psychiatric Interview." *Journal of Abnormal Psychology* 81 (1973) : 226-232.

Sixty psychiatric patients were given an initial interview by one of four physicians. Patient speech disturbances, rater-judged overt anxiety, and rater-judged anxiety content were measured. Patients were interviewed at three, six, or nine feet. Patient speech disturbance ratios showed a consistent increase with increased distance. In response to a questionnaire, patients reported that they did not get their points across as well and felt their speech to be unclear at nine feet. Patients talked more about their anxieties and felt surer of the therapists' reactions at six feet. All therapists preferred the six-foot distance.

820.   **Lavender, Joan; Davis, Martha; and Graber, Eden.** "Film/Video Research Recordings: Ethical Issues." *The Kinesis Report* 1 (Spring 1979) : 9-20. Illus.

This is an exploration of the ethical issues involved in filming or videotaping people for close behavioral analysis, particularly dilemmas of harm versus benefit assess ¼ ment, privacy and confidentiality, long-term control of the footage, and guidelines for protecting subjects. It is based on interviews with several researchers, a philosopher of ethics, members of protection-of-subjects panels, and a popular TV personality who broadcasts films of people unaware they are on camera.

821.   **Laver, John.** "Language and Nonverbal Communication." In *Handbook of Perception VII: Language and Speech,* edited by E.C. Carterette and M.P. Friedman, pp. 345-361. New York: Academic Press, 1976.

In this discussion of the nonverbal aspects of social interaction, the author divides the components of nonverbal communication into "audible paralinguistic features" such as tone of voice, pitch, and tempo, and "visible paralinguistic features" such as proximity, spatial orientation, posture, gesture, gaze, and facial expression. He reviews findings on interactional synchrony and interactional equilibrium. After considering the semantic, demarcative, and regulative functions of nonverbal communication, the author draws attention to its indexical function, that is, its role in furnishing information about interactants, their attributes and attitudes, while warning about the stereotyping of subjective judgments based on nonverbal phenomena.

822.   **Laver, John, and Hutcheson, Sandy,** eds. *Communication in Face to Face Interaction: Selected Readings.* Harmondsworth, England: Penguin, 1972.

This compilation of articles on nonverbal communication from different disciplines is selected on the assumption that there are three different kinds of information expressed: cognitive (which is primarily linguistic), indexical information (which tells something about the speaker and is mainly conveyed through nonverbal channels), and interaction-management (information which allows the participants to conduct interaction smoothly and is conveyed via both the verbal and nonverbal mode). The book includes articles on paralanguage, judgment of personality from nonverbal aspects of speech, cultural basis of emotions, the significance of posture in communication, eye-contact, distance, and ritual elements in social interaction. Among the authors represented in this volume are Michael Argyle, Adam Kendon, Ray L. Birdwhistell, Weston La Barre, Albert E. Scheflen, Edward T. Hall, and Erving Goffman.

823.   **Leathers, Dale.** *Nonverbal Communication Systems.* Boston, Massachussetts: Allyn and Bacon, 1976.

824.   **Leathers, Dale G.** "The Impact of Multichannel Message Inconsistency on Verbal and Nonverbal Decoding Behaviors." *Communication Monographs* 46 (1979) : 88-100.

This study examines the relative importance of the verbal and nonverbal behaviors in helping one to decipher inconsistent messages. Inconsistent messages were introduced into laboratory discussions. The resultant communication behaviors were videotaped, and these behaviors were subjected to detailed analysis. Among the results there is indication that individuals respond to such inconsistent messages in ways predicted by the double-bind theory of communication.

825.   **Le Compte, William F., and Rosenfeld, Howard M.** "Effects of Minimal Eye Contact in the Instruction Period on Impressions of the Experimenter." *Journal of Experimental Social Psychology* 7 (1971) : 211-220.

Fifty-six undergraduates were assigned to two conditions of eye contact. Male experimenters read them instructions on videotape and either failed to look up or did glance up on two specific occasions. Subjects then gave their impressions of the experimenter. Glancing up by the experimenter produced impressions of his being less nervous and less formal.

826.   **Lefebvre, Luc M.** "Encoding and Decoding of Ingratiation in Modes of Smiling and Gaze." *British Journal of Social and Clinical Psychology* 14 (1975) : 33-42.

In this first attempt to explore nonverbal aspects of ingratiation, 24 male college students interacted with one of two female confederates in an ingratiation or a control condition. Analyses of variance showed a higher percentage of smiles and gazes, a greater number of smiles, and longer gazes for subjects in the ingratiation condition than in the control but longer smiles and more frequent gaze only during the first task. In a second experiment, videotapes of the subjects of the first study were shown to naive observers. Ingratiation subjects were found significantly more likeable than controls but were rated higher on measures of strategic intent. There were no significant differences, however, on ratings of dishonesty or untrustworthiness.

827. **Leiderman, P. Herbert; Tulkin, Steven R.; and Rosenfeld, Anne,** eds. *Culture and Infancy: Variations in the Human Experience.* New York: Academic Press, 1977. 615 pp.

This important and fascinating book is a collection of theoretical explorations and empirical studies of cultural and class variations in childrearing practices by many of the major infancy researchers. Of particular interest are two articles by Mary D. Salter Ainsworth, "Attachment Theory and Its Utility in Cross-Cultural Research" and "Infant Development and Mother-Infant Interaction Among Ganda and American Families"; two by Melvin Konner, "Evolution of Human Behavior Development" and "Infancy Among the Kalahari Desert San"; "Implications of Infant Development among the Mayan Indians of Mexico" by T. Berry Brazelton; and "Infant Development and Mother-Infant Interaction in Urban Zambia" by Susan Goldberg. Also of great interest for nonverbal communication specialists are "Variance and Invariance in the Mother-Infant Interaction: A Cross-Cultural Study" by Michael Lewis and Peggy Ban; "Biological Variations and Cultural Diversity: An Exploratory Study" by Peter Wolff; "An Ecological Study of Infant Development in an Urban Setting in Britain" by M.P.M. Richards; and "Mother-Infant Interaction and Development in Infancy" by Leon J. Yarrow, Frank A. Pedersen, and Judith Rubenstein. A number of papers deal with socioeconomic influences on infant care and behavior: "Relationship of Infant/Caretaker Interaction, Social Class, and Nutritional Status to Developmental Test Performance Among Guatemalan Infants" by Robert E. Klein *et al.*; "Economic Change and Infant Care in an East African Agricultural Community" by P. Herbert Leiderman and Gloria F. Leiderman; "Relations between Maternal Attitudes and Maternal Behavior as a Function of Social Class" by Howard A. Moss and Sandra J. Jones; and "Social Class Differences in Maternal and Infant Behavior" by Steven R. Tulkin.

828. **Leone, James Paul.** "Body Movement and Gazing in Children's Conversations." Ph.D. dissertation, University of Virginia. 1978. 84 pp. (Order No. 79163-04)

Fifteen male and female pairs between the ages of four and 14 were videotaped in conversation. Movement of body parts, gaze direction, mutual gaze, and activity when speaking or listening were recorded and analyzed.

829. **Lester, Eldridge W.** "Assessing and Influencing the Attitude and Knowledge of Selected Post-Secondary Students Concerning Body Language." Ph.D. dissertation, North Texas State University. 1976. 124 pp. (Order No. 76-29,145)

This study was undertaken to develop an instrument to assess the attitude and knowledge of teachers and students concerning body language, as well as to develop instructional techniques for increasing students' understanding and awareness of body language.

830. **Lester, Eva P.** "A Two-Year-Old Girl with 'Tics': Theoretic and Therapeutic Considerations." *International Journal of Child Psychotherapy* 2 (1973) : 71-79.

According to this paper, conflict at the ages of two and three years produces behavioral phenomena often of a symbolic nature. The author discusses the theoretical framework for this idea and describes the case of a two-year-old who developed a facial 'tic' due to stress and conflict with the physiological problem accurately portraying the psychological reality.

831. **Leventhal, Gloria; Matturo, Michelle; and Schanerman, Joel.** "Effects of Attitude, Approach, and Sex on Nonverbal, Verbal, and Projective Measures of Personal Space." *Perceptual and Motor Skills* 32 (1971) : 27-33.

In this study of 120 undergraduates, invaders approached from the front or side in a positive, neutral, or negative manner. Effects of sex of invader and plane of approach are discussed in terms of societal norms and potential threat.

832. **Leventhal, Marcia B.** "Research in Movement Therapy." *Conference Proceedings of the American Dance Therapy Association* 8 (1974) : 126-143.

First, the body-image concept and its relationship to learning is discussed in this presentation of research on movement therapy as a treatment modality for disturbed children. Control and experimental groups were tested four times pre- and post-movement therapy sessions. Areas covered include movement pattern and developmental level, tension pattern organization, elements of focus and control, and body parts and sensory motor integration. The experimental group showed 30 percent overall improvement. The author's own Body Image ID test is presented.

833. **Leventhal, Marcia B.**, ed. *Movement and Growth: Dance Therapy for the Special Child.* New York: The Graduate Dance Therapy Program, New York University, 1980.

The proceedings of a conference honoring the UNICEF International Year of the Child 1979 is divided into three broad sections: theoretical considerations, methods of approach, and assessment tools. There are papers on psychoanalytic, humanistic, and ego psychology-oriented approaches to movement therapy with children. Case studies and therapeutic approaches with blind, learning disabled, and emotionally disturbed children are presented, and two rating instruments for assessment are described, the BRIAAC (Behavior Rating Instrument for Austistic and Other Atypical Children) developed by Bertram A. Ruttenberg, Beth Kalish, and their associates, and a nonverbal assessment of family systems developed by Dianne Dulicai.

834. **Levine, Marion Heineman, and Sutton-Smith, Brian.** "Effects of Age, Sex, and Task on Visual Behavior during Dyadic Interaction." *Developmental Psychology* 9 (1973) : 400-405.

Ninety-six subjects were divided into four age groups (ages four, five, and six years; seven, eight, and nine; ten, 11, and 12; and adults), and same-sex dyads in each age group were formed. Each dyad was then observed during both a conversation and a construction task. The results of recorded observation revealed significant age differences in the amount of gazing during conversation, yet no age changes in gazing occurred during the construction task. Significant sex differences, with females gazing more than males, were found during conversations. Significantly more gazing was found during conversation than the construction task.

835. **Lewis, David.** *The Secret Language of Your Child.* New York: St. Martins, 1978, Berkley Books, 1980. 287 pp. Illus.

Although written for a popular audience in a lively style, this book on the communication behaviors of children under five incorporates the work of many major researchers, including some such as the French researcher Hubert Montagner, whose work is not easily accessible elsewhere. Well illustrated with unposed photographs and videotape stills, the book covers topics such as context-sensitive "rules for successful child-watching" and a discussion of the complexities involved in "reading a smile." Child-child interactions are focused upon in chapters on leadership, aggression and anxiety. Developmental aspects of gesture and gaze, the role of adults in the learning of nonverbal behaviors, and the nonverbal analysis of family snapshots are also discussed.

836. **Lewis, Michael.** "State as an Infant-Environment Interaction: An Analysis of Mother-Infant Interaction as a Function of Sex." *Merrill-Palmer Quarterly* 18 (1972) : 95-121.

This article uses an interactive approach to redefine "state" in terms of an infant-environment interaction. Various types of interactive processes and analyses are explored and discussed to examine both state differences and individual differences in state. Empirical data support the idea that infant behavior alone was insufficient to describe state. Data are also presented on the state differences related to the sex of the child.

837. **Lewis, Michael, and Rosenblum, Leonard A.**, eds. *The Development of Affect.* New York: Plenum, 1978. 426 pp. Illus.

In addition to this work, Lewis and Rosenblum have edited a number of books related to topics covered in this bibliography, among them: *The Effect of the Infant on Its Caregiver* (Wiley, 1974), *Interaction, Conversation and the Development of Language* (Wiley, 1977) and *The Child and Its Family* (Plenum, 1979.)

838. **Libby, William L., and Yaklevich, Donna.** "Personality Determinants of Eye Contact and Direction of Gaze Aversion." *Journal of Personality and Social Psychology* 27 (1973) : 197-206.

Seventy subjects were compared according to scores on three personality variables (need for nurturance, intraception, and abasement). They were interviewed and their eye behavior observed and recorded. Subjects high in need for abasement looked away to the left more. Subjects high in need for nurturance held eye contact more than low-nurturance subjects.

839. **Liben, Lynn S.**, ed. *Deaf Children: Developmental Perspectives.* New York: Academic Press, 1978. 246 pp. Illus.

This collection of papers on the developmental effects of deafness contains several articles of special relevance to nonverbal behavior research: "Structural Properties of American Sign Language" by Ursula Bellugi and Edward S. Klima, "The Acquisition of Signed and Spoken Language" by Hilde S. Schlesinger, and "Current Research and Theory with the Deaf: Educational Implications" by Donald F. Moores.

840. **Lichstein, Kenneth L., and Wahler, Robert G.** "The Ecological Assessment of an Autistic Child." *Journal of Abnormal Child Psychology* 4 (1976) : 31-54.

The behavior of a five-year-old autistic child was observed in his natural environment. Observations were made in three settings, over approximately six months. Sixteen behaviors of the child and six behaviors of adults and peers were recorded. Inverse correlations between the child's self-stimulatory behaviors and his attentiveness to the environment were noted. Greater adult attention was consistently related to less child self-stimulatory behavior. This autistic child exhibited a diversity of behavior over time in a given setting and across settings.

841. **Lickiss, Karen P., and Wellens, A. Rodney.** "Effects of Visual Accessiblity and Hand Restraint on Fluency of Gesticulator and Effectiveness of Message." *Perceptual and Motor Skills* 46 (1978) : 925-926.

One member of a set of ten male and female dyads described a series of photographs via a voice intercom or two-way videotelephone, while hand movements were experimentally restrained or unrestrained. The partner selected duplicate copies from a set of similar pictures. The variables measured were the number of photographs correctly identified, numbers of words spoken, speech errors made, and gestures made; all interactions were videotaped. A series of two-way analyses of variance (visual accessibility × hand restraint) revealed that the conditions of free or unrestrained hand movement had no effect on the amount of speech output, verbal fluency, or task success. The mere visual presence of the interactant resulted in less efficient verbal communication than did hand restraint alone.

842. **Lieber, Lillian; Plumb, Marjorie; and Holland, Jimmie.** "Verbal and Non-Verbal Communications Among Persons Under Stress of Life-Threatening Physical Illness." *Archives of the Foundation of Thanatology* 5 (1975) : 473.

This paper examines certain aspects of verbal and nonverbal communications between advanced cancer patients and their families and friends; and among patients themselves. Data were obtained on frequency and intimacy and social interchange and physical contact, as well as on perceived changes in their actual interpersonal behavior. Comparable changes in communication between the patient and family members and friends were also studied.

843. **Lieth, Lars von der.** "Le geste et la mimique dans la communication totale." *Bulletin de Psychologie* 26 (1972-73) : 494-500.

Written in French, this article points to the importance of body language in total communication. Categorizing body language into facial movements, gestures (movements of arms and hands), and movements of the rest of the body, the author emphasizes the importance of redundancy through this medium. He distinguishes between two types of signals: those that carry linguistic information and those that carry expressive information. The more people perceive a given signal as a specific linguistic symbol, the more room there will be for redundancy, both on the part of the sender and the receiver. He briefly talks about the usefulness and drawbacks of notation systems and about the recent methodologies in research in nonverbal communication.

844. **Liggett, John.** *The Human Face.* London: Constable and Company Limited, 1974. 282 pp. Illus.

The author discusses the physiological, anatomical, psychological, cultural, and sociological aspects of the human face. Topics such as "beauty, health, and disease," and "sex, age, and race" are included.

845. **Lin, Barbara Weitzner, and Duchan, Judith.** "Using Movement to Differentiate Patterns of Interaction and Situational Understanding in the Verbal Productions of a Two-and-a-Half Year Old Child." *Sign Language Studies* 27 (1980) : 113-122.

In this study of the role of the context and person controlling the situation on the child's "construction of meaning," differences were found in large trunk movements accompanying spontaneous utterances. These were seen when the child was involved in interactions dominated by him but not so much during interaction dominated by an adult.

846. **Lindenfeld, Jacqueline.** "Verbal and Non-Verbal Elements in Discourse." *Semiotica* 3 (1971) : 223-233.

Analysis of syntactic and kinesic data from a film of a psychotherapeutic interview indicated that the kinesic movements were more closely related to surface structure than to the deep structure of language. Thirty-nine out of 128 kinesic units accompanying speech failed to coincide with syntactic units (thus violating the syntactic structure of speech), whereas 89 respected it.

847. **Lindenfeld, Jacqueline.** "Syntactic Structure and Kinesic Phenomena in Communicative Events." *Semiotica* 12 (1974) : 61-73.

The first of two studies reported here concerns "Mrs. C," a manic-depressive patient, in both depressed and remitted states. The number of movements respecting syntactic boundaries versus number violating syntactic boundaries in an interview were assessed. In the depressed interview 23 of the 42 kinesic units respected syntactic boundaries, while 19 did not. In the normal (remitted) interview 15 of the 41 kinesic units respected syntactic boundaries. This differed from the 1971 finding that 70 percent of the kinesic units respected syntactic boundaries. The second study involved four normals and eight manic-depressives (four in the manic state and four in the depressive state). The number of embedding transformations in 900-word speech samples; the number of head, hand, and foot movements; and total number of movements in eight-minute samples were tabulated. These preliminary findings indicated the existence of an inverse relationship between syntactic complexity and movement frequency in both the normal and depressed states; in the manic state the inverse relationship held only in head and hand movements, not in foot movements.

848.   **Ling, Daniel, and Ling, Agnes H.** "Communication Development in the First Three Years of Life." *Journal of Speech and Hearing Research* 17 (1974) : 146-159.

Behavior checklists were devised to record time-sampled behavior relating to eight modes of mother-to-child and child-to-mother communication. Forty-eight middle-class children (ages one month to three years) were observed interacting with their mothers. The frequency with which certain patterns of vocal and verbal behavior, eye contact, facial expression, body posture, action, "demonstration," and gesture were used relative to the children's age, sex, and position in the family are presented. Trends in relation to age were largely predictable, except that mothers of young babies verbalized as frequently as mothers of older infants. Mothers communicated significantly more often with first-born than with last-born children and with younger children more frequently than with older children.

849.   **Liss, Robert Alan.** "Personality Correlates of Mutual Glance Patterns in Dyadic Interactions." Ph.D. dissertation, New York University. 1971. 117 pp. (Order No. 72-13,385)

Students interacting in dyads for ten minutes were scored for frequency and duration of mutual glances. A significant negative correlation was found between duration of mutual glances in a dyad and the level of depression of the more depressed member.

850.   **Littlepage, Glenn E., and Pineault, Martin A.** "Detection of Deceptive Factual Statements from the Body and the Face." *Personality and Social Psychology Bulletin* 5 (1979) : 325-328.

Videotapes of two confederates giving truthful or untruthful answers were made with the camera focusing on face only or body below the neck only. Thirty-two students evaluated the tape segments as to degree of credibility, and they were shown to be more accurate at judging body than face, but only for dishonest statements.

851.   **Lo Castro, Joseph Samuel.** "Judgment of Emotional Communication in the Facial-Vocal-Verbal Channels." Ph.D. dissertation, University of Maryland. 1972. 120 pp. (Order No. 72-20,258)

Congruent and incongruent combinations of emotional stimuli expressed facially in photographs and vocally (tone of voice) and verbally in recordings were assessed. Vocal and verbal cues were found more significant than facial cues in anger-love combinations, and facial and vocal cues were more important than verbal cues in sadness-joy combinations.

852.   **Lock, Andrew,** ed. *Action, Gesture and Symbol: The Emergence of Language.* New York: Academic Press, 1978. 588 pp. Illus.

This collection of papers on the emergence of language from action and gesture and its acquisition within social interaction contains theoretical perspectives by M.P.M. Richard on "The Biological and the Social," John Newson on "Dialogue and Development," and John Shotter on "The Cultural Context of Communication

Studies: Theoretical and Methodological Issues." Cathy Urwin has contributed "The Development of Communication Between Blind Infants and their Parents." Two papers consider the background of evolution: a study of a natural gesture language of wild chimpanzees by Frans X. Plooij and a study of language in the orangutan by Keith Laidler. On early communicative actions and the development of gesture there are "Learning to Take an Object from the Mother" by Hilary Gray, "Secondary Intersubjectivity: Confidence, Confiding, and Acts of Meaning in the First Year" by Colwyn Trevarthen and Penelope Hubley, and "The Transition from Action to Gesture" by Roger A. Clark. Additional chapters include "Sensory-motor Intelligence and Language Development" by David Ingram, "Word and Gesture Usage by an Indian Child" by Alice Nokony, and "From Sensori-Motor Vocalizations to Words (in the second year)" by Anne Lindsay Carter. "Beyond Herodotus: The Creation of Language by Linguistically Deprived Deaf Children" by Heidi Feldman, Susan Goldin-Meadow, and Lila Gleitman and "Structure Parallels Between Language and Action in Development" by Patricia Marks Greenfield also deal with the transition from gesture to symbol. In the final section there is Derek Edwards' "Social Relations and Early Language," and Linda Ferrier, Susan R. Braunwald, and M.M. Shields have each contributed a paper on the development of symbolic competence within the social world.

853. **Lockard, Joan S., and Adams, Robert M.** "Peripheral Males: A Primate Model for a Human Subgroup." *Bulletin of the Psychonomic Society* 15 (1980) : 295-298.

In several nonhuman primate species males are observed to exhibit a subadult stage wherein, unlike females, they remain peripheral, associating largely with same-sex peers. The present study draws an analogy between this subadult stage of primates and a stage of human male adolescence. In the study, observers gathered data in two large shopping malls. More than 10,000 groups were observed, and the sex and age of the subjects were recorded. The results indicated that male groups (18-to 20-year-olds) of more than two members were seen with much greater frequency than female groups of comparable ages.

854. **Lockard, Joan S.; Daley, Paul C.; and Gunderson, Virginia M.** "Maternal and Paternal Differences in Infant Carry: U.S. and African Data." *The American Naturalist* 113 (1979) : 235-246.

This article addresses the specific question of whether adult females carry infants in a consistently different manner from adult males. In Seattle, Washington, 1,916 adult-child groupings were observed in a variety of public places, and in Dakar, Senegal, 2,419 Wolof family groupings were observed. The research findings indicated that in Dakar infants who are carried dorsally in backpacks show a left-side head placement with respect to their mothers' backs. Male adults rarely carry their children in public. The findings in Seattle indicate that adult females carry infants predominantly on the left side and that, when adult males and females are together, young infants are carried equally by either sex.

855. **Lockard, J.S.; Fahrenbruch, C.E.; Smith, J.L.; and Morgan, C.J.** "Smiling and Laughter: Different Phyletic Origins?" *Bulletin of the Psychonomic Society* 10 (1977) : 183-186. Illus.

The present study addressed the ethological problem of whether laughter is simply a more intense form of smiling or whether the two displays have different origins. The experimenters observed 141 dyadic interactions for smiling and laughter. A numerical value was assigned to the smile and/or laughter on the basis of its intensity. The findings support the hypothesis that "front-teeth smiling" and the more open-mouth expression associated with laughter may have different origins and functions.

856. **Lockard, J.S.; McDonald, L.L.; Clifford, D.A.; and Martinez, R.**
"Panhandling: Sharing of Resources." *Science* 191 (1976) : 406-408.

In order to study sharing of resources, several male and female college students posed as panhandlers. Two studies, altogether involving six panhandlers and 516 "targets," showed that male panhandlers were more successful in spring than summer and that panhandlers were generally successful only when submissively approaching individuals who were eating. The results are discussed in terms of reciprocal altruism and kinship selection.

857. **Loeb, Loretta R.; Loeb, Felix F. Jr.; and Ross, David S.** "Grasping as an Adult Communicational Signal." *Journal of Nervous and Mental Disease* 154 (1972) : 368-386.

Previous microanalytic research had identified a quick, purposeless grasp-like movement in adults similar to that made by infants while nursing. The movement was found to accompany speech referring to the nursing situation. In this study 103 subjects, including hospitalized psychiatric patients and hospital staff, viewed a film in which five of the grasp-like movements and four control movements were spliced together in a random order. Subjects recorded the meaning they attached to each movement. Analyses of the responses showed that certain categories of response originally identified with the movements such as "off-on," "negation," "finished," "anger," and "disgust" were much more often attributed to the experimental than the control stimuli. The authors speculate on how meaning of "negation" may become developmentally associated with the rooting and grasping reflexes of infants.

858. **Lofland, John Jr.** *Doing Social Life: The Qualitative Study of Human Interaction in Natural Settings.* New York: Wiley, 1976.

859. **Lofland, Lyn H.** *A World of Strangers: Order and Action in Urban Public Space.* New York: Basic Books, 1973.

860. **Lomax, Alan.** *Folk Song Style and Culture.* New Brunswick, New Jersey: Transaction Books, first paperback edition, 1978. 263 pp. Illus.

A paperback edition of the American Association for the Advancement of Science 1968 edition. Includes the Choreometric coding book for analysis of dance style in relation to diverse cultures and the Cantometric coding book for cross-cultural analysis of folk song style. Sound tapes to elucidate the Cantometrics coding book and films illustrating the results of the Choreometric project are available from: University of California Extension Media Center, 2223 Fulton Street, Berkeley, California 94720.

861. **Lomax, Alan; Bartenieff, Irmgard; and Paulay, Forrestine.** "Choreometrics: A Method for the Study of Cross-Cultural Patterns in Film." In *New Dimensions in Dance Research: Anthropology and Dance—the American Indians,* edited by T. Comstock, pp. 193-212. New York: CORD, New York University, 1974.

This article describes the work done by the authors to develop a scientific method for encoding and comparing dance movements from different cultures of the world, and includes some results of their research as well as a discussion of their procedures. It raises several questions regarding filming, editing, and preservation of filmed records, indexing of footage for maximum availability, and organization and exchange of material. It concentrates on what kinds of information relevant to social science can be systematically and reliably derived from film.

862. **Lomax, Alan, and Paulay, Forrestine.** *A Handbook of World Dance.* Tentative title, forthcoming.

This will be an index of dance style by culture with a geography of dance by area and chapters on the relationship of movement to social structure, movement to musical structure, male-female differentials in movement, and movement universals based on a factor analysis of the data from the "Choreometrics" research project. (information from the senior author)

863. **Lomranz, J., and Shapira, A.** "Communicative Patterns of Self-Disclosure and Touching Behavior." *Journal of Psychology* 88 (1974) : 223-227.

Questionnaires on self-disclosure and touching behavior were administered to 190 Israeli students, ages 17-19. The subject was instructed to indicate on a four-point scale the extent to which he or she had talked about each of several topics to four target persons: mother, father, friend of same sex, friend of opposite sex. The subject was also asked to indicate on a sketch the body region that he or she touches and is touched by each of the four target people. A significant positive correlation between the two measures was found, indicating that people who are high in self-disclosure are also high in touching behavior.

864. **Lomranz, Jacob; Shapira, Ariela; Choresch, Netta; and Gilat, Yitzchak.** "Children's Personal Space as a Function of Age and Sex." *Developmental Psychology* 11 (1975) : 541-545.

Personal space measures were obtained for 74 children aged three, five, and seven when they approached boys or girls of their own age. Results show that three-year-olds kept less distance than five- and seven-year-olds. No difference was found between boys and girls in the distances they kept, but all approached closer to girls.

865. **Loo, Chalsa M.** "The Effects of Spatial Density on the Social Behavior of Children" *Journal of Applied Social Psychology* 2 (1972) : 327-381.

The same group of 60 children ages four to five were studied in controlled, physical spaces, varying from 265.1 square feet to 90 square feet in size, in order to evaluate the effects of low and high density on social behavior. The specific behaviors analyzed were: dominance, aggression, resistance, submission, nurturance, solitary play, and the degree of social involvement. The results of the study indicate that spatial density plays an important role in determining a child's behavior and the quality of his social relations. Of particular interest was the finding that, in crowded situations (high density), children become less aggressive and tend to isolate themselves, interacting with fewer children.

866. **Loo, Chalsa.** "Important Issues in Researching the Effects of Crowding on Humans." *Representative Research in Social Psychology* 4 (1973) : 219-226.

The author discusses problems in doing research on the effects of crowding and density on humans. Differences in theory and terminology, differences in structuring a crowd situation, and directions for future research are addressed.

867. **Loo, Chalsa, and Kennelly, Denise.** "Social Density: Its Effects on Behaviors and Perceptions of Preschoolers." *Environmental Psychology and Nonverbal Behavior* 3 (1979) : 131-146.

The effects of social density on the behaviors and perceptions of five-year-old children in four- and eight-person groups were investigated. In addition, differential effects of density for sex and for preferred personal space were examined. From a factor analysis of observed behaviors and self-reported perceptions, five factors emerged: Activity-Aggression-Anger, Positive Interactions, Distress-and-Nonplay, Feeling Bad, and Avoidance. A multivariate analysis of variance was performed; significant main effects were found for density and for sex. A univariate analysis of variance for each factor demonstrated that in the crowded condition there was significantly more Actvity-Aggression-Anger, more Distress-and-Nonplay, and fewer Positive Interactions than in the uncrowded condition. In the high-density condition the frequency of Activity-Aggression-Anger for boys increased significantly more than it did for girls.

868. **Loo, Chalsa, and Smetana, Judi.** "The Effects of Crowding on the Behavior and Perception of 10-Year-Old Boys." *Environmental Psychology and Nonverbal Behavior* 2 (1978) : 226-249.

The present study integrated observational and self-report methods to investigate the effects of low and high spatial density on ten-year-old boys in an experimental setting. The differential effects of density on acquaintances versus strangers and on close versus far personal-space boys were analyzed. From a factor analysis of variables that were either rated during a free-play session or were scored responses from a postexperimental interview, five factors emerged: Discomfort and Dislike of Room, Active Play, Avoidance, Positive Group Interactions, and Anger and Aggression.

869. **Lord, Catherine.** "The Perception of Eye Contact in Children and Adults." *Child Development* 45 (1974) : 1113-1117.

Sixteen second-graders, 16 sixth-graders and 16 adults made judgments as to whether they were being looked in the eye by the experimenter, who looked at seven points on their faces, at near and far distances. Subjects showed greater accuracy at the far distance than the near. Error rates were high for all age groups but accuracy increased with age.

870. **Lothstein, Leslie Martin.** "Personal Space in Assault-Prone Male Adolescent Prisoners." Ph.D. dissertation, Duke University. 1972. 211 pp. (Order No. 72-23,244)

Personal space preferences of assault-prone male adolescent prisoners were found to be greater than those of nonassault-prone prisoners. Racial differences in the findings are also discussed.

871. **Lothstein, L.M.** "Human Territoriality in Group Psychotherapy." *International Journal of Group Psychotherapy* 28 (1978) : 55-71.

This article espouses the need for obtaining empirical data on human territoriality in group therapy. The importance of spatial variables in the group psychotherapy setting is discussed with particular attention to the therapy room, the arrangement of furniture, and "chair territoriality."

872. **Lowen, Alexander.** *Depression and the Body: The Biological Basis of Faith and Reality.* New York: Penguin, 1972. 318 pp. Illus.

Arguing that the treatment of depression begins in helping a person regain his or her energy, the book discusses the bioenergetic approach to the phenomenon of depression. Lowen discusses causes of depression, including the role of self-deception, the importance of being grounded in reality, and the body's energy dynamics during depression. He then presents a case study and the psychoanalytic view of depression. The book ends with four chapters which speak of the relationship of reality and faith and the human need for faith in the modern context; depression is here described as an issue of loss of faith and health is regarded as the result of faith in life. This book includes eloquent and articulate explanations of the interrelatedness of body and psyche.

873. **Lowen, Alexander.** *Bioenergetics.* New York: Penguin, 1975. 352 pp. Illus.

In this fourth book on bioenergetics, Lowen gives an overview of the therapeutic system he evolved from the work he did in Reichian therapy in the 1940s. He writes of this evolution and the fundamental concept of bio-energy which originated with Reich. He describes bioenergetic therapy and presents his arguments for its effectiveness, interspersing his discussion with specific exercises and personal experiences. Two chapters focus on the concepts of pleasure as "primary orientation" and reality as "secondary orientation." Ensuing chapters focus on specific issues including falling anxiety, stress and sex, self-expression and survival, and the concurrent unity and duality of consciousness.

874. **Lurçat, Liliane.** "Du geste au langage." *Bulletin de Psychologie* 26 (1972-73) : 501-505.

Does gesture precede language as a system of communication? In this French article the author deals with this question by investigating the origin of gestures in the development of the child. By distinguishing between three levels of activity: the practical level, the symbolic level, and the conceptual level, she finds gesture to be an intermediary step between practical actions and conceptual language. She states that at a certain age, and depending on their social class, most children will branch off toward either a more conceptual or a more practical orientation and that this will show in their use of movement. She concludes that, although a complete gestural language does not precede language, it derives from the same source and that the limits of a gestural language are twofold: it cannot conceptualize reality, and it cannot be transmitted like the written word.

875. **Maccoby, Eleanor E., and Jacklin, Carol Nagy.** "Stress, Activity, and Proximity Seeking: Sex Differences in the Year Old Child." *Child Development* 44 (1973) : 34-42.

Forty infants aged 13 to 14 months participated in two experiments. In experiment I subjects were observed with their mothers under a "low-stress" condition, an unfamiliar room filled with toys. Half the subjects were then placed near their mothers and half far away and given a "fear stimulus" (a loud angry male voice spoken over a loud speaker). In the second experiment the fear stimulus was varied. Among the results it was found that proximity to the mother increased substantially following the fear stimulus. Among several sex differences it was found contrary to expectation that boys moved more quickly under stress than girls towards the mother.

876. **Maccoby, Eleanor Emmons, and Jacklin, Carol Nagy.** *The Psychology of Sex Differences.* Vol. II, *Annotated Bibliography.* Stanford, California: Stanford University Press, 1974.

This excellent bibliography includes a number of fully summarized experimental studies of nonverbal sex differences including ones before 1971 that are not included in the present volume.

877. **Mach, Richard Stuart.** "Postural Carriage and Congruency as Nonverbal Indicators of Status Differentials and Interpersonal Attraction." Ph.D. dissertation, University of Colorado. 1972. 231 pp. (Order No. 73-1806)

Naturalistic observation via closed circuit television of dyads of marine scientists living and working underwater revealed a relation between higher status and less postural tension and between similarity of status within dyads and less average postural tension. Postural congruency was correlated with status similarity, dyadic liking, and to some extent with higher dyadic status levels.

878. **Mackey, Wade C.** "Parameters of the Smile as a Social Signal." *The Journal of Genetic Psychology* 129 (1976) : 125-130.

One hundred twenty-four subjects listened to a tape recording alone or with another same-sex subject. Smiling frequency and duration were noted. Females smiled more than males when isolated and smiled most when with other females. In a related field study 137 undergraduates each verbally greeted six strangers with or without an accompanying smile. Results showed that greater smiling provoked a reciprocal smiling response and that females responded with a smile more than males in both conditions.

879. **Maffeo, Gilbert F. Jr.** "The Variable of Proxemics in Audience Persuasion: A Multivariate Experimental Study." Ph.D. dissertation, Bowling Green State University. 1972. 128 pp. (Order No. 73011-14)

Scattered versus compact seating arrangements were investigated in this study of the variable of proxemics in audience persuasion.

880. **Magnusson, David,** ed. *Toward a Psychology of Situation: An Interactional Perspective.* Hillsdale, New Jersey: Lawrence Erlbaum Associates, 1981. approx. 490 pp.

881. **Mahl, George F.** "Body Movement, Ideation and Verbalization during Psychoanalysis." In *Communicative Structures and Psychic Structures,* edited by N. Freedman and S. Grand, pp. 291-310. New York and London: Plenum Press, 1977. Illus.

Mahl elucidates how the motoric action represents an unverbalized statement in the psychoanalytic situation. He sees kinesic behavior as a direct sensori-motor stimulation to the conscious communication process. The verbal manifestation of the message is apparent after the kinesic sequence "drops out" of the interaction.

882. **Maines, David R.** "Tactile Relationships in the Subway as Affected by Racial, Sexual, and Crowded Seating Situations." *Environmental Psychology and Nonverbal Behavior* 2 (1977) : 100-108.

Observations of touching behavior were made on a New York City subway line to determine whether homogeneous behavioral patterns exist in the subway. Direct observations of race, sex, and crowding on subway car benches were made. These factors were coded as variables that might affect touching among strangers. The data indicated the presence of tactile avoidance behavior in crowded situations, but statistical significance was achieved only in the case of racial and sexual heterogeneous relationships.

883. **Malandro, Loretta A.** *Your Every Move Talks: Experiences in Nonverbal Communication.* Dubuque, Iowa: Gorsuch Scarisbrick Publishers, 1977. 126 pp. Illus.

Unlike many exercises in nonverbal communication awareness, this series of experiences was developed based on the findings of researchers such as Birdwhistell, Hall, Henley, Ekman, Sommer, and Goffman and also includes illustrations of Sheldon physical types. Snappy illustrations accompany descriptions of active experiences to help participants focus on their own nonverbal actions and reactions, while the debriefing section to be used afterwards discusses possible reactions.

884. **Malandro, Loretta, and Barker, Larry L.** "Increasing Efficiency in Experimental Instruction: An Information Retrieval System for Exercise in Nonverbal Communication." *Communication and Education* 27 (1978) : 53-59.

This article states that a classification system with sufficient reliability and validity can be devised to code games and exercises. Moreover, the procedures for the design and testing of the classification system can be generalized to other areas of speech communication and nonverbal communication.

885. **Maletic, Vera.** "On the Aisthetic and Aesthetic Dimensions of the Dance: A Methodology for Researching Dance Style." Ph.D. dissertation, Ohio State University, 1980.

Phenomenological descriptions of the perception and experience of two modern dances are compared with investigation of the dances' structural components as articulated through formal movement languages and analysis systems. Implications for dance theory, research and education, for observations and recording of movement from film and videotapes, and for the study of choreographic style are extensively discussed. (from author's information)

886. **Mallenby, Terry W.** "Personal Space: Projective and Direct Measures with Institutionalized Mentally Retarded Children." *Journal of Personality Assessment* 38 (1974) : 28-31.

Two projective interaction measures were employed in order to establish whether 20 institutionalized, retarded children were aware of their disorder in their interactions with normals. The measures involved the children's choice of personal space in dyadic interaction with a normal. Results indicate that an institutionalized, retarded child's awareness of his disorder may affect his perceived acceptance by "normal" people. Additional findings indicate that a child's sex may also be an important variable in choice of personal space.

887. **Maloney, Clarence,** ed. *The Evil Eye.* New York: Columbia University Press, 1976. 335 pp. Illus.

This book is an exploration of the evil eye phenomenon—the belief that one can project harm by looking at another's person or property. The first 12 chapters are discussions of the belief as it is represented in major parts of the world. Chapter 13 surveys the traits associated with this belief across cultures and arrives at certain conclusions based on the data. Chapters 14 and 15 look further into the meaning of this belief and associated behaviors.

888. **Mann, Leon.** "The Effect of Stimulus Queues on Queue Joining Behavior." *Journal of Personality and Social Psychology* 35 (1977) : 437-442.

In Jerusalem where queueing is not customary, confederates formed a line at a bus stop to test for the drawing power of queues on commuters. The results indicated that the larger the queue the greater the influence on the bystander. It was found that a queue of at least six was required to induce a reliable number of commuters to join the line.

889. **Mar, Timothy.** *Face Reading: The Chinese Art of Physiognomy.* New York: Dodd, Mead & Company, 1974. 150 pp. Illus.

A fascinating if hard to accept presentation of Chinese physiognomy written by a retired Chinese diplomat, practitioner of Zen, and student of an eminent Central Chinese physiognomist. In this method of analyzing, personality, intelligence, and accomplishment from facial structure, the face is divided into zones and small areas taken to correspond to years in the person's life. Though they're obviously *a posteriori* analyses, the examples of face reading of famous people (West and East) are intriguing.

890. **Marcelle, Yvonne Marie.** "Eye Contact As a Function of Race, Sex, and Distance." Ph.D. dissertation, Kansas State University. 1976. 86 pp. (Order No. 76300-10)

The eye contact behavior of 80 blacks (40 males, 40 females) and 80 whites (40 males and 40 females) was examined. Differences in the frequency, duration, and average duration of eye contact between these groups were investigated.

891. **Marcos, Luis R.** "The Emotional Correlates of Smiling and Laughter: A Preliminary Research Study." *American Journal of Psychoanalysis* 34 (1974) : 33-41.

The author hypothesized that smiling and laughter are not necessarily correlated with pleasant emotions in this study of 24 psychotherapy patients videotaped during therapy sessions. Eleven experienced psychiatrists decided whether the expression displayed by the patient was a smile or laughter. The clinician recorded the approximate duration of the facial expression in seconds and its location in the hour in addition to rating the smile or laughter according to a three-point intensity scale. Later, patients were asked to respond to three questions while viewing themselves: What do you feel now that you're smiling/laughing? What words would you use to describe your feelings as you're smiling/laughing? and Do you want to keep the feeling or get rid of it? The hypothesis was confirmed.

892. Margenau, Henry; Sellon, Emily B.; and Milburn, Patrick. *Main Currents in Modern Thought* 31 (1974) : 1-40. Illus.

This issue of *Main Currents* is devoted to writing on the significance of human movement, and particularly the impact and implications of Rudolf Laban's work on movement analysis. There are articles on the phenomenology of movement by R.L. Tall and V.E. Cobey, Algis Mickunas, Elizabeth Behnke, and Martha Davis. There are chapters on effort analysis by Marion North, space harmony by Sylvia Bodmer, movement and phylogeny by Patrick Milburn, and neurophysiological correlates of Laban movement terms.

893. Marks, Harold Eugene Jr. "The Relationship of Eye Contact to Congruence and Empathy." Ph.D. dissertation, University of California—Los Angeles. 1971. 64 pp. (Order No. 71213-31)

An experiment to test the prediction that individuals more able to engage in eye contact would be more congruent and more empathic with others than individuals less able to engage in eye contact.

894. Marsh, Peter; Rosser, Elisabeth; and Harre, Rom. *The Rules of Disorder.* London: Routledge and Kegan Paul, 1978. 140 pp. Illus.

This book considers violence and disorder in British classrooms and football stadiums. The roles of territoriality, posture, gesture, and eye contact behaviors in precipitating violence are considered.

895. Marshall, Joan E., and Heslin, Richard. "Boys and Girls Together: Sexual Composition and the Effect of Density and Group Size on Cohesiveness." *Journal of Personality and Social Psychology* 31 (1975) : 952-961.

One hundred forty-two female and 142 male undergraduates participated in this study. Small groups were found to be more cohesive than large groups but only for same-sex and not for mixed-sex groups. Women in mixed-sex groups preferred large groups to small and crowded groups to uncrowded, and the reverse was true for same-sex groups.

896. Massie, Henry N. "Blind Ratings of Mother-Infant Interaction in Home Movies of Prepsychotic and Normal Infants." *American Journal of Psychiatry* 135 (1978) : 1371-1374.

Home movies of 13 infants later diagnosed as having early childhood psychoses and 15 normal infants were analyzed. Mothers' and infants' behaviors were rated on a scale of attachment indicators for the intensity of attachment in four modalities: feeding, holding, eye gaze, and touching. Judges also made overall assessments of the mothers and infants. Results indicated a trend toward lower attachment in all modalities for prepsychotic mother-infant pairs. There was a significant difference between normal and prepsychotic infants in the category of holding and between mothers of normal and prepsychotic infants in the categories of eye gaze and touching. There were no significant differences between overall assessment of infants in the two groups, but a significant difference between mothers in the two groups, with ten mothers of prepsychotic infants appearing poorly attached and three normally attached, compared to two poorly and 13 normally attached for the mothers of normal infants.

897. **Mathiot, Madeleine.** "Toward a Frame of Reference for the Analysis of Face-to-Face Interaction." *Semiotica* 24 (1978) : 199-220.

Part of an issue devoted to study of face-to-face interaction, this paper is concerned with formulating a theory and frame of reference for conducting analyses of face-to-face interactions. The author proposes conducting analysis in this order: macroanalysis, sign systems analysis, and then microanalysis; and the first two are extensively considered.

898. **Matson, Katinka.** *The Psychology Today Omnibook of Personal Development.* New York: William Morrow and Company, 1977. 500 pp.

A kind of encyclopedia/glossary on psychotherapies, body therapies, personalities, and concepts keynoting the human potential movement of the 1960s. Of note here are the pieces on Ray Birdwhistell and kinesics, dance therapy, face reading, Alexander Lowen/bioenergetic therapy, and sentics/Manfred Clynes.

899. **Matthews, Robert W.; Paulus, Paul B.; and Baron, Robert A.** "Physical Aggression After Being Crowded." *Journal of Nonverbal Behavior* 4 (1979) : 5-17.

Subjects were given an opportunity to aggress using a Buss machine either immediately or 30 minutes after competing or cooperating on a task in a crowded or uncrowded situation. It was found that for subjects who were allowed to aggress immediately, crowding reduced aggression under the competitive set but had no effect under the cooperative set. This effect of crowding was not found with the delay subjects. The results of this study are consistent with the findings of other studies that social withdrawal rather than aggression may occur in response to adversively dense conditions. The lack of crowding effect after a 30-minute delay suggests that the effect of the laboratory crowding experience is transient in nature and best generalized to short-term crowding experience such as those encountered on elevators and buses.

900. **Mayo, Clara, and Henley, Nancy,** eds. *Gender and Nonverbal Behavior.* New York: Springer Verlag, forthcoming.

This book presents original articles bearing upon the convergence of research on sex roles and nonverbal behavior. Topics include visual behavior (S. Ellyson, J. Dovidio, B.J. Fehr), movement (M. Davis and S. Weitz), spatial norms (Natalie Porter and F. Geis), and touch (B. Major). The book explores the concept of androgyny in nonverbal behavior with chapters by W. Ickes, M. LaFrance, B. Lott, and F. Crosby, W. Wang-McCarthy and P. Jose. A closing section presents emerging research frontiers for nonverbal behavior including chapters on the development of gender-identifying behaviors (J. Haviland, B. Malatesta, J. Umiker-Sebeok), on cross-cultural indicators of gender (M. Wex), on homosexual orientation and nonverbal behavior (P. Webbink), and on therapeutic change in gender stereotypic behavior (E. Robson). All chapters address both new research directions and application of the authors' findings. (by the first author)

901. **Mayo, Clara, and LaFrance, Marianne.** *Evaluating Research in Social Psychology: A Guide for the Consumer.* Monterey, California: Brooks/Cole, 1978. 316 pp.

This book is intended to teach the reader how to critically appraise and evaluate research in the field of social psychology. Each chapter contains a laboratory experiment and a field experiment. The theories, findings, and methods used in research on that particular topic are discussed. The book contains chapters on attraction, interpersonal distance, aggression, helping behavior, group decision making; "Extremity Shifts, Attribution, Attitude Change, and Attitude-Behavior Discrepancy"; "Prejudice and Racism"; and "How to Be an Intelligent Research Consumer." A helpful book for anyone reviewing the literature in nonverbal communication.

902. **Mayo, George Arnold.** "Use of Eye Contact During an Employment Interview." Ph.D. dissertation, University of Arizona. 1975. 56 pp. (Order No. 76015-96)

In this study four employment interview films were made in which a blind woman either made high eye contact or low eye contact with the interviewer. Businessmen rated the film as to the likelihood of the interviewee being hired. The study concluded that blind individuals can increase their likelihood of success in an employment interview by making high eye contact with the interviewer.

903. **Mazo, J.H.** *Prime Movers.* New York: Morrow, 1977. Illus.

This history of American modern dance focuses on major choreographers including Fuller, Duncan, St. Denis, Shawn, Humphrey, Graham, Cunningham, Nikolais, Ailey, Taylor and Tharp. It describes individual works in the context of the innovations and development of these major artists. It describes the moods, issues and conflicts of different eras of modern dance.

904. **McCall, Robert B.** "Smiling and Vocalization in Infants as Indices of Perceptual-Cognitive Processes." *Merrill-Palmer Quarterly* 18 (1972) : 341-347.

A review of literature on smiling and vocalization suggests that they indicate the infant possesses certain perceptual-cognitive predispositions that influence his response to new stimuli and that they may be predictive of later mental behavior. Furthermore, there may be sex differences in smiling and vocalization, such that they have different meanings for boy infants than girl infants.

905. **McCardle, Ellen Steele.** *Nonverbal Communication.* New York: Marcel Dekker Inc., 1975.

Subtitled "for media, library and information specialists," the content and organization of this monograph are unusual for general references on nonverbal communication. Rather than chapters organized by aspect of nonverbal communication (such as proxemics, facial expression, and so on), the volume is arranged by broad topics from a discussion of schools of communication theory to relevant principles from biology and ethology (including Darwin's principles of emotion expression) to learned behavior (including factors of culture) to aggression and nonverbal communication and, finally, "socio-sexual nonverbal behavior."

906. **McCauley, Clark; Coleman, Geoffrey; and De Fusco, Patricia.** "Commuters' Eye Contact with Strangers in City and Suburban Train Stations: Evidence of Short-Term Adaptation to Interpersonal Overload in the City." *Environmental Psychology and Nonverbal Behavior* 2 (1978) : 215-225.

Experimenters attempted to make eye contact with commuters as they approached an express train linking city and suburb and, 20 minutes later, as commuters left the same train. During both the morning rush from suburb to city and the evening rush from city to suburb, commuters were less willing to meet an experimenter's eye at the city train station than at the suburban station. These results support the hypothesis that reduced eye contact with strangers in the city is a short-term adaptation to interpersonal overload in the city.

907. **McClintock, Charles, and Hunt, Raymond.** "Nonverbal Indicators of Affect and Deception in an Interview Setting." *Journal of Applied Social Psychology* 5 (1975) : 54-67.

Male and female college students were interviewed on topics pretested to arouse in them pleasant involvement, passive involvement, and unpleasant involvement. Subjects were instructed to lie to the interviewer on issues of importance to them, to systematically assess patterns of deception and emotional states of respondents. Unpleasant involvement resulted in increased smiling, self-manipulations, and postural shifts. Deception resulted in decreased smiling but increased self-manipulation and postural shifts. Gesture did not vary, but eye contact was observed to indicate greater intensity of affect. Deception is discussed as a source of stress in the interview content.

908. **McCorkie, Ruth.** "Effects of Touch on Seriously Ill Patients." *Nursing Research* 23 (1974) : 128-132.

Thirty seriously ill patients were assigned to an experimental group and 30 to a control group. The experimental group subjects were touched while talking with the nurse investigator; control group subjects were not. Responses to the verbalization and touching were measured by four instruments (an Interactional Behavior worksheet, Bales Interaction Process Analysis, a postinteraction questionnaire, and electrocardiographic changes). The findings indicate the importance of touch for communicating the nurse's concern and care to seriously ill patients.

909. **McCroskey, James C.; Richmond, Virginia P.; and Daly, John A.** "The Development of a Measure of Perceived Homophily in Interpersonal Communication." *Human Communication Research* 1 (1975) : 323-332.

This paper reports the development of a measure of perceived homophily. In five studies employing samples from diverse populations, four dimensions of interpersonal communication were discussed. These dimensions were labeled attitude, morality, appearance, and background. The studies also indicated that opinion leaders are perceived as more homophilous than nonleaders on the dimensions of attitude, morality, and background.

910. **McDermott, Ray.** "Profile: Ray L. Birdwhistell." *The Kinesis Report: News and Views of Nonverbal Communication* 2 (Spring 1980) : 1-4, 14-16. Illus.

The prime mover in the study of kinesics that has so increased in the past 20 years, Birdwhistell explains his framework for the study of communication and the importance of context. There are some intriguing comments on communication as collusion and how he would study the nature of teaching.

911. **McDermott, Ray P., and Gospodinoff, Kenneth** "Social Contexts for Ethnic Borders and School Failure." In *Nonverbal Behavior: Applications and Culture Implications,* edited by A. Wolfgang, pp. 175-195. New York: Academic Press, 1979. Illus.

The authors argue that miscommunication (nonverbal and verbal) between groups is "no accident." Different communication codes alienate classes, and cultures yet exist because they represent "political adaptations." An analysis of what at first appears to be a miscommunication between a white teacher and a Puerto Rican boy in the first grade indicates that the pattern is a way of coping with an organizational structure (classroom) which is not conducive to learning or teaching. The authors point out that under the circumstances both the teacher and student benefit in the short run.

912. **McDermott, Ray P.; Gospodinoff, Kenneth; and Aron, Jeffrey.** "Criteria for an Ethnographically Adequate Description of Concerted Activities and Their Contexts." *Semiotica* 24 (1978) : 245-275. Illus.

Part of an issue devoted to the study of face-to-face interaction, this paper is primarily concerned with the contexts of the activity and group members' positionings examined as part of the context. The example for the discussion involved the activities of a small group of first-grade children and their teacher during an 11-minute reading lesson.

913. **McDermott, R.P., and Roth, David R.** "The Social Organization of Behavior: Interactional Approaches." *Annual Review of Anthropology* 7 (1978) : 321-345.

This review focuses on a growing literature of how people organize their social interactions. The authors argue that this work is critically important for reliable ethnographic descriptions of activities and their contexts. They include the treatment of such themes as conversational sequencing and facing formations (a sustained relationship between two or more people who, by their continuous orienting to each other, occupy an exclusive space). The authors demonstrate how the concern for communicative codes, "native knowledge," and information management has focused attention on the organization of social behavior and interaction.

914. **McDermott, R.P., and Wertz, Marjorie.** "Doing the Social Order: Some Ethnographic Advances from Communicational Analysis and Ethnomethodology." *Reviews in Anthropology* 3 (1976) : 160-174.

This is a review of two works: Albert E. Scheflen's *Communicational Structure: Analysis of A Psychotherapy Transaction* (1973) and *The Reality of Ethnomethodology* by Hugh Mehan and Houston Wood (1975). The authors discuss the uniqueness, historical importance, and implications of this greatly expanded version of Scheflen's 1965 monograph and explore his "context analysis" method as it is illustrated in this study of a family therapy session. The second book is reviewed as Mehan and Wood's particular view of ethnomethodology, built on "five features of reality." The book reviewers discuss how strikingly related these works are as efforts to rigorously record everyday activities despite the fact they share only three authors in common in their extensive bibliographies.

915. **McDowell, Joseph J.** "Interactional Synchrony: A Reappraisal." *Journal of Personality and Social Psychology* 36 (1978) : 963-975.

The author reports an attempt to observe William Condon's finding of "interactional synchrony" in a six-person discussion group. The probability of the movement boundaries of participants' body parts co-occurring within three frames was compared with that expected by chance for all combinations of participants from dyads to hexad. The hypothesis of greater co-occurrence of movement boundaries between friends than between strangers was not supported, nor was increased interactional synchrony observed at speaker-switching points between speakers. However, greater co-occurrence of movement boundaries was observed at speaker-switching points of short latency than at those of long latency or overlapping speech. In all, the co-occurrence of movement boundaries above chance was observed in only one of the 57 relationships analyzed.

916. **McDowall, Joseph J.** "Microanalysis of Filmed Movement: The Reliability of Boundary Detection by Observers." *Environmental Psychology and Nonverbal Behavior* 3 (1978) : 77-88.

This study investigated the reliability with which observers detected movement boundaries from films of human behavior. Five experienced observers microanalyzed 50-frame segments of film for each of 15 designated body parts, attempting to identify the frame on which a movement was initiated, terminated, or where it changed direction. Generally, inter- and intra-observer reliabilities were found to be low at the single-frame level of agreement; only 36 percent and 40 percent, respectively, of these observed values were significantly different from chance ($p<.05$) as determined using the binomial test. However, when the unit of agreement was extended beyond one frame, there was a trend for reliability to increase. From the evidence available, it is suggested that a three-frame unit of agreement might be the optimal balance between reliability magnitude and significance.

917. **McDowell, Kenneth.** "Violations of Personal Space." *Canadian Journal of Behavioural Science* 4 (1972) : 210-217.

Eighty-two students participated in this examination of behavioral responses to the violation of personal space. Changes in body orientation, variations in eye contact, and movement away from the violator were observed. Results indicate that a violation of personal space does produce movement away from the violator; but it does not seem to affect the victim's bodily orientation or his attitudes towards the violator.

918. **McDowell, Kenneth V.** "Accommodations of Verbal and Nonverbal Behaviors as a Function of the Manipulation of Interaction Distance and Eye Contact." *American Psychological Association Proceedings* 8 (1973) : 207-208.

Two hundred forty Canadian students interacted with a confederate at normal or close distances with "open," "normal," or "closed" (minimal) eye contact. Analysis of subjects' looking and speech behavior failed to support Argyle and Dean's notion of a reciprocal relationship between distance and eye contact. The eye contact manipulation failed to have an impact on subjects' eye behavior; however, they spoke more when interacting in the increased eye contact condition. Female confederates elicited longer eye contact and more speech from subjects.

919. **McGinley, Hugh; Lefevre, Richard; and McGinley, Pat.** "The Influence of a Communicator's Body Position on Opinion Change in Others." *Journal of Personality and Social Psychology* 31 (1975) : 686-690.

Ninety-six female undergraduates read a communicator's attitude questionnaire and then saw photographs of her discussing her beliefs. Half the subjects saw open and half saw closed body positions. Subjects' attitudes changed in the direction of the communicator's viewpont more often for those who saw the communicator in the open body position.

920. **McGinley, Hugh; Nicholas, Karen; and McGinley, Patsy.** "Effects of Body Position and Attitude Similarity on Interpersonal Attraction and Opinion Change." *Psychology Reports* 42 (1978) : 127-138.

One hundred sixty-five female undergraduates were pretested for attitude similarity and dissimilarity with a "communicator." Subjects were given a brief description of the communicator's attitudes and opinions and then were shown slides of the communicator displaying open and closed body positions. Those similar to the communicator in attitude evaluated her more positively than dissimilar subjects, and they evaluated her more positively on open than closed body positions. Changes in the subjects' attitude were most often in the direction of the attitude of a positively evaluated communicator.

921. **McGough, Elizabeth.** *Understanding Body Talk* (Original title: *Your Silent Language*). New York: Scholastic Book Services, 1974. 119 pp. Illus.

This inexpensive, illustrated paperback provides a factual, popular introduction to most kinds of nonverbal behavior, citing examples from researchers such as Birdwhistell, Hall, Scheflen, and Goffman.

922. **McGovern, Thomas, and Ideus, Harvey.** "The Impact of Nonverbal Behavior on the Employment Interview." *Journal of College Placement* 38 (1978) : 51-53.

To determine the effect of interviewee's nonverbal behavior on interviewer ratings, four staged interviews were videotaped and rated by 52 experienced interviewers. Interviewees either demonstrated low nonverbal behavior (little voice modulation, infrequent eye contact, smiling, head gestures and body movements, and frequent speech disturbances) or high nonverbal behavior (steady eye contact, voice modulation, fluid responses, frequent smiling, head gestures, body movement). Eighty-nine percent of the experienced interviewers stated they would have invited the interviewees with high nonverbal behavior for a second interview, whereas none would have invited those with low nonverbal behavior. These impressions were made during the first quarter of the videotape.

923. **McGrew, Penny L., and McGrew, W.C.** "Interpersonal Spacing Behavior of Preschool Children during Group Formation." *Man-Environment Systems* 5 (1975) : 43-48.

Thirteen preschool children, five returning and eight new additions, were observed for seven days at the beginning of a school year. Eight categories of proximity to peers and adults were scored during free play. Changes in the group over the period studied, differences in proximity behaviors of experienced and inexperienced children, and sex differences were analyzed and discussed.

924. **McGrew, W.C.** *An Ethological Study of Children's Behavior.* New York: Academic Press, 1972. 257 pp. Illus.

This early attempt to apply the theory and methods of ethology to human behavior begins with a review of research on children's social behavior in psychology, anthropology, sociology, and primatology and discusses the theoretical advantages of an ethological approach. In Chapter 4 the author devotes 76 pages to the construction of an ethogram or repertoire of preschool children's behavior patterns based on his own observations and the research of others. The 110 behavioral elements are grouped into six sections: facial patterns, head patterns, gestures, postures and leg patterns, gross patterns, and locomotion. The following five chapters report research conducted by the author in two nursery schools using these behavioral elements as units in the investigation of group structure, group formation, changes in individual social behavior as a result of introduction into a group, the behavioral effects of spatial and social density, and periodicities in social behavior. Comparisons with nonhuman primate research are made throughout.

925. **McGuire, Michael T., and Polsky, Richard H.** "Behavioral Changes in Hospitalized Acute Schizophrenics: An Ethological Perspective." *The Journal of Nervous and Mental Disease* 167 (1979) : 651-657.

Six acute schizophrenic patients were observed four hours a week over a four-week period. Observers were trained to record behaviors in terms of an 101-item ethogram. Analysis of the observations indicated the patients may be distinguished as to outcome early in hospitalization with those showing less diverse pathological behaviors and more "receiving" social behavior possibly predictive of good outcome.

926. **McNeill, David.** *The Conceptual Basis of Language.* Hillsdale, New Jersey: Lawrence Erlbaum Associates, 1979. 306 pp. Illus.

In this complex and difficult work dealing with "the relationship of speech to thought," the author argues that interiorized representations of action schemes control the articulation of speech and are part of the organization of meaning. In a chapter on gestures, he discusses evidence that gestures are synchronous with and homologous to this sensory-motor content of speech.

927. **Mehrabian, Albert.** *Nonverbal Communication.* Chicago: Aldine/Atherton, 1972. 226 pp. Illus.

This book explores the many subtle ways people convey their feelings and attitudes through nonverbal communication. In Mehrabian's formulation nonverbal behavior serves to communicate feelings, attitudes, and evaluations in a three-dimensional framework of positiveness, potency/status, and responsiveness, and the book is organized around these three dimensions. The author deals with posture and position, paralanguage, implicit rhetoric, nonverbal betrayal of feeling, inconsistent messages, implicit communication, social behavior, and child communication.

928. **Mehrabian, Albert.** *Public Places and Private Spaces: The Psychology of Work, Play and Living Environments.* New York: Basic Books, 1976. 354 pp. Illus.

This book is designed to acquaint the reader with environmental psychology. In section one the author explains the set of terms and working assumptions associated with this field. He argues that human emotions can be described and measured and can vary according to individual levels of arousal, pleasure, and dominance. One's desire to approach or avoid a particular environment is related to these three factors. In sections two through seven Mehrabian examines various types of environments (intimate, residential, work, therapeutic, play, and communal settings) within the environmental psychologist's framework.

929. **Mehrabian, Albert.** *Silent Messages: Implicit Communication of Emotions and Attitudes,* second edition. Belmont, California: Wadsworth Publishing Co., 1981. 192 pp.

This book "provides a framework for grouping various postures, positions, movements, and stylistic qualities of speech and then relates this framework to basic, viable dimensions of human feelings that are conveyed nonverbally or implicitly." Among others, there are chapters on liking and approach, dominance, social style, and applications. (from publisher's information)

930. **Mehrabian, Albert, and Ksionzky, Sheldon.** "Some Determiners of Social Interaction." *Sociometry* 35 (1972) : 588-609.

Two hundred fifty-six undergraduates participated in this study of some determinants of social interaction between same-sex pairs of strangers standing and waiting. Subjects filled out personality and attitude questionnaires. They then received questionnaires of another subject (confederate). After this the subject was asked to write a personality sketch of that partner-confederate based on the questionnaire responses. A second "exchange" meant the subject ostensibly received the partner's view of him/her, although in fact these sketches were designed to be positively or negatively reinforcing or neutral. Behaviors of the subject and confederate were then observed as they waited together for two minutes before ostensibly going into a cooperative or competitive task. Results analyzed the social interaction as composed of affiliative behavior, responsiveness, relaxation, ingratiation, distress, and intimacy. Among the results it was found that affiliative behavior was a function of one's affiliative tendency and the social reinforcers received, and was greater in the cooperative conditions.

931. **Meisels, Murray, and Dosey, Michael A.** "Personal Space, Anger-Arousal, and Psychological Defense." *Journal of Personality* 39 (1971) : 333-344.

One hundred sixty undergraduates were administered the Word Association Test and the Thematic Apperception Test. They then experienced an anger-inducing condition or a nonanger condition, followed by a close-space or comfortable-space condition. Results showed that under the anger-arousing condition some subjects counterattacked by invasion of the experimenter's territory. Subjects with stronger defenses against anger expression maintained larger spatial distances.

932. **Meissner, Martin, and Philpott, Stuart B.** "The Sign Language of Sawmill Workers in British Columbia," and "A Dictionary of Sawmill Workers' Signs." *Sign Language Studies* 9 (1975) : 291-347.

This paper and dictionary describe the language of manual gestures created by sawmill workers to coordinate their work as well as for personal conversation. The development of this occupationally specific sign language appears related to a combination of noise level and technical constraints such as restriction to a fixed place, level of mechanization of work, and necessity of rapid communication. The dictionary illustrates 133 signs.

933. **Melbin, Murray.** "Some Issues in Nonverbal Communication." *Semiotica* 10 (1974) : 293-304.

Starting with a review of Albert Mehrabian's 1972 book *Nonverbal Communication*, the author discusses the scope of nonverbal communication, the problem of defining and selecting nonverbal units, multichannel communication in nonverbal communication, and correlates of nonverbal behaviors.

934. **Meltzoff, Andrew N., and Moore, M. Keith.** "Imitation of Facial and Manual Gestures by Human Neonates." *Science* 198 (1977) : 75-78. Illus.

Two studies (one a refinement of the original) indicate that infants from 12 to 21 days old actively imitate adult facial movements such as lip protrusion, mouth opening, tongue protrusion, and sequential finger movement. The authors take special note that the imitation occurs when the stimulus is no longer visually present.

935. **Messer, Stanley B., and Lewis, Michael.** "Social Class and Sex Differences in the Attachment and Play Behavior of the Year-Old Infant." *Merrill-Palmer Quarterly* 18 (1972) : 295-306.

Thirty-three 13-month-old lower-class infants were observed and compared with the middle-class sample of the S. Goldberg and M. Lewis (1969) study. Fifteen minutes of free play activity were observed and recorded. Each five-second unit of this record was assessed according to length of time, frequency of time, and response latency of behavioral categories including attachment behaviors, style of play, toy preference, and movement. Results showed that of the visual, vocal, and proximity attachment behaviors observed, only the vocal showed a significant class difference, with lower-class infants vocalizing significantly less than middle-class infants. There were no class differences in style of play, but middle-class infants were significantly more mobile than lower-class infants. Sex differences in attachment behaviors were consistent across both groups with females showing a shorter latency to return to mother, greater frequency of returns, and more time touching mother than boys. There were no significant sex differences in toy preference for the lower-class sample, but there were for the middle-class. Lower-class girls were significantly more mobile than lower-class boys, a difference not seen in the middle-class sample.

936. **Michael, Robert P., and Crook, John H.,** eds. *Comparative Ecology and Behavior of Primates.* New York: Academic Press, 1973. 847 pp. Illus.

In addition to describing socioecological, sexual, and social behavior of nonhuman primates, the volume contains a section on primates and human ethology which includes "A Description of Some Human Greetings" (Adam Kendon), "Primate Ethology and Human Social Behavior" (M.J. Waterhouse and H.B. Waterhouse), "Sex Differences in Behavior of London and Bushman Children" (N.G. Blurton-Jones and M.J. Konner), "Temporal Clusters and Individual Differences in the Behavior of Pre-School Children" (Peter K. Smith), and "Sex Differences in the Activities and Social Interaction of Nursery School Children" (C. Brindley, P. Clarke, C. Hutt, I. Robinson, and E. Wethli).

937. **Michelini, Ronald L.; Passalacqua, Robert; and Cusimano, John.** "Effects of Seating Arrangement on Group Participation." *Journal of Social Psychology* 99 (1976) : 179-186.

One hundred ninety-eight men and women were used as subjects in this field experiment. Three-person groups were observed in natural settings on a college campus and in a town. Observers coded seating arrangement, initiation and direction of interaction, as well as eye contact and body movement. Results show that those sitting in central positions initiate more communication. High visibility seemed to be related to receiving communications. Those who were central and highly visible dominated the conversation.

938. **Middleman, Ruth R.** "The Impact of Nonverbal Communication of Affect on Children from Two Different Racial and Socio-Economic Backgrounds." Ed.D. dissertation, Temple University. 1972. 345 pp. (Order No. 72-20,200)

A teacher was trained to conduct the same lesson while varying her proxemic, visual, facial, movement, and vocal behavior in either positive, negative, or neutral modes. Ninety suburban middle-class children and 90 inner-city fourth graders participated in the study. The results are complex depending on type of task productivity, race, and class, but there is evidence that affect-style had no effect on white middle- and lower-class children, but for the drawing task "the black lower-socio-economic subjects were more productive in response to the negative affect-style."

939. **Middlemist, R. Dennis; Knowles, Eric S.; and Matter, Charles F.** "Personal Space Invasions in the Lavatory: Suggestive Evidence for Arousal." *Journal of Personality and Social Psychology* 33 (1976) : 541-546.

Micturation times were recorded for 60 subjects with a confederate standing immediately adjacent to subject, one urinal away, or absent. As hypothesized, close interpersonal distances delayed the start of and shortened the duration of urinating.

940. **Milberg, Daniel.** "Directions for Research in Dance Movement Therapy." *American Journal of Dance Therapy* 1 (1977) : 14-17.

Three methods of clinical research: descriptive, dynamic, and therapeutic are discussed in relation to dance therapy. The shortcomings of some dance therapy research are outlined, with suggestions for improvement.

941. **Miller, Robert E.; Giannini, A. James; and Levine, John M.** "Nonverbal Communication in Man with a Cooperative Conditioning Task." *Journal of Social Psychology* 103 (1977) : 101-113.

This study adopts a cooperative conditioning method of investigation for nonverbal sending and receiving ability, a design used with success in research with monkeys. Each of ten medical student subjects served as a "stimulus" and a "responder." Subjects' facial expressions were videotaped while they tried to solve a "slot machine task." Responders were shown the tape and used only the expressive cues of the stimulus subjects to solve the task. This method was apparently a good way to measure differences in nonverbal decoding and encoding ability.

942. **Miller, Ted L.** "Behavioral and Spatial Change in Response to an Altered Behavioral Setting." *Environmental Psychology and Nonverbal Behavior* 3 (1978) : 23-42.

A behavioral setting termed "free time" was identified in the dayroom of an institution for the retarded. The behavioral mapping technique was used to record behavior and spatial use within this setting. A three-week period was identified in which the second week served as treatment period, and the first and third served as nontreatment periods. The second period consisted of placing novel materials into the dayroom in four conceptually distinct groupings: arts and crafts, games, empty, and lounge. During treatment patients engaged in more active and socially involved behaviors, avoided isolated behaviors and empty dayroom areas, and evidenced adaptive behavior to novel environmental objects.

943. **Mitchell, Hawkins.** "A Study of Body Movement As Expression of Emotion." Ph.D. dissertation, Columbia University. 1979. 122 pp. (Order No. 79249-41)

Fifty-eight subjects participated in a test of whether there are regular shifts in qualities of body movement accompanying experiences of specific colors as assessed through effort-shape analysis. Age, sex, ethnicity, and class differences were explored.

944. **Modarresi, Taghi.** "Motor Organization and Symbolic Signification in Childhood Psychosis." *American Journal of Dance Therapy* 1 (1977) : 3-11. Illus.

Following a review of the development of motility patterns and their relation to adaptation, the author discusses the symbolic motor patterns found in psychosis. The symbolic postures and gestures of a ten-year-old psychotic girl are described in relation to a transcript of an interview of the girl by her therapist. Modarresi proposes that the adaptive motor functions of "intentionality, articulation, and modulation of motility" are most disturbed in psychotic children, which she compares to the normal communicative behavior of a 14-month-old child in play with her mother.

945. **Modigliani, Andre.** "Embarrassment, Facework, and Eye Contact: Testing a Theory of Embarrassment." *Journal of Personality and Social Psychology* 17 (1971) : 15-24.

Ninety-two male undergraduates experienced success or failure on a task in public or private. Self-reported embarrassment, change of proportion of eye contact, and "facework" (any statement calculated to save face) were recorded. Results showed some support for the hypothesis that embarrassment requires the presence of others, although some embarrassment was reported in the private condition. Greater embarrassment resulted in more facework and also in less eye contact, although the decrease in eye contact may have resulted from dislike of criticism by the confederate.

946. **Montagner, Hubert.** *L'enfant et la communication.* Paris: Pernoud/Stock, 1978.

The product of seven years of work by the author and his team of researchers, this book is a study of how imitation, posture, gesture, and vocalization, the means by which the young child regulates affective exchanges, link together to become messages. These messages of the child must be understood or they lead to aggression, fear, or isolation. On the basis of his research, Montagner has distinguished several behavioral profiles among children: the leader, the dominant-aggressive, the timid-submissive, and the child with fluctuating behavior. These are not considered hereditary but the result of the family's manner of relating to the child. The families of leaders, of submissive, and of aggressive children are described, as well as the ways in which these tendencies are reinforced or attenuated in school. Constructive suggestions for rethinking home and school life are included. In French. (from publisher's notice)

947. **Montagner, Hubert, and Henry, J. Ch.** "Vers une biologie du comportement de l'enfant." *Revue de Questions Scientifiques* 146 (1975) : 481-529. Illus.

The hypothesis of this charmingly illustrated French study is that pre-verbal children regulate relationships via mechanisms similar to those of other mammal species or even of birds. This ethological approach includes the investigation of appeasement behaviors (smiles, stroking, offering gestures, or reclining the head over one shoulder). Their function in redirecting aggression and prolonging communication is compared to that of other mammals. The authors also focus on menacing and aggressive behavior, such as biting, kicking, hair pulling, and so on. The study makes the distinction between dominant children showing aggressive displays and "leaders" who are characterized by a large repertoire of appeasement displays. It also comments on the tendency to synchronization of urine elimination when mother and child are reunited over the weekend.

948. **Montagu, Ashley, and Matson, Floyd.** *The Human Connection.* New York: McGraw-Hill, 1979. 211 pp.

The authors review the contribution of nonverbal communication to our understanding of human communication in a context of social and cultural commentary. In a lively style, they argue that the current collective rediscovery of this familiar material reflects an important transformation in our image of human beings. They offer specific examples of many types of nonverbal behaviors from many different cultures as they occur during different phases and types of human interaction.

949. **Morganstern, Barry F.** "A Nonverbal Communication Classification System for Teaching Behaviors." In *Communication Yearbook 2*, edited by B.D. Ruben, pp. 473-485. New Brunswick, New Jersey: International Communication Association, 1978.

The author examined three independently developed nonverbal communication classification systems for teaching behavior. Nonverbal teaching behaviors were defined, coded, and analyzed through the use of the Love and Roderick (1971), Grant and Hennings (1971), and Civikly (1973) category procedures. The results indicated that the combined use of these three systems provided a more comprehensive description of teaching behaviors than each would provide individually.

950. **Morris, Desmond.** *Manwatching: A Field Guide to Human Behavior.* London: Jonathan Cape, Ltd., 1977. 320 pp. Illus.

Written for the lay reader, this beautifully illustrated book describes the acquisition of nonverbal behaviors. Gestural, gaze, and other behaviors are presented in detail with reference to their emotional and social import.

951. **Morris, Desmond; Collett, Peter; Marsh, Peter; and O'Shaughnessy, Marie.** *Gestures.* New York: Stein and Day, 1979. 296 pp. Illus.

The results of an extensive study of the origins and geographical spread of 20 gestures, which have specific meanings and are consciously performed with or without word accompaniment. The authors discuss the antiquity, possible multiple meanings, "gesture boundaries," and forms of the gestures as they are traceable across parts of Western Europe and Central Europe. A chapter is devoted to each gesture and has illustrations, historical origins, distribution, and meaning. The gestures include, for example, the "cheek screw," the "vertical horn-sign," the "teeth flick," and the "nose tap." Final chapters discuss boundaries and distances with interesting regional and national examples.

952. **Morris, Kenneth T., and Cinnamon, Kenneth M.** *A Handbook of Verbal Group Exercises.* Springfield, Illinois: Charles C. Thomas, 1974. 347 pp.

Two hundred ten exercises and exercise variations, geared to a specific goal, are described in a standardized format. The exercises are listed according to their group application, taking into account such factors as group size, types of groups (encounter, personal growth, t-group, problem solving, and so on), member experience and age, and sex ratio. In addition, there are notes of time required (verbal and nonverbal ratio), materials needed, and room setting.

953. **Morsbach, Helmut.** "Aspects of Nonverbal Communication in Japan." *The Journal of Nervous and Mental Disease* 157 (1973) : 262-277.

Nonverbal communication in Japanese culture is discussed from many different aspects. Historical proscriptions, the effect of ranking and place on nonverbal behavior, examples of Japanese mother-child interactions, nonverbal expressions of intragroup solidarity, and specific examples of Japanese body motions, emblems, whole body movements (including bowing), facial expressions, paralanguage, and proxemics are presented.

954. **Murphy, Anthony J.** "Effects of Body Contact on Performance of a Simple Cognitive Task." *British Journal of Social and Clinical Psychology* 11 (1972) : 402-403.

This study examines effects on task performance of maintaining tactile contact with another person. In this experiment each of 40 student subjects held the hand of an ostensible co-subject, while simultaneously tracing a pathway through an insoluble maze with the dominant hand. Total maze-tracing time for each subject and the number of trials were recorded to the point where the subject gave up. (The subject and confederate were separated by a screen.) There were significant performance differences between the contact groups and an experimental control having no contact. Also, male subjects in contact with a female confederate spent more time in maze tracing than male subjects in contact with a male confederate. Female subjects in the no-contact situation spent more time in maze tracing than female subjects in the contact condition. Notably, subjects were unable to correctly guess the sex of the unseen confederate from touch.

955. **Myers, Gail E., and Myers, Michele Tolela.** *The Dynamics of Human Communication: A Laboratory Approach,* third edition. New York: McGraw-Hill Book Co., 1980. Illus.

This is a college textbook which includes chapters on effective listening and nonverbal communication (including brief discussion of silences, encoding and decoding, facial expression, touch, paralanguage, and contextual patterns for nonverbal messages).

956. **Myszka, Thomas J.** "Situational and Interpersonal Determinants of Eye Contact, Direction of Gaze Aversion, Smiling, and Other Nonverbal Behaviors During An Interview." Ph.D. dissertation, University of Windsor (Canada). 1975. (Order from National Library of Canada at Ottawa)

Interviewees were asked 48 questions by an interviewer of the same or opposite sex in a simulated socially embarrassing situation. Nonverbal behaviors including eye, head and hand movements, and facial expressions were assessed.

957. **Nahumck, Nadia Chilkovsky.** *Introduction to Dance Literacy: Perception and Notation of Dance Patterns.* Philadelphia, Pennsylvania: International Library of African Music, 1978. Illus.

A practical handbook in Labanotation and its application to diverse dance forms, particularly African and American dances. (Information from publisher)

958. **Nakdimen, Kenneth Alan.** "The Two Faces of Attention: Early Formulations." *Bulletin of the Menninger Clinic* 42 (1978) : 97-118.

One may distinguish between alloplastic attention (analytic attention) and autoplastic attention (nonanalytic attention) in an individual by reading his or her facial language. The alloplastic facial expression is also the face of a special kind of affect, anger, while the autoplastic face is also the face of wonder.

959. **Natale, Michael.** "A Markovian Model of Adult Gaze Behavior." *Journal of Psycholinguistic Research* 5 (1976) : 53-63.

Fifty-two university students were paired in same- and mixed-sex dyads. Subjects were asked to converse for five minutes about life at the university, and the conversations were taped and scored by an observer. Results show that mutual gaze behavior, although not conforming precisely to a Markovian chain, nevertheless fits dialogic time patterns.

960. **Naus, Peter J., and Eckenrode, John J.** "Age Differences and Degree of Acquaintance as Determinants of Interpersonal Distance." *Journal of Social Psychology* 93 (1974) : 133-134.

This study involved 54 students in an exploration of the effects of degree of acquaintance, age differences, and sex on interaction distances. Young people chose to interact with old people at a greater distance. As individual variables, degree of acquaintance and sex had no significant effect, but there were significant interaction effects of the three variables together.

961. **Navarre, Davida.** "Posture Sharing in the Interview Dyad." Ph.D. dissertation, SUNY/Buffalo. 1980.

In brief interviews student-interviewers were trained to assume mirror or neutral positions with student-interviewees. Posture mirroring was significantly related to subjects' ratings of rapport, and, when the posture sharing was not only a mirrored spatial position but a mirroring of the "effort" or intensity of the posture, it was also related to impressions of "sociability" of the interviewer. (from author's information)

962. **Neely, William Thomas.** "Eye Contact and Interpersonal Attraction in Cooperative and Competitive Situations." Ph.D. dissertation, University of Maine. 1975. 122 pp. (Order No. 76074-36)

Members of 32 male and 32 female dyads were asked to role play liking and disliking each other during two discussions; half of the dyads were told to cooperate and half to compete with each other. It was concluded that the relationship between eye contact and interpersonal attraction is affected by the context in which an interaction takes place.

963. **Nesbitt, Paul D., and Girard, Steven.** "Personal Space and Stimulus Intensity at a Southern California Amusement Park." *Sociometry* 37 (1974) : 105-115.

The proxemic behavior of individuals in lines for attractions at an amusement park was studied in two experiments. A male or female confederate wearing brightly colored clothing or conservative dress and wearing no scent or perfume/after shave lotion entered the lines. Subjects behind the confederates were observed to keep further distance from them when they wore the high-intensity stimuli (bright clothes) and also kept greater distance when the confederates wore a scent. Males were found to stand significantly closer to the female confederate than females did, predominantly in a night-time condition.

964. **Nevill, Dorothy.** "Experimental Manipulation of Dependency Motivation and Its Effects on Eye Contact and Measure of Field Dependency." *Journal of Personality and Social Psychology* 29 (1974) : 72-79.

Forty female and 40 male undergraduates were randomly assigned to a control condition or one where help was withdrawn. Results showed greater eye contact and field dependency was found in the "dependency arousal" group. Also, there were strong correlations between measures of field dependence, eye contact duration, and gender differences.

965. **Newman, Oscar.** *Defensible Space: Crime Prevention Through Urban Design.* New York: Macmillan Company, 1972. 264 pp. Illus.

In a broad sense this book is a study of how environment affects behavior. It is a study of forms of residential areas, particularly high-density ones, and how they contribute to or lessen victimization by criminals. This book outlines the problems produced by many familiar housing types; isolates factors affecting the behavior and attitudes of the people living in these dwellings; and suggests remedies for new and existing residential tracts.

966. **Newman, Robert C. II, and Pollack, Donald.** "Proxemics in Deviant Adolescents." *Journal of Consulting and Clinical Psychology* 40 (1973) : 6-8.

Sixty male high school students participated, 30 of whom were deviant and hostile toward authority and 30 of whom were "normal" and enrolled in a class for underachievers. An experimenter approached each subject from the front, rear, left, and right until the subject told him to stop at the point of discomfort. Analysis showed that the deviants demanded more interpersonal distance than normals. There was a significant difference across both groups between proxemic distance from the front and the rear, with subjects demanding more distance from the rear. Both groups' proxemic space when charted displayed the same geometric shape.

967. **Newtson, Darren.** "Attribution and the Unit of Perception of Ongoing Behavior." *Journal of Personality and Social Psychology* 28 (1973) : 28-38.

In experiment I 20 male college students viewed a five-minute videotaped behavior sequence. Subjects were instructed to segment the behavior into as "fine-units" of action or as "gross-units" of action as were natural and meaningful to them. On the basis of their unit judgments, the subjects were then divided into two groups. In comparison to "gross-unit" subjects, "fine-unit" subjects were more confident in their impressions, made more dispositional attributions, and had more differentiated opinions. In experiment II 20 male college students viewed either of two comparable sequences of problem-solving behavior; in one, an unexpected action was inserted. Results indicate that the unit of perception varies according to situational constraints. The author argues that attribution theories assuming constant units are seriously in error.

968. **Newtson, Darren; Engquist, Gretchen; and Bois, Joyce.** "The Objective Basis of Behavior Units." *Journal of Personality and Social Psychology* 35 (1977) : 847-862.

Twenty subjects were asked to segment seven action sequences into natural units. Sequences were then segmented into "as small actions as seem natural and meaningful" by the first 20 subjects and into "as large actions as seem natural and meaningful" by 19 other subjects. As with previous research, the results indicated that units are segmented at points of distinctive change from the previous boundary point.

969. **Nguyen, Tuan; Heslin, Richard; and Nguyen, Michele.** "The Meaning of Touch: Sex Differences." *Journal of Communication* 25 (1975) : 92-102.

Forty-one male and 40 female unmarried college students answered a questionnaire concerning the meaning of touch from their best opposite-sex friend. The question "What does it mean to me when a (close) person of the opposite sex touches a certain area of my body in a certain manner?" was answered in terms of each area of the body diagrammed in 11 sections, four modalities of touch (a pat, a squeeze, a brush, and a stroke) and five meaning categories (pleasantness, playfulness, warmth/love, friendship/fellowship, and sexual desire). It was found that best opposite-sex friends touch each other's sexual areas less often than nonsexual areas, although touch from the opposite-sex best friend was found to be highly pleasant and indicating warmth/love. Also, females discriminated between their body areas to a greater degree than males, while males were more sensitive to tactile modalities.

970.   **Nierenberg, Gerard U., and Calero, Henry H.** *How to Read a Person Like a Book; and What to do About it.* New York: Cornerstone Library, 1971. 184 pp. Illus.

A popularized paperback on how to interpret the significance of gestures and facial expressions, positions, and seating arrangements written by a lawyer and a businessman.

971.   **Nine-Curt, Carmen Judith.** *Non-verbal Communication.* Fall River, Massachusetts: National Assessment and Dissemination Center for Bilingual Education.

Differences in nonverbal behavior and cultural patterns between American and Hispanic cultures are contrasted; for example, smiling behavior, clothes, silence versus noise. Elementary and intermediate Puerto Rican school-age children in Brooklyn, New York, are observed for their linguistic and nonverbal characteristics. The author stresses that an understanding of cultural differences of nonverbal behavior and communication will enable teachers of bilingual education to more successfully engage their students.

972.   **Noll, A. Michael.** "The Effects of Visible Eye and Head Turn on the Perception of Being Looked At." *American Journal of Psychology* 89 (1976) : 631-644.

Forty adults observed photos of two female models. It was found that, with a turn of the head and direct gaze at the camera, the further eye appears to be looking at the observer, while the nearer eye appears to be looking away.

973.   **Nowicki, Stephen Jr., and Duke, Marshall P.** "Use of Comfortable Interpersonal Distance Scale in High School Students: Replication." *Psychological Reports* 30 (1972) : 182.

Using a paper-and-pencil technique described in an earlier study, 62 high-school students were asked to indicate a comfortable distance from stimulus persons. Same-sex, same-race persons were held farther away than opposite-sex, same-race persons. Males kept all persons farther away than females with the exception of opposite-sex, same-race persons. Blacks of the opposite sex were held farther away than blacks of the same sex.

974.   **Obudho, Constance E.** *Human Nonverbal Behavior: An Annotated Bibliography.* Westport, Connecticut: Greenwood Press, 1979. 197 pp.

This annotated bibliography is divided into two sections: Studies with Normal Individuals and Studies with Psychiatric Subjects. Included are articles and books about nonverbal behavior written between 1940 and 1978. Each entry includes a brief, uncritical description of the study, including the purpose, procedure, and results. There are 536 annotations.

975.   **O'Connor, John Regis.** "The Relationship of Kinesic and Verbal Communication to Leadership Perception in Small Group Discussion." Ph.D. dissertation, Indiana University. 1972. 120 pp. (Order No. 72-15,924)

Viewers rated discussants in small groups on four dimensions of kinesic communication: dynamism (arm and hand movement), alertness (head and facial movement), involvement (posture), and participation (mouth movement), as well as on verbal dimensions. When results were compared with discussants' ratings of individual influence, it was found that participation and dynamism were most closely related to leadership perception.

976. **Odom, Penelope B.; Blanton, Richard L.; and Laukhuf, Claire.** "Facial Expressions and Interpretation of Emotion-Arousing Situations in Deaf and Hearing Children." *Journal of Abnormal Child Psychology* 1 (1973) : 139-151. Illus.

The degree to which a child could infer from emotionally loaded situations what affect the person in that situation was experiencing and could match it with a facial expression appropriate to that emotion was assessed. Fifteen deaf (ages seven to eight) and 30 hearing children (ages five to seven) were compared for their ability to select a facial expression appropriate for given situations from a series of photographs. The deaf children did not match the faces to the situations as well as the hearing children. In a second experiment deaf and hearing children were compared for their ability to sort facial expressions into nine predetermined categories. The deaf children performed the same as the hearing children. Thus, it appeared that the deaf children were unable to analyze and interpret emotion-arousing events as well.

977. **Odom, Richard D., and Lemond, Carolyn M.** "Developmental Differences in the Perception and Production of Facial Expressions." *Child Development* 43 (1972) : 359-369.

The study was designed to investigate a developmental lag between perception and production of facial expressions. Sixty-four children from each of grades kindergarten through fifth were shown 32 photographs of the human face with the following expressions: fear, anger, disgust, joy, distress, shame, surprise, and interest. Among the results it was found that a lag between perception and production of certain facial expressions was seen for six of the eight expressions, and contrary to expectation there was no reduction in this lag with increased age.

978. **Olofson, Harold.** "Hausa Language About Gesture." *Anthropological Linguistics* 16 (1974) : 25-39.

This article succinctly discusses the West African Hausa language for terms relating to facial expressions, gaze, and hand gestures. The great majority of them pertain to sternness, annoyance, social withdrawal, anger and contempt according to the author's interpretation, showing they are a nonverbal means of communicating unacceptable feelings.

979. **O'Neal, Edgar C.; Brunault, Mark A.; Carifio, Michael S.; Troutwine, Robert; and Epstein, Jaine.** "Effect of Insult Upon Personal Space Preferences." *Journal of Nonverbal Behavior* 5 (1980) : 56-62.

After 60 male undergraduates individually were either insulted or not insulted by the experimenter, each was tested for body-buffer zone (the physical distance between themselves and an approaching person at which they first reported being uncomfortable) by either the experimenter or an assistant. The body-buffer zones of the insulted subjects were larger when tested by the experimenter than when tested by his assistant; but for those not insulted, there were no differences in body-buffer zone produced by the identity of the tester. The results are discussed in terms of the interaction between affect and interpersonal proxemics.

980. **Oshire, M.M.** "Eye Contact: An Annotated Bibliography." *Man-Environment Systems* 6 (1976) : 187-200.

An attempt to review most of the literature on eye contact from 1970 to 1976, this annotated bibliography contains 133 citations, grouped according to seven topics: methodology; interpretation of the individual based on eye behavior, normal or deviant, judged by outside observers; interpretation of the individual by eye behavior, judged by participants in the interaction; interpretation of an interaction by outside observers based on the eye behavior of the interactants; responses to eye contact; physiological, conditioned, affective, and implications for learning effectiveness; variations in eye contact relative to variations in the environment including manipulation; and intimacy equilibrium and the interaction of eye contact with other nonverbal behaviors. Within each section the author integrates the references into a general discussion of the research.

981. **Osofsky, Joy D.**, ed. *Handbook of Infant Development*. New York: John Wiley and Sons, 1979. 954 pp. Illus.

This important resource begins with an overview of the field of infancy research by Jerome Kagan. Part I on the neonate and early infant contains an overview of neonatal behavioral assessment by Patricia A. Self and Frances Degan Horowitz; an overview of early infant assessment by Raymond K. Yang; T. Berry Brazelton, Heidelise Als, Edward Tronick, and Barry M. Lester on the Brazelton Neonatal Behavior Assessment Scale; and Judith Rosenblinth on the Graham/Rosenblinth Behavioral Examination. Developmental perspectives in infancy include "Psychophysiological Development in Infancy: State, Sensory Function, and Attention" by W. Keith Berg and Kathleen M. Berg, "Infant Visual Perception" by Leslie B. Cohen, Judy S. DeLoache, and Mark S. Strauss, and "Socioemotional Development" by Alan L. Sroufe. The interactional dimension is covered in a discussion of mother-infant interaction by Joy D. Osofsky and Karen Connors, of the father-infant interaction by Ross D. Parke, and of infant-infant interaction by Edward C. Mueller and Deborah Vaudell. Gene P. Sackett has contributed "The Lag Sequential Analysis of Contingency and Cyclicity in Behavioral Infancy Research." Papers dealing with continuity and change in development include Michael Lewis and Mark D. Starr's "Developmental Continuity," Leila Beckwith's "Prediction of Emotional and Social Behavior," and Stephen W. Porges' "Developmental Designs for Infancy Research." Among the contributions on clinical issues, applications, and interventions are "Conceptual Issues in Infant Research" by Anneliese F. Korner, "Parent Infant Bonding" by John H. Kennell, Diana K. Voos, and Marshall H. Klaus, "Vulnerability and Risk in Early Childhood" by Albert J. Solnit and Sally Provence and several articles on supportive and intervention programs. A conclusion by Leon J. Yarrow on historical perspectives and future directions completes the volume.

982. **O'Sullivan, Maureen, and Guilford, J.P.** "Six Factors of Behavioral Cognition: Understanding Other People." *Journal of Educational Measurement* 12 (1975) : 255-271. Illus.

A battery of "behavioral-cognition" tests, many based on nonverbal behaviors, were given to 240 eleventh-grade students in an effort to devise valid tests of "social intelligence." Factor analysis of the results yielded six factors dealing with a person's "ability to understand other people's thoughts, feelings, and intentions." The factors are "cognition of behavioral units," "cognition of behavioral classes," "cognition of behavorial relations," "cognition of behavioral systems," "cognition of behavioral transformation," and "cognition of behavioral implications." The factors and their respective test loadings are discussed along with questions of test validity and application to education.

983. **Pack, Alice.** "Interpretations of Kinesics Are Cultural and Not Universal." *TESL Reporter* 6 (1972) : 6-7.

Part one of a three-part article on the relationship of kinesics to culture and language teaching. The author discusses the culture-specific nature of nonverbal communication and lists numerous examples of misunderstanding. Suggestions are made for the incorporation of kinesics into second-language education.

984.   **Papp, Peggy.** "Family Choreography." In *Family Therapy: Theory and Practice,* edited by P.J. Guerin. New York: Halsted Press, 1976.

985.   **Parke, Ross D., and O'Leary, Sandra E.** "Mother-Father-Newborn Interaction: Effects of Maternal Medication, Labor and Sex of Infant." *Proceedings of the Annual Convention of the American Psychological Association* 7 (1972) : 85-86.

Nineteen parents and their first-born children were observed soon after birth. Cries, vocalizations, movements, and looks at mother or father were recorded for the infant, and a range of behaviors including hold, look, smile, imitate, touch, and rock were recorded for both parents. Fathers were found to be very active in interacting with the infant, twice as likely to hold the infant as the mother, and equalling her in the other behaviors. Both parents touched boys significantly more than girls, and mothers' rates of touching, rocking, and holding the infant increased with increased amount of medication during labor.

986.   **Patray, JoAnn Howard.** "The Relationship of Sex and Temperament to Mutual Gaze Behavior in Early Parent-Infant Interactions." Ph.D. dissertation, The University of Florida. 1978. 87 pp. (Order No. 79-00,086)

Forty-two fathers and mothers and their first-born 13-week-old infants were videotaped in structured play. Raters coded their brief and prolonged mutual gazes, and parents completed a "Perception of Baby Temperament Scale." Results showed very little mutual gaze at this age in this laboratory situation and no effects by infant or parent sex on ratings of infant temperament.

987.   **Patterson, Miles L.** "Compensation in Nonverbal Immediacy Behaviors: A Review." *Sociometry* 36 (1973) : 237-252.

Does an increase in one of the components of interpersonal intimacy have to be compensated for by a decrease in one or more of the other components? For example, does a smaller distance between interactants mean less eye contact? The author concludes that this indeed happens in order to reach an equilibrium in nonverbal expression so that interaction can be maintained. Problems involved in evaluating relevant research and implications for further work are discussed.

988.   **Patterson, Miles L.** "Stability of Nonverbal Immediacy Behaviors." *Journal of Experimental Social Psychology* 9 (1973) : 97-109.

A study involving two 25-minute interviews of college students given at one-week intervals confirmed the hypothesis that the "immediacy" behaviors of approach distance and orientation, eye contact, and body lean are consistently expressed by an individual over time. Three other problems were also examined: compensatory relationships between the immediacy behaviors, the effect of sex of subject and sex of interviewer on the immediacy behaviors, and the relationship between personality variables and immediacy behaviors. Among the results it was found that eye contact was greater in same-sex than opposite-sex dyads and that females displayed greater eye contact than males. It was also found that subjects chose to sit relatively close or relatively distant as opposed to choosing a middle range. Subjects who remained distant were more anxious than those who approached closely.

989.   **Patterson, Miles L.** "An Arousal Model of Interpersonal Intimacy." *Psychological Review* 83 (1976) : 235-245.

Following an analysis and critique of equlibrium theory, the author proposes an arousal model to explain some of the exceptions to the equilibrium model predictions; namely, that sufficient changes in one person's intimacy behaviors will precipitate arousal change in the other. Depending on factors such as context, this arousal change may be considered positive or negative, but the model predicts that those considered positive will facilitate reciprocal or enhancing reactions, while those considered negative engender compensatory reactions.

990. **Patterson, Miles L.** "Interpersonal Distance, Affect, and Equilibrium Theory." *Journal of Social Psychology* 101 (1977) : 205-214.

Two studies are reported: a laboratory one using 24 males and 24 females and a field study of 24 pairs of adults. In the laboratory study an interviewer asked the subject questions at close, comfortable, and far distances. Closer approaches resulted in significantly less eye contact and direct body orientation. In the field study dyads were observed interacting while standing. These subjects also chose less directly confronting orientations at closer interpersonal distances.

991. **Patterson, Miles L.** "Tape-Recorded Cuing for Time-Sampled Observations of Nonverbal Behavior." *Environmental Psychology and Nonverbal Behavior* 2 (1977) : 26-29.

While much research on nonverbal components of social interaction effectively employs film or videotape recording, a variety of circumstances preclude their use. For those situations that require direct observation of ongoing interactions, a simple technique is proposed that facilitates the reliable judgment of diverse behaviors on a time-sampling basis. This particular technique involves the tape-recorded cuing of exact observation times and instructions, which direct the observer's visual attention to the critical behaviors of specific subjects. The implementation of this technique in one setting and its potential application are briefly discussed.

992. **Patterson, Miles L.** "Arousal Change and Cognitive Labeling: Pursuing the Mediators of Intimacy Exchange." *Environmental Psychology and Nonverbal Behavior* 3 (1978) : 17-22.

In recent years a considerable amount of research on nonverbal behavior has focused on identifying patterns of exchange in the component behaviors of interpersonal intimacy. The rapidly developing empirical research, occasionally giving hope for some convergence in the results, has precipitated efforts at explaining the processes underlying the exchange of intimacy. This paper attempts to analyze issues surrounding two of the more promising mediators of intimacy exchange—arousal change and cognitive labeling. This speculative discussion is offered as a means of stimulating several specific and empirically testable questions which may promote our understanding of the intimacy exchange process.

993. **Patterson, Miles L.; Mullens, Sherry; and Romano, Jeanne.** "Compensatory Reactions to Spatial Intrusion." *Sociometry* 34 (1971) : 114-121.

Eighty college students sitting alone at library tables were the subjects. Their behaviors were observed as a female confederate sat next, across, two seats adjacent, or three seats adjacent to them. Increased proximity (immediacy) by the confederate resulted in leaning and blocking responses and more glancing across at the intruder. Of the subjects who quickly left the scene of the invasion, the shortest latencies were in the condition of greatest immediacy.

994. **Pattison, Joyce E.** "Effects of Touch on Self-Exploration and the Therapeutic Relationship." *Journal of Consulting and Clinical Psychology* 40 (1973) : 170-175.

In this study of 20 female undergraduates who had requested counseling, subjects who were touched by counselors engaged in more self-exploration than no-touch subjects. No significant differences were found between the two groups on relationship inventories. The interviewers were trained to use a specific touch sequence involving a handshake, a touch on client's shoulder to usher him or her into the room, a hand on the client's forearm ten to 15 minutes into the session, a hand on the back of the client's hand 25-30 minutes into the interview, and a hand on the back as the client is ushered out.

995. **Paulk, Daniel Lester.** "Sex Effects in the Interpretation of Kinesic Behavior." Ph.D. dissertation, Georgia State University—School of Arts and Sciences. 1976. 69 pp. (Order No. 77-2934)

One hundred sixty subjects were shown two videotaped sequences without sound in which a male or female actor displayed "conjunctive" or "disjunctive" kinesic behavior. Subjects rated the actors in terms of attractiveness, appropriateness of behavior, and masculinity-femininity.

996. **Paulus, Paul B.; Annis, Angela B.; Seta, John T.; Schkade, Janette K.; and Matthews, Robert W.** "Density Does Affect Task Performance." *Journal of Personality and Social Psychology* 34 (1976) : 248-253.

The effects of group size, room size, and interpersonal proximity on task performance were studied in three experiments. Results showed that task performance was independently affected by increasing group size, decreasing room size, and decreasing interpersonal distance. There were no sex differences in the effects of group size and distance, although only males were affected by room size.

997. **Pedersen, Darhl M.** "Development Trends in Personal Space." *Journal of Psychology* 83 (1973) : 3-9.

Twenty-two children in each of six elementary school grades were studied using a children's version of the Pedersen Personal Space Measure. Each subject was asked to place a figure representing him or herself at a comfortable distance from figures representing a man, woman, boy, and girl, and then the converse. Males had larger personal space preferences at all grade levels for all four stimuli. The mean distance for male third-graders was significantly different from all other means.

998. **Pedersen, Darhl.** "Relations Among Sensation Seeking and Simulated and Behavioral Personal Space." *Journal of Psychology* 83 (1973) : 79-88.

Results of a study of 40 undergraduates show that simulated and behavioral personal space measures were highly correlated for men but not for women. Men and women who rated high on the Sensation Seeking Scale (SSS) showed greater space preferences on the simulated test, but high SSS women preferred closer *behavioral* personal space toward men.

999. **Pedersen, Darhl M.** "Self-Disclosure, Body-Accessibility and Personal Space." *Psychological Reports* 33 (1973) : 975-980.

Self-disclosure, body-accessibility, and personal space were measured for 170 male undergraduates. Correlations among body-accessibility scores showed an almost perfect relationship between the extent to which subjects touch and are touched by specific target persons. Body accessibility was found to be related to self-disclosure for all target persons and most highly related for best female friend. As with previous research, body accessibility with best female friend was not found to be related to body accessibility with parents and male friends.

1000. **Pedersen, Darhl M., and Heaston, Anne B.** "The Effects of Sex of Subject, Sex of Approaching Person, and Angle of Approach upon Personal Space." *Journal of Psychology* 82 (1972) : 277-286.

Forty university students (20 males, 20 females), aged 18-30, participated. Subjects were administered two personal space measures—one simulated and one in which they were actually approached by another person at varying angles. Subjects permitted females to approach more closely than males. Female subjects allowed a person to approach more closely on the sides than from the front, while males allowed greater approach from the front than on the sides.

1001. **Pedersen, Darhl M., and Shears, Loyda M.** "Review of Personal Space Research in the Framework of General System Theory." *Psychological Bulletin* 80 (1973) : 367-388.

Key concepts of general system theory (for example, open versus closed systems, input, throughput, output, information transfer) are applied to diverse research on personal space and nonverbal communication. The review is divided into studies dealing with the "person system" and those that consider the "group as a system."

1002. **Pedersen, Frank A.** *The Father-Infant Relationship: Observational Studies in Family Settings.* New York: Praeger, 1980.

1003. **Peery, J. Craig,** "Magnification of Affect Using Frame-by-Frame Film Analysis." *Environmental Psychology and Nonverbal Behavior* 3 (1978) : 58-61. Illus.

Frame-by-frame film analysis of social interaction enhances the observer's ability to make inferences about the affective component of the interaction by allowing a detailed and precise review of the interpersonal behavior. An example of leave-taking behavior between a parent and preschool child is presented. The magnification of the interaction by repeated slow-motion viewing allows one to draw out emotional behavioral components that occur too rapidly to be perceived at normal speed. The technique is applicable to any type of interpersonal analysis.

1004. **Peery, J. Craig, and Stern, Daniel N.** "Gaze Duration Frequency Distributions During Mother-Infant Interaction." *Journal of Genetic Psychology* 129 (1976) : 45-55.

Interactions of ten twin infants and their mothers were videotaped weekly during the infants' fourth month of life. Time spent gazing at or away from the other's face was recorded during play, bottle feeding, and spoon feeding. Frequency distributions of gaze durations for both mothers and infants were plotted, and the results in both cases approximated a straight line. The identical finding was obtained for frequency distributions of time spent not looking. The authors conclude that these findings reveal an invariant in this dimension of social behavior and question the appropriateness of techniques measuring mean gaze time, which assumes a normal distribution.

1005. **Peng, Fred C.C.** "Kinship Signs in Japanese Sign language." *Sign Language Studies* 5 (1974) : 31-47. Illus.

This paper examines the expression of kinship relationships in Japanese sign language as a first step in studying the relationships of the deaf and how they regard themselves and others.

1006. **Peng, Fred C.C.; Hongo, Tomoko; and Nakawaki, Masako.** "Nonverbal Expressions of Rituals in Japanese *Sumo.*" *Semiotica* 17 (1976) : 1-12. Illus.

The authors describe the proxemics of Japanese *sumo* wrestling in some detail, the nonverbal expression of the rituals, and offer interpretations of the cultural meanings.

1007. **Peng, Fred C.C., and Raffler-Engel, Walburga von,** eds. *Language Acquisition and Development Kinesics.* Hiroshima, Japan: Bunka Hyoron Publishing Co., 1978. 205 pp. Illus.

Three chapters are devoted to developmental kinesics. One describes the child's acquisition of kinesics as beginning with nursery games and culminating during puberty. Kinesic synchrony is said to be acquired gradually. A second chapter describes the kinesic, intonational, and semantic aspects of two-syllable utterances by a one-and-a-half-year-old. Finally, the interactional synchrony of 35 autistic and schizophrenic children is compared to age-matched normals. Movement was found to be distorted from its appropriate speech pattern.

1008. **Pesso, Albert.** *Experience in Action: A Psychomotor Psychology.* New York: New York University Press, 1973. 263 pp. Illus.

An in-depth look at what the author terms "psychomotor therapy." Proceeding from an exploration of philosophical and existential questions, the author examines the psychomotor process as a means of viewing emotional phenomena and behavior. The psychomotor process is based on the hypothesis that emotions tend to become actions and actions seek to find appropriate or satisfying interactions. Psychomotor group members are sensitized to their emotional actions and are helped to modify and adjust to the particular interaction. The work includes a sketch of the relationship of the body's activities to emotions and discussion of themes such as identity, rhythm, and interactional synchrony.

1009. **Peters, Michael, and Ploog, Detler.** "Communication Among Primates." *Annual Review of Physiology* 35 (1973) : 221-242.

This review examines communication among primates using Albert Scheflen's framework for the study of communication. It consists of a discussion of the methods of study, a description of the communication modes available to primates, and social interactions involving sexual behavior. A bibliography on other social interactions is also included.

1010. **Peterson, Carole L.; Danner, Fred W.; and Flavell, John H.** "Developmental Changes in Children's Responses to Three Indications of Communication Failure." *Child Development* 43 (1972) : 1463-1468.

Twenty-four preschool chldren and 24 first-graders participated in this experiment to see if children could recognize when a listener (adult) needed more information. Three conditions were used: a "Facial Feedback Condition," where the experimenter indicated "puzzlement" or "bewilderment"; an "Implicit Condition," where the experimenter told the child "I don't understand" and "I don't think I can guess that"; and "Explicit Condition," where the experimenter told the child how to help him. Among the results it was found that all children were able to give additional information when explicitly requested to do so but did not respond to the Facial Feedback Condition. Most first-graders but few of the preschoolers were able to respond to the implicit request.

1011. **Petofi, J.S.** "On the Comparative Structural Analysis of Different Types of 'Works of Art.'" *Semiotica* 3 (1971) : 365-378.

One section of this article contains a chart comparing movement and verbal languages.

1012. **Philips, Susan Urmston.** "Some Sources of Cultural Variability in the Regulation of Talk." *Language in Society* 5 (1976) : 81-95.

The way in which talk is regulated, both verbally and nonverbally, was investigated in two groups: the Indians of the Warm Springs Reservation in central Oregon and Anglos nearby. Many differences (and some very general similarities) were found, especially in the nonverbal regulation. Body motion, position shifting, facial movement and expression, gaze, the rhythmic relationship between speech and body movement, general versus specific address of listeners, and interactional synchrony were all found to be differently used as nonverbal talk regulators by the Anglos and the Indians.

1013. **Pike, Kenneth L.** "On Kinesic Triadic Relations in Turn-Taking." *Semiotica* 13 (1975) : 389-394. Illus.

Kinesic relationships involved in turn taking are discussed in a theoretical framework that parallels that previously developed for analyzing conversational turn taking in a triad.

1014. **Pitcairn, Thomas K., and Eibl-Eibesfeldt, Irenäus.** "Concerning the Evolu¼ tion of Nonverbal Communication in Man." In *Communicative Behavior and Evolution,* edited by M.E. Hahn and E.C. Simmel, pp. 81-113. New York: Academic Press, 1976.

The authors argue that, if animals have produced a communicative system that can be shown to have an evolutionary continuity along parts at least of the phylogenic tree, then it is reasonable to posit that the continuity of communication system extends into human behavior, particularly human nonverbal communication.

1015. **Pitcairn, Thomas K., and Schleidt, Margaret.** "Dance and Decision: An Analysis of a Courtship Dance of the Medlpa, New Guinea." *Behaviour* 58 (1976) : 298-316. Illus.

This study focuses on a courtship dance to assess the role of individual variation within tradition and partnership. Illustrated with wonderful photographs, it examines such questions as: how variable are the performance and pace of the dance both within and between pairs of dancers, and which partner controls these variations and how?

1016. **Pliner, Patricia; Krames, Lester; and Alloway, Thomas,** eds. *Nonverbal Communication of Aggression.* New York: Plenum Press, 1975. 189 pp.

The book contains the proceedings of the Fourth Annual Symposium of Communication and Affect held at the University of Toronto in 1974. The following papers are included: "Language and Communication – II: The View from '74" by Harvey Sarles; "Visual Behavior as an Aspect of Power Role Relationships" by Ralph V. Exline, Steve L. Ellyson, and Barbara Long; "Direct Gaze as a Social Stimulus: The Example of Aggression" by Phoebe C. Ellsworth; and "Patterns of Emotion and Emotion Communication in Hostility" by Carroll E. Izard. Additional chapters include "Communication and Aggression in a Group of Young Chimpanzees" by E.W. Menzel, Jr., "Nonverbal Expressions of Aggression and Submission in Social Groups of Primates" by Robert E. Miller; "Nonverbal Communication: The Effect of Affect on Individual and Group Behavior" by Benson E. Ginsburg; and "Animal's Defenses: Fighting in Predatory-Prey Relations" by Stanley C. Ratner.

1017. **Plutchik, Robert, and Kellerman, Henry,** eds. *Emotion: Theory, Research and Experience.* Vols. 1 and 2. New York: Academic Press, 1979.

1018. **Polhemus, Ted,** ed. *The Body Reader: Social Aspects of the Human Body.* New York: Pantheon Books, 1978. 324 pp. Illus.

The editors approach the study of the human body from a physio-psychosociological perspective. The book contains papers by authors from various disciplines; for example, Weston LaBarre, "The Cultural Basis of Emotions and Gestures"; Seymour Fisher, "Body Image"; Jane Richardson and A.L. Kroeber, "Three Centuries of Woman's Dress Fashion: A Quantitative Analysis"; and Ray Birdwhistell, "Kinesics." This book also contains a bibliography of nonverbal communication.

1019. **Poling, Tommy Hugh.** "Proxemic and Kinesic Behavior." Ph.D. dissertation, Oklahoma State Univeristy. 1974. 63 pp. (Order No. 75088-61)

Standing and seated personal space, postural openness, torso lean, eye contact, approach rate, and use of adaptors, illustrators, and emblems were studied in relation to subject's sex, "dominance," physical attractiveness, and sex of the confederate.

1020. **Polit, Denise, and LaFrance, Marianne.** "Sex Differences in Reaction to Spatial Invasion." *The Journal of Social Psychology* 102 (1977) : 59-60.

Male or female confederates sat next to each of 120 subjects and either asked if a seat was taken (invasive condition) or remained silent. Subjects' departure times were recorded. Females were found to depart sooner than males. No differences were found between the invasive and silent conditions.

1021. **Polsky, Richard H., and Chance, M.R.A.** "An Ethological Analysis of Long Stay Hospitalized Psychiatric Patients." *The Journal of Nervous and Mental Disease* 167 (1979) : 669-674.

Applying ethological methods to describing the behaviors of 24 chronic male patients' sending and receiving patterns of four molar behavioral groupings; "assertive, altruistic, cigarette, and verbal," are analyzed in terms of rank on a 3-level scale. A number of relationships are reported such as the finding that middle-third members received the greater portion of assertive behavior.

1022. **Polsky, Richard, and McGuire, Michael T.** "An Ethological Analysis of Manic-Depressive Disorder." *The Journal of Nervous and Mental Disease* 167 (1979) : 56-65.

Eight patients diagnosed bi-polar manic-depressive were observed for up to four weeks of their hospitalization. Trained observers coded various verbal and nonverbal actions and the context for half-hour periods in a systematic way allowing later qualitative analysis. A number of analyses of changes over time and behavioral profiles for the manic-improved, manic-not improved, and depressive patients are presented which show distinct differences.

1023. **Post, Barbara, and Hetherington, E. Mavis.** "Sex Differences in the Use of Proximity and Eye Contact in Judgments of Affiliation in Pre-School Children." *Developmental Psychology* 10 (1974) : 881-889.

Forty four-year-olds and 40 six-year-olds were shown two pictures of couples with varying eye contact and proximity and asked to choose which couple liked each other best. Girls were found to be more sensitive to both social cues than boys, with a rapid increase between ages four and six. In a second study 80 four-year-olds were presented similar pictures varying proximity between couples and asked the same question. However, half of the children were given discrimination training. No sex differences were found before training, but only the girls improved with training.

1024. **Poyatos, Fernando.** "Gesture Inventories: Fieldwork Methodology and Problems." *Semiotica* 13 (1975) : 199-227.

This review article primarily comments on the book *Handbook of Gestures: Colombia and the United States* (the 1973 *Approaches to Semiotics* series edition of the 1962 inventory by Robert L. Saitz and Edward J. Cervenka), although two other books are also dealt with: Jerald R. Green's *Gesture Inventory for the Teaching of Spanish* (1968) and David Efron's *Gesture, Race, and Culture* (1972). Many of the first book's shortcomings are discussed, as well as possible ways it might have been improved. An extensive discussion of the various sources of data, subjects, and recording techniques that were used in these books, with suggestions for a much more comprehensive plan, is presented.

1025. **Poyatos, Fernando.** *Man Beyond Words: Theory and Methodology of Nonverbal Communication.* Oswego, New York: New York State English Council (Monograph Number 15), 1976. 207 pp.

Following an introduction to issues in intercultural communication and analysis of the cultural context, the author explores "total body communication" in interaction and attempts to move toward an exhaustive description of it. There is a section on the "triple structure of human communication": language, paralanguage, and kinesics, followed by special concentration on paralanguage, kinesics, proxemics, and chronemics. Besides the author's distinctive efforts to theoretically integrate the subject, there is a unique section on nonverbal communication in narrative literature. A serious study of diverse researchers, the book includes a good reference list and subject index.

1026. **Poyatos, Fernando.** "Forms and Functions of Nonverbal Communication in the Novel: A New Perspective of the Author-Character-Reader Relationship." *Semiotica* 21 (1977): 295-337.

An analysis of how an author conveys the nonverbal aspects of what's going on in a scene, an interpersonal interaction, and so on. The communication process between the author and the reader, problems of translating nonverbal behaviors, and various reasons for including descriptions of nonverbal behavior are also discussed. Extensive quotations illustrate each point.

1027. **Poyatos, Fernando.** "The Morphological and Functional Approach to Kinesics in the Context of Interaction and Culture." *Semiotica* 20 (1977) : 197-228.

This article is concerned with the need to carry out both synchronic and diachronic cultural and cross-cultural analyses of kinesic material, and also with development of a methodological framework for systematic and exhaustive classification of the kinesic material to be analyzed and classified. Extensive kinesic classifications are suggested.

1028. **Poyatos, Fernando.** "Interactive Functions and Limitations of Verbal and Nonverbal Behaviors in Natural Conversation." *Semiotica* 30 (1980) : 211-244.

The author sets out to "delimit the boundaries and forms" of conversation and the covariation and interrelationship of various verbal and nonverbal channels. He presents his theoretical paradigm for these relationships and focuses on turn-taking patterns, rules and simultaneous behavior, and silence.

1029. **Poyatos, Fernando.** "New Perspectives for an Integrative Research of Nonverbal Systems." In *Nonverbal Communication Today: Current Research,* edited by M.R. Key, forthcoming.

The author outlines his personal approach to the difficult goal of integrating diverse disciplines, theories, and aspects of communication, verbal and nonverbal, under a theoretical superstructure illustrated here in two complex diagrams. Following a discussion of the semiotic approach to interaction, he discusses systems interrelationships, what he calls "culturemes," his "basic triple structure" formulation of communication, and categories of nonverbal behaviors. (from prepublication manuscript)

1030. **Price, Judy Martha.** "The Effects of Crowding on the Social Behavior of Children." Ph.D. dissertation, Columbia Univeristy. 1971. 79 pp. (Order No. 72-19,151)

Preschool and first-grade children were observed during free play under crowded and noncrowded conditions. Crowding was found to increase solitary behavior and decrease interaction but was unrelated to aggression. Males engaged in more social and aggressive behavior and females in more solitary behavior.

1031.　**Pritchard, Charles Harold.** "A Study of Manifested Counselor Nonverbal Behavior Within Counseling Subroles." Ed.D. dissertation, Oklahoma State University. 1972. 128 pp. (Order No. 73-15,216)

Sixteen nonverbal behavior categories were assessed to determine the characteristic nonverbal patterns of 30 secondary school counselors videotaped in actual counseling sessions. Specific behaviors characteristic of "sub-roles" such as "Probing" or "Information Giving" are reported.

1032.　**Prkachin, Kenneth M.; Craig, Kenneth D.; Papageorgis, Demetrios; and Reith, Gunther.** "Nonverbal Communication Deficits and Response to Performance Feedback in Depression." *Journal of Abnormal Psychology* 86 (1977) : 224-234.

In this study of a small group of depressed women and psychiatric and normal controls, videotapes of their elicited facial expressions were judged by them. Among the results was evidence that the depressed subjects were the most difficult to judge correctly.

1033.　**Prosser, M.H.** *The Cultural Dialogue: An Introduction to Intercultural Communication.* Boston, Massachusetts: Houghton-Mifflin, 1978. 344 pp. Illus.

A chapter on nonverbal behavior reviews its classifications and discusses cultural differences in the use of touch and the importance of the different senses.

1034.　**Prost, J.H.** "Varieties of Human Posture." *Human Biology* 46 (1974) : 1-19. Illus.

Arguing that language describes bodily postures as if they belonged to discrete classes, the author analyzes 590 postural poses from magazines, concluding that posture is rather a field phenomenon, the result of a combination of continuous variables, the placements allowed by the joints.

°1035.　**Putnam, Linda L., and McCallister, Linda.** "Situational Effects of Task and Gender on Nonverbal Display." In *Communication Yearbook IV,* edited by D. Nimmo. New Brunswick, New Jersey: Transactional Books, forthcoming.

The authors selected ten nonverbal categories which function to control conversations and to express attentiveness and which are linked to masculine or feminine behavior. The dominant behaviors (interruptions, long back channel behaviors, turn time, postural shift, and gesticulation) and warmth-attentiveness behaviors (head nods while listening, "mm-hmm" back channels, eye gaze, smiling, and laughing) of 423 undergraduate students were observed and measured as each worked with a partner on a task. Results indicated that both sexes employed dominance and attentiveness cues in accordance with the task situation and gender identity as measured by the Bem-Sex-Role Inventory (BSRI), a scale which classifies subjects into four psychological gender categories. (from a pre-publication manuscript)

1036.　**Quick, Alida Diane.** "The Effects of Sex and Anxiety in Invasion of Personal Space." Ph.D. dissertation, Michigan State University. 1975. 68 pp. (Order No. 75-20,882)

Lack of results in a study predicting that higher anxiety in female invaders evokes more invadee threat led to a discussion of the need for retesting with a multivariate approach in field experiments.

1037.　**Raffler-Engel, Walburga von.** "Developmental Kinesics: Cultural Differences in the Acquisition of Nonverbal Behavior." *WORD* 27 (1971) : 195-204.

In this article the author describes a study comparing and contrasting the French and English kinesics system of bilingual children. The author also gives examples of how the development of kinesics can be suppressed by social rules, as in Japanese society, or altered as in the Italian culture, where a great many specific forms of semantic gestures have to be learned.

1038. **Raffler-Engel, Walburga von,** ed. *Aspects of Nonverbal Communication.* Lisse: Swets and Zeitlinger B.V., 1980. 379 pp. Illus.

This excellent collection of original articles by major authors is divided into four sections: research foundations, acquisition of nonverbal communication, practical research methodology, and applied kinesics. The first section on theory and foundations includes an unusually extensive array of theoretical overviews by Albert E. Scheflen, Adam Kendon, Irenäus Eibl-Eibesfeldt, Starkey Duncan, Jr., Robert N. St. Clair, Fernando Poyatos, Michael T. McGuire, Michael Eric Bennett, and Elizabeth Nall, with a chapter on the conceptual framework for three classes of nonverbal behavior by Paul Ekman. The second section is devoted to a chapter on developmental kinesics by Walburga von Raffler-Engel. The third section on methodology includes a very practical paper by Heather Hilton and Steven Weinstein, brief methodological guidelines by Patrice L. French, use of computers in kinesic research by Larry H. Reeker, statistical methods by Lillian Christman, measurement of expression by Harald G. Wallbott, and an unsuccessful attempt to use a new high-speed film method to reproduce Condon's synchrony "effect" by C.D. Webster, H. Westerblom, J. Oxman, M.M. Konstantareas, and R. Rivers. The final section contains special topics such as rhythmic analysis of face-to-face interaction by Adrian T. Bennett, expression of emotion in theatrical performance by Carroll E. Izard and Barbara S. Izard, hand illustrations while giving directions by Akiba A. Cohen, storytelling illustrations by Janis Buckner, speaker adjustments to hearer by Brenda Hopson-Hasham, and nonverbal behavior in foreign language teaching by Leo Ward and Walburga von Raffler-Engel. Also included are chapters on facial muscles in expression by Charles Gregory Puckett, differences in group versus dyadic interaction by Susan Byrn and Betsy Van Vleck, "personality structure and communicative behavior—a comparison of Japanese and Americans" by Tetsuya Kunihuro, culture clashes by Bates Hoffer and Richard G. Santos, patient-nurse interaction by Diane Angelini, and blind nonverbal communication by Lisa Manly. This section concludes with chapters on female reactions to male invasion of their space by Perry Weisberg and Elizabeth B. Battey, and nonverbal behavior in job applicant evaluation by Walburga von Raffler-Engel, Keith Newman, Robin Foster, and Frank Gantz.

1039. **Raffler-Engel, Walburga von; Stewart, M.; and Elliott, J.** "White Reactions to the Black Handshake Under Three Experimental Conditions." In *Language and Ethnic Relations*, edited by H. Giles and B. St. Jacques, pp. 197-214. London: Pergamon Press, 1979.

1040. **Rago, William V. Jr.** "Eye Gaze and Dominance Hierarchy in Profoundly Mentally Retarded Males." *American Journal of Mental Deficiency* 82 (1977) : 145-148.

This study focused on aggression in 24 profoundly retarded institutionalized men to examine the function of mutual gaze in this social group and to provide evidence regarding the relationship between eye contact and an individual's rank in the group dominance hierarchy. Submissive individuals were found to maintain significantly longer eye contact than dominant individuals, which contradicts previous research on gaze and submissiveness in normal adults.

1041. **Rago, William V. Jr., and Cleland, Charles C.** "Relationship between Frequency of Touching and Status in Institutionalized Profoundly Retarded." *Bulletin of the Psychonomic Society* 11 (1978) : 249-250.

Fourteen institutionalized, profoundly mentally retarded adult males, members of the same group, were observed for a two-week period, and aggressive and touching (nonaggressive) interactions were recorded. Results showed that the subjects with lower status, that is, those who did not initiate aggression, touched other group members more frequently than higher-status subjects. Higher-status subjects seldom initiated touching but were often the recipients of it.

1042. **Rajecki, D.W.; Lamb, Michael E.; Obmascher, Pauline.** "Toward a General Theory of Infantile Attachment: A Comparative Review of Aspects of the Social Bond." *The Behavioral and Brain Sciences* 1 (1978) : 417-464.

Contemporary theories of bonding are reviewed in light of three phenomena (maltreatment, secure base, and separation effects) and research on birds, dogs, monkeys, and children. The authors suggest attention be paid to the infant's role in bonding, species differences in bonding, and a refined identification of different human infant emotions. Twenty-eight commentaries by other contributors are followed by the author's reply.

1043. **Ramsden, Pamela.** *Top Team Planning: A Study of the Power of Individual Motivation in Management.* New York: John Wiley and Sons, 1973. 262 pp. Illus.

This book constitutes an in-depth application of contemporary thought and research on nonverbal behavior to practical problem solving. Written by a management consultant, it includes four "action profiles" which express the individual's level of motivation in such terms as exploring, confronting and deciding, commitment, dynamism, and adaptablility. It then shows how action profiles are derived from movement patterns. The book also covers how to use the action profile; how to educate someone as to her/his own strengths and weaknesses; how to develop people's skills in accordance with these; how to protect from overactive behavioral tendencies; and how to develop a team within the perspective of individual profiles and desired team atmosphere.

1044. **Ramsey, Sheila J.** "Prison Codes." *Journal of Communication* 26 (1976) : 39-45.

This interesting article describes the ways in which nonverbal communication via dress, gesture, posture, touch, and so on, gains importance within the male prison environment. Differences in cultural subgroups, prisoner-guard communication, sexuality, personal space, privacy, and crowding are discussed. Interesting comments on visiting room behavior and on the experience of time and space are also included.

1045. **Rarick, G. Lawrence; Dobbins, D. Alan; and Broadhead, Geoffrey D.** *The Motor Domain and its Correlates in Educationally Handicapped Children.* Englewood Cliffs, New Jersey: Prentice-Hall, 1976.

This monograph reports two studies of the motor behavior of educable mentally retarded children. The first study was an investigation of the basic components underlying the motor abilities of this population. A large number of motor performance tests and measures of physical growth were administered to 135 educable mentally retarded boys and girls and 126 normal boys and girls ages six to nine years and to 145 educable mentally retarded boys and girls ages ten to 13 years. Scores on 39 motor performance and seven physical growth measures were factor analyzed to identify the factor structures of motor performance of both the educable mentally retarded and the normal children by age and sex. In the second study, the effects of individualized versus group-oriented physical education programs on the motor, physical strength, intellectual, social, and emotional development of educable mentally retarded and minimally brain-injured children ages six to 13 were studied.

1046. **Rasberry, R.W.** "A Collection of Nonverbal Communication Research: An Annotated Bibliography." *The Journal of Business Communication* 16 (1979) : 21-29.

1047. Rawls, James R.; Trego, Ronald E.; McGaffey, Charles N.; and Rawls, Donna J. "Personal Space as a Predictor of Performance under Close Working Conditions." *Journal of Social Psychology* 86 (1972) : 261-267.

Male university students, 56 for the psychomotor task, 48 for the math task, were pretested as to their need for personal space (high or low PS). Psychomotor test results indicated that high PS scorers' performance significantly decreased in crowded conditions, while low PS scorers' performance did not. Math test results indicate that low PS scorers worked more problems under crowded conditions, while problems worked by high PS scorers did not correlate with seating density. High PS scorers did more poorly while low PS scorers did better under high seating density.

1048. Redican, William K. "Facial Expression in Nonhuman Primates." In *Primate Behavior: Developments in Field and Laboratory Research,* vol. 4, edited by L.A. Rosenblum, pp. 103-194. New York: Academic Press, 1975.

Primate facial displays of threat, grimace, lipsmack, yawn, playface, and protruded lip face are described in terms of their appearance during infant primate development.

1049. Rejeski, Walter, and Lowe, Charles A. "Nonverbal Expression of Effort as Causally Relevant Information." *Personality and Social Psychology Bulletin* 6 (1980) : 436-440.

One hundred sixty-five subjects in groups of 20 watched a videotape of an athlete running on an exercise treadmill. The athlete either succeeded or failed and was either expressive or nonexpressive. The results showed the subjects attributed more effort to the expressive athlete than the nonexpressive athlete and judged the unsuccessful nonexpressive athlete to have less ability and more culpability for his failure.

1050. Rekers, George A., and Amaro-Plotkin, Hortensia D. "Sex-Typed Mannerisms in Normal Boys and Girls as a Function of Sex and Age." *Child Development* 48 (1977) : 275-278.

Eight gestures previously identified in gender-disturbed boys were recorded for normal children of two age groups (four to five years and 11 to 12 years) while they performed a standardized play task. A significant overall difference was found between the girls and boys on these measures, and three of the gestures significantly discriminated between the sexes.

1051. Research Centre for Movement Notation. *Movement Notation Survey 1976.* Holon, Israel: The Movement Notation Society, 1976. 30 pp. Illus.

A beautifully illustrated manual on the nature and uses of Eshkol-Wachman Movement Notation including description of where it is being applied. There is an annotated list of books on the notation and reference to where it is taught. Of particular note is the description of the University of Illinois project led by Heinz von Foerster and Noa Eshkol to transcribe the notation into a computer program which "would allow the machine to execute the movements by computing its trajectories and deliver these in numeric and graphic form."

1052. Resnik, Salomon. *Personne et psychose: Etudes sur le langage du corps.* Paris: Payot, 1973.

Nonverbal communication is the "thread of Ariadne" in the psychosis, the fundamental, underlying dimension. The analyst's task is to decode this language in its different forms: the language of the body, vocalizations, dramas, silence. The author analyzes the "syndrome of Cotard" — the mechanism of negation of the body, wherein the body becomes the container of internal projections.

1053. **Reynolds, John Stephen.** "A Study of Nonverbal Communication as Related to Three Educational Administration Situations." Ed.D. dissertation, University of Tennessee. 1971. 177 pp. (Order No. 72-15,543)

A videotape depicting an administrator interacting with a teacher in three administration situations was shown to 212 teachers and administrators. Among the results it was found that women were more perceptive than men in identifying nonverbal cues, and people over 40 are not as positive or negative in their reactions as people under 40.

1054. **Rich, Andrea L.** "Interracial Implications of Nonverbal Communication." In *Interracial Communication,* edited by A.L. Rich, pp. 161-190. New York: Harper & Row, 1974.

The importance of nonverbal communication in interracial settings is even more evident than in racially homogeneous settings because basic geographical and psychological separation of the races has made it difficult for them to get close enough to communicate verbally. This chapter examines the variables of environment, communicator appearance, and nonverbal behavior with respect to the manner in which these variables facilitate and/or disrupt interracial interaction. An exploration of dress, gesture, posture, kinesics, and territoriality patterns of blacks and whites is included.

1055. **Richer, J.M., and Coss, R.G.** "Gaze Aversion in Autistic and Normal Children." *Acta Psychiatrica Scandinavica* 53 (1976) : 193-210.

Ten autistic children were matched on the basis of age and sex with a group of normal school children. A male adult sat in a room with one child at a time. Whenever the child looked at the region of the adult's eyes, the adult pressed a foot switch producing a burst of white noise on the videotape soundtrack, so that duration of looking could be measured in the subsequent analysis of the videorecording. The autistic children's mean total "looking times" were lower and their "flight predominance" scores were higher than those of normal children.

1056. **Riley, Francis Terrill.** "The Effects of Seating Arrangements in the Dyadic Interaction Interview upon the Perceptual Evaluation of the Counseling Relationship Among Secondary Students." Ed.D. dissertation, University of Virginia. 1972. 103 pp. (Order No. 72-26,265)

One hundred forty-four high school students viewed counseling session videotapes in which seating arrangement (on opposite sides of a desk, at 45° angle to each other, away from the desk and opposite but at 45° angle from desk). No specific arrangement per se appeared optimal, but there were significant interaction effects of counselor × arrangement, suggesting the need to determine which arrangement is "most effective for individual counselors."

1057. **Rinck, Christine M.; Willis, Frank N. Jr.; and Dean, Larry M.** "Interpersonal Touch Among Residents of Homes for the Elderly." *Journal of Communication* 30 (1980) : 44-47.

In this study of touch patterns observed in four homes for the elderly, the rate of touch initiation was found to be higher for women than for men and higher for white than black residents. Women touched other women most frequently, followed by rate of women touching men, then rate of men touching women, with men touching other men the least often. Women and men were not found to differ as to which body areas were touched.

1058. **Rizzitiello, Theresa G.** *An Annotated Bibliography on Movement Education.* Washington: American Alliance for Health, Physical Education and Recreation, 1977. 49 pp.

1059. Robinson, Christine L.; Lockard, Joan S.; and Adams, Robert M. "Who Looks At a Baby in Public." *Ethology and Sociobiology* 1 (1979) : 87-91.

In two field studies, 7,134 subjects in a shopping mall were observed with regard to whether or not they looked for at least two seconds at an infant in proximity to her parent. Significant differences in looking were found to be a function of sex, with females more likely to look than males, and a function of age, with males under 15 and over 60 and females under 30 and over 60 more likely to look than other age/sex categories.

1060. Rodgers, Janet A. "Relationship between Sociability and Personal Space Preferences at Two Different Times of Day." *Perceptual and Motor Skills* 35 (1972) : 519-526.

A study investigating the relationship between sociability, personal space preference, and time of day. A sample of 100 undergraduates was given the Heron Personality Inventory and then was observed for interpersonal distance behaviors between 8:30 and 9:30 am and 2:30 and 3:30 pm. The findings confirmed that all subjects preferred more personal space in the morning than in the afternoon. In four out of six trials, low-sociability subjects manifested a significantly greater variability of scores than did high-sociability subjects.

1061. Rohner, Ronald P. "Proxemics and Stress: An Empirical Study of the Relationship Between Living Space and Roommate Turnover." *Human Relations* 27 (1974) : 697-702.

Fifty-eight pairs of males living in rooms in four men's dormitories were studied. The subjects either had twin or bunk beds. It was hypothesized that there would be greater turnover in roommates among the men having twin beds due to the increased crowding and decreased visual privacy this furniture arrangement entails. The hypothesis was confirmed.

1062. Romig, Dennis Arl. "The Relationship of Decreased Eye Contact Upon Anxiety and Recall in a Learning Task." Ph.D. dissertation, University of Texas-Austin. 1971. 114 pp. (Order No. 72196-59)

The effects of decreased eye contact on recall of complex learning material presented by a lecturer on videotape was investigated in this doctoral study.

1063. Rose, Carol-Lynne. *Action Profiling: Movement Awareness for Better Management.* Estover, Plymouth: MacDonald and Evans, 1978. 44 pp. Illus.

The author demonstrates that the study of movement can be profitably applied to the field of management, whether of a large industrial concern, research team, or household. By producing "action profiles" for an individual, it is possible to isolate areas of strength or weakness and build up a model management team with mutual compatible components. The assessment technique is based on R. Lagan and W. Lamb's effort-shape analysis of movement.

1064. Rosegrant, Teresa J., and McCroskey, James C. "The Effects of Race and Sex on Proxemic Behavior in an Interview Setting." *The Southern Speech Communication Journal* 40 (1975) : 408-420.

Two hundred forty students, equally stratified among blacks, whites, males, and females, were subjects. Four confederate interviewers, black male and female and white male and female, were used. The distances subjects placed their chairs from interviewers were noted. Male-male dyads kept the greatest distances. White interviewees kept greater distance from black interviewers than from white interviewers, but black interviewees made no similar distinction on the basis of race of interviewer. Female black interviewees maintained closer distances with all interviewers than did any other group.

1065. Rosenberg, Marc. "The Case of the Apple Turnover: An Experiment in Multichannel Communication Analysis." *Semiotica* 16 (1976) : 129-140.

A lexical transcript and a kinesic description of behaviors that occurred during a short husband-wife interchange are presented. The multichannel communication signals are discussed in terms of the metacommunicational signals occurring about the relationship.

1066. Rosenfeld, Howard M. "Conversational Control Functions of Nonverbal Behavior." In *Nonverbal Behavior and Communication,* edited by A.W. Siegman and S. Feldstein, pp. 291-328. Hillsdale, New Jersey: Lawrence Erlbaum Associates, 1978.

An excellent overview of research on regulation of conversation, turn-taking signals, and listening behavior. There are discussions of behavior segmentation and classification, units within speaker roles, nonverbal aspects of listener responses, and various conversational control signals.

1067. Rosenfeld, Lawrence B. *Human Interaction in the Small Group Setting.* Columbus, Ohio: Charles E. Merrill, 1973.

Relevant is a brief chapter on nonverbal communication in small groups, including exercises to enhance awareness and understanding of apparel, facial expressions, how to give meaning to posture, paralinguistics, territoriality, and body rhythms.

1068. Rosenfeld, Lawrence B., and Civikly, Jean M. *With Words Unspoken: The Nonverbal Experience.* New York: Holt, Rinehart & Winston, 1976. 254 pp. Illus.

An interesting presentation of the subject of "nonverbal experience," this book draws on scientific research, contemporary culture, and cross-cultural comparison. Among the topics included are biorhythms, body image, facial expressions, visual behavior, movement, touch, voice, personal space, physical environment, and time, including a "case study" of nonverbal experience in the American city.

1069. Rosenfeld, Lawrence B.; Kartus, Sallie; and Ray, Chett. "Body Accessibility Revisited." *Journal of Communication* 26 (1976) : 27-30.

The authors replicated a previous study by Jourard with a sample of 98 female and 103 male unmarried undergraduates, aged 18 to 22. Subjects were given a questionnaire and asked to report where they had been touched in the previous 12 months by their mothers, fathers, same-sex friend, and opposite-sex friend. Results were compared with Jourard's. Touching behavior varied little with regard to mothers, fathers, and same-sex friends. Opposite-sex friends were found to touch areas of the body with greater frequency than had been found previously.

1070. Rosensweig, Jane Stewart. "Eye Contact As a Variable of Temperament in Early Infancy." Ph.D. dissertation, California School of Professional Psychology. 1976. 106 pp. (Order No. 77065-79)

Forty-one low socioeconomic status black mothers and their infants participated in this study. Significant differences in infants' eye contact, smiling, and activity with novel-stranger and familiar-mother stimuli were observed.

1071. Rosenthal, Robert, ed. *Skill in Nonverbal Communication: Individual Differences.* Cambridge, Massachusetts: Oelgeschlager, Gunn and Hain, 1979. 288 pp.

Considering individual skill in encoding and decoding nonverbal behavior in the context of an "idiographic" as opposed to "nomothetic" approach, this book reports on a range of studies, many of which use the PONS test (Profile of Nonverbal Sensitivity). Sex differences and individual differences in PONS performance, decoding abilities of professionals such as physicians, relationships of decoding and encoding ability, and detecting deception are among the topics addressed. Contributing authors include: Howard S. Friedman, Judith A. Hall, Bella M. DePaulo, Shirley Weitz, Ross Buck, Miron Zuckerman and Deborah T. Larrange, M. Robin DiMatteo, and Robert Rosenthal. (from publisher's notice)

1072. **Rosenthal, Robert, and DePaulo, Bella M.** "Sex Differences in Eavesdropping on Nonverbal Cues." *Journal of Personality and Social Psychology* 37 (1979) : 273-285.

The authors describe a series of studies investigating females' superiority in decoding nonverbal cues. One series shows that female superiority in decoding visual cues decreases when the cues are of brief duration (250 milliseconds). A second series of studies shows that women are less effective at decoding less controllable ("leakier") nonverbal channels such as body movements or tone of voice. Women were found to interpret visual cues more than aural cues when faced with discrepant messages. Persons skilled at decoding leaky cues were perceived by others as less effective in interpersonal relationships. The third series of studies found that, in discrepant situations, women were more likely than men to decode nonverbal cues which the deceiver wanted to send rather than those revealing the sender's real feelings.

1073. **Rosenthal, R.; Hall, J.A.; Archer, D.; DiMatteo, M.R.; and Rogers, P.L.** *PONS (Profile of Nonverbal Sensitivity) Test Manual.* New York: Irvington, 1979.

1074. **Rosenthal, Robert; Hall, Judith A.; DiMatteo, M. Robin; Rogers, Peter L.; and Archer, Dane.** *Sensitivity to Nonverbal Communication: The PONS Test.* Baltimore, Maryland: The Johns Hopkins University Press, 1979. 407 pp. Illus.

This book describes the design and reliability of the Profile of Nonverbal Sensitivity (PONS) test, short PONS tests, and the influence of gender, age, culture, cognitive and psychosocial correlates, psychopathology and sensory impairment, role and relationships, practice and training, and interpersonal expectancy effects.

1075. **Rosenthal, Robert; Hall, Judith A.; and Zuckerman, Miron.** "The Relative Equivalence of Senders in Studies of Nonverbal Encoding and Decoding." *Environmental Psychology and Nonverbal Behavior.* 2 (1978) : 161-166.

As an aid to researchers who study encoding and decoding of nonverbal cues, we compared the relative equivalence of encoders sending a single scene with the relative equivalence of scenes when one encoder sent many scenes. Length-corrected internal consistency was identical in both cases, indicating that no necessary gain in generality results from employing more senders each of whom sends fewer scenes rather than one sender who sends more scenes.

1076. **Ross, Michael; Layton, Bruce; Erickson, Bonnie; and Schopler, John.** "Affect, Facial Regard, and Reactions to Crowding." *Journal of Personality and Social Psychology* 28 (1973) : 69-76.

Male or female groups of eight subjects were confined in a crowded or uncrowded room for either five or 20 minutes. During this time, they discussed a series of choice-dilemma problems. Observers recorded subjects' facial regard of others. After the experimental induction was over subjects rated the discussion room, the discussion, themselves, and other group members. Males tended to rate themselves and others more positively in the uncrowded condition; females responded just the opposite. Males tended to gaze at others' faces more in the uncrowded room, while females tended to gaze more in the crowded room.

1077. **Rothbart, Mary K.** "Laughter in Young Children." *Psychological Bulletin* 80 (1973) : 247-256.

This study reviews studies of laughter in children and describes a model for the conditions that elicit laughter. Drawing on past research results, the author proposes an arousal-safety model that laughter follows arousal once the situation has been judged safe or inconsequential. Laughter is seen as an important social response of the child and a signal that a given stimulus is within a child's tolerable limits of arousal.

1078. **Rousseau, G., and Rousseau, G.** *La communication: Son rôle dans le travail social et éducatif et la rencontre personnelle.* Toulouse: Privat, 1973. 180 pp.

In these reflections on interpersonal communication the authors discuss communication as an expression of life. Nonverbal channels are discussed as "modes and supports" of communication, and the concept of feedback and its importance are elaborated.

1079. **Rowe, Patricia A., and Stodelle, Ernestine,** eds. *Dance Research Annual X:* CORD, 1979.

This annual of the Congress on Research in Dance (CORD, located at New York University, New York City) is entitled "Dance Research Collage, a variety of subjects embracing the Abstract and the Practical." Among the articles is a paper by Marcia B. Leventhal on a dance therapy model for personality integration.

1080. **Royce, Anya Peterson.** *The Anthropology of Dance.* Bloomington, Indiana: Indiana University Press, 1977. 238 pp. Illus.

This book explores dance as an aspect of human behavior inextricably bound with culture. This anthropological approach to dance involves the observation, description, and analysis of dance data. The author, in presenting some methods and techniques for collecting dance data, treats dance in terms of its structure and function. A chapter on dance history introduces the technique of the comparative method and its application to dance. The Zapotic dance, the American Indian powwow dance, and American colonial dance all serve as case studies for the anthropological approach. A final chapter on dance's meaning offers an illustrated comparison between the communicative aspects of dance behavior and other means of expression.

1081. **Rozelle, Richard, and Baxter, James.** "Impression Formation and Danger Recognition in Experienced Police Officers." *Journal of Social Psychology* 96 (1975) : 53-63.

Uniformed police officers of varying seniority answered a series of open-ended questions concerning cues they utilize to interpret citizen behavior in dangerous and nondangerous situations. In dangerous circumstances cues such as spatial arrangements and proximity were considered most important while, in nondangerous situations, the officers report focusing on dispositional characteristics such as facial expression.

1082. **Rozelle, Richard M., and Baxter, James C.** "The Interpretation of Nonverbal Behavior in a Role-Defined Interaction Sequence: The Police-Citizen Encounter." *Environmental Psychology and Nonverbal Behavior* 2 (1978) : 167-180.

Videotapes of staged police-citizen interactions were shown to subjects. Nonverbal behaviors of the citizen were programmed to reflect empirically derived reactions to spatial intrusion versus nonintrusion conditions by the police officers. In the first study subjects made attributional ratings of the citizen based on the nonverbal behaviors only with the physical distance between the interactants held constant. Citizens exhibiting spatial intrusion reaction behaviors were judged to be significantly more deceptive, guilty, anxious, and generally more suspicious and unfavorable than citizens not exhibiting such behaviors. In the second study physical distance was explicitly manipulated to create a close versus distant condition. Many replications of results from the first study were obtained indicating that the preponderant cause of impression formation of the citizen was based upon spatial intrusion behavioral cues, regardless of the perceived physical distance between the interactants. However, significant interaction effects between proximity and behavioral cue conditions were obtained and confirmed an attribution theory prediction regarding degree of confidence in impression-formation ratings made of the citizen.

1083. Rubin, Gary Neil. "A Naturalistic Study in Proxemics: Seating Arrangement and Its Effect on Interaction, Performance, and Behavior." Ph.D. dissertation, Bowling Green State University. 1972. 161 pp. (Order No. 73011-19)

Eighty-four sixth-grade students were randomly assigned to seats rearranged by the teacher each week for six weeks. Seating arrangement was found to affect the performance attitudes and behavior of students.

1084. Ruby, Jay. "Franz Boas and Early Camera Study of Behavior." *The Kinesis Report: News and Views of Nonverbal Communication* 3 (Fall 1980) : 6-11, 16. Illus.

This account of anthropologist Boas' field trips to film the dances and everyday activities of the Kwakiutl Indians as early as 1930 makes a case for Boas being one of the fathers of visual anthropology in general, and cultural study of body movement in particular. In a fascinating bit of sleuthing from the literature and personal communication with those who worked with Boas, the author proposes that Boas envisioned a film museum display of the "motor habits" of different cultures.

1085. Rudden, Maria Rita, and Switzer, David E. "Studies of Nonverbal Behavior: An Evaluation and Recommendation." *Communication Quarterly* 26 (1978) : 2-12.

Citing examples from articles published between 1965 and 1975, the authors criticize research on nonverbal behavior for lack of progression from previous literature, insufficient justification for variable manipulation, and an inadequate concern for conceptual foundations. They propose a general theory of human behavior derived from the concept that communication involves acting according to rules and constructs.

1086. Ruesch, Jurgen. *Semiotic Approaches to Human Relations.* The Hague: Mouton, 1972.

1087. Ruffner, Michael, and Burgoon, Michael. *Interpersonal Communication: A Revision of "Approaching Speech Communication."* New York: Holt, Rinehart & Winston, 198. 324 pp. Illus.

This textbook has an extensive section on nonverbal communication by Judee K. Burgoon with discussion of proxemics, chronemics, kinesics, appearance, touch, and paralanguage. There is also a discussion of the function of nonverbal communication vis-a-vis symbolic displays, metamessages, self-presentation, structuring interaction, and manipulating others. Well-illustrated with photos and drawings, it has an interesting summary of key points, study questions and exercises.

1088. Russo, Nancy Felipe. "Eye Contact, Interpersonal Distance, and the Equilibrium Theory." *Journal of Personality and Social Psychology* 31 (1975) : 497-502.

Twenty-four boys and 24 girls from kindergarten, third-, and sixth-grade classes were placed in same-sex dyads. The experimenter wanted to determine the effect of grade, sex, friendship, and distance on percentage of time engaged in eye contact and mean length of eye contact. Percentage of time engaged in eye contact increased significantly with distance and was greater for females than males to a highly significant degree. The mean length of mutual eye contact was significantly higher for females and for friends but did not significantly increase with distance.

1089. **Ruttenberg, B.; Kalish, B.; Wenar, C.; and Wolf, E.** "A Description of the Behavior Rating Instrument for Autistic and Other Atypical Children. (BRIAAC)." *Conference Proceedings of the American Dance Therapy Association* 9 (1975) : 139-142.

The BRIAAC, an instrument for measuring the behavior of atypical children, consists of eight scales ranging from severely autistic to normal 4½-year-old behavior. The scales measure relationships, communication, vocalization, speech and sound reception, social functioning, body movement, psychosexual development, and drive for mastery. Seven of the scales are briefly described, and the body movement scale is explained in detail.

1090. **Rutter, D.R.** "Visual Interaction in Psychiatric Patients: A Review." *British Journal of Psychiatry* 123 (1973) : 193-202.

An interesting article reviewing studies on visual interaction among psychiatric patients. The author presents an insightful critique of current research methodologies and findings. The paper points to the need for carefully controlled, standardized, experimental studies which incorporate methods of direct observation.

1091. **Rutter, D.R.; Morley, Ian E.; and Graham, Jane C.** "Visual Interaction in a Group of Introverts and Extroverts." *European Journal of Social Psychology* 2 (1972) : 371-384.

Ten introverts and ten extroverts were selected from a college population on the basis of their responses to the Eysenck Personality Inventory. The groups contained five men and five women and were matched for neuroticism. Each person took part in two four-minute conversations (one with a male, one with a female), and their visual and speech behavior was recorded by two trained observers on an event recorder. The results of the experiment indicated that extroverts "looked," that is, showed visual behavior which elicited "face-reactions" in the partner more frequently than introverts. Extroverts also spoke more frequently than introverts. No sex differences in eye movement patterns were found.

1092. **Rutter, D.R., and Stephenson, G.M.** "Visual Interaction in a Group of Schizophrenic and Depressive Patients." *British Journal of Social and Clinical Psychology* 11 (1972) : 57-65.

Twenty schizophrenic and 20 depressive psychiatric patients were interviewed and a continuous record of their visual interaction recorded and compared to normals. Both types of patients spent less time looking than normals. This was true whether the subject was speaking or not. Schizophrenics exhibited shorter glances than depressives.

1093. **Rutter, D.R., and Stephenson, G.M.** "Visual Interaction in a Group of Schizophrenic and Depressive Patients: A Follow-up Study." *British Journal of Social and Clinical Psychology* 11 (1972) : 410-411.

Nine men and one woman (six of whom were alcoholic, one who was manic, one who was highly anxious, and two who had no clear diagnosis) served as subjects. Visual interaction was recorded, measured, and compared to a matched group of normals and to the schizophrenic or depressed patients in a previous study. The decrement in looking behavior found in the schizophrenic and depressed patients of the first study was not found in the second study group.

1094. **Rutter, D.R., and Stephenson, G.M.** "The Role of Visual Communication in Synchronising Conversation." *European Journal of Social Psychology* 7 (1977) : 29-37.

Twelve male pairs and 12 female pairs were recorded in conversation either face-to-face or over an audio intercom with no visual communication. Conversations were analyzed for number and word-length of utterances, number of floor changes, noun-verb ratio of utterances, incidence of questions and attention signals, filled pause ratio, and speech disturbance ratio. Analyses of variance showed that, contrary to prediction, simultaneous speech occurred significantly more frequently and for longer total time in the face-to-face condition and that there were no differences between conditions in duration of mutual silence. The mean length of utterances was greater in the audio condition, and there was a greater incidence of speech disturbance in the audio condition as predicted. Men used proportionately more filled pauses, had a greater incidence of speech disturbance, and used fewer attention signals than women.

1095. **Rutter, D.R.; Stephenson, G.M.; Ayling, K.; and White, P.A.** "The Timing of Looks in Dyadic Conversation." *British Journal of Social and Clinical Psychology* 17 (1978) : 17-21.

Thirty-six subjects were used in a first study and 48 in a second. In the first study subjects were paired (in same- and mixed-sex combinations) and asked to converse on a topic for 20 minutes. In the second study, subjects brought friends and were then paired with a friend or stranger of the same sex. These pairs eventually participated in competitive-persuasive or cooperative discussions. Although results showed that the majority of utterances leading to a floor change ended with the speaker looking at the listener, other findings indicated that this alone is not sufficient to justify A. Kendon's analysis of the looking-turntaking relationship. Kendon responds to this paper on pp. 23-24 of the same volume.

1096. **Ryan, John Albert.** "A Study to Determine the Effects of Body Movement Exercises on the Body Percept and Body Boundaries of Young Children." Ph.D. dissertation, University of Detroit. 1978. 212 pp. (Order No. 79280-86)

Fifty-six second-grade students participated in this study of the influence of a body movement exercise program, "Dramakinetics," on self-concept, body percept, and body boundary definiteness.

1097. **Ryen, Allen H., and Kahn, Arnold.** "The Effects of Intergroup Orientation on Group Attitudes and Proxemic Behavior. *Journal of Personality and Social Psychology* 31 (1975) : 302-310.

Spatial relations within and between groups and members' evaluations of their own and other groups were studied for five types of group orientation (solitary, coacting, cooperating, competing with no feedback, and competing with win-lose feedback). Subjects in solitary and coacting groups chose random seating patterns. Members of cooperating groups sat near both members of their own groups and members of the other group, while members of groups competing without feedback sat far from members of the other group. The group with winning feedback sat closer than the group with no feedback, and losers tended to sit as far from the winners as possible.

1098. **Sabatelli, Ronald M.; Dreyer, Albert S.; and Buck, Ross.** "Cognitive Style and Sending and Receiving of Facial Cues." *Perceptual and Motor Skills* 49 (1979) : 203-212.

Seventeen dating couples participated in an experiment which tested the sending and receiving accuracy of facial cues. Field-dependence/field-independence of each person was measured using the Embedded-Figures Test. The results showed that, although there were no relationships between several measures of receiving accuracy and cognitive style, field-dependent individuals were better senders of facial expressions.

1099.   **Sackheim, Harold A.; Gur, Ruben C.; and Saucy, Marcel C.** "Emotions Are Expressed More Intensely on the Left Side of the Face." *Science* 202 (1978) : 434-436.

Photographs of the human face portraying seven emotions were constructed from mirror reversals split down the middle into left-side composites and right-side composites. The results indicated that observers judged the left-side composites as expressing emotions more intensely than the right-side composites.

1100.   **Sackett, Gene P.,** ed. *Observing Behavior.* Vol. I, *Theory and Applications in Mental Retardation.* Baltimore, Maryland: University Park Press, 1978. 416 pp. Illus.

The papers included in this, the first of a two-volume set, concern theoretical and methodological issues in direct observation of behavior for research. They concentrate on how it can be used to enlarge the descriptive base of facts about the behavior of retarded people, and test specific hypotheses under laboratory conditions and in the everyday environment of retarded people. Volume I opens with articles on two basic theoretical approaches, one ethological and one ecological. The body of this volume consists of examples from a variety of research areas including parent-infant interaction, cognitive development, language development, group processes, and behavior in community settings. These models utilize a wide range of observational methods and illustrate research strategies to form testable questions, design behavioral coding and sampling systems for measuring interest, and choose environmental settings likely to yield relevant data.

1101.   **Sackett, Gene P.,** ed. *Observing Behavior.* Vol. II, *Data Collection and Analysis Methods.* Baltimore, Maryland: University Park Press, 1978. Illus.

The second volume of this set, which brings together the work of scientists interested in developing a systematic science of behavioral observation, concentrates on the technical aspects of collecting and analyzing observational data. It brings together information on the basics of observational methodology which has previously been scattered among books and journals and has often been presented in highly technical or mathematical form. This book includes papers offering criticisms of methodological issues raised in Volume I and suggestions for improving the research methodologies of the experiments presented there.

1102.   **Sacks, Oliver.** *Awakenings.* Garden City, New York: Doubleday, 1974. 249 pp.

From the pandemic of encephalitis between 1916 and 1927, there were survivors who had a special form of Parkinsonism. Some lived more than 40 years in virtual cessation of movement and thought. The author describes 20 such people and their responses to the introduction of the drug L-DOPA over a period of four years. Some literally awoke decades later, their personalities and memories frozen at the age they became ill. A dramatic and harrowing account of the complexities of neurophysiology, personality, and movement, it vividly illustrates how such motor symptoms are inextricably interwoven with the personalities and environments of each patient.

1103.   **Saegert, Susan,** ed. "Crowding in Real Environments," Special Issue of *Environment and Behavior* 7/2 (1975).

Among the articles in this special issue are "Toward a Redefinition of Density" by Amos Rapoport on the importance of perceived density; "The Role of Group Phenomena in the Experience of Crowding" by Andrew Baum, R. Edward Harpin, and Stuart Valins, a study of the impact of groups on the perception of crowding; and "Two Studies of Crowding in Urban Public Spaces" by Susan Saegert, Elizabeth Mackintosh, and Sheree West, a study of task performance in crowded conditions. Also included are "Room Size, Group Size and Density: Behavior Patterns in a

Children's Psychiatric Facility" by Maxine Wolfe; "Spatial and Perceptual Components of Crowding: Effects on Health and Satisfaction" by Larry M. Dean, William M. Pugh, and E.K. Eric Gunderson; and "Psychophysiological Responses to Crowding" by Davis A. D'Atri, an overview of research on blood pressure and spatial density.

1104.   **Saine, Thomas J.; Levine, Madlyn A.; and McHose, Gaylynn E.** "Assessing the Structure of Nonverbal Interaction." *The Southern Speech Communication Journal* 40 (1975) : 275-287.

Two research assistants recorded the frequency and duration of six nonverbal behaviors for each of 42 college subjects (arm symmetry, arm asymmetry, rocking, chair swivel, gesticulation, and self-manipulation) asked to speak with a stranger. Comparisions were made of distributions for subjects differing on the basis of speech anxiety scores, duration of speech, and sex. Results showed that duration measures, not frequency, significantly reflected differences between the speech anxious subjects and the other subjects.

1105.   **Saitz, Robert L., and Cervenka, Edward J.** *Handbook of Gestures: Colombia and the United States.* The Hague: Mouton, 1972. 164 pp. Illus.

Many gestures are the same in form and meaning for Colombians as for North Americans. While there are gestures unique to each group, still other gestures are the same in form for each group but different in meaning. Each of the specific, easily recognizable gestures in this handbook has been labeled and accompanied by an illustration. This inventory of more than 100 gestures is presented in both English and Spanish.

1106.   **Salkin, Jeri.** *Body Ego Technique: An Educational and Therapeutic Approach to Body Image and Self Identity.* Springfield, Illinois: Charles C. Thomas, 1973. 200 pp. Illus.

The ego is first and foremost a body ego. Its mental representations, the body image and sense of identity, must derive from bodily sensations, since every new experience is perceived through the body. Salkin develops this body-ego theme from her viewpoint as a modern dancer starting with an outline of the underlying concepts of "Body Ego Technique" and its relationship to early childhood development. In subsequent chapters, she discusses the fundamental elements that are employed in her approach — movement, form, space and rhythm — how they may be used by the teacher, and what is required of the teacher herself. She then describes how Body Ego Technique is used with infants, preschool children, and older children; with adults and with the mentally handicapped, mentally ill, deaf, and culturally deprived. Special chapters are devoted to teacher training and sample classes. The author presents many vivid details of procedure, materials, and technique throughout.

1107.   **Sallagoity, Pierre.** "The Sign Language of Southern France." *Sign Language Studies* 7 (1975) : 181-202.

This article describes "Marseilles Sign Language" used by some 1,000 persons in the south of France despite attempts to discourage its use since 1880.

1108.   **Sallop, Marvin B.** "Language Acquisition: Pantomime and Gesture to Signed English." *Sign Language Studies* 3 (1973) : 29-38.

The author posits a language hierarchy in deaf sign language: pantomine and gesture; "holophrastic" signs and signs with gestures; combined signs in the simple "Pivot-Open" structure; strings of signs in "Topic-Comment" constructions; signs ordered in accordance with the natural grammar of American Sign Language; and signed English as a second language.

1109. **Samovar, Larry A., and Porter, Richard E.**, ed. *Intercultural Communication: A Reader*. Second edition. Belmont, California: Wadsworth Publishing Co., 1976. 391 pp.

This interesting and diverse collection of readings on intercultural communication contains several important articles on cultural dimensions of nonverbal communication: "Paralanguage, Kinesics, and Cultural Anthropology" by Weston LaBarre; "Nonverbal Behavior: Some Intricate and Diverse Dimensions in Intercultural Communication" by Fathi S. Yousef; "Nonverbal Signs for 'Yes' and 'No'" by Roman Jakobson; "Aspects of Nonverbal Communication in Japan" by Helmut Morsbach; "Black Kinesics: Some Non-Verbal Communication Patterns in the Black Culture" by Kenneth R. Johnson; and "Culture Patterning of Tactile Experiences" by Lawrence K. Frank.

1110. **Samuels, Arlynne S.** "Movement Change through Dance Therapy—A Study." *American Dance Therapy Association Monograph No. 2* (1972) : 50-77.

A case study of a 21 year old male patient in dance therapy with description of 12 weekly sessions. Of note is the inclusion of a Movement Observation Scale devised by the author following Labananalysis principles and M. Davis' Movement Diagnostic Scale, which were used to assess the patient's movement patterns pre- and post-dance therapy treatment.

1111. **Sandel, Susan L.** "Reminiscence in Movement Therapy with the Aged." *Art Psychotherapy* 5 (1978) : 217-221.

Research studies have shown that reminiscing by the aged is an adaptive response which should be encouraged in appropriate circumstances. Reminiscing, as it occurs within movement therapy sessions with the aged, appears to stimulate short-term cognitive reorganization among disoriented patients and socialization among patients with a wide range of physical and mental disabilities. The pervasive playfulness of the sessions permits the patients to distance themselves from the content of their reflections.

1112. **Sandel, Susan L.** "Sexual Issues in Movement Therapy with Geriatric Patients." *American Journal of Dance Therapy* 3 (1979) : 4-14.

Group movement therapy sessions in which mutual touching, the expression of memories, and the sharing of feelings are encouraged provide one place where nursing home residents may explore their sexuality. Issues, such as the longing for companionship and warmth, are explored in the supportive environment of the group.

1113. **Sandel, Susan, and Johnson, David.** "Indications and Contra-Indications for Dance Therapy in a Long-Term Psychiatric Hospital." *American Dance Therapy Association Monograph 3* (1974) : 47-61.

The subjects of this study were 44 inpatients, 13 to 30 years of age, who were diagnosed schizophrenic or severe character disorders and had an average hospitalization of one year. Subjects were rated as to potential benefit from dance or sociodrama therapy, prior participation, and degree of familiarity with therapist. Psychological test data and standardized treatment plans of the patients were also compared. Diagnosed schizophrenics rated higher on potential for deriving benefit from dance therapy; those with higher IQs rated higher on benefiting from sociodrama; and highly medicated patients rated higher on benefiting from dance therapy.

1114. **Sanders, Gerald David.** "Heart Rate Change During Eye Contact As a Function of Intimacy in Married Couples." Ph.D. dissertation, Pennsylvania State University. 1978. 87 pp. (Order No. 79091-23)

A study of the hypothesis that the physiological response of married couples during eye contact would reflect the extent of psychological intimacy is reported.

1115. **Sanders, Jeffrey L.** "Duplicity by a Friend and its Effect on Simulated Space." *Perceptual and Motor Skills* 42 (1976) : 426.

Each of three groups of male and female undergraduates read "inadvertently overheard evaluations" of them made by a hypothetical same-sex friend. Evaluations, divided by group, were positive, negative, and neutral. The 99 subjects then indicated how close they would want this hypothetical friend to approach. Means for positive, negative, and neutral evaluations indicate that "friends" making negative evaluations were kept farthest away.

1116. **Saral, Tulsi B.** "Cross-Cultural Generality of Communication Via Facial Expressions." *Comparative Group Studies* 3 (1972) : 473-486.

A theoretical and historical overview of research on facial expressions and cross-cultural differences. The author cites Osgood's work on the relationship between perceived linguistic symbols and perceived facial expressions.

1117. **Sarles, Harvey B.** "Facial Expression and Body Movement." In *Current Trends in Linguistics,* Vol. 12, edited by T.A. Sebeok, pp. 297-310. The Hague: Mouton, 1974.

The study of facial expression and body movement is still in its infancy, especially with regard to possible linguistic relationships. The author argues that reasons for the neglect of such obvious aspects of behavior are various, but the most important are traditions of thought and conceptualization of problems to which linguists are heir. Careful description, while necessary, will not itself solve the mysteries of expression and communication.

1118. **Savitsky, Jeffery C.; Izard, Carroll E.; Kotsch, William; and Christy, Lo.** "Aggressor's Response to the Victim's Facial Expression of Emotion." *Journal of Research in Personality* 7 (1974) : 346-357.

Ninety-six male undergraduates whose opinions were disagreed or agreed with by a confederate were instructed to deliver unspecified levels of electric shock to that confederate in a staged learning experiment. Subjects viewed the facial responses of their "students" who showed expressions of anger, fear, joy, or neutrality in response to varying levels of shock. The opinion of the confederates showed no significant relationship with the level of delivered shock. The expression of enjoyment significantly increased levels of subsequently delivered shock, while expressions of anger significantly decreased the level of shock. The expressions of fear or neutrality were not significantly associated with changes in the level of delivered shock.

1119. **Scaife, M., and Bruner, J.S.** "The Capacity for Joint Visual Attention in the Infant." *Nature* 253 (1975) : 265-266.

Thirty-four infants, ages two to 14 months old, and their mothers participated in the experiment. Mothers played with their infants for a short time and then turned them over to an experimenter who then interacted with them. During this interaction, the infant's ability to follow changes in eye movement by the experimenter was noted. As well, the direction of the infant's gaze and degrees of head rotation were recorded. Results showed that the older the infant the more likely he was to look in the same direction as the experimenter. How soon and where the infants looked did not systematically change with age.

1120. **Schaffer, H.R.,** ed. *Studies in Mother-Infant Interaction.* London: Academic Press, 1977. 478 pp. Illus.

A collection of articles for the lay and professional reader based on presentations at the 1975 Loch Lomond Conference on "Maternal-Infant Interactions," it provides an in-depth understanding of current research on the developmental origins of par-

ticular behaviors and mental processes within the infant's earliest social relationships. Articles by several authors address the reciprocal nature of early mother-
infant communication. Convincing evidence is presented that the infant is capable of
a higher degree of social interaction and organization than previously identified.
Methodological problems involved in the study of infant social behavior are also
raised and discussed. Of particular note for nonverbal communication research are
the chapters by William Condon; R.A. Hinde and J. Herrmann; Daniel Stern,
Beatrice Beebe, Joseph Jaffe, and Steven L. Bennett; A. Fogel; and the section on
"Communicative Performance" which includes articles by C. Trevarthen, J.S.
Bruner, G.M. Collis, and C.M. Murphy and D.J. Messer. There is also a chapter on
communication with Down's syndrome infants by O.H.M. Jones.

1121. **Scheflen, Albert E.** *Communicational Structure: Analysis of a
Psychotherapy Transaction.* Bloomington, Indiana: Indiana University Press, 1973.
378 pp. Illus.

This fascinating volume presents a context analysis of a filmed therapy session involving two psychotherapists, a schizophrenic, and her mother. A wealth of
methodologies and notation systems, including a multimodality transcript of the first
5½ minutes, are discussed within the text. The introduction describes the search for
appropriate theoretical frameworks from which to examine small group communication. The author discusses at length how communicative behaviors are integrated to
enact social process. The first part is divided into three sections: discussion of the
communicative positions of the four participants, analysis of these positions and
their language component, and synthesis of the first two sections. The second part
focuses on special aspects of the behavioral communication, including a discussion
of psychotherapy.

1122. **Scheflen, Albert E.** *How Behavior Means. Exploring the Contents of Speech
and Meaning: Kinesics, Posture, Interaction, Setting and Culture.* New York: Jason
Aronson, 1974. 222 pp. Illus.

The author discusses the meaning of kinesic patterns in terms of cultural, personal, and institutional contexts. People form "behavior gestalts" to communicate
and inform. They announce relationships through kinesic behaviors, such as gaze,
posture sharing, and body orientation. Courtship and quasi-courtship behavior is
discussed. Scheflen elaborates further on "emic" or cultural variants in kinesics; individual variants due to health and mood, and so on; and "metacommunications,"
such as laughter and sobbing. He concludes the work with a comparison of current
kinesic research with Einsteinian physics, proposing a structural and systems approach to the study of human communication activity. The book includes an extensive bibliography and index.

*So the mode of explanation we are justified in using depends upon the focus and the
scope of our conscious observation. But we can turn this interdependent relation
around. If we wish to feature a particular mode of explanation, we can manipulate
what we consciously see. We can look at one person alone or a particular dyad or at a
sequence of three people's behavior. And we can look forward from what just happened to what happened next or backward from what is happening to what just did
occur.*
Albert E. Scheflen from "Susan Smiled," *Family Process* 17 (1978) : 62.

1123. **Scheflen, Albert E.** "Susan Smiled: On Explanation in Family Therapy."
Family Process 17 (1978) : 59-69.

Beautiful in its simplicity and clarity, this paper explores the validity and implications of diverse perspectives of the same behavior—the smile of a young daughter
during a family therapy session. Scheflen pursues some philosophical issues on the

nature of explanation in behavioral science with the device of recounting the diverse interpretations of the same behavior by therapists viewing a videotape.

1124. Scheflen, Albert E., with Ashcraft, Norman. *Human Territories: How We Behave in Space-Time.* Englewood Cliffs, New Jersey: Prentice-Hall, 1976. 210 pp. Illus.

How humans form nonverbal territories, create links with others, show relationship, orientation, and commitment to events is the subject of this clearly illustrated book. Scheflen points out that orientations, defined by body positions or gaze, are space-time events defining territories. The subtle angles and positions of body regions reflect social, emotional, and political conscious and unconscious messages. Cultural territorial requirements are discussed, and the stress in urban multi-cultural areas as a result of different territorial needs and subtle, nonverbal communication problems is noted. Included is a glossary of relevant terms.

1125. Scheflen, Albert E., and Scheflen, Alice *Body Language and the Social Order: Communication as Behavioral Control.* Englewood Cliffs, New Jersey: Prentice Hall, 1972. 208 pp. Illus.

This book remains faithful to daily experience and contemporary realities while developing a complex and subtle system of insights. Its format is based on the evolutionary development of communication. Part I describes reciprocal behaviors, territoriality, face-to-face communication, and kinesic behavior accompanying speech. Part II discusses more complex human reactions in terms of regulatory functions of kinesic behaviors that serve to maintain or change a given transaction. Part III describes how territorial, reciprocal, and kinesic behavior, combined with language, are used in the political control of thought and behavior in the social institution. Part IV discusses the role of communication in the creation of social deviancy. The material is clearly organized, well-illustrated, and succinctly stated.

1126. Schegloff, Emanuel A. "Sequencing in Conversational Openings." In *Directions in Socio-Linguistics: The Ethnography of Communication,* edited by J.J. Gumperz and D. Hymes, pp. 346-380. New York: Holt, Rinehart and Winston, 1972.

Who speaks first, and what does the first speaker say? Schegloff's analysis of conversational openings as summons and answer covers nonverbal as well as verbal behavior, such as gestures and knocking on a door.

1127. Scherer, Klaus R. *Nonverbal Communication.* Cologne: Kiepenheuer and Witsch Verlag, forthcoming.

In German.

1128. Scherer, Klaus; Scherer, Ursula; Hall, Judith A.; and Rosenthal, Robert. "Differential Attribution of Personality Based on Multi-Channel Presentation of Verbal and Nonverbal Cues." *Psychological Research* 39 (1977) : 221-247.

This is an experimental study of the differential effects of various channels of perception of personality characteristics. Various visual and verbal cues were masked or distorted in videotapes of 15 subjects. Judges rated individual subjects participating in a simulated jury discussion based on verbal script, content filtered speech, voice frequency obliterated speech, still photographs or video clips of the behavior sample. Ratings were made on five dimensions: conscientiousness, emotional stability, extroversion, assertiveness, and agreeableness. Among the results it was found that presence or absence of visual cues is salient for the judgments of conscientiousness and emotional stability.

1129. Scherer, Shawn E. "Influence of Proximity and Eye Contact on Impression Formation." *Perceptual and Motor Skills* 38 (1974) : 538.

Forty male subjects sat in pairs for ten minutes at distances of 3.5 and eight feet from each other and at a 0° or 60° orientation. Results from questionnaires completed by the subjects identified partners as likeable, interesting, and pleasant in the eye contact condition, and likeable and pleasant in the close proximity condition. All subjects gave the most positive ratings to partners who were 3.5 feet away at a 60° orientation.

1130.   **Scherer, Shawn E.** "Proxemic Behavior of Primary School Children as a Function of their Socioeconomic Class and Sub-Culture." *Journal of Personality and Social Psychology* 29 (1974) : 800-805.

Two experiments involved 13 black and 20 white dyads, 31 lower-class and 37 middle-class dyads of primary school children photographed in a school yard. Results showed no racial difference in interaction distance, but lower-class children stood closer together while conversing than did middle-class children.

1131.   **Scherer, Shawn Elliott.** "The Influence of Linguistic Style, Interpersonal Distance and Gaze on Attitude Acquisition." Ph.D. dissertation, University of Toronto. 1975. (Order No. 03129-06)

The effects of distance and of communicator's gaze and "linguistic style" on the communicator's persuasiveness and the listener's perceptions of and feelings about the communicator were investigated. Results suggest that persuasiveness is affected by congruence or incongruence of communicator's nonverbal cues.

1132.   **Scherer, Shawn E., and Schiff, Myra R.** "Perceived Intimacy, Physical Distance and Eye Contact." *Perceptual and Motor Skills* 36 (1973) : 835-841.

Thirty male subjects rated 54 photographic slides on the degree of intimacy of the two males shown seated at a cafeteria table. Ten other subjects rated the slides for intimacy and amount of eye contact. Head and body positions and distance varied, with side-to-side and corner-to-corner seating arrangements. Results show that perceived intimacy is related to physical closeness and visual contact. Corner-to-corner seating was judged more intimate than side-to-side.

1133.   **Schiff, William, and Thayer, Stephen.** "An Eye for an Ear? Social Perception, Nonverbal Communication, and Deafness." *Rehabilitation Psychology* 21 (1974) : 50-70.

Recent research has revealed systematic differences in deaf and hearing subjects' perception and judgment of social stimuli. This article reviews recent research in social information processing bearing on the interplay of verbal, vocal, and visual information during interactions between deaf and hearing people.

1134.   **Schiffenbauer, Allen.** "Effect of Observer's Emotional State on Judgments of the Emotional State of Others." *Journal of Personality an Social Psychology* 30 (1974) : 31-35.

Sixty undergraduate students were divided into five groups. Each subject received an "emotional arousal manipulation." They then judged a series of facial expression slides as to the type of emotion conveyed and the intensity of the emotion. Evidence is presented that the emotion experienced by the subject colors his or her subsequent judgment of facial expressions.

1135.   **Schiffenbauer, Allen.** "When Will People Use Facial Information to Attribute Emotion. The Effect of Judge's Emotional State and Intensity of Facial Expression on Attribution of Emotion." *Representative Research in Social Psychology* 5 (1974) : 47-53.

The study confirmed the hypothesis that emotionally aroused subjects are more likely to judge facial stimuli as emotionally aroused than will nonaroused subjects. The results also indicated that subjects will spontaneously utilize facial information to make emotional attributions about others, but the conditions under which the judgments are made should be taken into consideration.

1136. Schiffrin, Deborah. "Handwork as Ceremony: The Case of the Handshake." *Semiotica* 12 (1974) : 189-202.

The handshake in social occasions and relationships is discussed as ritual ceremony. Three types of handshake are designated: (1) the "collapsed" handshake of the election campaign which functions as an introduction, greeting, and farewell collapsed into one ritual performance; (2) opening handshakes, where it functions as an "access ritual," participants then having more access to each other than before; and (3) the closing handshake where the participants take leave of each other. The handshake as a signifier and as a sign are discussed.

1137. Schlesinger, I.M., and Namir, Lila, eds. *Sign Language and the Deaf: Psychological, Linguistic, and Sociological Perspectives.* New York: Academic Press, 1978. 380 pp. Illus.

This introductory work reviews research on the linguistic, psychological, social, and educational aspects of sign language. In addition to discussing the evolution of sign language, the authors include such varying topics as sign language acquisition by children, the grammar of sign language, and the relationship of sign language research to disciplines such as psycholinguistics and sociolinguistics. A final chapter is devoted to methodology.

1138. Schmais, Claire, and Felber, Diana Jacoff. "Dance Therapy Analysis: A Method for Observing and Analyzing a Dance Therapy Group." *American Journal of Dance Therapy* 1 (1977) : 18-25.

A method for observing and analyzing dance therapy sessions, based on a synthesis of Chapple's interaction chronography, Bales' Interaction Process Analysis, Scheflen's context analysis, and Labananalysis is presented. Parameter choice and research procedure are carefully outlined. A sample dance therapy group session is analyzed according to the method, revealing developmental patterns, leadership styles, and synchronous behavior.

1139. Schnelle, John F.; Kennedy, Martha; Rutledge, Alvin W.; and Golden, Stanford B. Jr. "Pupillary Response as Indication of Sexual Preference in a Juvenile Correctional Institution." *Journal of Clinical Psychology* 30 (1974) : 146-150.

Twenty female adolescents incarcerated at a state vocational training school participated in the study. Each resident was seated in a dimly lit room before a project screen. Of 55 slides projected for viewing, 13 were stimulus slides and included 7 pictures of nude or near-nude females and six pictures of nude or near-nude males. A TV camera (connected to a SONY pupillometer model 830) focused on the subject's left eye. A significant difference was found toward the direction of increased female slide interest between the score distributions of test I and test II administered three months apart.

1140. Schoop, Trudi, with Mitchell, Peggy. *Won't You Join in the Dance? A Dancer's Essay into the Treatment of Psychosis.* Palo Alto, California: Mayfield Publishing Company, 1974. 208 pp. Illus.

Written and illustrated in a lively, ingenuous style, this is a presentation of the author's dance therapy practice with psychiatric patients in a state hospital and some students in her private studio. With many clinical examples, she illustrates her approach to dance therapy and her psychological interpretations of disturbances in breathing, alignment, tension, rhythm and spatial patterns.

1141. **Schopler, John, and Stockdale, Janet E.** "An Interference Analysis of Crowding." *Environmental Psychology and Nonverbal Behavior* 1 (1977) : 81-88.

The behavioral consequences of crowding are analyzed in terms of mediation by the amount of interference experienced in a setting. It is argued that the amount of interference is the major determinant of crowding stress and one of several determinants of the subjective feeling of being crowded. Research implications of this analysis are discussed.

1142. **Schuham, Anthony I., and Freshley, Harold B.** "Significance of the Nonverbal Dimension of Family Interaction." *Proceedings of the 79th Annual Convention of the American Psychological Association* 6 (1971) : 455-456.

Mother-father-child triad interactions (two of a normal child and two of a borderline psychotic child) were analyzed using the Bales Interaction Process Analysis scoring system under verbal (transcript) and verbal-nonverbal (videotape) conditions. When nonverbal activity was additionally assessed behaviors formerly classified as instrumental were reclassified as negative tension indicators, agreement behaviors decreased slightly, and tension-release activity increased. Thus the incorporation of nonverbal behavior into analysis of family interaction shifts the interpretation toward affective communication.

1143. **Schulman, David; and Schontz, Franklin C.** "Body Posture and Thinking." *Perceptual and Motor Skills* 32 (1971) : 27-33.

One hundred sixty female and male undergraduates were individually tested in standing, sitting-erect, sitting-bent, and supine posture. Results show that the number of problems solved, pace of talking, number of self-referent statements, and proportion of posture-related words remembered were significantly affected by type of posture. There were significant gender differences reported for some tasks.

1144. **Schulz, Richard, and Barefoot, John.** "Non-Verbal Responses and Affiliative Conflict Theory." *British Journal of Social and Clinical Psychology* 13 (1974) : 237-243.

Interpersonal distance and topic intimacy were manipulated in interviews with 36 male college students. The amount of time the subject made eye contact with the interviewer, the frequency of smiles and of manipulative and demonstrative gestures, and several paraverbal variables were measured. Among the results it was found that looking decreased significantly as intimacy increased but only for looking while talking, not listening. Increased looking occurred in the far condition only while listening, not talking. Of the smile and gesture variables only smiling varied and only in the distance condition: the ratio of smiling to total response time was higher in the close condition than in the far. Subjects spoke longer in response to questions of higher intimacy and spoke less in the close condition than in the far.

1145. **Schützenberger, Anne Ancelin.** *Contribution à l'étude de la communication non-verbale.* 2 Vols., Atelier Reprod. des Thèses, Université de Lille III, Lille, 1978. Illus. Diffusion Librairie Honoré Champion, 7 Quai Malaquais, Paris.

This is an extensive two-volume work in French, largely theoretical in nature. In the first chapter, the author makes a point of defining "communication," verbal and nonverbal, in which she adheres to the notion that communication consists of complex relational dynamics between two or more individuals, both being subject and object alternately. Therefore, there is no distinction between communication and expression. She defines nonverbal communication as every action of individuals in relation to each other and, therefore, includes subjects as far reaching as socioeconomic context, art, institutions, and so on. She states, however, that her own work has been essentially limited to the social aspect of nonverbal communication. She includes an extensive historical overview, discusses the major "schools" of nonverbal communication, and the primary fields of research, such as proxemics, facial expressions, interaction rituals, and so on. Her personal contribution is to be found in the exposition of a theory of nonverbal communication, in which she states that the meaning is created by the constant shifting of figure and ground between three dimensions: the object of research, the researcher, and the context. She bases her research on the study of psychodrama groups viewed on film, illustrated here with photographs, and analyzes certain moments of the interaction using the context analysis method. There is a brief discussion of the advantages of the use of audiovisual equipment and an extensive bibliography of approximately 3,000 references.

1146. **Schwartz, G.E.; Fair, P.L.; Greenberg, P.S.; Mandel, M.R.; and Klerman, G.L.** "Facial Expression and Depression: An Electromyographic Study." *Psychosomatic Medicine* 36 (1974) : 458.

This abstract reports the use of facial electromyography (EMG) as a means of quantifying not only overt facial expression but covert expressions as well. By recording surface EMG from four groups of facial muscles, one can discriminate whether normal female subjects are generating happy or sad, angry or cheerful affects even when no expressions are apparent to the observer.

1147. **Schwartz, G.E.; Fair, P.L.; Greenberg, P.S.; Mandel, M.R.; and Klerman, G.L.** "Facial Expression and Depression II: An Electromyographic Study." *Psychosomatic Medicine* 37 (1975) : 81-82.

An exploration of the use of facial electromyography to assess change in mood during four weeks of antidepressant drug treatment. EMG patterns were recorded from four facial muscle groups while subjects (1) rested with eyes closed; (2) exhibited self-generated happy and sad facial imagery with no requirement to "reexperience" the sensations; (3) generated happy and sad imagery with the instruction to "reexperience" the sensations; (4) made overt happy and sad faces to express recent feelings; and (5) produced the largest overt happy and sad expressions possible. As predicted, patients showed attenuated EMG patterns for the happy conditions, particularly in conditions 2 and 4. Also relative to the matched normals, the facial EMG pattern for the depressed patients during quiet resting was one of sadness.

1148. **Schwartz, Gary E.; Fair, Paul P.; Salt, Patricia; Mandel, Michel R.; and Klerman, Gerald L.** "Facial Muscle Patterning to Affective Imagery in Depressed and Nondepressed Subjects." *Science* 192 (1976) : 489-491.

Six depressed and 12 nondepressed volunteers had surface electrodes placed at four facial locations and were asked to imagine a typical day and happy, sad, and angry occurrences in the past. Later they were also asked to make happy, sad, and angry faces. The facial patterning distinguished depressed from nondepressed subjects in a number of predictable ways which are reported.

1149. **Schwebel, Andrew I., and Cherlin, Dennis L.** "Physical and Social Distancing in Teacher-Pupil Relationships." *Journal of Educational Psychology* 63 (1972) : 543-550.

Subjects were students in kindergarten through fifth grade classes at two elementary schools and one class of educable retarded children. The behavior of students who had been assigned seats in the front, middle, and back rows of their classroom was assessed through observation and teacher interview. After a time the subjects were assigned new seats and reevaluated. Results showed that students in the front row were more attentive to class activity than students in other rows. Teachers perceived students who were moved forward as becoming more attentive and more likeable than those who were moved backward. Students in the front row were perceived more positively by their teachers, peers, and themselves.

1150. **Seaford, Henry W. Jr.** "Maximizing Replicability in Describing Facial Behavior." *Semiotica* 24 (1978) : 1-32. Illus.

The author suggests that facial behavior can best be described with reference to the contractions of the various muscles involved. A literature review of facial behavior follows. Muscular contractions were found useful in describing and delineating the recurring facial expressions of 62 Virginians in a study of over 10,000 yearbook photographs. Many photographs illustrated the recurring southern facial patterns.

1151. **Seals, James M., and Prichard, Charles H.** "Nonverbal Behavior as a Dimension of Counselor Subroles." *Counselor Education and Supervision* 13 (1973) : 150-154.

Videotapes of 30 experienced secondary school counselors were made in each counselor's office and then judged to locate and label 12 counselor subroles and their transition points. Following this, trained observers determined the presence or absence of 16 nonverbal behaviors within these school counselor subroles. Judges could be trained successfully to locate the transition points and to label counselor subroles directly from the videotapes. Units of verbal and nonverbal behavior could be easily separated for use in individual evaluation of interview behavior. Within this sample, counselors tended to use different nonverbal behaviors with significantly different frequencies in all subroles, with the exception of "reflecting." Counselor nonverbal behaviors in this study were characterized by high percentages of hand movements and talk behavior and by low frequencies of head support, head support shift, position shifts, and talk shift.

1152. **Sebeok, Thomas A.** ed. *Linguistics and Adjacent Arts,* I. *Current Trends in Linguistics,* Vol. 12. The Hague: Mouton, 1974. 626 pp.

Part 2 of this massive work deals with semiotics. Included are "Semiotics: A Survey of the State of the Art" by Thomas A. Sebeok, which outlines the scope and history of the field and gives a classification of signs and sign systems; "Facial Expression and Body Movement" by Harvey B. Sarles, which argues that these dimensions are an integral part of the study of language; and "Proxemics" by O. Michael Watson, which discusses parameters for the classification of proxemic behavior. William C. Stokoe, Jr. has contributed "Classification and Description of Sign Languages," and W. John Smith, "Zoosemiotics: Ethology and the Theory of Signs."

1153. **Sebeok, Thomas A.** *Contributions to the Doctrine of Signs.* Studies in Semiotics, Vol. 5. Bloomington, Indiana: Research Center for Language and Semiotic Studies, and Lisse: Peter de Ridder Press, 1976. 271 pp.

Sebeok's integration of semiotics and biology provides a theoretical framework within which to study nonverbal communication. Papers in this collection deal with the history of semiotic research, the possibility of a comparative study of human and animal semiotic strategies, and "zoosemiotics," the communicative capacities humans share with other animals.

1154. **Sebeok, Thomas A.,** ed. *How Animals Communicate.* Bloomington, Indiana: Indiana University Press, 1977. 1128 pp. Illus.

This massive volume contains 38 chapters and a vast amount of information on the communicative behaviors of animals. Theoretical perspectives are provided by Philip Lieberman on the phylogeny of language, Donald R. Griffin on expanding horizons in animal communicative behavior, Anthony Robertson on cellular communication, Peter Marler on the evolution of communication, Gordon M. Burghardt on the ontogeny of communication, and George W. Barlow on modal action patterns. Included among the mechanisms of communication discussed in Part 2 are pheromones by Harry H. Shorey, bioluminescence by James E. Lloyd, visual communication by Jack P. Hailman, tactile communication by Frank A. Geldard, and electric communication by Carl D. Hopkins. The third and longest section presents the communication patterns of selected groups from cephalopods to human and nonhuman primates, including crustaceans and arachnids, lepidoptera, fishes, amphibians and reptiles, birds, dogs, cats, and cetaceans. There are several chapters on primates, and Roger S. Fouts and Randall L. Rigby have contributed a chapter on human-chimpanzee communication. The book ends with "Zoosemiotic Components of Human Communication" by Thomas A. Sebeok.

1155. **Sebeok, Thomas A.** *The Sign & Its Masters.* Austin, Texas: University of Texas Press, 1979. 339 pp. Illus.

This wide-ranging collection of papers includes much of interest to the student of body movement. Sebeok's integration of biology and semiotics is discussed here in chapters on "Semiosis in Nature and Culture" and "Semiotics and Ethology." "Zoosemiotic Components of Human Communication" provides a typology of communication channels and a discussion of those channels that humans share with other animals. The "Clever Hans effect" and the workings of interpersonal influence in face-to-face interaction are discussed. Included here is also "Aboriginal Sign 'Languages' from a Semiotic Point of View" with D. Jean Umiker-Sebeok, which analyzes Plains sign language and the Australian aboriginal sign language.

1156. **Serber, Michael.** "Teaching the Nonverbal Components of Assertive Training." *Journal of Behavior Therapy and Experimental Psychiatry* 3 (1972) : 179-183.

Specific nonverbal behaviors can be taught via behavior modeling and practice, and this method is described. A case example of a 21 year old male is given illustrating the kinds of nonverbal behavior changes that were taught during a three-week period, using a total of five 45-minute training sessions and diligent practice between sessions.

1157. **Seta, J.; Paulus, P.; and Schkade, J.** "The Effects of Group Size and Proximity Under Cooperative and Competitive Conditions." *Journal of Personality and Social Psychology* 34 (1976) : 47-53.

In two experiments the effects of group size and proximity were studied on arousal induction and reduction as indicated by performance on novel tasks. Subjects with a cooperative task performed better when seated close together as opposed to far apart. The opposite was true of subjects with competitive tasks.

1158. **Severy, Lawrence J.; Forsyth, Donelson R.; and Wagner, Peggy Jo.** "A Multimethod Assessment of Personal Space Development in Female and Male, Black and White Children." *Journal of Nonverbal Behavior* 4 (1979) : 68-86.

In order to obtain evidence of the effects of demographic parameters and measurement techniques on personal space, several different assessments were used to determine the impact of subject age, race, and sex on interpersonal distancing. Thirteen different variables representing stimulation, paper-and-pencil, and behavioral techniques indicated that as age increased, personal space requirements decreased, particularly for whites. Blacks as compared to whites required less space at age seven, and mixed-sex dyads tended to require more space than same-sex dyads. The results thus indicate that, while some previous findings appear to be measurement method specific, others show intermethod consistency.

1159. **Sewell, Alan, and Heisler, James.** "Personality Correlates of Proximity Preferences." *Journal of Psychology* 85 (1973) : 151-155.

On entering an interview room, 35 male college students were asked to "pull up a chair," and they were asked to complete a Personality Research Form. Subjects who scored high on the "Exhibition" scale or on the "Impulsivity" scale placed their chairs closer to the interviewer than those who scored lower on these scales.

1160.   **Shapiro, Jeffrey G.** "Variability and Usefulness of Facial and Body Cues." *Comparative Group Studies* 3 (1972) : 437-442.

Thirty judges rated 18 photographs of five counselors during interview sessions for degree of genuineness, empathy, warmth, evaluation, potency, activity, and helpfulness. Subjects were divided into three groups of five females and five males each. The photographs each group rated differed according to head only, body only, and whole person. Among the results, it was found that judges reached higher agreement rating bodies alone than faces alone. However, they reported that they did not use body cues when rating the whole person.

1161.   **Shaw, Marvin E.; Bowman, Thomas; and Haemmerlie, Frances M.** "The Validity of Measures of Eye-Contact." *Educational and Psychological Measurement* 31 (1972) : 437-442.

An opposite-sex dyad was used to test whether two people can accurately judge the frequency and duration of mutual eye contact. During two ten-minute discussions, each person pushed a button connected to an Esterline Angus Event recorder when he or she believed that he or she had made eye contact and released the button when he or she believed eye contact had been broken. The results showed that two people tend to know when they are looking into each other's eyes. The study went on to test whether an observer can validly judge when two other persons are making eye contact. An interviewer, maintaining as much eye contact as possible, engaged a subject in a discussion for approximately ten minutes. Both an observer and the interviewer recorded eye contact. It was found that the observer was less accurate and there was substantial variation between the 18 interviews assessed.

1162.   **Shea, Marilyn, and Rosenfeld, Howard.** "Functional Employment of Nonverbal Social Reinforcers in Dyadic Learning." *Journal of Personality and Social Psychology* 34 (1976) : 228-239.

A study to identify natural behavioral responses, specifically face and head movements, of 40 "teacher-learner" dyads of unacquainted college students. The goal was to increase the performance of the learner through different tasks. It was predicted that, when feedback failed to facilitate learning, the teacher would use nonverbal behaviors (emblems) as feedback on performance. The effectiveness of the emblems was expected to increase if the listener was aware of their usage. It was also predicted that nonverbal cues from teachers would be less subtle when not acknowledged. The extensive results are discussed.

1163.   **Shepherd J.W.; Ellis, H.D.; McMurran, Mary; and Davies, G.M.** "Effect of Character Attribution on Photofit Construction of a Face." *European Journal of Social Psychology* 8 (1978) : 263-268.

"Photofit" is a method police use to construct out of numerous possible facial details one the witness judges as a likeness of the suspect. This is a report of a study in which subjects constructed a photofit from recall of a photograph of a man described as either a lifeboatman or a murderer. Their respective photo constructions were judged differently by independent raters with those for the "murderer" much less favorable.

1164.   **Sherman, Richard C.; Croxton, Jack; and Smith, Meredith.** "Movement and Structure As Determinants of Spatial Representations." *Journal of Nonverbal Behavior* 4 (1979) : 27-39.

Subjects were exposed to an experimental environment in which some locations were separated either by an opaque or a transparent barrier and other locations were not separated by any barrier. As subjects learned where the locations were, they were required to follow a specific route that allowed travel between some locations in each category but not others. Afterward subjects were asked to reproduce from memory the separation between pairs of locations. Recalled distance between locations was significantly affected by both movement patterns of subjects and structural aspects of the environment (type of barrier and actual separation between locations). These results are interpreted in terms of the types of information made available through particular movement patterns and the corresponding salience of that information.

1165. **Sherrod, Drury R.** "Lateral Eye Movements and Reaction to Persuasion." *Perceptual and Motor Skills* 35 (1972) : 355-358.

The eye movements of 300 college students were observed while they responded to word and number tasks. The direction of the first eye movement made immediately following each question was scored. A predominance of left eye movements was associated with more extreme reaction in either a pro or con direction, while right eye movements were associated with more moderate or hesitant reactions.

1166. **Sherrod, Drury R.** "Crowding, Perceived Control, and Behavioral After-effects." *Journal of Applied Social Psychology* 4 (1974) : 171-186.

Groups of high school girls performed simple and complex tasks in three conditions: noncrowded, crowded, and crowded with perceived control. Immediately afterwards, all three groups worked on two tasks testing frustration tolerance and proofreading ability respectively. Performance on simple or complex tasks was not affected by the crowding conditions. There were significant negative aftereffects during the frustration tolerance task for the crowded group, but this negative aftereffect was less for the crowded-with-perceived-control group. The proofreading task showed no negative aftereffects of crowding.

1167. **Sherzer, Joel.** "Verbal and Non-Verbal Deixis: The Pointed Lip Gesture Among the San Blas Cuna."*Language in Society* 2 (1972) : 117-131. Illus.

The pointed lip gesture used among the Cuna Indians of San Blas, Panama, consists of looking in a particular direction and raising the head while the mouth is opened and closed. Although the gesture occurs in various contexts and appears to have several unrelated meanings, an analysis of the context reveals that the meaning "pointing" is always present. Further meanings are derived from the discourse structures in which the pointed lip gesture is found.

1168. **Shields, Stephanie A., and Stern, Robert M.** "Emotion: The Perception of Bodily Changes." In *Perception of Emotion in Self and Others,* edited by P. Pliner, K.R. Blankstein, and I.M. Spigel. New York: Plenum Press, 1979.

The author discusses the relationship between perceived and physiological responses. Research examining the perception of bodily change and its implications for the study of emotion is reviewed.

1169. **Shimoda, Kimiko; Argyle, Michael; and Ricci-Bitti, Pio.** "The Intercultural Recognition of Emotional Expressions by Three National Racial Groups: English, Italian, and Japanese." *European Journal of Social Psychology* 8 (1978) : 169-179.

Groups of students in England, Italy, and Japan rated videotapes of subjects from each of these countries who were asked to portray 12 expressions (happy, angry, friendly, and so on). Members of one culture were able to recognize expressions of another in all cases except that the Italian and English could not recognize Japanese expressions well. Additional interesting differences in Japanese expression and recognition patterns, are reported which the authors interpret as evidence of different display rules.

1170. **Shotland, R. Lance, and Johnson, Michael P.** "Bystander Behavior and Kinesics: The Interaction Between the Helper and Victim." *Environmental Psychology and Nonverbal Behavior* 2 (1978) : 181-190.

One hundred eighty subjects participated in a factorial field experiment designed to study the effects of body orientation, eye contact, and sex upon helping behavior in a situation where a male victim fell. An eye-contact x body-orientation interaction and a sex x body-orientation interaction were found. Eye contact raised the rate of help; and women helped more often than men, but only when the victim and subject were approaching each other. The cue value of the front side of a person, eye contact acting as a plea for help, and the salience of responsibility norms were discussed.

1171. **Showronski, Suzanne.** *"Proxemics and Nursing Care."* Hospital Progress 53 (1972) : 72-77.

This article discusses aspects of nonverbal behavior from the perspective of one in the nursing profession. The author notes cultural variation in communication through gestures, posture, space, and touch. She examines German, English, French, and Eastern differences. She also notes the emphasis of hospital design on functional rather than spatial considerations.

1172. **Shultz, Jeffrey.** "It's Not Whether You Win or Lose, It's How You Play the Game." In *Language, Children, and Society,* edited by O. Garnica and M. King. Oxford: Pergamon Press, 1979.

This chapter presents a microethnographic analysis of a game played by a teacher and three of her students during the first week of school. While playing a game of tic-tac-toe, the observer focused on the behavior of one student who had never attended school before and compared this student's verbal and nonverbal behavior with that of the two other students. The purpose of the study was to demonstrate the value and feasibility of microethnographic analyses of classroom behavior. (from a pre-publication manuscript)

1173. **Shultz, Jeffrey, and Florio, Susan.** "Stop and Freeze: The Negotiation of Social and Physical Space in a Kindergarten/First Grade Classroom." *Anthropology and Education Quarterly* 10 (1979) : 166-181.

This study used microethnographic techniques to discover and describe important aspects of the social competence acquired by children in a kindergarten/first-grade classroom. Analyses of 70 hours of videotaped classroom interaction showed the importance of the teacher's role in contextual changes. By performing a set of behaviors in a systematic fashion, the teacher communicates to students when they should pay attention to her and when they do not need to pay attention to her. The use of space is one behavior the teacher employs to communicate effectively.

1174. **Shultz, Jeffrey; Florio, Susan; and Erickson, Frederick.** "Where's the Floor?: Aspects of the Cultural Organization of Social Relationships in Communication at Home and at School." In *Ethnography and Education: Children In and Out of School,* edited by P. Gilmore and A. Glatthorn. Philadelphia: University of Pennsylvania Press, in press. Illus.

The interactions of Italian-American children were analyzed both at home during the dinner hour, and at school during a math lesson. Results showed that the children reacted to the contexts of the family dinner hour and the math lesson as similar (that is, these contexts evoke similar behavioral sequences and responses from the children), although their parents and their teacher respond differently (indicating that different behavior was expected in what the children apparently perceived as similar situations). The "floor" refers to who has the "floor" as speaker. A typology of the various participation structures was described and outlined.

1175. **Shuman, Malcolm K.** "The Sound of Silence in Nohya: A Preliminary Account of Sign Language Use by the Deaf in a Maya Community in Yucatan, Mexico." *Language Sciences* (1980) : 144-173. Illus.

This is a well-illustrated article on the sign language lexicon, syntax, and grammar used by the deaf in a Maya Indian village useful for comparison with sign language and gesture patterns of other cultures.

1176. **Shuter, Robert.** "Proxemics and Tactility in Latin America." *Journal of Communication* 26 (1976) : 46-52.

About 394 couples, fairly equally divided in number among the countries of Costa Rica, Panama, and Colombia, were used. Observers noted the sex, distance, angle of orientation and touching behavior of all pairs. The angle of orientation and distance of Costa Ricans was smaller than the other groups. Females were found to interact with more direct orientation, at a significantly closer distance, and with more touching and holding than male and male/female pairs. There were also differences in the amounts of contact in the three cultures, with Costa Ricans tending to touch and hold more than the Colombians or Panamanians.

1177. **Shuter, Robert.** "A Study of Nonverbal Communication Among Jews and Protestants." *The Journal of Social Psychology* 109 (1979) : 31-41.

Protestants are stereotypically rigid and staid, whereas Jews are said to be emotionally expressive, aggressive, and frequently gesticulating. To test the validity of these notions dyads were observed in churches and synagogues during social interaction. Analysis of gesture and touch behavior revealed only that Episcopalians tended to gesticulate far from the body, while Jews tended to use gestures in front of the torso. Sex differences were apparent in the analysis.

1178. **Shuter, Robert.** "Gaze Behavior in Intraracial and Interracial Interaction." In *International and Intercultural Communication Annual,* vol. 5, edited by N.C. Jain, pp. 48-55. Falls Church, Virginia: Speech Communication Association, 1979.

Mixed and same-race pairs of students from a sample of 100 black and 100 white undergraduates were videotaped in five minute conversations. Duration of other-directed gaze was measured. During speaking and listening whites in all dyads gazed more than blacks, and females gazed more than same-race males. Blacks gazed most when listening.

1179. **Shuter, Robert** "The Dap in the Military: Hand-to-Hand Communication." *Journal of Communication* (1979) : 136-142. Illus.

The "dap" was a series of hand movements performed by blacks serving overseas in the U.S. military during the '60s and early '70s. It served to identify those blacks who could be trusted and was a way of signifying racial solidarity. Social consequences resulted for those blacks who did not dap and for those few whites who did dap. Ninety-five enlisted men and officers, 25 whites, and 70 blacks were interviewed for this study.

1180. **Siegel, Elaine V.** "Movement Therapy as a Psychotherapeutic Tool." *Journal of the American Psychoanalytic Association* 21 (1973) : 333-343.

A healing of the split between psyche and soma becomes the aim of this mode of therapy. The dance movement therapist searches for the somatic expressions of felt experiences, particularly in the muscular tensions and locomotive behavior of the patient, in order to help her or him recreate homeostasis between psyche and soma — that delicate balance in which action and thoughts function interdependently and smoothly under the direction of a well-defined ego.

1181. **Siegel, Elaine V.** "Developmental Levels in Dance-Movement Therapy." *Conference Proceedings of the American Dance Therapy Association* 8 (1974) : 31-40.

A good explanation of nonverbal manifestations of developmental levels as seen through the eyes of a psychoanalytic dance-movement therapist. The article contains a review of the levels and accompanying movement rhythms, as well as brief case histories.

1182. **Siegel, Elaine V.** "The Treatment of Depressive States During Movement Therapy." *American Dance Therapy Association Monograph No. 3* (1974) : 76-86.

In this brief article on the treatment of depression by dance/movement techniques, physical cues to the somatization of depression and postural changes and rhythmic patterns observed in patients suffering from depression are described. The symbolic and expressive meaning of these nonverbal messages is also discussed.

1183. **Siegel, Marcia B.** *The Shapes of Changes: Images of American Dance.* Boston: Houghton-Mifflin Co., 1979. 386 pp. Illus.

This book is concerned with the preservation and documentation of twentieth-century American dance heritage. The underlying thread of inquiry is what had made this dance tradition characteristically American. The author discusses specific dances with detailed notes of gestures, positions, and movements. She discusses famous as well as less well known works, selecting only those she has actually seen performed and studied in detail. In addition, she draws on many sources to sketch the dominant issues and backgrounds of different choreography, trends, and epochs.

1184. **Siegel, Marcia B.** "Profile: Irmgard Bartenieff." *The Kinesis Report: News and Views of Nonverbal Communication* 2 (Summer 1980) : 1-5, 14-16. Illus.

This interview on the occasion of Irmgard Bartenieff's 80th birthday concentrates on her early career as a dancer and movement notation expert in Europe. Her subsequent work in physical therapy in the 60s, and particularly her application of Laban movement analysis to psychiatric research and cross-cultural analysis of movement styles ("Choreometrics") are then discussed.

1185. **Siegman, Aron W., and Feldstein, Stanley,** eds. *Nonverbal Behavior and Communication.* Hillsdale, New Jersey: Lawrence Erlbaum Associates, 1978. 400 pp.

This collection of essays designed for advanced undergraduate and graduate students and researchers is organized in four parts: biological considerations, "coverbal" behavior, vocal behavior (particularly paralanguage), space and time, and "chronography of conversation" (such as turn-taking). There are chapters on facial expression by Paul Ekman, visual interaction by Ralph V. Exline and B.J. Fehr, pupillary changes by E.A. Hess and S.B. Petrovich, space in interaction by Miles L. Patterson, and animal communication by Petrovich and Hess. Also of note are "The Role of Body Movement in Communication" by Allen T. Dittmann, "Conversational Control Functions of Nonverbal Behavior" by Howard M. Rosenfeld, and "A Chronography of Conversation: In Defense of an Objective Approach" by Stanley Feldstein and Joan Welkowitz.

1186. **Siegman, Aron W., and Feldstein, Stanley,** eds. *Of Speech and Time: Temporal Speech Patterns in Interpersonal Contexts.* Hillsdale, New Jersey: Lawrence Erlbaum Associates, 1979. 230 pp.

Including papers presented at a 1976 symposium on "Temporal Aspects of Speech and Conversation" and contributions by other researchers, this volume deals with the temporal patterning of communication on several levels. A prescript to Chapter 1, "Communication Rhythms and the Evolution of Language" by Joseph Jaffe and Samuel W. Anderson, deals with the theory of the gestural origin of language and reviews evidence that leads the authors to posit the capacity for rhythmic entrainment as a key to the evolution of human communication. Chapter 1 is "The Kinesic Rhythm of Mother-Infant Interactions" by Beatrice Beebe, Daniel Stern, and Joseph Jaffe, which reports a study identifying precursors of conversational structures in the kinesic patterns of mother-infant interaction. "Recent Studies on Cognitive Rhythm" by Brian Butterworth and Frieda Goldman-Eisler reports research using speech-focused body movements and findings on gaze in interaction to investigate the planning-execution rhythmic cycle underlying speech.

1187. **Sielski, Lester M.** "Understanding Body Language." *Personnel and Guidance Journal* 57 (1979) : 238-242.

Nonverbal communication is explained for counselors, including messages sent by gestures (18 types are listed), posture, facial expressions, eye movements, proxemics, "appearance," time, and culture of communicator.

1188. **Silverman, Alan F.; Pressman, Mark E.; and Bartel, Helmut W.** "Self-Esteem and Tactile Communication." *Journal of Humanistic Psychology* 13 (1973) : 73-77.

The study examined the relationship between self-esteem and tactile communication in 80 female and male undergraduates paired with a confederate to form mixed- and same-sex dyads. Both confederate and subject read a card which indicated an emotion to be communicated nonverbally to the partner as if he or she were a friend. Among the results it was found that, as self-esteem increased, so did intimacy, and that subjects with high self-esteem found tactile communication easier than those with relatively low self-esteem.

1189. **Silverstein, C.H., and Stang, D.G.** "Seating Position and Interaction in Triads: A Field Study." *Sociometry* 39 (1976) : 166-170.

How do leadership-seeking individuals seat themselves in a triad, and how does acquaintanceship influence interaction among subjects? This study shows that these individuals seat themselves in a visually and physically central location and that subjects who know each other do not necessarily communicate more.

1190. **Silverthorne, Colin; Noreen, Cynthia; Hunt, Tani; and Rota, Leslie.** "The Effects of Tactile Stimulation on Visual Experience." *The Journal of Social Psychology* 88 (1972) : 153-154.

It was hypothesized that tactile communication would enhance the aesthetic ratings of neutral stimuli, particularly when the examiner and subject were of the opposite sex. Ninety-seven college students were given a booklet containing four scales, one for each slide they viewed, and were instructed to rate each slide on its aesthetic qualities. On two of the four slides the examiner gently placed a hand on the subject's shoulder for three seconds. The difference in the effect for same- vs. opposite-sex pairs was slight, with all subjects preferring the slides they viewed when they were touched.

1191. **Simon, William E.; Primavera, Louis N.; Klein, Bernard; and Cristal, Robert M.** "Personality and Nonverbal Rigidity: Some Preliminary Findings." *The Journal of Psychology* 82 (1972) : 127-132.

This study of 176 college women examined relationships between nonverbal rigidity as assessed by the Breskin Rigidity Test (BRT) and ordinal position of birth, psychological need structure, and self-evaluation. With regard to psychological need structure, nonverbal rigidity was found to be positively related to the needs for "deference," "order," "abasement," and "endurance."

1192. **Simpson, W.E., and Crandall, Sally J.** "The Perception of Smiles." *Psychonomic Science* 29 (1972) : 197-200.

Subjects measured the extent to which they perceived the face to be smiling in photographs shown for various durations. It was found that little time was necessary for perceiving the magnitude of a smile and that increased exposure did not alter judgments.

1193. **Siple, Patricia,** ed. *Understanding Language Through Sign Language Research.* New York: Academic Press, 1978. 378 pp. Illus.

Each of the chapters in this volume explores some aspect of American Sign Language (ASL) to better understand language and language processing. Topics include the linguistic structure of ASL, implications of ASL for neurolinguistics and psycholinguistics, and sociolinguistic and cultural aspects of ASL. The initial chapter provides an introduction to the language itself and an overview of sign language research.

1194. **Sivadon, P.** "Attitudes corporelles et relations spatiales dans la relation médecin-malade." *Psychotherapy and Psychosomatics* 21 (1972-73) : 107-110.

This article discusses different aspects of proxemics as it applies to interaction between psychotherapist and patient, especially the violent patient. It is a good synopsis and introduction to discoveries in the field. In French.

1195. **Skelly, Madge; Schinsky, Lorraine; Smith, Randall W.; Donaldson, Robert C.; and Griffin, John M.** "American Indian Sign: A Gestural Communication System for the Speechless." *Archives of Physical Medicine and Rehabilitation* 56 (1975) : 156-160.

American Indian Sign (Amerind) was successfully adapted and used as a communication system serving the daily needs of deficient patients, many with unfavorable prognosis for oral speech rehabilitation. Various videotape samples of patients using signing in everyday situations were shown to viewers with no or minimal prior exposure to this communication system. Viewers' selections of one-word meanings resulted in an accuracy varying from 65 to 100 percent. Errors were limited to substitutions of associated words.

1196. **Skelly, Madge; Schinsky, Lorraine; Smith, Randall W.; and Fust, Rita Solovitz.** "American Indian Sign (Amerind) as a Facilitator of Verbalization for the Oral Verbal Apraxic." *Journal of Speech and Hearing Disorders* 39 (1974) : 445-456.

Six oral apraxic patients were first instructed in the use of American Indian Sign (Amerind) to facilitate their daily communication with others in their treatment situation and to help prevent isolation. Amerind was then used to help facilitate verbalization in these patients. Five of the six patients made progress in using speech accompanying their Amerind signing, as measured at the end of a six-month period, with their gestural and verbal achievement again assessed by the PICA (Porch Index of Communicative Ability).

1197. **Skotko, Vincent P., and Langmeyer, Daniel.** "The Effects of Interaction Distance and Gender on Self-Disclosure in the Dyad." *Sociometry* 40 (1977) : 178-182.

One hundred thirty-eight male and female undergraduates were assigned to same-sex dyads interacting at two, four, or ten feet. Subjects were asked to converse on topics varying in intimacy. Conversations were taped and later rated for self-disclosure. Self-reports of degree of disclosure were also taken. Males tended to increase intimacy as interaction distance increased. An opposite trend was seen with females.

1198. **Skupien, Janet.** "Profile: Thomas A. Sebeok." *The Kinesis Report: News and Views of Nonverbal Communication* 3 (Fall 1980) : 1-5. Illus.

From his writings and an interview the author reports on the work of this principal American semiotician. Sebeok's perspectives on semiotics, of which he considers "body language" a part, and particularly his work on zoosemiotics (nonverbal signs occurring within or across animal species), and current writing on "the Clever Hans Phenomenon" and trainer or experimenter effects are explored.

1199. **Smith, Brenda J.; Sandford, Fonda; and Goldman, Morton.** "Norm Violations, Sex, and the 'Blank Stare.'" *Journal of Social Psychology* 103 (1977) : 49-55.

Thirty-two male and female subjects studying in the library were stared at for 15 minutes by female and male confederates. Women left sooner and more often than men, especially when the starer was a man. Male subjects returned the stare more frequently, especially when the starer was a woman.

1200. **Smith, David E.; Willis, Frank N.; and Gier, Joseph A.** "Success and Interpersonal Touch in a Competitive Setting." *Journal of Nonverbal Behavior* 5 (1980) : 26-34.

Early observations of interpersonal touch among American adults have revealed rates of touch well below that of many European and Latin American countries. Conclusions drawn from these results, however, mandate caution since touch has been shown to be affected by age, gender, race, and setting. Observation of mens' televised sports has revealed that high rates of touch often follow a successful performance. The present study attempted to quantify touch within a mixed-gender, competitive setting in both black and white subcultures. Interpersonal touch following a success and otherwise occurring was observed among bowlers during league play. Overall rates of touch were much higher than those reported for other public settings. High rates of touch following a success were reported only for blacks. Unlike previous studies females initiated cross-gender touch as often as did males.

1201. **Smith, Dennis R., and Williamson, L. Keith.** *Interpersonal Communication: Roles, Rules, Strategies, and Games.* 2nd ed. Dubuque, Iowa: Wm. C. Brown Co., 1981, 370 pp.

A college textbook in which communication theories are discussed in terms of "four primary message systems": language, gesture, speech, and sexuality/intimacy. Within a transactional model of interpersonal communication, the authors explore the structure, ecological nature, and congruency/incongruency of communication behavior. Chapter 8 in particular deals with gesture very broadly defined and Chapter 9 with space, territoriality, and proxemics. Chapter 8 has sections on silence, manners, visual behavior, gender signals, instrumental and denotative gestures, and movements that monitor, define roles and contexts, or modify other messages.

1202. **Smith, Edward W.L.** "Postural and Gestural Communication of A and B 'Therapist Types' During Dyadic Interviews." *Journal of Consulting and Clinical Psychology* 39 (1972) : 29-36.

In this study of 12-minute simulated interviews involving male students pre-tested as A or B therapist types, it was found that As as a group varied their posture and gestures more than Bs, while Bs reflected greater interpersonal approach and affiliation nonverbally then As. The A and B types are described, and the specific nonverbal behaviors recorded by trained observers are listed so it is possible to posit the nonverbal communicative styles of each for further research. A table of correlations between specific actions and ratings as a source for assessing their psychological meanings is included.

1203. **Smith, Euclid O.**, ed. *Social Play in Primates.* New York: Academic Press, 1978.

1204. **Smith, Howard A.** "Nonverbal Communication in Teaching." *Review of Educational Research* 49 (1979) : 631-672.

School-related research is reviewed under seven categories of nonverbal communication: environmental factors, proxemics, kinesics, touching behavior, physical characteristics, para-language, and artifacts. Problems of educational research and of conducting nonverbal communication research within an educational setting as well as a process-product paradigm for research are discussed.

1205. **Smith, W. John.** *The Behavior of Communicating: An Ethological Approach.* Cambridge, Massachusetts: Harvard University Press, 1977. 545 pp. Illus.

This book focuses on the interactional messages or information shared by animals through their displays. Deeply rooted in the ethological tradition of naturalistic observation, the author argues that virtually all subhuman animal displays can be interpreted as transmitting messages not about the environment but about the communicator. These messages may make information public about the displaying animal and thus make possible responses that are quite specific. Such displays are evolutionarily adaptive in providing specific, specialized information that otherwise might remain private. The three major levels of semiotics were followed in presenting the material: the syntactic or signal level; the semantic (informational, message, referent) level; and the pragmatic (usage, actual communication) level. Formalized interactions, as well as several examples from human nonverbal communication are examined.

1206. **Smith, W. John; Chase, Julia; and Lieblich, Anna Katz.** "Tongue Showing: A Facial Display of Humans and Other Primate Species." *Semiotica* 11 (1974) : 201-246. Illus.

Tongue showing was examined in : nursery school children; all age groups in a broad range of situations primarily in Philadelphia; people in Panama and the Canal Zone; captive gorillas and orangutans; one infant using "tongue balling" and protrusion over a period of about 60 weeks; and a survey of the primate literature. Results showed that tongue showing occurs during an absorbing or somewhat difficult activity; where aversion to social activity might occur, such as before or during a scolding; when the person has foregone the physical control by which he or she could avoid or modify social interactions; and in mocking or teasing.

1207. **Smythe, Mary-Jeanette.** "Eye Contact as a Function of Affiliation, Distance, Sex, and Topic of Conversation." Ph.D. dissertation, Florida State University. 1973. 131 pp. (Order No. 74094-98)

Two hundred thirty female and male college students participated in this study of the effects of distance, intimacy of conversation topic, sex of interactants, and need for affiliation on eye contact.

1208. **Snortum, John R., and Ellenhorn, Lewis J.** "Predicting and Measuring the Psychological Impact of Nonverbal Encounter Techniques." *The International Journal of Group Psychotherapy* 24 (1974) : 217-229.

Forty-three college students and 44 adult members of sensitivity training groups completed the Myers-Briggs Type Indicator. Following each of 12 nonverbal exercises, subjects rated their feelings on 12 bipolar adjectives. A repeated measures analysis of variance yielded significant differences between exercises on each of the three factors: evaluation, potency, and activity. It was found that extroverted subjects tended to find the training session a more pleasant experience than subjects who were assessed as introverted.

1209. **Snyder, Allegra Fuller.** "Some Aspects of the Nature of the Rhythmic Experience and its Possible Therapeutic Value." *American Dance Therapy Monograph No. 2* (1972) : 128-149.

The author discusses the biological and historical aspects of rhythm. Examples from empirical studies and traditional cultures are used to illustrate how song and dance relate to the bodily rhythms of pulse rate, respiration, and muscle tension. Further discussion focuses on so-called convulsive or ecstatic dance and its ability to cause frustration in the human rhythmic structure by its ever-accelerating pulse. The resultant personality changes are detailed.

1210. **Snyder, Mark.** "Self-Monitoring of Expressive Behavior." *Journal of Personality and Social Psychology* 30 (1974) : 526-537.

A reliable measure of individual differences in self-monitoring (self-observation and self-control) behavior was developed. The construct validity of the instrument was investigated in four studies involving peer perception ratings, "criterion group membership," self-control of facial and vocal expressive behavior, and social comparison information.

1211. **Snyder, Mark; Grether, John; and Keller, Kristine.** "Staring and Compliance: A Field Experiment on Hitchhiking." *Journal of Applied Social Psychology* 4 (1974) : 165-170.

To ascertain whether staring induces altruistic or compliance behavior, a field experiment was conducted in which a male alone, a female alone, or a male-female couple attempted to hitch automobile rides at four locations differing in traffic characteristics while staring directly or not staring at a driver. Two hundred drivers were included in the study. Staring increased the probability of a ride being offered. The lone female was more likely to be offered a ride than either the male or couple in the stare condition only.

1212. **Sommer, Robert.** "Spatial Parameters in Naturalistic Social Research." In *Behavior and Environment,* edited by A.H. Esser, pp. 281-290. New York: Plenum Press, 1971.

This author discusses the social use of space and territoriality and man's response to increased density and spatial deprivation from an environmental perspective. This article is a summary of Sommer's work on small group ecology and personal space invasion.

1213. **Sommer, Robert.** *Tight Spaces: Hard Architecture and How to Humanize It.* Englewood Cliffs, New Jersey: Prentice-Hall, 1974. 150 pp. Illus.

This book concerns the extensive use of hard architecture and its subsequent dehumanizing effects on society. Hard architecture is that which is resistant to human imprint and is often characterized by a lack of permeability between the inside of buildings and the outside world (no windows). It is expensive to construct, alter, or raze. It is usually a response to needed increases in security. Preferable to hard architecture is a soft architecture that allows one to make an imprint on his surroundings. Soft architecture is responsive to the user, designed to welcome and reflect the presence of human beings. Sommer notes extensive use of hard architecture in prisons, hospitals, zoos, airports, classrooms, public buildings, work environments, and dormitories. He also discusses ways of softening these rather impersonal hard environments.

1214. **Sorce, James F., and Campos, Joseph J.** "The Role of Expression in the Recognition of a Face." *American Journal of Psychology* 87 (1974) : 71-82.

The experiment was designed to test for accuracy and confidence of facial recognition. Eighty undergraduate students were shown photographs of a female face with different facial expressions. Among the results it was found that facial expression is a factor influencing the recognition of a face.

1215. **Sorenson, E. Richard.** "Anthropological Film: A Scientific and Humanistic Resource." *Science* 186 (1974) : 1-8. Illus.

Interest in a broad understanding of the human condition has led anthropologists to adapt and use modern cameras and film to study the variety of ways of life and to prepare anthropological film as a permanent scientific record. Anthropological films can preserve lifestyles that are now disappearing. Anthropological film records permit continued reexamination of past human conditions and permit an ongoing scientific and public view.

1216. **Soucie, Robert Maurice.** "Anxiety, Status and Sex Influences on Visual Intimacy in Interpersonal Encounters." Ph.D. dissertation, Indiana University. 1971. 81 pp. (Order No. 72-10,008)

Students in high and low anxiety conditions interacted with a confederate of high or low "status." Frequency and duration of mutual gaze was recorded, and effects of status, anxiety, sex, and confederate were analyzed.

1217. **Sousa-Poza, Joaquin Fausto.** "Effects of Different Communicative Tasks and Cognitive Style on Verbal and Kinesic Behavior." Ph.D. dissertation, State University of New York, Downstate Medical Center. 1975. 172 pp. (Order No. 76146-26)

Patterns of object- and body-focused hand and arm movements were recorded while 32 male subjects from a homogeneous sociocultural background spoke on somewhat intimate topics and on emotionally neutral topics in a semistructured interview. Determinants of kinesic behaviors other than cultural and situational factors and types of verbal-kinesic relationships are discussed.

1218. **Sousa-Poza, Joaquin F., and Rohrberg, Robert.** "Body Movement in Relation to Type of Information (Person- and Nonperson-Oriented) and Cognitive Style (Field Dependence)." *Human Communication Research* 4 (1977) : 19-29.

The subjects were college students identified as field-dependent (16) or field-independent (16) on the group Embedded Figures Test and the Portable Rod-and-Frame Test. They were asked to speak during a one-hour interview on four topics, two person-oriented and two nonperson-oriented. Interviews were recorded, and a five-minute segment from each topic was scored for object-focused movements (distinguished as either speech primacy or motor primacy representational) and body-focused movements (distinguished as continuous hand-to-hand touching, continuous body touching or discrete body touching). Continuous body focused movement was significantly more prevalent during speech on person-oriented topics, and the rate of total object-focused movement was significantly higher during the nonperson-oriented topics. Motor primacy object-focused movements were significantly more frequent during nonperson-oriented topics, and speech primacy movements were significantly more frequent during person-oriented topics. Field-dependent subjects produced more continuous body touching movements than those testing as field-independent.

1219. **Sparhawk, Carol M.** "Contrastive-Identificational Features of Persian Gestures." *Semiotica* 24 (1978) : 49-86. Illus.

Persian emblems (hand gestures having a specific verbal definition) were studied, listed, and classified using a method similar to phonemic analysis. They were compared and contrasted with those of American Sign Language. Fifteen citizens of Tehran were presented with a message and asked if they knew any emblems conveying that message, as well as any other emblems. Eight to ten informants (including some of the encoding informants, after a few months' time) observed the author perform each emblem. Ninety-eight emblems were verified, four were probable, and 24 were ambiguous. An appendix lists the emblems and includes illustrations of contrastive features in the emblems.

1220. **Speer, David C.**, ed. *Nonverbal Communication*. Beverly Hills, California: Sage Publications, 1972. 137 pp.

Originally published as a special issue of *Comparative Group Studies,* this collection of papers includes discussion of counselor education in nonverbal behavior by R.A. Heimann and H.M. Heimann, social behavior categories by A. Mehrabian and S. Ksionzky, facial expression of affect by D. Cucegloglu, and exercises for sensitivity training by M.S. Weinstein and H.B. Pollack. Also of note are the chapters assessing the "Validity of Verbal and Nonverbal Cues in Accurately Judging Others" by V.B. Cline, J. Atzet, and E. Holmes, "Variability and Usefulness of Facial and Body Cues" by J.G. Shapiro, and "Cross-Cultural Generality of Communication via Facial Expressions" by T.B. Saral.

1221. **Spiegel, John, and Machotka, Pavel.** *Messages of the Body.* New York: Macmillan, 1974. 440 pp. Illus.

This book is an interesting combination of behavioral research and art analysis, making use of the relative consistency of posture and implied movement in art works through history. The first half of the book concentrates on developing a theory and vocabulary descriptive of standard body movements. Chapters include: "Various Concepts of Expressive Movement," "Stylized Movement: Dance, Mime," "Research Strategies," "Structure of Events," "Cognitive Aspects of Presenting Behavior," "Somatotactics: the Group of Body Movement Categories," and "Visual-Motor Coding and Linguistic Coding." The second half of the book discusses the results of a study designed to verify the theoretical framework posited based on subjects' interpretations of particular works of art. Topics discussed include: "The Arms of Venus," "Presentations of Apollo," "Direction of Gaze," "Arm Positions and Dominance," "Acrotropic Superiority and Dominance," and "Male-Female Encounter," In addition, a related study is included in which subjects were asked to reverse the process, assuming a position or movement from verbal cues.

1222. **Spinetta, John J.; Rigler, David; and Karon, Myron.** "Personal Space as a Measure of a Dying Child's Sense of Isolation." *Journal of Consulting and Clinical Psychology* 42 (1974) : 751-756.

Twenty-five leukemic children and 25 chronically ill school-age children were asked to place figures of nurse, doctor, mother, and father at their usual place in a hospital room replica. The leukemic children placed them at a significantly greater distance from the child/patient than did the control group. The authors propose that the fatally ill child not only perceives a growing distance from those around him or her but may have a need for this.

1223. **Spotnitz, Hyman.** "Touch Countertransference in Group Psychotherapy." *The International Journal of Group Psychotherapy* 22 (1972) : 455-463.

The innovative use of touch for therapeutic purposes, like other types of experimental procedures now being employed, runs the risk of providing emotional gratification instead of promoting client growth. Continual study of the dynamics subsumed in what the author calls "touch countertransference" helps the group therapist use touch therapeutically. The danger of employing touch for the therapist's own gratification is minimized through the "analyzing out" of the subjective touch countertransference.

1224. Sproule, J. Michael. *Communication Today.* Glenview, Illinois: Scott, Foresman & Co., 1981. 376 pp.

One of several introductory college textbooks on communication that has a section on nonverbal communication. This one has a lively potpourri of photos, cartoons, and anecdotes sprinkled throughout a discussion of the nonverbal code, its function and forms.

1225. Sroufe, L. Alan, and Wunsch, Jane Piccard. "The Development of Laughter in the First Year of Life." *Child Development* 43 (1972) : 1326-1344.

This article reports on a series of observational studies of the development of laughter in the infant. The reactions of infants four to 12 months old to 24 test items that varied according to modality employed, intensity, and cognitive complexity were rated on a six-point scale from crying to laughter. A notable increase of laughter with age was observed. An analysis of the types of items eliciting laughter showed a change in the modality of stimulus eliciting laughter with age. Older infants laughed more in response to visual and social items, younger infants more in response to auditory and tactile items.

1226. Starkweather, C. Woodruff. "Disorders of Nonverbal Communication." *Journal of Speech and Hearing Disorders* 42 (1977) : 535-546.

This article explores the notion of nonverbal communication disorders. It isolates types of conditioning as roots of different types of nonverbal communication disorder and recommends behavioral therapy for their rectification.

1227. Stein, R.B.; Pearson, K.G.; Smith, R.S.; and Redford, J.B. *Control of Posture and Locomotion.* Advances in Behavioral Biology, vol. 7. New York: Plenum, 1973. 635 pp.

This volume was produced in connection with an International Symposium of the University of Alberta in 1973 on new developments in the study of motor control. There are three parts, each beginning with a chapter which reviews the field: "Motor Units and Muscle Spindles," "Control of Posture," and "Control of Locomotion." Discussion papers and discussion summaries are included.

1228. Stein, R. Timothy. "Identifying Emergent Leaders from Verbal and Nonverbal Communication." *Journal of Personality and Social Psychology* 32 (1975) : 125-135.

College student subjects were able to accurately identify the emergent task and socio-emotional leadership hierarchies of videotaped task groups when given either complete audio and visual information, scripts of the verbal transactions, visual information without the audio, or visual information with content-filtered audio. Subject/observers retained significance in three of the four information conditions when their knowledge of the group members' participation rates was controlled by covariance, indicating the presence of leadership cues independent of participation rates. The author proposes that the emergence of leaders be studied from the perspective of group members selecting leaders by verbal and nonverbal cues rather than that of individuals achieving leader status by emitting characteristic leadership behaviors.

1229. **Steinfatt, Thomas M.** *Human Communication: An Interpersonal Introduction.* Indianapolis, Indiana: Bobbs Merrill, 1977. 301 pp.

This work includes a chapter on nonverbal communication, nonverbal behavior, and animal communication which has a brief discussion of the Clever Hans phenomenon and discussion of bird, bee, and chimp communication. There is also a survey of paralanguage, kinesics, proxemics, touch, and the functions of nonverbal behavior.

1230. **Steingart, Irving, and Freedman, Norbert.** "The Organization of Body-Focused Kinesic Behavior and Language Construction in Schizophrenic and Depressed States." *Psychoanalysis and Contemporary Science* 4 (1975) : 423-450.

This study of eight psychiatric patients identifies two speech/motion "clusters" which may be useful in diagnostic assessment: specific finger/hand movements accompanying fragmented language as exhibited by schizophrenic patients and continuous body touching with specific narrative language which tends to be exhibited by depressives.

1231. **Steingart, Irving; Grand, Stanley; Margolis, Reuben; Freedman, Norbert; andBuchwald, Charles.** "A Study of the Representation of Anxiety in Chronic Schizophrenia." *Journal of Abnormal Psychology* 85 (1976) : 535-542.

This study examines the communication behavior of 16 male chronic schizophrenic patients during interviews and demonstrates a relationship between their communication behavior and types of anxiety expression. It is part of a series of interrelated studies conducted with normal and clinical populations which uses gestural and verbal aspects of communication behavior as evidence concerning cognitive organization.

1232. **Steklis, Horst B.; Harnad, Stevan R.; and Lancaster, Jane,** eds. *Origins and Evolution of Language and Speech.* Annals of the New York Academy of Sciences 280. New York: New York Academy of Sciences, 1976.

The result of a conference held by the New York Academy of Sciences in September, 1975, this volume deals with language and its origins from a wide variety of directions including behavioral continuities with primates and other nonhumans, the theory of the gestural origin of language, the linguistic properties of sign language, and the linguistic competence of primates. Among the many researchers who have contributed are Gordon W. Hewes, Ashley Montagu, William C. Stokoe, Ursula Bellugi, Edward S. Klima, David Premack, Duane M. Rumbaugh, and Roger S. Fouts.

1233. **Stephenson, G. M.; Rutter, D.R.; and Dore, S.R.** "Visual Interaction and Distance." *British Journal of Psychology* 64 (1973) : 251-27.

Pairs of 54 undergraduate students in England held five-minute conversations at two, six, or ten feet apart. Interactions were videotaped with subjects' looking and speech scored by observers. Nether the duration nor amount of looking at the other was affected by distance, but the duration of *mutual focus* increased with distance.

1234. **Stern, Daniel N.** "A Micro-Analysis of Mother-Infant Interaction: Behavior Regulating Social Contact Between a Mother and her 3½-Month-Old Twins." *Journal of The American Academy of Child Psychiatry* 10 (1971) : 501-517.

Using a method of frame-by-frame film analysis, the interactions between a 25 year-old mother and her 3½-month-old fraternal twin sons were studied. Particular attention was given to the nonverbal communication of "overstimulating" and "controlling" behaviors on the part of the mother. The ability of the infants to regulate social contact with the mother through visual motor behaviors was also studied. Of

particular interest was the finding that certain maternal and infant behaviors produce repetitive interaction sequences.

1235. **Stern, Daniel N.** "Mother and Infant at Play: the Dyadic Interaction Involving Facial, Vocal, and Gaze Behavior." In *The Effect of the Infant on its Caregiver,*
edited by M. Lewis & L.A. Rosenblum, New York: Wiley and Sons, 1974.

The author describes research on mother-infant interaction during the third and
fourth months of life. Infant-elicited maternal behavior differs greatly from normal
interpersonal behavior in that interpersonal space is reduced and the paralinguistic
and facial expressions are exaggerated and lengthened. The author posits that this
serves to match the infant's perceptual and speech-production capabilities. The infant's primary contribution to the regulation of stimulation is his control of mutual-
gaze behavior. It was found the 94 percent of all mutual gazes are initiated and terminated by the infant. Finally, the author discusses how much of the play activity
appears devoted to criss-crossing the upper and lower boundaries of arousal in order
to develop early coping and defensive mechanisms.

1236. **Stern, Daniel N.** "The Goal and Structure of Mother-Infant Play." *Journal
of the American Academy of Child Psychiatry* 13 (1974) : 402-421.

Stern presents a structure for viewing mother-infant play. An exploration of the
role of facial expressions, vocalization, movement, touch, spacing, and mutual vision in their communication is also discussed. Issues pertaining to the significance of
mother-infant play are examined.

1237. **Stern, Daniel N.** *The First Relationship.* Cambridge: Harvard University
Press, 1977. 149 pp.

A fascinating and intelligible account of how infants learn the basic "rules" of
social interaction during the first six months of life. Facial expressions, gaze
behavior, and vocalizations of both caregiver and infant during periods of free play
are investigated. The author lists four functions of bodily expressions as regulators
of social interaction, namely the initiation, maintenance, termination, and
avoidance of communication, and discusses the consequences of regulatory failures
as in cases of overstimulation, understimulation, or paradoxical stimulation. The
author also discusses the infant's innate mechanism for eliciting parenting behavior
in adults and the virtues of what he calls "messing up" during the interaction for
developing coping mechanisms.

1238. **Stern, D.N.; Beebe, B.; Jaffe, J.; and Bennett, S.L.** "The Infant's Stimulus
World During Social Interaction: A Study of Caregiver Behaviors with Particular
Reference to Repetition and Timing." In *Studies in Mother-Infant Interaction,*
edited by H.R. Schaffer, pp. 177-193. London: Academic Press, 1977.

A chapter reporting detailed analyses of the temporal patterning and sequential
structure of vocal and kinesic behaviors manifested by mothers with infants in
maternal-infant free play. Particular attention was given to the role of maternal
repetition in vocalizations, nonverbal behaviors, and tactile stimulation in infant
development. Three different structural units for gaze, expression, vocalization, and
face presentation were described. The importance of temporal and sequential patterning of vocal and kinesic stimuli for the infant was examined.

1239. **Stern, Daniel N.; Jaffe, Joseph; Beebe, Beatrice; and Bennett, Stephen L.**
"Vocalizing in Unison in Alternation: Two Modes of Communication within the
Mother-Infant Dyad." *Annals of The New York Academy of Sciences* 263 (1975) :
89-100.

A paper focusing on the simultaneous vocalizations of mother and infant as
forerunner to the development of speech by the infant. There is a secondary focus on
the role of mutual gaze and posture sharing in vocalization.

1240. Sterrett, John H. "The Job Interview: Body Language and Perceptions of Potential Effectiveness." *Journal of Applied Psychology* 63 (1978) : 388-390.

Subjects included 160 midlevel managers (100 male, 60 female). Videotapes were prepared for viewing using the same two actors as interviewer and job applicant, with applicant's answers remaining the same, but with eye contact, hand gestures, type of clothing, and pause length varying in intensity. Each of the eight resulting tapes was viewed by 20 managers who rated the applicant on eight scales. Among the results it was found that females rated applicants using high-intensity body language as low on ambition and ranked those using low-intensity body language as high on ambition, while males rated in the opposite manner.

1241. Stewart, Denton J., and Patterson, Miles L. "Eliciting Effects of Verbal and Nonverbal Cues on Projective Test Responses." *Journal of Consulting and Clinical Psychology* 41 (1973) : 74-77.

The experiment was designed to investigate the role of verbal ("good") and nonverbal (eye contact and body lean) cues as reinforcers under far and close conditions of interpersonal distance. Their effects were measured according to number of responses to the Thematic Aperception Test (TAT). Among the results it was found that eye contact served as a social reinforcer in the far condition. The number of thematic responses at either far or close distance for body lean was not affected.

1242. Stillwell, Thomas, and Hailman, Jack P. "Spatial, Semantic, and Evolutionary Analysis of an Animal Signal: Inciting by Female Mallards." *Semiotica* 23 (1978) : 193-228.

The authors begin with a literature review of previous examinations of inciting behavior by female ducks. Questions raised in this literature are examined using field observation methods and a notation developed by the authors. The details of interaction between consort pair and intruder are presented along with a hypothetical tracing of evolutionary changes in the semantic content of animal (duck) signals.

1243. Stokoe, William C. Jr. *Semiotics and Human Sign Language,* Approaches to Semiotics Series, No. 21. The Hague: Mouton, 1972. Illus.

1244. Stokoe, William C. Jr. "Motor Signs as the First Form of Language." *Semiotica* 10 (1974) : 117-130.

In this consideration of the theory that man's first language was gestural, the author introduces a new term: gSign. The letter "g" here refers to gestural manifestation, and "sign" is intended as a shortened version for "sign-vehicle in a semiotic system." A gSign is considered as a symptom and signal as well as an index because one can make the basic assumption that gSign activity, like the expression of emotions in men and animals, has social and hence survival value. Communication by gSigns is assumed to have begun (far back in phylogeny) as analogic or iconic, evolved into denotative, linguistic, arbitrary, and digital communication, and is superseded in this function by sSigns (where "s" stands for speech), so that gSign finally remained or reverted back to its earlier function.

1245. Stokoe, William C. "Sign Language and the Monastic Use of Lexical Gestures." *Semiotica* 24 (1978) : 181-194.

This is a book review of Robert A. Barakat's *The Cistercian Sign Language: A Study in Non-Verbal Communication* (Cistercian Studies Series II, Kalamazoo, Michigan: Cistercian Publications, 1976, 220 pp.). The possibility of monastic sign languages having been the beginnings of sign languages for the deaf is discussed and rejected. American Sign Language and the monastic Cistercian sign language are compared, and American Plains Indian sign language and a sign language of sawmill workers in the Pacific coastal forests are also discussed.

1246. **Stokols, Daniel.** "The Relation Between Micro and Macro Crowding Phenomena: Some Implications for Environmental Research and Design." *Man-Environment Systems* 3 (1973) : 139-149.

The author discusses recent work on density and crowding done on the micro or psychological level and questions its utility for macro considerations of environmental design. Parallels between the two approaches are discussed as well as contrasts in the temporal dimensions involved and in the operational criteria for measuring crowding stress. Directions for future research are suggested.

1247. **Stone, L. Joseph; Smith, Henrietta T.; and Murphy, Lois B.,** eds. *The Competent Infant: Research and Commentary.* New York: Basic Books, 1973. 1,314 pp. Illus.

This massive volume combines edited versions of 202 previously published reports of infancy research with commentary. It is meant to be a handbook of readings providing an overview of the explosion of infancy studies in the '60s and early '70s. It is possible only to give a sample of the various dimensions of body movement covered in this book. As a collection of articles on the "competent infant," it focuses on the abilities and capacities of infants and their development to age 15 months. Smiling, laughing, sucking, and attention are covered in sections on "Individuality in Development" and "Prenatal and Perinatal Development." A section on "Capabilities of the Newborn" includes articles on animal newborns and imprinting. A chapter on "Motor Development and Maturational Changes" is included in the section "Development During Year One," as well as articles on race and ethnic differences in development. "Early Experience: Deprivation and Enrichment" provides an overview of research on class differences, and a final section on the "Social Infant" includes research on attachment behaviors and sex differences.

1248. **Storms, Michael D., and Thomas, George C.** "Reactions to Physical Closeness." *Journal of Personality and Social Psychology* 35 (1977) : 412-418.

Male students were used as subjects in three experiments. In the first study a confederate with similar or dissimilar attitudes sat close or at a normal distance to subjects. In the next two experiments the experimenter sat close or at a normal distance to subjects and acted in a friendly or hostile way. In all three studies subjects' reactions revealed an interaction between distance and the experimental manipulation. The experimental was liked more when he sat close and was friendly or similar and liked less when he was close and hostile or dissimilar.

1249. **Strachwitz, Elisabeth von.** "Über averbale Prozesse in der Kindertherapie." *Praxis der Kinderpsychologie und Kinderpsychiatrie* 22 (1973) : 33-37.

The author describes the functions of nonverbal processes in child therapy as to symbolize meanings that cannot be verbalized and to provide the emotional experience of closeness. These functions are illustrated with examples of children the author has seen in her therapeutic practice. Written in German.

1250. **Stratton, Lois O., and Horowitz, Mardi J.** "Body Buffer Zone: A Longitudinal Method for Assessing Approach Distances and Patterns of Psychiatric Patients."*Journal of Clinical Psychology* 28 (1972) : 84-86.

Five female psychiatric patients participated in the experiment. They were asked to approach a female experimenter frontally, backwards, and sideways. The distance at which they stopped was measured two or three times per week for four to six weeks and correlated with behavioral observations made by the nursing staff. Previous research revealed that for normal females approaching a female at the closest approach is made with the back, the next closest the front, followed by the left side, and then the right side. This pattern almost never occurred with the psychiatic patients. On occasions on which patients were rated as depressed or withdrawn, the greatest distance was noted for front and left approaches. On occasions of "bizarre" behavior (hallucination, irrationality), the greatest distance was kept with the back. When aggressive behavior was noted, the greatest distance was kept with the right side.

1251. **Strong, Stanley R.; Taylor, Ronald G.; Bratton, Joseph C.; and Loper, Rodney G.** "Nonverbal Behavior and Perceived Counselor Characteristics." *Journal of Counseling Psychology* 13 (1971) : 554-561.

Two experienced male counseling psychologists were trained to exhibit high and low frequencies of nonverbal behavior in ten-minute simulated counseling sessions with a male confederate client. Nonverbal behaviors consisted of movements of head, eyes, face, body posture, extremities, and body positions. Sessions were recorded in one of four conditions: video- and audiotaping of high and low movement sessions, and audiotaping only of high and low movement sessions. Eighty-six female students were assigned randomly to one of the four conditions and required to complete an adjective checklist on their impressions of the counselor. Analyses of variance revealed that subjects who both heard and viewed counselors described counselors more negatively than those only hearing them. Low frequency of movement resulted in more negative descriptions than high movement.

1252. **Summerfield, Angela B., and Lake, J.A.** "Non-Verbal and Verbal Behaviours Associated with Parting." *The British Journal of Psychology* 68 (1977) : 133-136.

Twenty-four pairs (some friends, some strangers) were seated at a table facing each other. At the end of 20 minutes, one or both subjects were requested to go to other rooms. A significant effect was obtained for acquaintance indicating that friends spoke significantly more words at parting than did strangers. Also, friends looked longer at their partners at parting. No other significant effects were found.

1253. **Sundstrom, Eric.** "An Experimental Study of Crowding: Effects of Room Size, Intrusion, and Goal Blocking on Nonverbal Behavior, Self-Disclosure, and Self-Reported Stress." *Journal of Personality and Social Psychology* 32 (1975) : 645-654.

Groups of three male undergraduates and three male confederates were placed in large or small rooms. Each subject interacted with a confederate who introduced intrusive actions and goal blocking. Analysis of the videotaped interactions and subjects' reports of stress and self-disclosure showed that the small room produced feelings of discomfort and crowdedness and less self-disclosure. Intrusion produced discomfort leading to decreased facial regard and goal blocking (inattention and speech interruptions) led to a decrease in facial regard, gesturing, and head nodding. Room density did not affect stress responses to intrusion and goal blocking.

1254. **Sundstrom, Eric.** "A Test of Equilibrium Theory: Effects of Topic Intimacy and Proximity on Verbal and Nonverbal Behavior in Pairs of Friends and Strangers." *Environmental Psychology and Nonverbal Behavior* 3 (1978) : 3-16.

This experiment examined verbal and nonverbal behavior by pairs of female friends and strangers as they discussed either intimate or nonintimate topics at face-to-face distances of approximately 2.5 or 4.5 feet. On the basis of equilibrium theory and Altman and Taylor's (1973) theory about interpersonal exchange, strangers were expected to react to intimate topics or close proximity or both with discomfort and decreased affiliative behavior (facial regard, gesturing, speech). Friends were expected to show increased affiliative behavior. Results indicated that both strangers and friends showed signs of discomfort and low levels of affiliative behavior while discussing intimate topics, that is, *compensation*. Discomfort with intimate topics and compensation decreased over time, indicating *adaptation*. This finding suggests that compensation for intimate topics may occur only during the initial phases of an encounter.

1255. Sundstrom, Eric, and Sundstrom, Mary Graehl. "Personal Space Invasions: What Happens When the Invader Asks Permission?" *Environmental Psychology and Nonverbal Behavior* 2 (1977) : 76-82.

Male or female college students seated outdoors and alone on a university campus were approached by a same-sexed "invader" who sat nine inches and 18 inches away. The invader asked permission before sitting down or said nothing. An unobtrusive observer recorded the amount of time before subjects left and the presence of compensatory reactions (moving away, interposing barriers, orienting away, leaning away, or leaning forward). Results showed that males left more quickly with silent invaders; females tended to leave more quickly if permission was asked. Compensation was greatest among closely invaded subjects who remained in their seats longest (males who were asked; females who were not asked). These findings agree with equilibrium theory.

1256. Sussman, Nan M., and Rosenfeld, Howard M. "Touch, Justification and Sex: Influences on the Aversiveness of Spatial Violations." *The Journal of Social Psychology* 106 (1978) : 215-225.

Hall's pioneering studies designated discrete zones of interpersonal space appropriate to levels of intimacy within a culture. This study consisted of two experiments in which a confederate touched half of the subjects who sat six inches away. The results showed that the violations of Hall's intimate zone were more aversive to males than females when lacking prior justification.

1257. Szasz, Suzanne. *The Body Language of Children.* New York: W.W. Norton and Company, 1978. 160 pp. Illus.

This is a beautiful photographic essay of infants and children's behavior: the photographs are arranged according to the feelings conveyed, accompanied by a description of the child's and/or parent's nonverbal behavior and the situational context.

1258. Takala, Martti. "Consistencies of Psychomotor Styles in Interpersonal Tasks." *Scandinavian Journal of Psychology* 16 (1975) : 193-202.

A study designed to investigate the influence of group situations and tasks on individual psychomotor behavior. Four different groups were observed for 11 psychomotor behaviors that were divided into three general categories: (1) temperamental acts; (2) psychomotor indications of tension; and (3) movements controlling interaction. Overall findings indicate that individual consistencies in psychomotor behavior are most apparent in self-inititated tasks. Consistency in individual psychomotor styles was also found in the utilization of narrow and large space and in the total tension scores.

1259. Tautermannová, M "Smiling in Infants." *Child Development* 44 (1973) : 701-704. Illus.

Seven infants were observed two times a day for two days at age eight weeks and then at four week intervals until 24 weeks. Smiling duration was noted to vary widely across individuals and to increase with age and close presence of the adult.

1260. Taylor, Allan Ross. "Nonverbal Communications Systems in Native North America." *Semiotica* 13 (1975) : 329-374. Illus.

Several nonverbal communication systems were used by the various native peoples of North America. The direct signaling systems discussed here include the American Indians' Plains Sign language, various means of distance signaling (including audible signals such as cries of birds or animals, smoke and fire signals, visual signaling, and mirror signaling), body signals used by the Plains Indians, and picture writing (both mnemonic and notificational). Indirect signaling systems (speech surrogates) discussed include the whistle speech of the Mexican Kickapoos and the Aleut wig-wag, which was a type of arm and body semaphore system. The impact of Native American direct signaling systems on Euro-American civilization is also discussed.

1261. **Taylor, Orlando, and Ferguson, Dianna.** "CAL Research Report 2: A Study of Cross-Cultural Communication Between Blacks and Whites in the U.S. Army." *The Linguistic Reporter* 17 (1975) : 8,11.

This investigation of black-white communication problems within the U.S. Army outlined nine major problem areas, six of them verbal (dialect features, paralanguage, conversational topics, discourse rules, conversational rules and speech acts [pragmatics]) and three of them nonverbal (proxemics, haptics, and kinesics). Specific cross-cultural communication problems found during the research were then listed. Interviews, field observations, and a Cross-Cultural Communications Questionnaire were used in the research.

1262. **Taylor, Ralph B., and Ferguson, Glenn.** "Solitude and Intimacy: Linking Territoriality and Privacy Experiences." *Journal of Nonverbal Behavior* 4 (1980) : 227-239.

The further advancement of privacy models depends upon clarifying two issues: the relationship between privacy and territoriality and the degree to which different types of privacy have distinct behavioral and cognitive correlates. Two types of privacy experiences — solitude and intimacy — were investigated. Given the divergent function of these two forms of privacy, it was expected that each would be sought in different types of territories. It was also expected that where people seek a form of privacy depends in part upon the quality of the immediate social environment: a territory will be used less for privacy experiences as the understandings that regulate usage of the space erode. Students were asked where they went for solitude, where they went for intimacy, and to describe their experiences in these two places. Results supported the hypotheses. In addition, a substantial and coequal linkage between privacy and territoriality appeared.

1263. **Tedesco, J.F., and Fromme, D.K.** "Cooperation, Competition, and Personal Space." *Sociometry* 37 (1974) : 116-121.

Eighteen male undergraduates participated in cooperative, competitive, or neutral games with confederates. As predicted, the measures of seating distance were largest relative to the competitive situation.

1264. **Templer, Donald I.; Goldstein, Rhonnie; and Penick, S.B.** "Stability and Inter-Rater Reliability of Lateral Eye Movement." *Perceptual and Motor Skills* 34 (1972) : 469-470.

Two observers judged the eye movements of 19 female clinical workers while they were asked reflective questions during two sessions one week apart. Previous research indicated that upward eye movement consistently either to the right or the left accompanies reflective thinking. In the present study, inter-rater reliability of judging eye movement was found to be less than acceptable. In addition, stability in direction of eye movement for the two sessions was not found.

1265. **Tepper, Donald Thomas.** "The Communication of Counselor Empathy, Respect, and Genuineness through Verbal and Non-Verbal Channels." Ed.D dissertation, University of Massachusetts. 1972. 177 pp. (Order No. 73-6710)

Thirty-two interactions on a videotape of an actor-counselor and actor-client varying eye contact, postural lean, intonation, facial expression, and verbal content were
rated by judges for degree of empathy, respect, and genuineness. Forward lean,
maintained eye contact, "concerned" tone and facial expression received high ratings
in all measurements. The nonverbal behaviors proved far more influential than verbal ones.

1266. **Tepper, Donald T. Jr., and Haase, Richard F.** "Verbal and Nonverbal Communication of Facilitative Conditions." *Journal of Counseling Psychology* 25 (1978)
: 35-44.

Using the same actor-counselor and the same actor-client, a videotape stimulus
was prepared consisting of 32 role-played interactions that varied one verbal and five
nonverbal cues. After seeing the videotaped interactions, 15 experienced male
counselors and 15 male counseling students ("clients") rated all 32 interactions on the
three dependent measures of empathy, respect, and genuineness (facilitative conditions as defined by Carkhuff). Nonverbal cues accounted for significantly greater
message variance than did verbal cues. "Clients" differed significantly from
counselors in their perceptions of the cues, and these differences depended heavily
on the remaining cues' presence or absence. Facial expression and vocal intonation
proved to be significant contributors to the final judgments of the facilitative conditions.

1267. **Teresa, Joseph Gerald.** "The Measurement of Meaning as Interpreted by
Teachers and Students in Visuo-Gestural Channel Expressions through Nine Emo-
tional Expressions." Ph.D. dissertation, University of Michigan. 1971. 210 pp.
(Order No. 72-4992)

This study used semantic differential scale to determine the meaning of nine emotional expressions in the visual-gestural channel for teachers and students. Significant differences between students and teachers were found for the factors calm-
excitable and still-active. Sex and IQ did not yield significant differences, although
the author interprets a significant difference for socio-economic status.

1268. **Ter Vrugt, Dick, and Pederson, David R.** "The Effects of Vertical Rocking
Frequencies on the Arousal Level in Two-Month-Old Infants." *Child Development*
44 (1973) : 205-209.

Sixty-four infants were rocked at four different rates and rated at 15-second intervals on level of arousal on a six-point scale from quiet sleep to agitated with severe
crying and grasping. Movement transducer scores were also recorded. Other
variables included sex of the infant and prestimulus state. Analysis of observer
ratings showed that at higher frequencies of rocking more infants slept and fewer
cried. There was a positive relationship between frequency and effectiveness of rocking. No sex differences were found.

1269. **Tewes, Uwe.** "Einige Bedingungen für Diskriminactionsleistungen bei der
Wahrehmung des Gefühlsausdrucks." *Zeitschrift für Experimentelle und
Angewandte Psychologie* 20 (1973) : 317-346.

This study of the factors determining the interpretation of emotional facial expressions found that the appeal of the stimuli, subjects' knowledge of the situation portrayed in the photograph, and subjects' emotional instability affected their ability to
discriminate facial expression. Written in German.

1270. **Thayer, Stephen.** "The Effect of Facial Expression Sequence upon
Judgments of Emotion." In *Proceedings of the National Conference on Body
Language* (tentative title), edited by S. Thayer, in preparation.

One hundred forty white, female college students were shown a series of five separate photographs of facial expression showing either the same emotion for five trials or four separate photographs of the same emotion followed by a fifth photograph showing a different emotion. Analysis showed that the students' judgments were influenced by the sequence of facial expressions: the judged intensity of identical expressions was significantly increased when preceded by a sequence of contrasting expressions. (from pre-publication manuscript)

1271. **Thayer, Stephen, and Alban, Lewis.** "A Field Experiment on the Effect of Political and Cultural Factors on the Use of Personal Space." *The Journal of Social Psychology* 88 (1972) : 267-272.

Male pedestrians were approached for help with directions in a conservative and a liberal neighborhood during a period of intense clash over the war issue preceding the 1970 New York State senatorial elections. The questioner wore either a large American flag button or a peace button. An observer noted the distance assumed by the pedestrian from the questioner immediately after the request. Results showed significantly smaller interaction distances with the flag button wearer in the conservative neighborhood and no significant differences in the liberal neighborhood.

1272. **Thayer, Stephen and Schiff, William.** "Observer Judgment of Social Interaction: Eye Contact and Relationship References." *Journal of Personality and Social Psychology* 30 (1974) : 110-114.

Male and female subjects were shown films of college-age "actors" in a library setting in which one of the actors turns and looks at the other. The manipulated factors were duration of gaze (long or short), reciprocity of gaze (reciprocated or not reciprocated), and sex of the interacting pair (male looks at male, male looks at female, female looks at female, female looks at male). Subjects were then asked to judge the extent of prior relationship. In general, judgments of a more enduring relationship were related to longer and/or reciprocated gaze. However, significant differences in judgment based on the sexes of the interacting pairs and the sex of the observer are also indicated when these factors are correlated with duration and reciprocity.

1273. **Thayer, Stephen, and Schiff, William.** "Eye-Contact, Facial Expression, and The Experience of Time." *The Journal of Social Psychology* 95 (1975) : 117-124.

This study examines the impact of interpersonal processes on temporal judgment. Forty-eight female undergraduates were asked to judge the amount of time that had passed while they looked at a confederate's eyes. During the eye-contact interval the confederate maintained one of two facial expressions: negative-unpleasant and positive-pleasant for either 12 or 36 seconds. Results showed that time was experienced as passing more slowly (overestimation relative to clocktime) when combined with a negative facial expression, an effect most pronounced for female-female encounters.

1274. **Thayer, Stephen, and Schiff, William.** "Gazing Patterns and Attribution of Sexual Involvement *The Journal of Social Psychology* 101 (1977) : 235-246.

One hundred seventy-one undergraduate students rated 16 brief, filmed encounters as to the degree of sexual involvement apparent in each encounter. Results indicated that longer and reciprocated gazes resulted in attributions of greater sexual involvement. Also, within every gaze condition, female judges made greater attributions of some established sexual relationship for opposite-sex pairs.

1275. **Theeman, Margaret.** "Research Ethics (To Do or Not to Do, and If So, How to Do)." *Conference Proceedings of the American Dance Therapy Association* 8 (1974) : 91-102.

A personal and theoretical discussion of the ethics involved in nonverbal research and particularly dance-movement therapy research. The author cites examples from her own research on the sociology of expressive body movement and poses ethical questions for consideration.

1276. **Thoman, Evelyn B.**, ed. *Origins of the Infant's Social Responsiveness.* New York: Halsted Press, 1979.

1277. **Thoman, Evelyn B.; Leiderman, P. Herbert; and Olson, Joan P.** "Neonate-Mother Interaction During Breast Feeding." *Developmental Psychology* 6 (1972) : 110-118.

This study involved 20 primaparous and 20 multiparous mothers with their 48-hour old infants. Results of observation during breast feeding show that primaparous mothers spent more time in nonfeeding activities and spent more time feeding male infants, while multiparous spent more feeding time with females. Primaparous mothers also changed activity more often, provided more general stimulation for their infants, and talked more to them during breast feeding. Primaparous mothers talked much more to female infants, but multiparous mothers talked more to male infants. Longitudinal observations showed that the number of weeks these infants were breast fed was related to the amount of time the mothers talked to the infant during the two-day observation.

1278. **Thompson, Donna E.; Aiello, John R.; and Epstein, Yakov M.** "Interpersonal Distance Preferences." *Journal of Nonverbal Behavior* 4 (1979) : 113-118.

The utility of various curvilinear "comfort" models of interpersonal distance was examined in a study employing subjects' responses to a broad range of videotaped, seated distances. Results obtained provided considerable support for these models. Intermediate distances were rated as more comfortable, preferable, and appropriate than more extreme close or far distances. This pattern of results was manifested for interaction situations involving both two- and four-person groups.

1279. **Thompson, James J.** *Beyond Words: Nonverbal Communication in the Classroom.* New York: Citation Press, 1973. 208 pp.

The author considers proxemics, facial expression, eye movement, posture, gesture, touch, and responses to time in relation to teaching.

1280. **Thomsen, Curtis E.** "Eye Contact by Non-Human Primates Toward a Human Observer." *Animal Behavior* 22 (1974) : 144-149.

An investigation of the utility of a quantitative measure of eye contact for nonhuman primates. The frequency with which nonhuman primates return the gaze of a human observer was studied in relation to the following variables: age, sex, environment, rearing conditions, and species. The overall findings from four separate experiments indicate that eye contact is a reliable and quantifiable measure of behavior for nonhuman primates. Further results suggest that for nonhuman primates, eye contact is decreased: As distances are increased; in new environments; and when reared by surrogates. Young male rhesus monkeys made less contact than females.

1281. **Thornton, Sam.** *A Movement Perspective of Rudolf Laban.* London: Mac-Donald and Evans, 1971. 134 pp.

The book is a full account of Rudolf Laban's contributions to the field of movement education. There is a short biography and a thorough discussion of his philosophies, ideas, and principles that have influenced "movement in education," "movement notation," and "movement education."

1282. **Tiegerman, Ellen Morris.** "A Comparison of Three Play Procedures in The Manipulation of Gaze Behavior and Object Use with Autistic Children." Ph.D. dissertation, City University of New York. 1979. 166 pp. (Order No. 8006476)

This study involving six autistic children ranging from four to six years investigated the effectiveness of three play procedures and found that gaze behavior of autistic children is modifiable. Play experiences are recommended as an integral part of therapy.

1283. Timney, Brian, and London, Harvey. "Body Language Concomitants of Persuasiveness and Persuasibility in Dyadic Interaction." *International Journal of Group Tensions* 3 (1973) : 48-67.

Twenty pairs of female students were asked to serve on a simulated jury hearing a case concerning a negligence suit for damages. Each of the two subjects received a different legal analysis of the case. The behavior of the subjects was videotaped. One pair of subjects, both of whom disagree with the legal analysis, were focused on. Three categories of behavior were rated and reported on: gesticulation, self-manipulation, and gaze behavior of "persuaders" and "persuadees."

1284. Tisch, Frederick E., Huston, Ted L., and Undenbaum, Eugene A. "Attitude Similarity, Attraction, and Physical Proximity in a Dynamic Space." *Journal of Applied Social Psychology* 3 (1973) : 63-72.

The attraction of female subjects to female confederates as measured by the Interpersonal Attraction Survey, physical distance during the interaction, subjects' chair and body angles, and verbalization latency were examined. These measures were correlated to perceived attitude similarity and liking as rated on seven-point scales. Similarity of attitude was manipulated by means of false attitude information and fixed-effects analysis of variance. Results indicate a direct relationship of attitude similarity to both attraction and liking but not to proximity in dynamic space.

1285. Tissot, Franck. "La morphopsychologie face à la typologie jungienne: Deux voies convergentes." *La Revue de Morphopsychologie* 2 (1980) : 41-63. Illus.

The author reviews the bases of morphopsychology, the study of psychological traits through the analysis of facial characteristics, and shows its compatibility with Jung's theory of psychological types. The face is seen as the "living schema of the psychic functions," and each of these psychic functions—thought, feeling, sensation and intuition—is represented in a specific area of the face. In combination with the two opposed but complementary forces of life, extraversion-expansion and introversion-retraction, they produce eight principal Jungian types. The article concludes with a charming morphopsychological interpretation of the facial characteristics of these types as guests at a dinner party, which is illustrated.

1286. Trochim, William M.K. "The Three-Dimensional Graphic Method for Quantifying Body Position." *Behavior Research Methods and Instrumentation* 8 (1976) : 1-4.

The method for quantifying body position described in this paper uses a series of observer procedures to collect body position data from videotaped records to be used in conjunction with FORTRAN computer programs. The data can be represented graphically from any angle and can be analyzed mathematically to provide information on topics such as interpersonal distance and body activity level. The graphic presentation of the data makes possible feedback to the observer for an accuracy check.

1287. Tronick, Edward; Brazelton, T. Berry; and Als, H. "The Structure of Face-to-Face Interaction and Its Developmental Functions." *Sign Language Studies* 18 (1978) : 1-16.

The authors observed several behaviors such as facial expressions, vocalizations, head positions, and direction of gaze of mother and infant during interactions videotaped in a split-screen image. Infants seem to have different body attitudes when interacting with people, as opposed to objects. In the former, the goal is to reciprocate in an affective interchange, whereas in the latter the goal is to reach out and explore. They postulate that one of the major tasks of the infant over the first several months is to order his behavior in reciprocal monadic phases so that it becomes synchronous with the interactant and so that the infant can communicate and decode information.

1288.　**Trott, D. Mary Lee.** "Expressive Movement Style and Personality Characteristic." *Conference Proceedings of the American Dance Therapy Association* 9 (1975) : 124-130.

Fifty-five female students having beginning level dance experience with an average age of 24.6 performed a series of 20 movements after verbal description and videotaped demonstration of the variables. Three trained observers rated the movers on a 7-point scale as to their interpretation of the movement variables. A personality questionnaire was given to the students following their performance. Interobserver reliability was .40 to .68. Correlations were found between expressive movement style and personality traits. No correlation was found between movement preference and level of dance training.

1289.　**Trout, Deborah L., and Rosenfeld, Howard M.** "The Effect of Postural Lean and Body Congruence on the Judgment of Psychotherapeutic Rapport." *Journal of Nonverbal Behavior* 4 (1980) : 176-190.

Naturalistic studies have implicated both forward postural lean and interpersonally congruent limb configurations as nonverbal indexes of social rapport, although both variables have been confounded with verbal and other nonverbal concomitants. In the present study direction of postural lean and congruence of body positions were systematically manipulated in each of six 40-second videotaped segments of simulated client-therapist interactions. participating in the study of 30 male and 30 female undergraduate students, each of whom viewed one of six orders of the segments and rated the level of rapport in each interaction. A 2 x 3 x 2 x 6 analysis of variance on factors of Congruence, Lean, Sex, and Order revealed main effects of the Lean and Congruence variables (p<.001 and p<.05, respectively), and no significant main effects of Sex or Order. Both congruent limbs and forward-leaning postures on the part of the therapist and client were significant contributors to attributions of rapport.

1290.　**Tubbs, Stewart L., and Carter, Robert M.,** eds. *Shared Experiences in Human Communication.* Rochelle Park, New Jersey: Hayden Book Co., 1978. 304 pp.

Among the 37 articles in this reader, there is an overview of nonverbal communication by Mark L. Knapp adapted from his 1972 book, a chapter by Julius Fast on "The Silent Language of Love" and body language in courtship from his 1970 book, and a reprint of an article on how to tell Type A personalities who have an increased risk of coronaries from Type B personalities based on nonverbal behavior, written by cardiologist Meyer Friedman and Ray Rosenman.

1291.　**Tubbs, Stewart L, and Moss Sylvia.** *Human Communication,* 3rd. ed. New York: Random House, 1980. 464 pp. Illus.

This textbook has a richly illustrated chapter on spatial and time cues, visual behavior, touch, gestures and movements, and paralinguistics. Written for college students, it surveys the work of many researchers and has numerous examples from familiar sources such as movies. The chapter concludes with a discussion of three functions of nonverbal messages and a brief section of exercises for study.

1292. **Tucker, James Allan.** "An Investigation into the Relationship Between Personal Space and Various Stress Indices in Educational Environments." Ph.D. dissertation, The University of Texas at Austin. 1972. 182 pp. (Order No. 73-7659)

In studies involving 285 college students and 203 elementary school children from schools and residence halls varying in crowdedness, the author investigated the relation of crowding to mental health, to subgrouping patterns as in size of lunch groups, and to individual responses to the spatial approach of a confederate. Results give tentative support for the "concept of personal space."

1293. **Turner, Roy,** ed. *Ethnomethodology.* Harmondsworth, England: Penguin, 1974. 287 pp.

This book includes papers written from 1964 to 1974, and it is meant to present the range of research concerns and strategies of ethnomethodology. The second section of the book focuses on interaction, and, of these articles, one, "Notes on the Art of Walking," deals directly with nonverbal communication.

1294. **Tway, Patricia.** "Verbal and Nonverbal Communication of Factory Workers." *Semiotica* 16 (1976) : 29-44. Illus.

Nonverbal communication among factory workers of different levels in different situations is described and illustrated with photos. Communicative situations and styles varied from formal to informal, and each had its own nonverbal components, including the "sign off" indicating the end of a formal situation and beginning of an informal one and the "sign on" indicating the reverse case. Influence of territory, topic, "mock gestures," shifting verbal and nonverbal styles, and various adaptive behaviors were described and discussed.

1295. **Umiker-Sebeok, Jean.** "Nature's Way? Visual Images of Childhood in American Culture." *Semiotica* 27 (1979) : 173-220. Illus.

Advertising photos were examined to show the way they visually represent stereotyped ideas about the roles of adults and children. Various parent-child relationships and families of different sizes were examined and illustrated.

1296. **Umiker-Sebeok, D. Jean, and Sebeok, Thomas A.,** eds. *Aboriginal Sign Languages of the Americas and Australia,* vols. 1 and 2. New York: Plenum Press, 1978. 442 pp. Illus.

Volume 1 contains three articles written in the 1880s by Garrick Mallery. A detailed description of North American sign language and signals is followed by a discussion of the similarities to gestural motion during verbalization. Volume 2 contains articles on gestures and sign languages used by Plains and Salishan North American Indians, the South American Urubus, and several Australian aboriginal tribes.

1297. **Uno, Yoshiyasu, and Rosenthal, Robert.** "Tacit Communication Between Japanese Experimenters and Subjects." *Psychologia* 15 (1972) : 213-222.

Five Japanese studies of experimenter effects of research outcomes are summarized. For example, in an experiment where subjects rated the behavior of the experimenter, those who obtained the greatest expectancy effects were seen by subjects as more active gesturally, more expressive facially, somewhat less courteous, less enthusiastic, less fair and honest, and less professional. Noting that the results are the exact opposite of similar Western experiments, it was hypothesized that the subjects used in this series of experiments were of the rebellious generation that participated in Japan's student riots and that this rebelliousness influenced the experiments. Nonverbal behavior in Japan was discussed within a context of Japan's religious beliefs.

1298. **Valins, Stuart, and Baum, Andrew.** "Residential Group Size, Social Interaction, and Crowding." *Environment and Behavior.* 5 (1973) : 421-439.

The authors discuss evidence that corridor-design dormitories can be considered overloaded social environments: the interior architecture of these dormitories requires many residents to share common facilities; residents frequently report meeting people when interaction is not wanted; and residents consider their dormitories to be crowded. The authors suggest that long-term exposure to these environments may lead residents to become hypersensitive to social stimulation and to experience negative affect at relatively low levels of social stimulation. Social interaction experiments indicate that residents adapt to the high levels of social stimulation that they experience by developing ways to reduce involvement with others.

1299. **Vande Creek, Leon, and Watkins, John T.** "Responses to Incongruent Verbal and Nonverbal Emotional Cues." The Journal of Communication 22 (1972) : 311-316.

Ninety-eight subjects judged 40 20-second videotape segments of actors portraying conflicting verbal-nonverbal cues and rated them on a nine-point scale from calm to stressed. Most subjects could be differentiated reliably as either verbal or nonverbal responders, while a few responded to the general level of stress without preferring either the verbal or nonverbal mode.

1300. **van Hooff, Jan A.R.A.M.** "The Comparison of Facial Expression in Man and Higher Primates." In *Methods of Inference from Animal to Human Behavior*, edited by M. von Cranach, pp. 165-196. Chicago, Illinois: Aldine Publishing Co., 1977. Illus.

In a concise and well illustrated article van Hooff shows how comparison of facial expressions between man and animals leads to the assumption that they are homologous. The major types of nonhuman facial expressions are found in humans, but the reverse is not the case. The main difference in usage of facial expressions between humans and nonhuman primates is found in the context of reporting about the environment rather than acting on it. Thus expressions such as surprise and disgust are found in man only, having evolved under the same pressures that caused the evolution of speech according to the author.

1301. **van Meter, William Isaac.** "Spatial Proximity, Sociability, and Topic Intimacy Factors Influencing the Affect and Behavior of Participants in Small Discussion Groups." Ph.D. dissertation, West Virginia University. 1971. 108 pp. (Order No. 72-14,086)

Distance (intimate or personal) and topic (casual or intimate) were not found to influence affect and behavior of persons interacting in small groups in this study. There was, however, a significant difference between high sociability and low sociability subjects on perceived affect.

1302. **Vávra, V.** "Is Jakobson Right?" *Semiotica* 17 (1976) : 95-110. Illus.

Two conflicting systems for the mimic expression of assent were explored in a number of experiments: System A (used by the great majority of Europeans) and System B (found primarily in Bulgaria). The direction of the initial movement in the assenting action was examined in relation to hand, eye, and ear laterality.

1303. **Vávra, V.** "The Self and Body Movement Behavior." *Semiotica* 21 (1977) : 1-22. Illus.

The body movements of the speaker while referring to him or herself as "I" or as "you" were investigated. The most striking movement differences were found in the movement of the head and in the face around the eyes. Investigations were then carried out as to whether this movement behavior might correlate with measures of field dependence and field independence.

1304. **Veague, Pamela Chiles.** "Non-Verbal Communication: Quasi-Courting." *Smith College Studies in Social Work* 43 (1972) : 68.

This study was designed to explore the subject of quasi-courting in clinical interviews, and Scheflen's observations that behaviors appear in psychotherapy similar to those found in American courtship (for example, "preening" behaviors of stroking the hair or adjusting clothes, head cocking, crossing legs).

1305. **Veno, Arthur.** "Response to Approach: A Preliminary Process Oriented Study of Human Spacing." *Social Science Information* 15 (1976) : 93-115.

One hundred twenty unaccompanied adult males and females waiting to ride trollies in San Francisco were used in the study. A confederate invaded the subjects' space, and their responses were judged as aggressive or submissive. Subjects' body orientation and the distance at which they responded to invasion of space by the confederate were estimated. Results showed that most subjects exhibited submissive behavior. Younger adults responded more aggressively than older.

1306. **Vernon, McCay, and Miller, William G.** "Language and Nonverbal Communication in Cognitive and Affective Processes." *Psychoanalysis and Contemporary Science* 2 (1973) : 124-135.

The paper discusses studies of deafness which suggest that verbal language is not as relevant a variable in cognition and the communication of affect as body language or paralanguage. The author discusses the hypothesis in the context of the often unsuccessful results of conventional psychotherapy.

1307. **Villa-Lovoz, Thomas Richard.** "The Effects of Counselor Eye Contact, Fluency, and Addressing on Client Preference." Ph.D. dissertation, University of Wyoming. 1975. 102 pp. (Order No. 75223-41)

The effects of counselor eye contact, speech fluency, and form of address on clients' preference for the counselor were assessed. Among the results it was found that higher levels of eye contact enhance client regard.

1308. **Vine, Ian.** "Social Spacing in Animals and Man." *Social Science Information* 12 (1973) : 7-50.

In this ethological analysis of territoriality in man and animals, Vine argues that the results of animal crowding studies may give clues to the results of human crowding. There is a strong relation between territorial behavior and aggressiveness, but the strength of the relation isn't as clear in man as it is in animals. To cope with urban invasion of space Vine disucsses how we may often see others as non-persons.

1309. **Vine, Ian.** "The Role of Facial-Visual Signalling in Early Social Development." In *Social Communication and Movement*, edited by M. Von Cranach and I. Vine, pp. 195-298. London: Academic Press, 1973. Illus.

In this chapter Vine analyzes research related to the ontogeny and development of human facial-visual signals. He discusses methodological issues of the research, the development of facial perception, and the development of social smiling. He also examines the relation between face schema and social attachment as understood from various perspectives.

1310. **Vine, Ian.** "Territoriality and the Spatial Regulation of Interaction." In *Organization of Behavior in Face-to-Face Interaction,* edited by A. Kendon, R. Harris, and M.R. Key, pp. 357-387. The Hague: Mouton, 1975.

An overview of the literature on territoriality and proxemics in animals and man, it includes a discussion of fixed and "semi-fixed-feature space," the effects of territoriality on face-to-face interactions, effects of crowding, "group space" and invasion of space.

1311. **Waksler, Frances Chaput.** "The Essential Structure of Face-to-Face Interaction: A Phenomenological Analysis." Ph.D. dissertation, Boston University. 1973. 281 pp. (Order No. 73-14,187)

Applying E. Husserl's phenomenological method to the question of what the "actor" must "know" to engage in face-to-face interaction, the author explores this through descriptive works in the social sciences.

1312. **Waldron, Joseph.** "Judgement of Like-Dislike from Facial Expression and Body Posture." *Perceptual and Motor Skills* 41 (1975) : 799-804.

Composite photos of combinations of facial expressions showing like, neutrality, and dislike with two body postures of women showing like or dislike were judged by 30 female undergraduates. A complex relationship between facial expression and body posture is noted. It was posited that body posture moderates the information communicated by the face.

1313. **Walker, David N.** "Openness to Touching: A Study of Strangers in Nonverbal Interaction." Ph.D dissertation, University of Connecticut. 1971. 179 pp. (Order No. 71-18,454)

Pairs of strangers were asked to interact in specific ways. Among the results it was found that male-male dyads were the least comfortable in touching interactions, while female-female dyads were most comfortable.

1314. **Walker, David N.** "A Dyadic Interaction Model for Nonverbal Touching Behavior in Encounter Groups." *Small Group Behavior* 6 (1975) : 308-324.

Thirty male-male, 30 male-female, and 30 female-female dyads were observed at three different times during nonverbal touching interaction. Two raters, watching from behind a one-way mirror, rated each subject on categories of bodily movement, type of touch employed, degree of personal involvement, and reaction to being touched. The subject's subjective affective state was influenced by the nonverbal touching interaction. Males in male dyads were significantly less open for all openness scoring categories than were females in female dyads. Openness scores were higher at rating period three than at periods one and two.

1315. **Ward, Louise Mallory.** "Body Language: Aspects of the General Communication System As Revealed in a Therapeutic Impasse." Ph.D. dissertation, George Peabody College for Teachers. 1974. 275 pp. (Order No. 74291-91)

A 15-minute videotape of a psychotherapy session with a 15 year old boy was analyzed. Gestures relating to the nature of the therapeutic impasse were identified, including spatial arrangement of interactants, approach and withdrawal motions, and lack of postural congruence.

1316. **Washburn, Paul V., and Hakel, Milton D.** "Visual Cues and Verbal Content as Influences on Impressions Formed After Simulated Employment Interviews." *Journal of Applied Psychology* 58 (1973) : 137-141.

One hundred twenty-two undergraduate subjects' ratings of interviewers and applicants were more favorable when interviewers displayed "enthusiasm" through greater use of gestures, eye contact, and smiling. Differences in judgments of audiovisual, visual-only, and transcript presentations are discussed.

1317. **Waterman, Darwin Earle.** "Remediation of Word Attack Skills in Slow Readers by Total Body Movement Learning Games." Ed.D. dissertation, University of Tulsa. 1973. 85 pp. (Order No. 74006-62)

Two groups of public school children, aged six to 14 participated in this study. An experimental group was given "Total Body Movement Learning Games" to help with remedial reading problems. No statistical differences in reading skills between the two groups were found after the movement games intervention.

1318. **Waters, Everett; Matas, Leah; and Sroufe, L. Alan.** "Infants' Reactions to an Approaching Stranger: Description, Validation, and Functional Significance of Wariness." *Child Development* 46 (1975) : 348-356.

Twenty-six five-month-old and 11 seven-month-old infants were part of a study designed to establish descriptive categories of infant wariness toward strangers. Very interesting and subtle indicators of infant behavior were delineated. Negative reactions were validated with measures of heart rate acceleration and responses to the mother's approach. Results indicate that negative responses to approaching strangers are linked to age.

1319. **Watson, O. Michael.** "Conflicts and Directions in Proxemic Research." *Journal of Communication* 22 (1972) : 443-459.

The author discusses different methods of proxemic research. Using his own research as a springboard for discussion, he examines the use of observational and laboratory studies, the use of paper and pencil tests, and the need for visual recording devices. He also discusses the advantages of limiting research to dyads, the use of foreign students as subjects, and the inclusion of same- and mixed-sex and race groups. The author concludes with an examination of future directions in proxemic research.

1320. **Watson, Sharon Gitin.** "Judgment of Emotion from Facial and Contextual Cue Combinations." *Journal of Personality and Social Psychology* 24 (1972) : 334-342.

The experiment was designed to test the relationship between verbal context and facial expression in the judgment of emotion. Eighty-two male and 90 female college students were shown 72 stimulus cue combinations of one facial expression and one context line. Subjects then rated these combinations for six categories of emotion and five bipolar scales of emotional expression. Among the results it was found that facial cues dominated the combination ratings.

1321. **Watson, Wilbur H.** "The Meaning of Touch: Geriatric Nursing." *Journal of Communication* 25 (1975) : 104-112.

This study reports differences in touching behavior of geriatric nurses in a home for the elderly. The author describes touching as selective with respect to where the resident is touched, the sex and social status of the persons involved, and physical stigma in the touched person. There was more touch between same-sex pairs; and staff of higher status initiated touch more.

1322. **Waxer, Peter.** "Nonverbal Cues for Depression." *Journal of Abnormal Psychology* 83 (1974) : 319-322.

The study's intent was to examine the value of nonverbal cues as a diagnostic tool. Sixty-seven psychology faculty, graduates, and undergraduates viewed silent videotapes of five depressed and five nondepressed psychiatric patients and attempted to identify the depressed patients on the basis of nonverbal cues alone. Two independent raters scored the patients' frequency and duration of eye contact. Results indicate that nonverbal cues are an aid in identifying depression; depressed patients maintained contact for much less time than nondepressed patients. Further findings suggest the duration of eye contact, not the frequency, may be an indicator of depression.

1323. **Waxer, Peter.** "Nonverbal Cues for Depth of Depression: Set Versus No Set." *Journal of Consulting and Clinical Psychology* 44 (1976) : 493.

A brief report on two studies investigating untrained raters' ability to identify depression based on nonverbal cues from psychiatric patients. Findings suggest that nonverbal cues may provide additional criteria for diagnosis.

1324. **Waxer, Peter H.** "Nonverbal Cues for Anxiety: An Examination of Emotional Leakage." *Journal of Abnormal Psychology* 86 (1977) : 306-314.

In an effort to determine the value of nonverbal cues in identifying emotional states, particularly anxiety, 46 raters scored 20 silent one-minute videotape clips of 20 psychiatric patients. Results indicate that raters are able to identify the presence and intensity of anxiety based solely on nonverbal cues. Included is an interesting discussion of the significance of "emotional leakage" and the role of microanalysis in this study.

1325. **Waxer, Peter H.** *Nonverbal Aspects of Psychotherapy.* New York: Praeger, 1978. 105 pp.

This book gathers literature on nonverbal behavior pertinent to clinical psychology and psychotherapy, including research, theoretical, and practical approaches. The first part includes chapters on "Early Scientific Thought," "Early Clinical Thought: the Analytic Tradition," "Contemporary Therapy Systems," and "Nonverbal Therapy Techniques." The second part of the book gives detailed information on research into specific nonverbal behaviors in chapters entitled: "Clinical Descriptive Studies," "Nonverbal Behavior in Basic Psychodiagnosis," "Nonverbal Cues of Therapeutic Progress," "Reliability and Validity of Nonverbal Communication," "Therapist-Generated Nonverbal Cues," and "Modeling for Psychological Growth." In the closing chapter, the author argues for an empirically based strategy for developing nonverbal behavior awareness pertinent to the therapeutic context.

1326. **Webbink, Patricia Glixon.** "Eye Contact and Intimacy." Ph.D. dissertation, Duke University. 1974. 99 pp. (Order No. 75024-37)

The effect on the level of intimacy between a female subject and a confederate of three minutes of silent eye contact versus three minutes looking at another body part (hand) or maintaining silence without eye contact was assessed. Women who had made eye contact expressed more feelings of intimacy and empathy than those with no contact.

1327. **Weber, Judy Walker.** "The Effects of Physical Proximity and Body Boundary Size on the Self-Disclosure Interview." Ph.D. dissertation, University of Southern California. 1972. 157 pp. (Order No. 73-789)

Forty-eight female high school students were subjects in this study designed to assess how the degree of self-disclosure in an interview setting is affected by the variables of body boundary size and physical proximity.

1328. **Weil, Pierre, and Tompakov, R.** *O Corpo Fala.* Petropolis, Brazil: Editora Vozes, 1973.

A popularized, illustrated vocabulary of body attitudes with their unconscious meanings. Written in Portuguese. There is a French translation, *Votre corps parle,* Brussels: Marabout, 1975.

1329. **Weinberg, Sanford** *Messages: A Reader in Human Communication,* 3rd ed. New York: Random House, 1979. 321 pp.

Of particular note here are Part 3, which has separate overview chapters by Albert Mehrabian and Mark L. Knapp and one on nonverbal communication of emotions by Ross Buck; Part 4, which has a chapter on self-disclosure by Sidney M. Jourard; Part 5, with a chapter on responsive listening by John Steward and Gary D'Angelo;

and Part 9, with a chapter on intercultural communication by Larry A. Samovar and Richard E. Porter, in which the authors discuss use and organization of space, time conceptualization, and nonverbal expression.

1330. **Weiner, Carole T., and Spero, Ruth.** "The Results of a Creative Arts Therapy Program for Mentally Retarded Children." *Conference Proceedings of the American Dance Therapy Association* 8 (1974) : 50-53.

Fourteen retarded children, ages six years eight months to nine years seven months, received an exceptional educational curriculum and language development sessions. Seven of the children also received 202 art therapy sessions (music—two per week; dance—two per week; drama—one per week; art—one per week). Both groups were pre- and post-tested with the Illinois Test of Psycholinguistic Abilities (ITPA), Draw a Person (DAP), and Hunt Effort (movement analysis) Protocol. Both groups showed improvement, but the experimental group showed significantly greater improvement in the six "representational level" sub-tests. Researchers conclude that language development and socialization improved as a result of creative arts therapy input and suggest further testing with a modified DAP and Effort protocol to measure change in personal identity and movement style.

1331. **Weinstein, Carol S.** "Modifying Student Behavior in an Open Classroom through Changes in the Physical Design." *American Educational Research Journal* 14 (1977) : 249-262.

The study observed the spatial distribution of activity in a second/third-grade open classroom before and after a change in the physical design. Over a two-week period, the activities and locations of the students were recorded on a floor-plan of the room before the change. The same activities and locations were charted for two weeks after the change. Analysis indicates that minor changes in the physical environment can produce predictable changes in student behavior.

1332. **Weinstein, Carol S.** "The Physical Environment of the School: A Review of the Research." *Review of Educational Research*, in press.

This article examines the current status of research on the impact of the educational environment on student behavior, attitudes, and achievement. The review is limited to investigations actually done in schools. It includes a focus on the effects of environmental variables (classroom design, seating position, windows, and so on); a review of ecological studies; and a review of the literature on the influence of open space designs on students and teachers. (from pre-publication manuscript)

1333. **Weiten, Wayne, and Etaugh, Claire F.** "Lateral Eye Movement As Related to Verbal and Perceptual-Motor Skills and Values." *Perceptual and Motor Skills* 36 (1973) : 423-428.

Forty college students, all but two of whom were right-handed, participated in this study. The subject sat straight in a chair directly facing the experimenter and answered a series of questions as quickly and as accurately as possible. The direction of initial eye movement following the completion of each question was recorded as right, left, invalid, or none. Each subject then completed a concept-identification task as well as an inverted alphabet-printing task. Subjects made valid lateral eye movements on 76.1 percent of 800 trials, with an average of 79.9 percent of an individual's lateral eye movements going in the same direction. Relative to left-movers, right-movers performed significantly better on the concept-identification task; showed significantly greater math-verbal discrepancy on the Scholastic Aptitude Test; and performed more poorly on the inverted alphabet-printing task.

1334. **Weitz, Shirley.** "Sex Differences in Nonverbal Communication." *Sex Roles* 2 (1976) : 175-184.

Twenty-four male and 24 female graduate students paired in opposite-sex dyads were videotaped during an unstructured interaction and while discussing the topic of Watergate. Ten naive raters then judged the videotapes according to various dimensions. Among the results it was found that liberalism in sex role attitudes correlated with nonverbal warmth in men and that women on the whole elicited more nonverbal warmth and men more nonverbal anxiety. There was also evidence indicating that women may adjust their nonverbal communication to fit that of their male partners.

1335. **Weitz, Shirley**, ed. *Nonverbal Communication: Readings with Commentary*. 2nd ed. New York: Oxford University Press, 1979. 434 pp. Illus.

This excellent collection of readings in nonverbal communication includes many papers and selections that have already become classics in the field as well as articles written for this volume by major researchers. Chapters dealing with the principle areas of nonverbal communication research are prefaced by comprehensive overviews that place the readings within the context of the major issues and trends in the field. Each chapter includes an extensive bibliography. Included in the section on facial expression and visual interaction are "Similarities and Differences between Cultures in Expressive Movements" by I. Eibl-Eibesfeldt, an excerpt from "The Expression of the Emotions in Man and Animals" by Charles Darwin, "Facial Expression and Imagery in Depression: An Electromyographic Study" by Gary E. Schwartz, Paul L. Fair, Patricia Salt, Michael R. Mandel, and Gerald L. Klerman, "Measuring Facial Movement" by Paul Ekman and Wallace V. Friesen, and "Gaze and Mutual Gaze in Social Encounters" by Mark Cook. Research on body movement and gesture is represented by Ray L. Birdwhistell's "Toward Analyzing American Movement," Adam Kendon's "Movement Coordination in Social Interaction: Some Examples Described," Albert E. Scheflen's "Quasi-Courtship Behavior in Psychotherapy," William S. Condon's "An Analysis of Behavioral Organization," George F. Mahl's "Body Movement, Ideation, and Verbalization During Psychoanalysis," Martha Davis' "Laban Analysis of Nonverbal Communication," and "The Body and the Group: The New Body Therapies" by Anne Ancelin Schützenberger and Yannick Geffroy. Contributions to the study of proximity behaviors are "Proxemics" by Edward T. Hall, "Hard Architecture" by Robert Sommer, "The Skin, Touch, and Human Development" by Ashley Montagu, and "Human Exocrinology: The Olfactory Component of Nonverbal Communication by Harry Wiener. Lastly, included in a section on multichannel communication are "The PONS Test: Measuring Sensitivity to Nonverbal Cues" by Robert Rosenthal, Judith A. Hall, Dane Archer, M. Robin DiMatteo, and Peter L. Rogers, "Dimensions of Dyadic Communication" by Myron Wish, "Working the Other Side of the Sequence: Studying Interaction Strategy" by Starkey Duncan, Jr., "Sentics: Communication and Generation of Emotion Through Dynamic Expression" by Manfred Clynes, and "Biological Rhythms as Information Channels in Interpersonal Communication Behavior" by Paul Byers. There are also five articles on paralanguage.

1336. **Wellens, Rodney A.** "Recording Methods and Instrumentation 10 (1978) : 458-459.

This short article suggests the use of sound-activated relays and counters to record the frequency and duration of subjects' talking and listening times.

1337. **Wellens, A. Rodney.** "An Interactive Television Laboratory for the Study of Social Interaction." *Journal of Nonverbal Behavior* 4 (1979) : 119-122. Illus.

A brief description of the set-up and research uses of interactive television (IATV) at the University of Miami.

1338. **Wenar, Charles.** "Executive Competence and Spontaneous Social Behavior in One-Year-Olds." *Child Development* 43 (1972) : 256-260.

Three 15-minute filmed intervals for each of 26 infants, approximately one year of age, were analyzed according to the categories of executive competence activities (explorations of the physical environment), child-initiated "spontaneous social behaviors," and mother-initiated social behaviors. Behaviors were scored according to complexity of activity and kind and intensity of affect. Results showed that executive competence activities were more frequent than spontaneous social behaviors and lasted longer, both to a highly significant degree. Spontaneous social behaviors showed more affect to a highly significant degree, but intensity was the same for executive competence activities. There was no significant relation between level of executive competence and amount and intensity of spontaneous social behavior.

1339. **Westbrook, Mary** "Sex Differences in the Perception of Emotion." *Australian Journal of Psychology* 26 (1974) : 139-146. Illus.

Nine hypotheses were tested, examining sex differences in accuracy of judgment of emotion, attention paid to emotional cues, and type of error made when incorrectly judging emotions. Little evidence of sex differences was found from testing 49 males and 51 females. However, males were found to make more evaluative errors when judging positive and negative emotions expressed by women.

1340. *Western Journal of Speech Communication* 43/2 (1979). "Assessments of Nonverbal Behavior," Special Issue.

Among the articles in this special issue are "Expectancies, Discrepancies, and Courtesies in Nonverbal Communication" by Robert Rosenthal and Bella M. DePaulo, "A Review of Nonverbal Behaviors of Women and Men" by Marianne LaFrance and Clara Mayo, and "Need-Fulfillment and Consistency Theory: Relationships Between Self-Esteem and Eye Contact" by John O. Greene and Kenneth D. Frandsen. Timothy G. Hegstrom has contributed "Message Impact: What Percentage is Nonverbal?," Stanley E. Jones and John R. Aiello, "A Test of the Validity of Projective and Quasi-Projective Measures of Interpersonal Distance," and Judee K. Burgoon, Don W. Stacks and W. Gill Woodall "A Communicative Model of Violations of Distancing Expectations."

1341. **Wexley, Kenneth N.; Fugita, Stephen S.; and Malone, Michael P.** "An Applicant's Nonverbal Behavior and Student-Evaluators' Judgments in a Structured Interview Setting." *Psychological Reports* 36 (1975) : 391-394.

Seventy-eight male and female undergraduates were asked to rate hypothetical applicants for suitability of a bank loan based on objective background financial data and nonverbal behavior. Three levels of financial background were presented in written form and two levels of nonverbal enthusiasm (measured as high or low amounts of eye contact, gesturing and smiling, and appropriate voice tone) were shown on videotape. Significant differences occurred for levels of financial background and levels of nonverbal behavior. Applicants exhibiting enthusiasm were rated significantly higher than those not exhibiting enthusiasm.

1342. **Whalen, Carol K.; Flowers, John V.; Fuller, Mary J.; and Jernigan, Terry.** "Behavioral Studies of Personal Space During Early Adolescence." *Man-Environment Systems* 5 (1975) : 289-297.

This article reports three studies of personal space preferences among sixth- to eighth-graders. Experimenters tested personal space in three modes: subject approaching a confederate peer, and confederate approaching the subject until subjects signals verbally, or nonverbally. Two studies found that older students preferred less personal space than younger. Space required was found to vary by mode: least with subject approach and most with nonverbal signal. Subjects kept more space with female confederates than with male. Between sixth and eighth grade, distance kept with a member of the opposite sex decreased. A third study found that popularity or unpopularity of the target person significantly affected distance. Boys rated as underachievers or disruptive by their teachers used more personal space, as did first-born females.

1343. **White, Michael J.** "Interpersonal Distance as Affected by Room Size, Status, and Sex." *The Journal of Social Psychology* 95 (1975) : 241-249.

A study exploring the effects of room size, sex, and status on interpersonal distance in seated conversation. Eighty college freshmen were observed conversing with confederates in familiar settings. Results indicate that females sat closer to confederates than did males. Further findings suggest that subjects sit closer together in a large room than in a small room.

1344. **White, Willo,** ed. *Resources in Environment and Behavior.* Washington, D.C.: American Psychological Association, 1979.

This book is an overview of and vocational guide to the field of environmental psychology. It has a listing of graduate programs, teaching innovations, career opportunities, federal and private funding, related journals, related organizations, a personal interest inventory, and an annotated bibliography.

1345. **Whiteside, Robert.** *Face Language.* New York: Frederick Fell Publishers, 1974, and New York: Pocket Books. 1977.

1346. **Wiemann, John M., and Knapp, Mark L.** "Turn-taking in Conversations." *Journal of Communication* 25 (1975) : 75-92.

Eighteen university students divided into dyads – three all male, three all female, and three mixed – were videotaped while engaging in a discussion. A random sample of 72 interaction sequences were analyzed twice, once each for subject as speaker and once each subject as listener. The data are then discussed in relation to turn-taking, back channel, and the verbal and nonverbal cues utilized in those mechanisms.

1347. **Wiemann, Mary O., and Wiemann, John M.** *Nonverbal Communication in the Elementary Classroom.* Urbana, Illinois: ERIC Clearing house on Reading and Communication Skills, 1975. 38 pp.

An original and practical guide for elementary school teachers, this booklet contains an overview of theory on the proxemic, kinesic, facial, and vocal components of nonverbal communication. The second half of the book contains 22 exercises dealing with topics such as the awareness of "personal space," how personal space is related to crowding, how space is used to indicate status, and the effects of spatial arrangements on interaction. Exercises related to the understanding of facial expression and eye behavior include recognizing emotions, identifying cues that communicate emotions, identifying cues that influence decisions, and establishing good eye contact. Body movement and orientation are treated in exercises on the nonverbal behaviors associated with interpersonal attitudes, the elements of greeting behavior, and the use of body control.

1348. **Wiener, Morton; Devoe, Shannon; Rubinow, Stuart; and Geller, Jessie.** "Nonverbal Behavior and Nonverbal Communcation." *Psychological Review* 79 (1972) : 185-214.

A critique of nonverbal communication literature based on a model presented by the authors. Attention is given to the establishment of definitions and criteria for nonverbal communication research. Using their model, the authors have identified suppositions implicit in the orientations of current researchers and attempted to reformulate specific issues relating to methodology. An interesting application of their model to the study of hand and arm movements is included.

1349. **Wiggers, T. Thorne.** "The Effects of Client Sex, Counselor Sex and Counselor Role on Selected Client Nonverbal Behaviors in a Counseling Analogue." Ph.D. dissertation, University of Rochester. 1978. 145 pp. (Order No. 7820421)

Male and female college students role-played counseling situations with a male and a female counselor. Albert Mehrabian's indexes of affiliation and relaxation were used to analyze subjects' behavior but were found not useful for his data. A post hoc analysis found no main or interaction effects for sex but a significant overall effect for time segment, suggesting that changes in the counselor's role over the duration of the session affected the nonverbal behavior of the "clients."

1350. **Wilbur, R.** *American Sign Language and Sign Systems.* Baltimore, Maryland: University Park Press, 1979.

1351. **Wilkinson, Louise Cherry, and Rembold, Karen L.** "Preschool Children's Production of Gestural Directives." *Language Sciences* 2 (1980) : 127-143.

A study of the gestures accompanying requests or verbal directives in three boys from age two to 2½ years. Videotapes in free play with parents were coded as to form of the gesture, eye contact, and function. The authors provide a glossary of the coded terms and case examples of each child at age two then 2½. Developmental trends toward increasing social complexity of these behaviors are discussed.

1352. **Willems, Edwin P., and Campbell, David E.** "One Path Through the Cafeteria." *Environment and Behavior* 8 (1976) : 125-140.

Four position papers—I. Altman's on analysis of privacy, J. Edney of "Human Territories," D. Stokols' concept of crowding, and G. Evans' and W. Eichelman's models of spatial behavior—are reviewed, compared, and evaluated. According to the authors, there remains some confusion about the ways in which the concepts and processes relate to each other. Secondly, in terms of theoretical emphasis the authors prefer psychological phenomena (cognition, attitude, motivation) to behavior (in the sense of adaptive performance). Thirdly, there remain some very complex problems of measurement, definitions, and identification of phenomena. Finally, the authors find it unclear how the cluster of psychological phenomena discussed by the above authors will bear directly on the understanding of human performance in the everyday environment.

1353. **Williams, Drid.** "The Arms and Hands, with Special Reference to an Anglo-Saxon Sign System." *Semiotica* 21 (1977) : 23-73. Illus.

An early system of counting using fingers, hand, and arms (preserved and illustrated in an Anglo-Saxon manuscript) is described and transcribed into Labanotation.

1354. **Williams, Ederyn.** "An Analysis of Gaze in Schizophrenics." *British Journal of Social and Clinical Psychology* 13 (1974) : 1-8.

Twenty-five schizophrenics formed an experimental group and 25 nonschizophrenic patients and normals were the control group. While ostensibly waiting for an experimenter, subjects were given the opportunity to watch television and then to converse with a female confederate who gazed continually into the subjects' eyes while attempting to engage them in conversation. Results indicate that schizophrenics show partial gaze aversion whether talking or listening. Gaze avoidance on the part of schizophrenics was shown to be person-avoidance and not nonhuman stimulus-avoidance.

1355. **Williams, Evalina.** "Effects of Inter-Group Discussion on Social Distance and Personal Space of Black and White Students." Ph.D. dissertation, The University of Texas at Austin. 1972. 118 pp. (Order No. 73-7677)

Ninety-six subjects assigned to six-week discussion groups and 96 controls completed a "Racial Attitude Survey" which had social distance and personal space projective measures. The discussion group significantly effected re-test scores.

1356. **Williams, Sharon J., and Willis, Frank N.** "Interpersonal Touch Among Preschool Children at Play." *Psychological Record* 28 (1978) : 501-508.

Two hundred seventy-four preschoolers were observed for this study of the effects of race and social class on touch. Results showed that in indoor play areas touch was more frequent for low-income children and for same-gender pairs and in outdoor play areas touch was higher for black same-gender pairs. Comparisons with studies of touch rates in older children and adults from America and from other cultures are noted.

1357. **Willis, Frank N.; Carlson, Roger; and Reeves, Dennis.** "The Development of Personal Space in Primary School Children." *Environmental Psychology and Nonverbal Behavior* 3 (1979) : 195-204.

Personal space in school cafeteria lines was observed for 1,047 children in kindergarten through sixth grade in seven public schools. It was found that children segregate themselves both racially and sexually in the lines. In three of the schools that were racially mixed, the children stood closer in the lower grades than in the higher grades, they stood closer to same-sex children than to other-sex children, but there was no racial difference. In three of the schools where all of the children were white, there was an increase in personal space across grades for all sex combinations except male to male. In two of the schools where all of the children were black, there was no significant increase in personal space across grades. The children in the white schools had greater line distances than children in the black schools throughout the upper grades. In general, the results were similar to those obtained in other studies involving observation in natural settings and different from results obtained using simulated interaction.

1358. **Willis, Frank N. Jr., and Hamm, Helen K.** "The Use of Interpersonal Touch in Securing Compliance." *Journal of Nonverbal Behavior* 5 (1980) : 49-55.

Direct gaze and a personal approach distance have been shown to increase compliance in a face-to-face situation. In the present study touch was varied along with gender and difficulty of request to assess the effects upon rate of compliance. The results indicated that touch was important in securing compliance, more so if the request was more difficult, and most important in securing same gender compliance.

1359. **Willis, Frank N., and Hofmann, Gale E.** "Development of Tactile Patterns in Relation to Age, Sex, and Race." *Developmental Psychology* 11 (1975) : 866.

The present study is concerned with the changes in touch interaction in primary school children. Two observers recorded the frequency of touch on school cafeteria lines of children in kindergarten through sixth grades. An examination of line adjacencies indicated that sexual and racial segregation begins early in primary school. A child was more likely to stand behind a child of the same sex and of the same race. There was a greater variety of body areas touched in same-sex pairs than in different-sex pairs.

1360. **Willis, Frank N., and Reeves, Dennis L.** "Touch Interactions in Junior High Students in Relation to Sex and Race." *Developmental Psychology* 12 (1976) : 91-92.

Students were observed in school cafeteria lines in seven junior high schools. Two observers recorded the sex and ethnic group (black, white, chicano) of each child as well as any instance of touching another child. A student was more likely to stand behind another of the same sex and the same race. In male-male interactions, blacks were more likely to touch, and in female-female interactions black girls were significantly more likely to touch others. In female-male interactions, black girls were significantly more likely to touch boys.

1361. **Wilson, E.** "The Evolution of Communication: A Review of R.A. Hinde, ed., *Nonverbal Communication.*" *Science* 176 (1972) : 625-627.

This review succinctly discusses the ethological and cultural concerns raised in Hinde's anthology, including several interesting behavioral observations. It also discusses the study group responsible for this book in the context of cooperative work in human ethology.

1362. **Wilson, Edward O.** *Sociobiology: The New Synthesis.* Cambridge, Massachusetts: The Belknap Press of Harvard University Press, 1975. 697 pp. Illus.

Embedded in this large and ambitious volume is a great amount of information on social behaviors of animals and humans. Part 2 on "Social Mechanisms" contains chapters on functions, origins, and evolution of communication, aggression, territoriality, dominance systems, and parental care. The final section deals with animal species from microorganisms to nonhuman primates, and with human society, including bonding, role-playing, communication, territoriality, and social evolution.

1363. **Wilson, Ronald S., and Harpring, Eileen B.** "Mental and Motor Development in Infant Twins." *Development of Psychology* 7 (1972) : 277-287.

The mental and motor development of 261 pairs of twins were tested at six intervals up to age two years. Results showed that twins had the same rate of development as single children. Twins showed high in-pair correlation throughout, with the correlations for monozygotic twins significantly higher than those for fraternal twins.

1364. **Wilson, Stanley Douglas.** "Eye Contact and Self-Disclosure As a Function of Interpersonal Proximity and Eye Directional Classification." Ph.D. dissertation, California School of Professional Psychology. 1978. 111 pp. (Order No. 79157-77)

This study attempted to integrate two approaches to eye behavior research: gaze, and as a facilitator of social interaction and eye directionality as an indicator of personality differences.

1365. **Wing, Lorna,** ed. *Early Childhood Autism: Clinical Educational and Social Aspects.* 2nd ed. Oxford: Pergamon Press, 1976. 342 pp.

This collection of papers on Kanner's syndrome includes a clinical description of the developmental manifestations of childhood autism (Chapter 2). An appendix to the chapter gives a scheme for clinical description and diagnosis including impairment in nonverbal communication, abnormalities in touch sensitivity and attention, and problems of motor imitation and control. Chapter 4, by Derek M. Ricks and Lorna Wing, includes a description of the development of nonverbal dimensions such as facial expression, gestures and nonverbal comprehension in the autistic child. Chapter 6, by Marian K. DeMyer, reports the results of a study of the motor and perceptual-motor skills of autistic chidren; and Chapter 7 by Lorna Wing touches on methods for teaching motor skills and expressive movements in remedial education. Also of interest is Chapter 10, "The Severely Retarded Autistic Child," by Janet Carr.

1366. **Wohlstein, Ronald T.** "Filming Collective Behavior and the Problem of Foreshortened Perspective: A Corrective Method. *Studies in the Anthropology of Visual Communication* 4 (1977) : 81-85.

The author discusses a method for correcting the problem of foreshortened perspective in filming collective behavior, which will make possible the measurement of such factors as velocity of movement and spatial arrangement from the film record.

1367. **Wolff, Peter, and Gutstein, Joyce.** "Effects of Induced Motor Gestures on Vocal Output." *Journal of Communication* 22 (1972) : 277-288.

The relationship between gestural and vocal components was studied by imposing an arbitrary gesture on a speaker and examining its effect on his verbal output. One hundred twenty subjects either performed or viewed a circular or linear gesture and were required to simultaneously produce either short stories or words in restricted categories. Analysis of the story protocols showed a significant effect of gesture type in both the observed and produced conditions. No such effect was found for word production. These results suggest that meaning was conveyed by the gestures and that the gestural and vocal systems are not independent during the communicative act.

1368.   **Wolff, Peter, and Wolff, Elizabeth Ann.** "Correlational Analysis of Motor and Verbal Activity in Young Children." *Child Development* 43 (1972) : 1407-1411.

Fifty-five children four to five years old in two nursery school classes and one kindergarten participated in this study. Teachers rated students on gross motor activity; fine motor activity; manual dexterity; verbal output; and verbal skill. Correlations among dimensions with age and sex were nonsignificant. Vocal output was significantly related to gross motor activity, but verbal skill was not. Fine motor activity and manual dexterity were significantly related to verbal skill much more than to verbal output. The results tend to support the hypothesis that gross motor activity and fine motor activity correlate with independent perceptual functions.

1369.   **Wolfgang, Aaron.** "Projected Social Distances as a Measure of Approach-Avoidance Behavior Toward Radiated Figures." *Journal of Community Psychology* 1 (1973) : 226-228. Illus.

Fourteen patients receiving radiation treatments and 14 nonradiated military personnel drew simple stick figures (representing themselves) at distances they would feel most comfortable from various others. The nonradiated Ss projected the greatest social distances from the radiated figures. Radiated Ss projected significantly greater social distance from figures accidentally exposed to radiation than they did toward normal figures. The radiated Ss showed significantly less apprehension or fear about approaching persons accidentally exposed to radiation than did the nonradiated Ss, as expressed in their selected distances.

1370.   **Wolfgang, Aaron** "Basic Issues and Plausible Answers in Counseling New Canadians." In *Education of Immigrant Students: Issues and Answers* edited by A. Wolfgang, pp. 139-148. Toronto: Ontario Institute for Studies in Education, 1975.

Counselors need to become sensitive to the problems that new immigrants to Canada have, including the students' differing ways of coping with their new situation. The counselor should become aware of both the students' and their own nonverbal behavior. Counseling models don't help in counseling with these students, nor does testing, so the author suggested some proposals for counselors to prepare themselves to help in counseling with these immigrant students.

1371.   **Wolfgang, Aaron.** "The Silent Language in the Multicultural Classroom." *Theory into Practice* 16 (1977) : 145-152.

We communicate simultaneously on at least three levels in interpersonal situations: verbal, nonverbal, and the cultural level, (which moderates and shapes the other two). Teachers can prepare for the multicultural or multiracial classroom by understanding their own culture, values, and nonverbal behaviors; learning about their own nonverbal behavior and its effects upon others; and facilitating communication between themselves and their students of different backgrounds by being aware of different learning styles in different cultures and by spelling out their expectations very clearly. Specific examples of differing nonverbal behaviors are given in this article along with specific nonverbal behaviors that teachers could utilize.

1372.   **Wolfgang, Aaron,** ed. *Nonverbal Behavior: Applications and Cultural Implications.* New York: Academic Press, 1979. 225 pp. Illus.

The following topics are discussed: an epistemological approach for understanding human communication by A. Scheflen; cross cultural studies of expressive behaviors that show evidence for the universality of fundamental emotions and facial expressions by I. Eibl-Eibesfeldt and C. Izard; and a comprehensive overview of the various categories and levels of nonverbal behavior by M. Davis. Additional chapters include discussion of the PONS test by R. Rosenthal; a research technique for examining the "listening response-relevant moment" during interracial interviews by F. Erickson; ways that nonverbal behavior research can be utilized in therapy, counseling, and social interactions by P. Waxer. An article by M. Argyle on five important functions of nonverbal behavior includes discussion of why humans use nonverbal behavior signals, 25 ways that social performance can fail, and several different methods that have been used in training individuals to improve their social skills. There is a chapter by A. Wolfgang on ways that teachers can become sensitized to the role of nonverbal behavior in communication, and its impact in the multicultural classroom; one by R. McDermott and K. Gospodinoff proposing that it is no accident that miscommunication occurs within a multicultural classroom; discussion of and suggestions for helping teachers become more aware of the influences and effects of their nonverbal behavior on others by C.M. Galloway; and discussion of some of the popular misconceptions that people have about nonverbal communication by R.M. Soucie.

1373. Wolfgang, Aaron, and Josefowitz, Nina. "Chinese Immigrant Value Changes with Length of Time in Canada and Value Differences Compared to Canadian Students." *Canadian Ethnic Studies* 10 (1978) : 130-135.

Fifty-six Canadian-born students and 53 Chinese-born students who had immigrated to Canada completed a 40 item scale on values as regards family, sex and marriage, nonverbal communication, education, and personal attitudes. Among the results it was found that the longer they are in Canada, the more the Chinese students adopt Canadian values of individualism, while simultaneously becoming more traditional in their view of family life and more concerned that their social interactions be smooth. These seeming contradictions were discussed. In the nonverbal area, the Chinese indicated significantly more often than not that touching is not a good way to show affection.

1374. Wolfgang, Aaron, and Weiss, David S. "A Locus of Control and Social Distance Comparison of Canadian and West Indian Born Students." *International Journal of Intercultural Relations* 5 (1980) : in press. Illus.

Three hundred and seventy-nine seventh and tenth grade students, 281 from the West Indies and 98 from Canada, completed the Rotter's Locus of Control Scale (LOC) and the Wolfgang Interpersonal Distance Test (WIDT). LOC is used to measure the amount of control an individual perceives he has over his own behavior (internally controlled) versus the control of luck or fate (externally controlled), while WIDT uses participants' stick figure drawings to indicate interpersonal distances preferred when approaching significant others to discuss personal matters. West Indian students were more internally controlled and showed more approach behavior toward significant interpersonal figures than did the Canadian students. In both groups females showed more approach behavior toward mother, while males showed more approach toward teachers. West Indian males showed more approach toward fathers than did Canadian males. Lack of correlation between the locus of control and social distance suggested that these are two separate constructs.

1375. Wolfgang, Aaron, and Wolfgang, Joan. "Exploration of Attitude via Physical Interpersonal Distance Toward the Obese, Drug Users, Homosexuals, Police and Other Marginal Figures." *Journal of Clinical Psychology* 27 (1971) : 510-512. Illus.

In experiments in which subjects drew stick figures at "comfortable" distances from various figures, it was found that male Ss positioned themselves significantly closer to female than to male figures; Ss positioned themselves significantly farther from marijuana users, drug addicts, obese persons, and homosexuals (either present or former) than from normal peers; there were no differences in the interpersonal distances between normal peers, heart disease patients, and male policemen; and Ss selected distances farther from female police then they did from female normals.

1376. **Wood, Barbara S.** *Children and Communication: Verbal and Nonverbal Language Development.* Englewood Cliffs, New Jersey: Prentice-Hall, 1976. 321 pp.

Several chapters are devoted to the development in childhood of gestural, proxemic, and prosodic language behaviors, with particular attention to the roles of emotional growth and sex differentiation. A second edition is in press.

1377. **Woodruff, Dianne L.**, ed. *Essays in Dance Research. Dance Research Annual*, vol. 9, 1978 (Congress on Research in Dance, New York University, New York City).

These proceedings from the Fifth CORD Conference of 1976 include four sections: "Studies in Dance History," "Labanalysis as a Research Tool," "Dance and Anthropology," and "Psychology, Biomechanics and Computer Studies."

1378. **Woodward, James; Erting, Carol; and Oliver, Susanna.** "Facing and Hand(l)ing Variation in American Sign Language Phonology." *Sign Language Studies* 10 (1976) : 43-51.

Alternation between facial and hand signs is considered here as ordered (implicationally) and conditioned by phonological features. There is systematic variation in American Sign Language according to region and race: New Orleans signers used more facial variants, while Atlanta signers used more hand variants; white signers used more facial variants than black signers; and black signers used hand and facial variants evenly.

1379. **Woolfolk, Anita E.** "Student Learning and Performance Under Varying Conditions of Teacher Verbal and Nonverbal Evaluative Communication." *Journal of Educational Psychology* 70 (1978) : 87-94.

Two male and two female teachers presented "microlessons" in each of four combinations of verbal and nonverbal (positive and negative) evaluative modes to 128 sixth-grade students. Among the results it was found that students with negative teacher nonverbal behavior performed better as measured by their writing significantly more sentences.

1380. **Woolfolk, Anita E.; Abrams, Lindsay M.; Abrams, David B.; and Wilson, G. Terence.** "Effects of Alcohol on the Nonverbal Communication of Anxiety: The Impact of Beliefs on Nonverbal Behavior." *Environmental Psychology and Nonverbal Behavior* 3 (1979) : 205-218.

Three males and three female raters were shown videotapes of 29 male subjects who were speaking to a silent female confederate. Raters were asked to make ten judgments about the subjects' behavior. The subjects had been assigned to one of two expectancy conditions in which they were led to believe the drink they consumed prior to meeting the confederate contained alcohol and tonic or tonic only. Actually, half of the subjects in each expectancy condition received alcohol and half received tonic only. Judgments of the female raters viewing the videotapes were congruent with physiological measures of the subjects' anxiety. Those subjects who believed they received alcohol were perceived by female raters as more relaxed, less anxious, less inhibited, and more dominant than subjects who believed they received tonic. The actual content of the drink had no significant effects on the raters' judgments of the subjects' behavior. Male raters were unable to discriminate among the experimental conditions.

1381. **Woolfolk, Anita E.; Garlinsky, Karen S.; and Nicolich, Mark J.** "The Impact of Teacher Behavior, Teacher Sex, and Student Sex Upon Student Self-Disclosure." *Contemporary Educational Psychology* 2 (1977) : 124-132.

Experimental teachers varied the style of a "microlesson" to be either verbally and nonverbally positive, verbally positive and nonverbally negative, verbally negative and nonverbally positive, and verbally and nonverbally negative. While the results of this study involving 126 sixth graders show a positive relationship between verbal "positiveness" and student's willingness to self-disclose, the relationships between nonverbal behavior and self-disclosure were partly mediated by student sex and partly functions of the teacher experimenter and hence more ambiguous.

1382. **Woolfolk, Robert L., and Woolfolk, Anita E.** "Effects of Teacher Verbal and Nonverbal Behaviors on Student Perceptions and Attitudes." *American Educational Research Journal* 11 (1974) : 297-303.

After removing the "highly disruptive" students, 80 students were chosen on the basis of their scores in the Piers-Harris Self-Concept Scale. A 24 year old female served as teacher for the experimental microlessons. The experimental manipulations consisted of varying teacher verbal and nonverbal behavior (both positively and negatively) during evaluations following work done on vocabulary. Contrary to expectation, the verbal channel had more impact on students' perceptions of the teacher's feelings and attitudes toward them than did the nonverbal channel.

1383. **Woolfolk, Robert L., and Woolfolk, Anita E.** "Nonverbal Teacher Behaviors: A Rejoinder." *American Educational Research Journal* 11 (1974) : 307-309.

This article is a response to Charles Galloway's (1974) critique of the authors' 1974 experiment showing (unexpectedly) that the verbal channel had more impact than did the nonverbal channel. Each of Galloway's criticisms is answered directly.

1384. **Woolfolk, Robert L.; Woolfolk, Anita E.; and Garlinsky, Karen S.** "Nonverbal Behavior of Teachers: Some Empirical Findings." *Environmental Psychology and Nonverbal Behavior* 2 (1977) : 45-61.

The effects of systematically varied verbal and nonverbal components of teachers' evaluative behavior upon children's perceptions and attitudes were studied within an experimental classroom. Subjects were 126 sixth-grade students who were removed from their classrooms to participate in a vocabulary lesson. Within each experimental condition a teacher employed one of four evaluative styles: verbally and nonverbally positive; verbally positive and nonverbally negative; verbally negative and nonverbally positive; or verbally and nonverbally negative. The data analysis indicated that teachers' verbal behavior influenced student perception and attraction. Nonverbal behavior influenced student perception and attraction but only when the teacher was female.

1385. **Worchel, Steven, and Teddlie, Charles.** "The Experience of Crowding: A Two Factor Theory." *Journal of Personality and Social Psychology* 34 (1976) : 30-40.

Three hundred fifteen male undergraduates participated in a study which compared close versus far distances, high versus low densities, and bare walls versus walls with pictures as affecting the experience of crowding. Interaction distance was found to be more closely related than density to crowding, and pictures reduced the experience of crowding only in the close distance condition.

1386. Word, Carl O.; Zanna, Mark P.; and Cooper, Joel. "The Nonverbal Mediation of Self-Fulfilling Prophecies in Interracial Interaction." *Journal of Experimental Social Psychology* 10 (1974) : 109-120.

In simulated interviews black high school student/candidates received less "immediate" behaviors (as measured by sitting and leaning farther away, less eye contact, and less direct orientation) than white students. In a second experiment white applicants received behaviors (from trained interviewers) like those the blacks or whites received in the first study. Judges rated those treated like blacks as more nervous and less adequate in performance; those subjects rated the interviewers poorer than subjects treated like the whites in the first experiment.

1387. Worth, Sol, and Adair, John. *Through Navajo Eyes: An Exploration in Film Communication and Anthropology.* Bloomington, Indiana: Indiana University Press, 1972. 286 pp. Illus.

The introduction of filmmaking to the Navajos was ethnographically described and chronicled in this book, from the first introduction of the idea to the general community, through the selection of who would do the filmmaking, the introduction of the use of the moviemaking tools to the novice filmmakers, the recording of the Navajo impressions throughout all of this, and, finally, the actual taking, making, and editing of the finished films. Not only did this book record the beginning of moviemaking by the Navajos, but it also chronicled an experimental test of the Whorfian hypothesis, using both visual and verbal modes for comparison across cultures. (According to the Sapir-Whorf hypothesis each culture's structuring of reality would be specifically related to the structuring of the culture's language.) By using the novice Navajo films as examples of how the Navajos visually structured their reality, the authors then compared this visual mode with the verbal mode structured in the Navajo language. The authors then contrasted the Navajo visual structurings with films by other novices under somewhat similar conditions. Novice black and Anglo films were compared and contrasted with each other and with the Navajo films in terms of how the filmmaking group structured itself, what movie topics were selected or avoided, which activities were filmed and which were avoided by each group, what the themes and topics of the movies were, and how each group constructed, structured, and portrayed the final visual images of the movies.

1388. Wundt, Wilhelm. *The Language of Gestures.* (Reprinted from 1921 edition) The Hague: Mouton, 1973. 149 pp. Illus.

This prodigious work of Wilhelm Wundt examines the development of gestural communication, beginning with gestural communication among deaf-mutes and among primitive peoples. From the demonstrative gestures of the Neapolitans to the connotative gestures of Cistercian monks, the author develops a psychological classification of gestures. He draws parallels between the workings of the central nervous system of the human body and the psychological processes that accompany human experiences, and proposes that gesture is the link and key to these parallel systems.

1389. Wylie, Laurence, and Stafford, Rick. *Beaux Gestes: A Guide to French Body Talk.* Cambridge, Massachusetts: The Undergraduate Press, 1977. 79 pp. Illus.

Following a very readable introduction to cultural differences in gesture, the monograph contains a series of photographs of various formal French gestures or emblems accompanied by brief descriptions of their precise meaning. It has good black and white photos of the first author in somewhat exaggerated but clear demonstrations of each motion.

1390.   **Young, D., and Beier, E.G.** "The Role of Applicant Nonverbal Communication in the Employment Interview." *Journal of Employment Counseling* 14 (1977) : 154-165.

1391.   **Young, David M.; Korner, Kim M.; Gill, J.D.; and Beier, Ernst G.** "Marital Communication: Beneficial Aggression." *Journal of Communication* 27 (1977) : 100-103.

Twenty-three married couples participated in mock fights using pillow-clubs that could record hitting pressure. Results show that the discord of the spouses, as measured on a questionnaire, was negatively related to the synchrony of the game bout behavior and the amount of fighting. Wife hit intensity correlated with husband ratings of disagreement and unhappiness. The longer the marriage, the less aggression was demonstrated by the wife.

1392.   **Young, Gerald, and Gouindecarie, Therese.** "An Ethology-Based Catalogue of Facial/Vocal Behavior in Infancy." *Animal Behavior* 25 (1977) : 95-107.

A study exploring 42 different facial expressions and vocalizations in infants and how, which, what, when, and why the expressions are used. They are analyzed according to the expressive elements of the brow, the eyes, the mouth, and other facial regions and the way these expressions combine with each other in different situations.

1393.   **Young, Laurence R., and Sheena, David.** "Surveys of Eye Movement Recording Methods." *Behavior Research Methods and Instrumentation* 7 (1975) : 397-429. Illus.

This comprehensive article begins with a description of the types of known eye movements and the characteristics of eyes that are amenable to measurement. The authors then discuss the major approaches to the measurement of eye movement in terms of the basic technique, specific implementations, technology involved, and an evaluation of the method. Methods discussed are: electro-oculography; corneal reflection; limbus, pupil, and eyelid tracking; contact lens method; point of regard measurement; measurement of eye rotation by double Prukinje image method; measurement of fixation pont by determining the rotation of a plane attached to the eye; and measurement of head movement to obtain point of regard. There is included a table of comparison of the measuring techniques to assist selection of instrumentation.

1394.   **Youngerman, Suzanne.** "The Translation of a Culture Into Choreography." From Essays in Dance Research edited by Dianne L. Woodruff, *Dance Research Annual* 9 (1978) : 93-110. Illus.

This article, subtitled "A Study of Doris Humphrey's 'The Shakers' Based on Labananalysis," is written by an expert in Laban Movement Analysis interested in its applications to anthropology.

1395.   **Zabor, Margaret Ruth.** "Essaying Metacommunication: A Survey of Contextualization of Communication Research." Ph.D. dissertation, Indiana University. 1978. 384 pp. (Order No. DDK 78-05345)

Two general paradigms of communication research were described and elaborated so that their metacommunicational assumptions were made explicit: the "psychological" and the "social" paradigms. Research developed within each of these paradigms was described, concentrating on the "natural history" approach developed within the "social" paradigm, as exemplified by the work done in *The Natural History of the Interview*. A kinesic "microtranscription" system based on the one by Birdwhistell was developed. Also included were film-frame tracings showing examples of various motions and interactions including interactional synchrony and position shifts in posture that may have signaled the punctuation of discourse units. Also included are the author's notation system for the "micro-kinesic" transcription on the "etic" level, and a discussion of the implications for educational research of this type of research.

1396. **Zelazo, Phillip R.** "Smiling to Social Stimuli: Eliciting and Conditioning Effects." *Developmental Psychology* 4 (1971) : 32-42.

In the first of two experiments, a female and a male experimenter conducted one session for "base rate" and five sessions of conditioning of ten infants, age 11 to 13 weeks over three to four days. For a "base rate" they gave no response to the infants' smiles; then each infant smile received contingent smiling, talking, and touching. Results show there was differential smiling to experimenters and a significant decline in smiling to contingent stimulation.

1397. **Zelazo, Philip R.** "Smiling and Vocalizing: A Cognitive Emphasis." *Merrill-Palmer Quarterly* 18 (1972) : 349-365. Illus.

The research discussed in this paper emphasizes the cognitive components of smiling and vocalizing. The demonstration that these responses have cognitive correlates carries the implication that they are reflecting basic characteristics of cognitive activity. It appears that the specification of the properties of smiling may help define the process of "recognitory" assimilation.

1398. **Zelazo, Philip R.** "Reactivity to Perceptual-Cognitive Events: Application for Infant Assessment." In *Infants at Risk: The Assessment of Cognitive Functioning* edited by R. Kearsley and I. Sigel. New York: Lawrence Erlbaum Associates, 1978. Illus.

The theories underlying traditional tests of infant development are limited, and the tests do not incorporate current research knowledge about infant behavior. A reexamination of old data and new experimental results implies that year-old infants undergo a cognitive metamorphosis that enables them to make specific associations to specific situations. The new perceptual-cognitive assessment procedures, rather than relying on traditional neuromotor measures, study the infant's responses — smiling, vocalizing, looking time, heart-rate increases and decreases — in order to assess the infant's cognitive status. Though a valid instrument has yet to be developed, a theory of perceptual-cognitive development provides a new approach to infant assessment. (from author's manuscript)

1399. **Zern, David, and Taylor, Amie Lou.** "Rhythmic Behavior in the Hierarchy of Responses of Preschool Children." *Merrill-Palmer Quarterly* 19 (1973) : 137-145.

Thirty-six children aged two years nine months to four years nine months were observed over two semesters. The occurrence and type of rhythmicities (defined as rhythmically repetitive patterns of body movement not directed toward a task) were recorded at ten-second intervals during five-minute periods. Also noted was whether the rhythmicity occurred during a structured or a free activity. One-third of the ten-second intervals were found to be marked by rhythmicity. There were significantly more rhythmicities in structured than in free activities. There were no significant sex, age, or semester differences, but there was some support for the hypothesis of a change in the frequency of different types, that is, a decrease in oral rhythmicities and an increase in nonoral with age.

1400. **Zharen, Windy L. von.** "The Education of Junior College Evening Students in the Humanities: A Modular Approach Utilizing Proxemics Emphasizing Tactility." Ph.D. dissertation, University of Florida. 1976. 240 pp. (Order No. 77-6911)

1401. **Zieger, Robyn Sue.** "Gaze Aversion As An Unobtrusive Measure of Homophobia." Ph.D. dissertation, University of Maryland. 1978. 88 pp. (Order No. 7824006)

This study investigated the frequency and/or duration of gaze aversion as a measure of homophobia in female college students.

1402. **Zimmerman, Barry, J., and Brody, Gene H.** "Race and Modeling Influences on the Interpersonal Play Patterns of Boys." *Journal of Educational Psychology* 67 (1975) : 591-598.

Seventy-eight fifth-grade boys, 40 white and 38 black, assigned to racially homogeneous or heterogeneous dyads, were observed during five-minute play periods and rated according to five measures of interaction. Racially mixed dyads were further exposed to a videotaped modeling episode of a racially mixed dyad playing together in either a warm or cold manner. The children were then observed again at play. Results of the initial observations indicated that all-black dyads interacted at a significantly greater interpersonal distance and faced each other less directly than all-white dyads. Black youngsters faced white boys significantly more directly than they did other black boys. Racially mixed dyads were intermediate in interpersonal distance compared to all-white dyads and all-black dyads. For mixed dyads who were exposed to the videotaped sequence, all five indexes of interaction were affected, with boys in the warm interaction condition displaying significantly more talk, eye contact, cooperation and greater proximity, and tending to face each other more directly after the viewing than boys who were exposed to the cold interaction.

1403. **Zimmerman, Linda Ellen Swanson.** "First Impressions as Influenced by Eye Contact, Sex, and Demographic Background." Ph.D. dissertation, University of Nevada, Reno. 1976. 106 pp. (Order No. 77129-78)

This study investigated the effects of eye contact and awareness of eye contact, among other variables, on first impressions as measured by a semantic rating analysis and a free response interview.

1404. **Zivin, Gail.** "On Becoming Subtle: Age and Social Rank Changes in the Use of a Facial Gesture." *Child Development* 48 (1977) : 1314-1321. Illus.

This study notes the similarities between a facial gesture children make (the "plus face") and the threat stares of nonhuman primates. Videotaped interactions of 23 four to five year olds and 26 seven to ten year olds confirms that higher-ranking children (based on "touchness" rankings) make more of these faces than lower-ranking ones.

1405. **Zlutnick, Steven, and Altman, Irwin.** "Crowding and Human Behavior." In *Environment and the Social Sciences: Perspectives and Applications,* edited by J. Wohlwill and D. Carson, pp. 44-60. Washington, D.C.: American Psychological Association, 1972.

This article is a discussion of the behavioral problem of human crowding. The authors pose and answer three questions with regard to this phenomenon. First, "What scientific knowledge exists regarding the effects of crowding on human social and psychological functioning?" Second, "What does crowding mean and what factors affect its impact?" Third, "What are some directions of analysis and alleviation of any negative effects of crowding?"

1406. **Zuckerman, Miron; DeFrank, Richard S.; Hall, Judith A.; and Rosenthal, Robert.** "Accuracy of Nonverbal Communication as Determinant of Interpersonal Expectancy Effects." *Environmental Psychology and Nonverbal Behavior* 2 (1978) : 206-214.

The person perception paradigm was used to address the effects of experimenters' ability to encode nonverbal cues and subjects' ability to decode nonverbal cues on magnitude of expectancy effects. Greater expectancy effects were obtained when experimenters were better encoders and subjects were better decoders on nonverbal cues, and the separate contributions of experimenter's and subject's nonverbal skills were of similar magnitude.

1407.   **Zuckerman, Miron; Hall, Judith A.; DeFrank, Richard S.; and Rosenthal, Robert.** "Encoding and Decoding of Spontaneous and Posed Facial Expressions." *Journal of Personality and Social Psychology* 34 (1976) : 966-977.

This study examines the relationship between posed and spontaneous facial expressions and between encoding and decoding ability in the same person. Thirty female and 30 male undergraduates were videotaped without their knowledge while watching two pleasant and two unpleasant scenes. Communication occurring under three conditions was examined: Spontaneous encoding (facial expressions while the sender watched the scenes), "talking encoding" (where the sender describes his or her reactions to the scenes), and posed encoding (where the sender poses the facial expression for each of the scenes). The senders were then presented their videotaped facial expressions for decoding. Among the results it was found that females were significantly more accurate decoders than males and that the capacity to decode posed cues was significantly correlated with the ability to decode spontaneous cues.

1408.   **Zuckerman, Miron; Lippets, Marsha S.; Koivmaki, Judith H.; and Rosenthal, Robert.** "Encoding and Decoding Nonverbal Cues of Emotion," *Journal of Personality and Social Psychology* 32 (1975) : 1068-1076.

Twenty-seven males and 13 female college students served as senders and 72 students were judged in a study examining the relationship between encoding and decoding nonverbal cues. Senders performed two tasks. The first task involved visual sending: the subject was photographed the moment the word "really" was spoken while reading sentences that expressed one of six emotions (anger, happiness, sadness, fear, surprise, disgust). In the second task (auditory sending) subjects recited the sentence "I have to leave now" for each of the above emotions. Among the results it was found that decoding and encoding ability were significantly related for both visual and auditory cues. Decoding a specific emotion in the visual channel was related to decoding of the same emotion in the auditory channel. Also, females were better encoders than males; auditory cues were better identified; and personally knowing the sender increased accuracy among male judges but not female judges.

1409.   **Zuckerman, Miron, and Przewuzman, Sylvia J.** "Decoding and Encoding Facial Expressions in Preschool-Age Children." *Environmental Psychology and Nonverbal Behavior* 3 (1979) : 147-163.

Preschool-age children drew, decoded, and encoded facial expressions depicting five different emotions. Each child was rated by two teachers on measures of school adjustment. Facial expressions encoded by the children were decoded by college undergraduates and the children's parents. Results were as follows: accuracy of drawing, decoding, and encoding each of the five emotions was consistent across the three tasks; decoding ability was correlated with drawing ability among female subjects, but neither of these abilities was correlated with encoding ability; decoding ability increased with age, while encoding ability increased with age among females and slightly decreased among males; parents decoded facial expressions of their own children better than facial expressions of other children, and female parents were better decoders than male parents; children's adjustment to school was related to their encoding and decoding skills and to their mothers' decoding skills; and children with better decoding skills were rated as being better adjusted by their parents.

1410. **Zunin, Leonard, and Zunin, Natalie.** *Contact: The First Four Minutes.* New York: Ballantine, 1975.

1411. **Zweigenhaft, Richard L.** "Personal Space in the Faculty Office: Desk Placement and the Student-Faculty Interaction." *Journal of Applied Psychology* 61 (1976) : 529-532.

Seventy-four male and female faculty members at a small southern coeducational college provided experimenters with diagrams of furniture arrangement in their offices. Faculty members who placed their desks between themselves and students with whom they interacted tended to be older and of higher academic rank. These were also rated by students less highly on items such as encouraging different viewpoints in students and were given lower overall ratings as instructors.

SUBJECT INDEX

A

Acquaintance, familiarity: degree of, 46, 51, 75, 116, 168, 286, 524, 533, 634, 644, 714, 868, 960, 1088, 1189, 1252, 1254, 1272

Acting, theater, drama, 254, 331, 444, 518, 519, 520, 528, 650, 746, 1038

Activity, amount of, 147, 177, 217, 473, 570, 583, 935, 1286, hyperactivity, 83

Adolescents, high school students, 99, 354, 370, 382, 463, 633, 641, 753, 754, 853, 870, 966, 982, 1139, 1342

Adult education, 555

Advertisements, advertising, 529, 637, 1295

Aesthetics, 291, 776, 1190

Affect, 24, 103, 382, 396, 466, 481, 534, 536, 573, 682, 784, 837, 907, 938, 1003, 1016, 1115, 1273, 1301. *See also* Anger; Anxiety; Emotion negative, 297, 474, 524, 644, 979; positive, *See* Smiling; Approval; Positivity

Affiliation, affiliative behavior, 3, 42, 425, 522, 548, 802, 810, 930

Age differences, 3, 8, 69, 83, 116, 191, 236, 324, 358, 389, 432, 461, 557, 585, 615, 634, 635, 676, 681, 700, 829, 834, 844, 848, 864, 869, 943, 960, 976, 977, 997, 1023, 1050, 1053, 1059, 1074, 1158, 1225, 1259, 1280, 1305, 1318, 1342, 1359, 1399, 1404, 1409

Aggression, aggressiveness, 49, 111, 147, 179, 198, 224, 280, 375, 384, 402, 403, 427, 456, 515, 516, 517, 537, 593, 594, 606, 633, 671, 784, 835, 865, 867, 868, 899, 901, 931, 946, 947, 978, 1016, 1030, 1041, 1118, 1305, 1308, 1362, 1391

Aging, aged, 206, 214, 624, 1057, 1111, 1112, 1321

Alcohol, alcoholic, 160, 632, 1093, 1380

Analogic vs. digital, 80, 268

Anatomy, 73, 74

Androgyny, 666, 900. *See also* Sex differences

Anger, 402, 633, 867, 931, 958, 978, 1118

Animals, 22, 43, 80, 180, 196, 230, 280, 309, 384, 421, 450, 477, 527, 650, 1042, 1153, 1154, 1155, 1205, 1229, 1232, 1247, 1308, 1310, 1362, birds, 65, 1242; dogs, 24; horses, 163; primates, 24, 81, 97, 125, 166, 200, 209, 210, 228, 261, 288, 311, 352, 388, 576, 642, 852, 853, 924, 936, 1009, 1014, 1016, 1048, 1203, 1206, 1232, 1280, 1300, 1404; rodents, 24

Anthropology, 48, 58, 80, 139, 312, 578, 654, 790, 1215, 1394. *See also* Cultural characteristics

Anxiety, 13, 23, 55, 146, 156, 159, 181, 238, 339, 353, 485, 540, 640, 652, 662, 683, 698, 706, 713, 720, 749, 798, 819, 825, 835, 964, 1036, 1062, 1104, 1216, 1226, 1231, 1324, 1334, 1380; at being observed, 152, 552, 798; separation, 410

Appearance, clothing, 41, 43, 203, 357, 484, 624, 963

Approach-withdrawal, 102, 704, 1038, 1369

Approval, disapproval, 16, 42, 79, 197, 198, 431, 443, 485, 530, 645, 711, 713, 715, 1379, 1381, 1382, 1384

Apraxia, 1195, 1196

Architecture, 13, 96, 117, 328, 965, 1213, 1298, 1335. *See also* Environmental psychology

Arousal, 16, 407, 505, 752, 928, 939, 989, 992, 1077, 1134, 1135, 1157, 1268

Art, 120, 650, 1011, 1221

Assertiveness, 6, 156, 1021, 1156

Attachment behavior, 19, 20, 24, 177, 230, 252, 695, 751, 810, 896, 935, 1042, 1247

Attention, 79, 169, 200, 217, 259, 265, 510, 528, 534, 537, 700, 711, 958, 981, 1149, 1173, 1247

Attitude, 43, 52, 172, 212, 382, 441, 468, 499, 506, 525, 683, 717, 909, 920, 1097, 1248, 1284, 1332, 1355, 1375, 1382

Attraction, attractiveness, 23, 151, 160,

N

O

ADDITIONAL AUTHORS INDEX

APPENDIX

FOR FURTHER REFERENCE

Certain journals have consistently included articles on nonverbal communication in recent years and are good sources for future work. Also, various organizations have begun to publish reference lists, abstracts, or news items related to the subject which are likely to be updated regularly. The reference works and periodicals listed below have been important sources for the present volume. However, some, such as *Human Ethology Abstracts*, do not extensively overlap with this bibliography, and these constitute closely related sources good for additional references.

American Journal of Dance Therapy
    Editors: Claire Schmais
                Elissa Q. White
    Publisher: American Dance Therapy Association
                2000 Century Plaza
                Columbia, Maryland 21044

Child Development
    Editor: E. Mavis Hetherington
    Publisher: University of Chicago Press
                5801 Ellis Avenue
                Chicago, Illinois 60637

Dance Research Journal
    Publisher: Congress on Research in Dance (CORD)
                Dance Department
                Education Building 675D
                New York University
                35 West 4th Street
                New York, New York 10003

Dance Therapy Bibliography 1981

>   Editor: Linni Silberman
>   Publisher: American Dance Therapy Association
>   2000 Century Plaza
>   Columbia, Maryland 21044

Environment and Behavior

>   Editor: Gary H. Winkel
>   Publisher: Sage Publications
>   275 South Beverly Drive
>   Beverly Hills, California 90212

FIND: Frye's Index to Nonverbal Data

>   (1980 Bibliography; custom computer searches and up-
>   dated bibliography in progress)
>   Editor: Jerry K. Frye
>   Publisher: University of Minnesota
>   Computer Center
>   University of Minnesota, Duluth
>   Duluth, Minnesota 55812

Human Ethology Abstracts

>   (published in *Man-Environment Systems*)
>   Volume I edited by C.B. Travis, D. Dowell, M.P. Cook,
>   and E. Meares in *Man-Environment Systems* 17
>   (1977):3-34.
>   Volume II edited by C.B. Travis in *Man-Environment
>   Systems* 7 (1977):227-273.
>   Volume III edited by R.M. Adams in *Man-Environment
>   Systems* 9 (1979):57-164.

Human Ethology Newsletter

>   Editor: Joan S. Lockard (R1-20)
>   Department of Neurological Surgery
>   University of Washington
>   Seattle, Washington 98195

The Journal of Communication

    Produced by: International Communication Association
    Publisher: The Annenberg School of Communication
         3620 Walnut Street
         Philadelphia, Pennsylvania 19104

Journal of Human Movement Studies

    Editors: H.T.A. Whiting and Marily G. Whiting
    Publisher: Henry Klimpton Publishers Ltd.
         7 Leighton Place
         L.P. London NW5 2QL England

The Journal of Nonverbal Behavior

    Editor: Randolf M. Lee
         Department of Psychology
         Trinity College
         Hartford, Connecticut 06106
    Publisher: Human Sciences Press
         72 Fifth Avenue
         New York, New York 10011

The Journal of Personality and Social Psychology

    Editor: Interpersonal Relations and Group Processes
         Section
         Ivan D. Steiner
         Department of Psychology
         University of Massachusetts
         Amherst, Massachusetts 01003

Kinesis: News and Views of Nonverbal Communication

    Publisher: Trinity University
         San Antonio, Texas
    Sponsor: The Institute for Nonverbal Communication
         Research
         25 West 86 Street
         New York, New York 10024

Man-Environment Systems
> Editor: Aristide H. Esser
> ASMER
> P.O. Box 57
> Orangeburg, New York 10962

Semiotica
> Editor: Thomas A. Sebeok
> Publisher: Mouton Publishers
> Walter de Gruyter Inc.
> 200 Saw Mill River Road
> Hawthorne, New York 10532

Sign Language Studies
> Editor: William C. Stokoe
> Publisher: Linstock Press Inc.
> 9306 Mintwood Street
> Silver Spring, Maryland 20901

Smithsonian Science Information Exchange
> Nonverbal Communication Packet DL07 Notices on
> Research Projects
> Room 300
> 1730 M Street, N.W.
> Washington, D.C. 20036

Videoinformationen
> Editors: Dr. Heiner Ellgring
> Max-Planck-Institut fur Psychiatrie
> Kraepelinstrasse 10
> 8000 Munchen, West Germany
> Dr. Harald Wallbott
> Fachbeieich Psychologie
> Universitat Giessen
> Otto-Behaghel-Strasse 10F
> 6300 Giessen, West Germany